AN INTRODUCTION TO PHILOSOPHY

BY

RIGHT REV. MSGR. PAUL J. GLENN, PH.D., S.T.D.

PRESIDENT OF COLLEGE-SEMINARY OF
ST. CHARLES BORROMEO, COLUMBUS, O.

B. HERDER BOOK CO.
15 & 17 SOUTH BROADWAY, ST. LOUIS 2, MO.
AND
33 QUEEN SQUARE, LONDON, W. C.

IMPRIMATUR

✠ *James J. Hartley, D.D.*
Bishop of Columbus

Dec. 16, 1943

Reprinted 1958
Library of Congress Catalog Card Number: 44-6182

Vail-Ballou Press, Inc., Binghamton and New York

THIS VOLUME IS DEDICATED

WITH AFFECTION AND REVERENCE

TO

MY FIRST TEACHERS AND MY LIFELONG FRIENDS,

THE MOTHER SETON SISTERS OF CHARITY

of Seton Hill, Greensburg, Pennsylvania

PREFACE

An Introduction to Philosophy ought to live up to its name. It should tell the young collegian, and the presumably older non-collegian who takes it up with serious intent, a number of important things. It should answer the questions naturally to be expected of the person who wishes to be introduced,—questions such as these: What is philosophy? How did it come into existence? What interesting things have happened to develop it or to hinder its development? What great names are identified with its effort? What have the bearers of these names done for philosophy? Is there a single true philosophy? Can there be a really false philosophy? Can one know true from false? What, in outline, are the things philosophy speaks of?

Some such litany of inquiries, duly adapted, would be recited, —at least inaudibly in his own mind and heart,—by any normally curious human being about to be introduced to a Personage. And philosophy is as interesting and as exciting as any Personage, even if he were spelled in capitals throughout.

This book attempts to introduce the reader or student to philosophy by answering the sort of questions just listed. It tells, in the somewhat dry and dusty fashion exacted by the needful compression of much in small space, the story of philosophy: its birth, its experiences, and even discusses its ancestry. It sets forth numerous samples of the language of philosophy, and insists upon a clear understanding of these terms. It tells of true philosophy, and of many a system of doctrines that tries to justify itself as true philosophy. It follows the winding course of philosophy through the centuries and down to our own. Then it sets forth the content of philosophy, the seven master sciences which are the departments of philosophy in its rounded and complete form. All this the present manual attempts to do. Such value as the book may have lies all in this attempt. The introduction may be a stumbling and half-inarticulate thing, but if it brings minds into familiar and appreciative communion, it can claim value despite its defects and stutterings.

It is hoped that this Introduction will really introduce many minds to the Queen of Human Sciences. After that is done, the personal efforts of each individual must determine whether he is to retire to the remembrance of a regal smile, or to be held as a favored courtier close to the queenly throne.

P.J.G.

College of St. Charles Borromeo,
Columbus, Ohio.

CONTENTS

PART FIRST

The Origin and Growth of Philosophy

PART SECOND

The Questions of Philosophy

AN INTRODUCTION TO PHILOSOPHY

INTRODUCTION

1. The Name *Philosophy;* 2. Definition of Philosophy; 3. Object of Philosophy; 4. Importance of Philosophy; 5. Identification of the True Philosophy; 6. Division of This Treatise.

1. THE NAME *PHILOSOPHY:* The word *philosophy* is a combination of two Greek nouns, *philia* which means "love" or "friendship," and *sophia* which means "wisdom." We may therefore translate the word *philosophy* as "the love of wisdom." A *philosopher,* consequently, is "a lover of wisdom."

Translating a word is one way of expressing its *nominal definition.* For a nominal definition (called so from the Latin *nominalis* which means "having reference to a *nomen* or *name*") tells what a name means. A nominal definition explains a name, but sometimes it tells very little about the thing which has the name. Of much greater value and importance is *real definition* (called so from the Latin *realis* which means "having reference to a *reality* or *thing*"). For while nominal definition explains the name of a thing, real definition explains the thing itself. Still, there is sometimes much enlightenment to be found in studying aptly formed names. This is so in the case of *philosophy.* We shall therefore pause briefly to consider the nominal definition of philosophy. Afterwards we shall study its real definition.

We have legend, if not history, to tell us that the word *philosophy* was coined by Pythagoras in the 6 century B.C. This ancient Greek teacher is praised for his humility or his clear-sightedness,

—which comes to much the same thing,—in recognizing the fact that a man, by the use of his unaided natural powers, can never attain to wisdom pure and simple. He can be, and should be, a lover of wisdom, a seeker after wisdom. But he may never presume to call himself absolutely wise. And hence Pythagoras called his own deep studies, not wisdom, but the love or the quest of wisdom; that is, he called these studies *philosophy*.

Not long after Pythagoras there appeared in Greece men of wide influence but of inferior mind who proudly called themselves "the enlightened" or "the wise" (as who should say "the intelligentsia"); the name in Greek is *sophoi*. History has permitted these persons to keep the name thus usurped, and knows them as *The Sophists*. But it is a tidy piece of irony that the name *Sophist* has come to mean, not a man truly wise, but a pretender and a quack. "Thus the whirligig of time brings in his revenges." We wonder what lies in store for the prideful modern "intellectuals" who make a religion of the latest apparent findings of material science. Doubtless their place is already set among the antic-comedians on the stage of coming time, and futurity will use them for its mirth, yea, for its laughter.

Philosophy, *nominally* or by virtue of the word as a name, means the love of wisdom. The words *love* and *wisdom* call for a moment's attention.

Love, in its fundamental meaning, is the tendency or drive of the will towards an object. It is an act and a state of the will, not a tender sentiment or affection. Sometimes, indeed, the will-act and the will-state of love are attended by soft feeling, but this is not always or necessarily the case. It is important to notice and to remember this fact in a day when the cinema and light fiction have distorted and almost destroyed the true meaning of the word *love.*—Love is of two types, called by the learned *desiring love* and *well-wishing love* (or, in the ancient Latin terminology, *amor concupiscentiae* and *amor benevolentiae*). *Desiring love* tends to possess its object; *well-wishing love* tends to do good to its object. Manifestly, the love of wisdom which we call *philoso-*

phy is desiring love. It is love which finds expression in effort, in quest, in striving to possess and to retain wisdom.

And what is this *wisdom* which philosophy seeks? Wisdom is not the same as knowledge, for a person might know much and still be unwise. Wisdom indeed involves knowledge, but it also includes the ability, the inclination, and the steady purpose of putting knowledge to good use. St. Thomas Aquinas (1225–1274) says in his book *Summa Contra Gentiles* that a man is to be called wise when he knows what he has to do and plans and manages to do it well. Thus wisdom involves several things: an end or purpose to be attained; an appreciative knowledge of this purpose; an ability, an inclination, and a steadfast effort to achieve the known purpose in the best possible manner. Thus it is *wisdom* to work for a known good purpose in a steady, devoted, and enlightened way. Such is wisdom considered *subjectively,* that is, in its *subject,* in the person who possesses it. Taking the term *wisdom* in an *objective* sense (that is, as a thing in itself, independent of a possessor) and regarding it in a most general way, we may say that wisdom is the sum-total of the things worth knowing and working for, which can attract the best efforts of the best minds and wills. This is the wisdom which philosophy pursues. This is that deepest knowledge, that *altissima scientia,* of which philosophy is the love and the untiring quest.

2. Definition of Philosophy: The real definition of philosophy, as contrasted with the nominal definition already discussed, tells us that philosophy is *the science of all things naturally knowable to man's unaided powers, in so far as these things are studied in their deepest causes and reasons.* We shall presently ponder each phrase of this definition. But first it will be well to inspect the meaning of the term *philosophy* as it is loosely employed in casual speech.

We often hear such expressions as these: "the philosophy of education," "the philosophy of religion," "business philosophy," "the philosophy of history," "the American philosophy of life," "the philosophy of style." Now what does the term *philosophy* mean in all these uses, or what, at least, does it suggest? It suggests, first of all, a body of reasoned truths or of conclusions regarded as truths. Further, it suggests that these truths are the background, the basis, and the ultimate explanation of the thing to which they are referred as "a philosophy." Thus the expression "the philosophy of education" suggests a body of reasoned truths (or principles, or "values") which give meaning to the word *education,* which show the worth of education, and which indicate, in a basic way, the best means of achieving and imparting it. Again, the expression "the philosophy of style,"—that is, of literary style,—means, as it does in Herbert Spencer's little book which bears that title, the root-reasons which are back of all the rules of grammar and rhetoric. Therefore, "the philosophy" of anything suggests the sum-total and system of reasoned truths which are back of the thing and give it meaning. Of any activity or procedure, of any plan, of any programme, of any "way of life," *the reasoned basis* is called its *philosophy*. Here, of course, we have the term *philosophy* in a very restricted meaning, even a metaphorical meaning; philosophy thus restricted comes close to what people usually mean when they use that horrible misnomer *ideology*. We have no quarrel with such a restricted use of the term, but it is not in this sense that we employ it in the present treatise. In this study we use the term *philosophy* to indicate the science of all things knowable, the science which is "man's ultimate effort to interpret the universe"; we do not use the term to mean the basis of some one effort or some one phase of human activity or interest. We do not speak of *the* philosophy of this or that; we speak of *philosophy*. Our concern is philosophy in its first meaning as the *universal* science, not in its restricted or metaphorical meaning as a special or particularized science.

Reverting now to the real definition of philosophy, we find that we have called it the science of all things naturally knowable to man's unaided powers in so far as these things are studied in their deepest, their ultimate, causes and reasons. This definition must be learned with care; we must be sure of the precise meaning of its every phrase.

a) Philosophy is a *science.—Science,* considered objectively, is a body of related data, set forth systematically, expressed with completeness, and presented together with the evidence (proofs and explanations) which justifies and establishes these data as certain and true. *Science,* considered subjectively, is scientific knowledge in the mind of a person; it is knowledge that is rounded, systematic, evidenced, and complete.

A science is (objectively) any branch or department of things knowable which presents *related data* with *certitude, proof, system, completeness. A* science (subjectively) is a person's certain, evidenced, systematic, rounded knowledge of things knowable.

When we say that philosophy is a science, we take the term *science* objectively. We mean that philosophy is a body of related data that is systematic, complete, evidenced, and certain.

It is to be noted in passing that the evidence or proof requisite for a science is not merely experimental or laboratorian evidence. Evidence may also be (as in the case of pure mathematics) *reasoned* or *rational* evidence. This point is important because many teachers of our times have presumed to limit science to the domain of the laboratorian and the statistician, arbitrarily ruling out rational evidence from the realm of true science. Such a ruling is blind and brazen impudence; it is also self-contradictory. For no amount of laboratorian data, no number of experiments, no catalogue of statistics, can amount to scientific evidence unless reason reduces them to unity and order and draws conclusions from them. And neither the nature and value of reasoning nor the basic force of the conclusions drawn by reason can be tested by laboratorian devices or proved by experimental methods. We therefore reject the *positivistic, sensistic, materialistic,* and *empiricist* doctrine that pure reasoning is of no scientific value. Philosophy is a rational or reasoned science, not a laboratorian science. Philosophy does indeed use the findings of the laboratorian sciences, but it is not confined or hampered by their limitations. It sheds its great light upon the data of the laboratory sciences, serving the scientist as daylight serves the laborer or the mechanic, and, in its turn, it draws from them illustration and even direction for its efforts. But it is not fettered by their methods or subjected to their special requirements.

b) Philosophy is the science of *all knowable things*.—In a day of intense specialization, it seems silly to say that there is a single science of everything. Nearly all the sciences we know of, and notably the positive sciences which keep our laboratorians busy, are partial or departmental sciences. Each of these deals with a branch of knowledge, and each is divided into almost endless departments and sub-departments. In the face of this bewildering maze of sciences, how can we think of *one* science which embraces in its scope every possible object of human knowing? Yet there inevitably *is* such a science. Even those who scoff at the assertion of its bare possibility are forced to assume its existence and to build their findings upon it as a necessary base. A little thought will convince anyone that there must be such a science; the difficulty suggested by the variety and multiplicity of partial sciences is merely a seeming difficulty. Cardinal Mercier has an enlightening word to say on this point in his *Manual of Modern Scholastic Philosophy* (p. 2): "Philosophy does not profess to be a particularized science with a place *alongside* other such sciences and a restricted domain of its own for investigation; it comes *after* the particular sciences and ranks *above* them, dealing in an ultimate fashion with their respective objects, inquiring into their connections and the relations of these connections, until it finally arrives at notions so simple that they defy analysis and so general that there is no limit to their application. So understood, philosophy will exist as long as there are men endowed with the ability and energy to push the inquiry of reason to its furthest limit. So understood, it is a living fact, and it has a history of more than two thousand years."

Indeed. as the Cardinal goes on to point out, it is impossible to have any particularized science without some fundamental grasp or some assumption of universal truths. The very existence of particularized or partial sciences affirms the existence of a non-particularized science, that is, of philosophy. For it is as impossible to have a partial science without reference to a universal science as it is impossible to have words without reference to a language, or even to have parts without reference to a whole. Not that philosophy is the simple sum-total of partial sciences. No, the relation of the particular sciences to philosophy is not the relation of constituent parts or elements to a totality which is their sum; rather, it is the relation of elements to a reality which is other and greater than themselves. Somewhat similarly, a building which is called a triumph of architecture is something other and something greater than any or all of the bricks and beams used in constructing it. A living plant is something more than a simple sum of parts. A language is more than a list of words; a literature more than a sum of sentences. The glorious harmonies of a musical masterpiece make something other and greater than a sum of notes. To dwell for a moment on the last illustration, we may notice that the harmonies of a musical composition "come after and rank above" the individual notes that make it up. The composition is not a simple addition of note to note; it involves more than single notes or chords sounded in sequence; it involves notes and chords in their relations, their interpretations, their fusions in a reality which is both *other* and *greater* than themselves. So philosophy which is the science of all things, and therefore includes all other sciences and their objects, comes *after* and ranks *above* the partial sciences, and is *other* and *greater* than the sum-total of all these. Philosophy achieves its place *by drawing into basic unities* the vast and bewildering world of knowables with which all other sciences deal piecemeal.

c) Philosophy is the science of all things *naturally knowable* to man.—Philosophy investigates all that man can know by the use of his unaided knowing-powers; that is, by the use of his intellect or reason working upon the data gathered by his senses. Philosophy does not investigate what man has come to know by Divine Revelation, except, indeed, in so far as he could have known this without such revelation. For this reason philosophy is called *a human science* in contrast with *the divine science* of Christian Theology. Philosophy, indeed, is the queen of human sciences.

Sometimes philosophy is described as "the handmaid of theology." This title is most honorable, and it is thoroughly justified. For the truths which philosophy discovers, discusses, and proves are in perfect alignment with truths divinely revealed. Philosophical truths, moreover, help a person to grasp and appreciate revealed truths. Further, the systematic procedure of philosophy suggests itself as the best and noblest instrument for setting forth the truths of theological science. Thus, in these several ways, philosophy *serves* theology, or, more precisely, serves man in his study and appreciation of theology. Since this service of philosophy to theology is the service of the *human* to the *divine* science, it is aptly described as the service of a handmaid. Now, certain mistaken minds,—some of which are malicious as well as mistaken,—interpret the phrase "the handmaid of theology" to mean "the slave of theology." These minds, out of an abundance of ignorance which misses the clearest truths of history, suggest that Catholic philosophers, in times past, have bent and twisted philosophy to make it support revealed truth. Nothing could be further from the fact. True philosophy does support Revelation. Naturally so. For the power of reason by which man discovers and proves truths is a gift of the same God who has supernaturally revealed certain truths. There is no contradiction in God; hence there can be no contradiction in His manifestations of truth, whether these be made naturally through the activity of sound minds or supernaturally through His revealed Word. No twisting or bending of philosophy is required to make it serve theology. Philosophy is by nature the devoted handmaid of theology, not its shackled and tortured slave.

d) Philosophy is the science of all things naturally knowable to man *inasmuch as these are studied in their deepest causes and reasons.*—The quest of philosophy is an ultimate one. Philosophy seeks bed-rock for the edifice of human knowledge. Every science looks for causes and reasons to evidence its data; philosophy seeks the last, the ultimate, the deepest causes and reasons. Philosophy, therefore, stands unique among human sciences. The partial or particularized sciences,—such as physics, chemistry, biology,—must be satisfied with proximate causes and reasons, that is, with those that are more or less ready to hand. For each of the partial sciences works in a very restricted field, and must find justification for its data within that field or in immediately related fields. Philosophy, however, is not so restricted; philosophy is not immediately or necessarily concerned with proximate causes; it wants the ultimate, the root-deep evidence for its truths.

To illustrate the contrast between the particular sciences and philosophy, consider a block of limestone. Mathematical science is interested in it solely as *quantity*. Physics looks to its *mass* and and *inertia*. Chemistry wants to know the substantial bodily constituents (the *elements*) that compose it. Now, philosophy ignores quantity, physical properties, and chemical constitution (although it does not deny these things). Philosophy poses an ultimate question; it asks, "What, in the deepest sense of the inquiry, is this thing called a block of limestone?" Philosophy does not, like mathematics, inquire about the size or measurement of the limestone. It does not, like physics, investigate qualities or properties of limestone. It does not, like chemistry, seek to know which other bodily realities (called *elements*) make up this bodily reality called limestone. Philosophy asks what this limestone *is*. The other sciences accept the basic fact, the deepest reality, of the block of limestone; they take this for granted; they do not seek to investigate it. But it is precisely this deepest reality, ignored or blindly assumed by the partial sciences, that focusses the inquiry of philosophy. Philosophy asks, "What, ultimately, *is* this limestone?" Well, it is a thing or reality; it is a substantial reality; it is a bodily reality. Fundamentally, ultimately, this limestone is *a substantial reality of the bodily order;* more briefly, it is *a body.* And as such, as *a body,* the limestone block engages the attention of philosophy. Notice here what an immense world of knowable things is *drawn into unity* in the one concept or idea of *body.* Notice too how truly *ultimate* is the quest of philosophy as contrasted with the effort of partial sciences to gain *proximate* justification for their conclusions. We have here something that should give us a grasp of the truth that philosophy can be, and is, a science of all things knowable (despite the endless variety and multiplicity of these things), and that philosophy penetrates as deeply as the human mind can go in its investigation of reality.

Philosophy seeks to trace things actual and things possible to their last discernible causes and reasons. Now *a cause* is anything that contributes in any way to the producing or the maintaining of a reality. *A reason* is whatever helps in any way to explain a reality to the inquiring mind. A cause contributes to the *becoming* or the *being* of a reality; a reason contributes to a person's *understanding* of a reality. In a word, a cause produces or maintains, a reason explains.

All reality must be either produced or unproduced. If produced, *it is caused,* it is *an effect.* One effect may, in turn, become the cause of a further effect. But the chain of cause-and-effect is not endless, nor can it be endless. Working back along this chain, we inevitably must come to a First Cause which is not produced, not an effect of a prior cause (for it is *first*). There must be a First Cause, existing of its own necessity, by its own unbounded and supreme excellence. And this Cause is, and must be, *one.* There is only one First or Primary Cause. All other causes in the universe, whether actual or merely conceivable, are *effects* before they are *causes.* As causes then they are not primary, but *secondary.* The one First or Primary Cause is God. God is First; He has no cause or causes of Himself; He is unproduced; He is not an effect. Yet God is somehow knowable (even as He is here shown to be knowable in the present train of argument); God is recognizable; God is explainable to the inquiring mind. All of which proves that while there are no *causes* of God, there are *reasons* which explain to the mind the existence and the excellence of God. Notice and remember this truth: All reality other than God has *both causes and reasons;* God has no causes but only *reasons.*

Now, when we know the cause of anything we have at least a partial explanation of that thing; therefore, *every cause is a reason.* But there are reasons other than causes; therefore, *not every reason is a cause.* Further, a reality, even if it lack causes (as does God) cannot lack reasons; for reality as such is knowable, graspable, understandable. Hence, *everything* is explainable; everything has its *reasons;* this is true even if the reasons elude the grasp of man's imperfect mind. In a word *nothing can exist without a sufficient or fully-accounting reason for its existence.* This is the meaning of the familiar Latin axiom *Nihil sine ratione sufficienti existentiae suae.* Literary folk like to refer to this truth as the necessity for a *raison d'être.*

Causes are of four chief types; these are called, respectively, *material, formal, effecting, final.* A bodily reality is the product or effect of all four types of cause; a spiritual reality is the effect of the last three types, for a spirit has no material cause. A *material* cause is the bodily stuff out of which a body is made. A *formal* cause gives "form" or character or definiteness or determinateness to a reality, making it that thing *formally* or *as such;* and this, whether one considers a substantial or an accidental reality; hence a formal cause is either *a substantial formal cause* (such as that which makes a silver statue *silver*) or *an accidental formal cause* (such as that which makes a silver statue six inches high). An *effecting* cause produces an effect by its activity or operation. A *final* cause is the goal which invites or indicates the aim of the activity of the effecting cause.

Philosophy is interested in all types of causes and in all reasons, but only in so far as these are *ultimate* or serve as means to the discovery of the ultimate explanation of reality. Herein we notice once more one of the *unifying* characteristics of philosophy, and we are enabled to grasp something of the possibility of a single science which deals with all knowables. For the multitude of sciences that exist today to amaze us with their endless variety are largely a tissue of *proximate causes and effects,* and of *reasons immediate and often provisional.* Philosophy, by entering the *ultimate* realms of investigation, is able to unify, clarify, and enhance the many and various findings of the particular sciences.

3. Object of Philosophy: When we speak casually of "an object" we may mean a reality or thing, as when we talk of "visible objects" or "objects of value" or "objects of art." Or we may mean the end, aim, or purpose of an action, fact, or event, as when we speak of "the object of a visit" or "the object of a plan or programme" or "the object of a meeting."

Now, when we speak of *the object of a science* we employ the term *object* in an ancient technical sense. First of all, the object of a science is what the science treats of; it is what we loosely call "the subject-matter" of the science. In this sense the object of a science is known as *the material object.* Thus, for example, the material object of the science of geology is the earth; the material object of the science of physiology is the human body; the material object of the science of astronomy is the world of heavenly bodies. Hence when we speak of *the material object* of a science we name, in general, the field in which the science works.—In a second and more penetrating meaning, the object of a science is what gives the science its precise character, its "form" as the ancients would say. It is that which makes a science this determinate science, *formally* or *as such,* and marks it off from other sciences in the same general field. In this sense the object of a science is called *the formal object.* Now, that which gives a science its accurate and determinate character is its point of approach, its aim and purpose, and the principles which guide it or light its way. Thus geology which studies the earth as its material object is concerned with *the rocky structure of the earth,* and not with the shape or size of fertility or divisions of the earth. We say: the material object of geology is the earth; the formal object of geology is the rocky structure of the earth.

Many sciences may work in the same field; therefore many sciences may have the same material object. But no two sciences deal with the material object in precisely the same way and with the same end in view; should they do so they would coalesce as *one* science. Hence no two sciences can have the same formal object. Sciences are distinguished one from another by their objects, and, in last analysis, by their complete formal objects. To illustrate this, consider the sciences of anatomy, physiology, and hygiene. All three of these sciences have the same material object, namely, the organs of the human body. But these three sciences have not the same formal object. Anatomy studies its material object for the purpose of knowing *structure;* physiology studies the same material object for the purpose of knowing *function;* hygiene studies the same material object for the purpose of knowing how to maintain *normality and health.*

The material object of philosophy is *reality,* that is, "all things knowable." The formal object of philosophy is *reality in its final explanation,* that is, "studied in its deepest, its ultimate causes and reasons." Philosophy is at one with all sciences in its material object, for all sciences deal with reality, although each particular science has but a limited part of reality in its scope while philosophy has all. But philosophy stands alone, stands unique, in its quest of *ultimate* causes and reasons. Philosophy is distinguished from every other science by its formal object.

There was once great confusion on the question of the distinction between philosophy and theology. The difficulty was this: Philosophy deals with all knowables in an ultimate manner. So does theology. For all knowables may be summed up in two words, *Creator* and *creature,* or in two equivalent words, *God* and *the universe.* It would seem then, since both theology and philosophy deal with God and the universe in an ultimate way, that these two sciences coalesce as one. St. Thomas Aquinas (1225–1274) cleared up the difficulty. He showed that the formal object is itself twofold: the formal object as *aim, purpose,* or *special aspect,* and the formal object as *guiding principle or light.* The former he called "the formal object *which*" (*objectum formale quod*); the latter he called "the formal object *whereby*" (*objectum formale quo*). Now, philosophy deals with all knowables (its material object) in an ultimate manner (formal object *which*) under the unaided light of the human mind (formal object *whereby*). Theology, on the other hand, deals with its material object (all knowables—God and creatures) in an ultimate manner (formal object *which*) under the light of Divine Revelation (formal object *whereby*). Stating the principle: *sciences are distinguished one from another by their respective formal objects and ultimately by the formal object "whereby,"* St. Thomas drew a clear line of distinction between philosophy and theology.

We may state the object of philosophy as follows:

Material Object: all things knowable; all reality;

Formal Object *Quod:* reality as knowable in its ultimate explanations;

Formal Object *Quo:* reality knowable in its ultimate explanations under the light and effort of man's unaided reasoning power.

4. Importance of Philosophy: On the face of things, it is unquestionably important for us to know what man has accomplished through the centuries by the closest and most intense use of his mind. It is manifestly important to know something of man's quest into the heart of reality and to read some of the results of that quest.

We all acknowledge the importance of knowing man's deeds, his dreams, his plans and policies, his management of affairs, his aspirations. Still greater must be the importance of knowing man's achievements in the high domain of the intellect. To follow the course of human efforts to learn ultimate truth; to be culturally enriched by a knowledge of what these efforts have won; to be helped by this knowledge to avoid the calamitous mistakes of the past; to achieve in all this a real enlightenment of mind,—surely this is to pursue most noble aims. Now, the earnest study of philosophy and its course through history is the one direct means of pursuing such aims. Can there be any doubt then that philosophy is a science of tremendous importance?

Father Stanislaus Lortie in his *Elementa Philosophiae Christianae* (Vol. I, p. 4 f.) says that philosophy is of great importance (*a*) to individual persons, (*b*) to human society, (*c*) to the Christian Faith, and (*d*) to all the particular sciences.—(*a*) The individual finds in the study of philosophy a splendid means of exercising both understanding and will: the understanding is stimulated by the quest of ultimate truth; the will is stirred by basically known truth to choose what is truly good. (*b*) Human society finds its condition improved as its members advance in the knowledge of truths fundamental to the social order, to sound economics, to solid political science. (*c*) The Christian Faith is benefited by philosophy inasmuch as this science demonstrates the truths which the Fathers of the Church called "The Preamble of the Faith"; further, philosophy is a splendid instrument for the scientific exposition of the truths of Faith, and it illuminates sacred doctrine by apt analogy and telling similitude. Philosophy also defends the Faith against those who presume to attack it in the name of reason; for true philosophy shows that there is, and must be, completest harmony between faith and reason, between religion and science. (*d*) The particular sciences find in philosophy,—as M. Jacques Maritain points out,—their judge, their defender, and their governor. Yet, though philosophy uses the particular sciences as instruments, and furnishes to them their requisite basis of reasoned principles, it never loses its queenly independence; it remains ever superior to the particular sciences and is "pre-eminently free."

These, then, are the points in which philosophy shows its tremendous importance: its intrinsic character; its necessity to man in individual and social life; its service to religion and to scientific study; its rank and independence as the queen of human sciences.

No one should go unwillingly to the study of philosophy, surrendering reluctantly to its imperious claims and taking up the work as a dull and heavy duty. For philosophy is not only inescapably important for the person who seeks education and culture; it is also one of the most attractive and absorbing studies that can engage the attention of any mind.

5. The Identification of True Philosophy: We have defined philosophy as the science of all things naturally knowable viewed in their last discernible causes and reasons. Pondering this definition, we conclude that a considerable amount of time must have been required for the necessary viewing and discerning. Philosophy, the greatest of human sciences, was not developed in a day. It must have come to whatever objective perfection it may now possess through the expenditure of great effort long sustained.

Now, it is hardly conceivable, in this clamoring, arguing world, that the development of philosophy has been a manifest and steady growth, like that of a tree in a garden, a thing to be recognized by every observer, and not to be mistaken or denied. No, there must have been in ages past, there must be still today, many and various philosophical *efforts,* some copiously fruitful, some largely futile and false. Man has been slow of mind since the original Fall; he has been in ignorance, subject to pride and prejudice; he has been wildly capricious and wilful. Even the story of man's most serious and studious thinking cannot be a simple record of steady achievement and constant agreement. Quite the contrary, in fact. Hence there have been, and there are now, multitudes of theories and of systems of theories which are not true philosophy at all. There are, to use a graceless phrase, many "false philosophies." Grains of truth are everywhere, of course; no system of thought, however mistaken, can be so wholly false as to exclude altogether every element of truth. But there are endless systems and theories in the world (many of them exhumed from ancient books and presented as sparklingly new "interpretations of the universe") which, in general character, and in their speculative and practical conclusions, are false and harmful to minds and souls. On the other hand, however, much of man's philosophical effort through the ages has led to the discovering of ultimate truth; much of man's mental labor has been successful labor. And, since the effort to systematize findings has been as continuous as the effort to know root-causes, we must reasonably expect to find, somewhere in the world, *a comparatively complete and ultimate system which alone is entitled to the name of philosophy.* In a word, there must be available now for the mind a *true philosophy.* It may not be wholly perfect; indeed, we cannot expect it to be that, since it is a human achievement and will necessarily bear the mark of human limitations. But, after two thousand years of tireless questing, there must be now available a system of ultimate thought, of reasoned truths, of which we say, "This is the best that the mind of man has been able to achieve; this system, more than any other, meets at all points the requirements of fact, and of reason in its most penetrating investigation of reality." The philosophy of which these words can justly be said is the true philosophy. Nor is it true in any mere metaphorical sense, true because it seems acceptable, true because it is comparatively better than other systems. It must be true in fact, true actually, true in very truth. If it be not so, then truth is simply not attainable by man's mind. For if two thousand years of the best efforts have produced a best and tested system which is not a true system, how can we hope that truth will be attained in two thousand years more, or in two million? How can we hope that man's mind can achieve philosophy at all? Unless we are prepared to accept the self-contradiction and the insanity of complete skepticism, we must admit, on the one hand, that the mind is capable of attaining truth, and, on the other hand, we must acknowledge some success where that capability has been exercised for studious centuries. That man can go on learning is certain, but that man can utterly change the pattern of his knowing, and can abandon all the most certain and fundamental principles and data of his knowledge, is so impossible as to be inconceivable. The true philosophy, then, imperfect but still *true* and *relatively perfect,* must be here in the world for the energetic and adequate mind to discover and embrace.

The modern mind is subject to a benighting influence in the steady advance of experimental science. It is likely to conclude that light and truth lie all ahead, and that the past was all a groping and mistaken time. One thought should serve to correct this sort of blindness. If there is no eternal, unchanging, unaging meaning in the words *truth, knowledge, certitude,* how do we even know what we are after in all our splendid experiments? How do we even know our aims, however far off in a glorious future we choose to set their attainment? This thought should lead to another: that philosophy is a system of *ultimate* truths which must stand up, and stand unchanged, under all the new findings of all the new sciences. True philosophy will throw its light around the findings of the partial sciences, and will take illustration of ultimate truths from what they offer. But this is only saying what has already been said: "True philosophy must meet at all points the requirements of fact and of reason." True philosophy welcomes and fosters the development of all sciences; the light of its ultimate truth finds new glories in them, as the light of the sun flashes with new beauty when the prisms which refract its ray are multiplied in number and variety.

We assert then that true philosophy *exists in the world,* and that it is *available to the human mind.* Yet much "false philosophy" is here too. How shall the true philosophy be known? What criteria have we for identifying the true philosophy?

First of all, true philosophical doctrine must exhibit itself as *enduring,* as *historically continuous.* Truth endures; error tends to fall away, although it tends also to recur and reappear in new guises. A doctrine which has managed *to last,* to weather storms of skepticism and direct attack, to stand up and stand firm under all the advances and extensions of human knowledge, has a claim on our attention as true doctrine. It has proved its mettle; it is authentic ware. Further, doctrine which involves a necessity of truth in itself, and has endured because it cannot be rationally doubted or denied, is necessarily part of the true philosophy.

Again, in addition to lastingness, a true philosophical doctrine will fit in with others of its kind in a sort of interlocking security, so that there is a true *consistency* in the system of such truths. Philosophical truths cannot be like individual survivors riding individual planks; they must rather be amicable and mutually helpful survivors in a single boat,—the one ark of intellectual salvation.

Still again, in addition to lastingness and interlocking consistency, true philosophical doctrines must be *changeless in themselves;* they are not to be trimmed or shaded, contracted or expanded. As the world grows older, as the sum of human knowledge is extended, as science opens new doors and windows, the truths of philosophy must show themselves over and over again, and in more and more detail, to be the rays of a single glorious sun. Truth is always truth. There is no such thing as a doctrine becoming more true or less true, although, of course, there is always the possibility of man's learning more about what is in itself changelessly true. Truth is eternally *there.* It may be discovered in successive and increasingly larger views, but, in itself, it neither grows, nor does it fade into falsity. Further, no truth can be in conflict with any other truth. Where such conflicts seem to exist, they are apparent, not real conflicts, or one of the conflicting things is falsity and not truth.

The course of human history shows a successive discovery and application of ultimate truths. We discern, moving down through the centuries, the stream of man's philosophical achievement. Sometimes the stream is clear and clean; sometimes it is muddled with intermingled error. In one place its course is straight and plain; in another it moves through bewildering loops and curves. Here it is open, there it lies concealed by some rank growth that obscures its channel. But the stream flows on, flows ever, continuous, consistent, enduring.

Now, of all the doctrines propounded and defended by many men of many ages, which are those that constitute this ever-flowing stream of true philosophy? Which are the truths that make the perennial philosophy, the *philosophia perennis,* the philosophy which runs a course unbroken through the centuries? Well, we shall find that this philosophy is mainly *Greek* in its origins, and mainly *Aristotelian* in its Grecian character. We shall find that this philosophy has come, in the main, from Socrates, Plato, and Aristotle,—but chiefly from Aristotle,—and that it moved into Christian times to take new light and power in the day of Christianity which succeeded the night of pagan antiquity. We shall find it enriched by the genius of St. Augustine in the 4 century; carried forward by religious men,—sole preservers of things of the mind during the true Dark Ages,—into the 9 century and the Revival of Learning under Charlemagne and Alcuin. We shall find it taking more complete form under the labor of the eloquent Roscelin, the deeply learned St. Anselm, the keen but hesitant William of Champeaux, the fiery and erratic Abelard. We shall find it rounding into perfection under the power of the unequalled genius of the 13 century when the greatest minds gave it their best efforts,—William of Auvergne, Alexander of Hales, St. Bonaventure, St. Albert the Great, St. Thomas Aquinas, John Duns Scotus. After the 13 century, the *philosophia perennis,*—henceforth known as *the Scholastic philosophy* or *the philosophy of the schoolmen,*—moved through the years to our own day, often obscured, often ignored, often and for long periods despised as outmoded by those who knew little or nothing of its doctrines and their compelling evidence. Despite continued and recurring obstacles and obscurities, this philosophy has ever been coming newly into view, ever striving to assume and maintain its rightful place of pre-eminence and control. Today it challenges the attention of the best minds, and its influence widens hourly. Many of its most notable modern exponents are called, perhaps regrettably, *the Neo-Scholastics,*—the "neo" being a concession to current fashion and a call for attention which, without it, would hardly be bestowed.

The Scholastic philosophy, or, more precisely the Greco-Scholastic philosophy, survives in the world today as *the only continuously existent and consistent system of philosophic thought that man may find in all the records of his race.* It represents the best that man has been able to do in his tireless quest of root-reality. It is the one system that has any roundness or completeness in its expression of the human philosophic effort, that is, of the effort of the deepest and most earnest human thought upon *the ultimate unities* which embrace all knowable reality within their mighty scope. This blunt statement is ever provocative of indignation and denial among non-Scholastics with their broken and partial philosophies. But there the thing stands. Like it or hate it, it is fact and not fiction. This is no dictum of partisan minds, but the irrefutable declaration of human history.

Nor is this perennial philosophy, this acme of human achievement in "interpreting the universe," a dry and dusty system of statistical truths, set in an iron fixity that leaves nothing for the student but the task of memorizing, and balks constructive thinking or advance in philosophic knowledge. No one who knows anything of the Scholastic philosophy could so utterly misconceive it or so slanderously misrepresent it. The Scholastic philosophy has been likened to a stream; it is no stagnant pool. It is a running, living, vitalizing stream, and its springs are ever-flowing, fresh, clear, new as well as old. Indeed, it is the non-Scholastic welter of philosophies that resembles the stale standing water that can do no more than dry away and leave but fruitless and hardened clay. These futile "philosophies," with their opinions, their views, their approaches to this subject and to that, can never give the human mind the certainty it requires for constructive thinking; they can never bring knowledge to flower or truth to glorious fruitfulness. It is these, and not the perennial philosophy, which give a show of reason to the layman's notion that philosophers are mere idlers and misty-eyed dwellers in a world of unreality.

Now, why should there be indignation and denial when the unique claims of the Scholastic philosophy are presented? There are many minor reasons: the resentment of prideful minds against any claim to uniqueness; the current substitution of fashion for thought, which finds anything with the mark of the past upon it an object for scoffing and derision; the ineptitude that ignores history, and reduces knowledge to a set of charts on the walls of a laboratory. Plain, brazen, unblinking ignorance is another reason. But the major reason for modern resentment against the claims of Scholasticism lies in this fact: the great Scholastics of the past were Catholics and, for the most part, churchmen, who, finding that divinely revealed truth may have in philosophy a noble instrument for exposition and scientific elaboration, applied their philosophic doctrines in the realm of theology. Because, as a fact, Scholastic philosophy stands in agreement with Catholic doctrine (and how could it be otherwise, since both are true?) biassed minds have declared that the Scholastics forced and twisted their philosophy to fit with their religion; that they warped its tenets into place as "Catholic philosophy"; that they shackled and enslaved philosophy to serve a set system of theology. All this is, of course, quite untrue. The *philosophia perennis* has not been warped or twisted; it fits naturally and nobly into its place as the free-serving and devoted *ancilla theologiae*. Just as grace supposes nature and builds upon it, so does Revelation suppose reason and ennobles and enlarges its efforts and its scope. Yet the modern non-Scholastic will have none of this. To him, Scholastic philosophy is Catholic philosophy. And Catholic philosophy is theological philosophy. Now, nothing is more distasteful to the modern mind than theology. For the first mark of pride is that it resents God, and the modern mind is sadly tainted by pride.

Strictly speaking, there is no such thing as Catholic philosophy. That is to say, there is no system of philosophical doctrines built up for the purpose of supplying a reasoned basis for Catholicity. True philosophy actually supplies such a reasoned basis, but it has not been elaborated for that purpose. True philosophy is naturally and inevitably the reasoned basis for true theology. But, as it is the fate and the glory of the Catholic religion to resemble its Divine Founder in being the object of hatred, abuse, contempt, and misrepresentation on the part of those who do not know and will not investigate its character, claims, and history, so it is the fate and glory of the true philosophy which naturally supports Catholicity to be the object of like evil sentiments and activities on the part of persons who reject, with the smallest and most cursory investigation, its irrefutable claims upon the human mind.

At the outset of our study we assert the claims of Scholastic philosophy to be the true philosophy. As we have said, there are elements of truth scattered through many doctrines and many systems and schemes of theories. But in the Scholastic philosophy we find truths systematized, correlated, set forth in a rounded completeness which covers the whole ground of rational inquiry. We do not assert that the Scholastic philosophy is wholly perfect. We must admit that certain departments of it, and notably that called Natural Philosophy or Cosmology, are subject to development and improvement. But in its basic principles, in its rounded character, in its coherence and continuity, in its reasoned conclusions, it is a unique thing in the world. If there can be true philosophy at all, and surely there can be, then this is the true philosophy. Our studies, as we advance, will help to show the justice of this claim.

From the standpoint of Scholastic philosophy we shall view

and criticize the development of philosophic thought as we endeavor to trace, in an elemental and sketchy manner, the progress of the *philosophia perennis* through human history.

6. Division of This Treatise: The first part of the present study is descriptive and historical. We shall, in this part, look into the beginnings of philosophy, its development, its coming of age. The second part of our study turns upon the essential questions of philosophy; it turns upon what may be called the diversified function of philosophy. If we choose, we may say that the first part of this study is *historical,* the second part *functional.*

The treatise is therefore divided into two Parts. These, with their subjoined Chapters are set forth in the following scheme:

PART FIRST

The Origin and Growth of Philosophy

Chapter I. The Beginnings of Philosophy
Chapter II. The Development of Philosophy
Chapter III. The Perfecting of Philosophy
Chapter IV. The Course of Philosophy to Our Times

PART SECOND

The Questions of Philosophy

Chapter I. The Logical Question
Chapter II. The Critical Question
Chapter III. The Ontological Question
Chapter IV. The Cosmological Question
Chapter V. The Psychological Question
Chapter VI. The Theological Question
Chapter VII. The Ethical Question

PART FIRST

The Origin and Growth of Philosophy

The Part gives some account of the roots of philosophic endeavor, and of the emergence and development of philosophy. It gives a summary description and criticism of notable philosophical doctrines from the most ancient times to the present day. These matters are discussed in four Chapters, as follows:

CHAPTER I

THE BEGINNINGS OF PHILOSOPHY

The present Chapter discusses *the roots of philosophy* found in man's rational nature and in some primeval manifestation to man of the meaning of reality, particularly of his own existence. Further, the Chapter studies *the first emergence of philosophy* among the ancient Orientals and the early Greeks. The Chapter is accordingly divided into two Articles:

Article 1. The Roots of Philosophy
Article 2. The Emergence of Philosophy

Article 1. The Roots of Philosophy

a) Man's Rational Nature; b) Primitive Revelation and Tradition.

a) Man's Rational Nature

Philosophy, the loving quest of wisdom, the tireless pursuit of knowledge to its deepest origins and roots, comes into being, first and foremost, because the human mind is forever seeking to *know,* and to grasp the ultimate *how's* and *why's* of what it knows. Man has a quenchless thirst for knowledge. Nor is this a desire for mere data, for bare facts and events; it is a desire for data with their explanations, their justifications, their evidence, their proofs. And if a proof or explanation is not in itself an evident and inescapable reality, the mind looks for proof of that proof. So the search for solid and reliable knowledge,—for *truth,* in a word,—is carried forward, or naturally tends to be carried forward, towards fulfillment. The mind proves truth by truth; it holds truths in relation and connection; it delves deep to unify and clarify its findings in an ultimate understanding. Thus man is, by his very nature, philosophical.

The incessant questions of a child are manifest proof of *the natural thirst for knowledge* in which philosophy finds its first root. And though the child, unspoiled and trusting, will accept any explanation as satisfactory, and will find, for instance, no difficulty in the story of a fat Santa Claus coming down a narrow chimney or in the leap that carried the cow over the moon, the young mind will presently inquire further for evidence as extended experience makes its first willing acceptance give place to doubts. In its immaturity, in its lack of time and experience to draw into understandable unity the endless wonders of the world about it, the child accepts any explanation of any fact, and accepts fantastic tales quite casually as no more wonderful than the reality of this most wonderful world. But the child accepts each explanation, each wondrous tale, because it regards these things as true. Truth is what the mind is after; truth is what the mind desires; truth is what the mind is *for.* And the quest of truth, down to its last foundations, is a philosophical quest. Here is discerned the first root of philosophy.

Nor can it be successfully objected that many minds are indifferent, careless, unconcerned about the quest for truth and the explanation of facts. Such an objection is far from exact. No normal mind, however incurious, is without special interests in which it has the tendency to *know* and to *understand,* even though enervation or lack of energy hinders the full exercise of this tendency. There are indeed countless persons who have no direct or conscious interest in what are loosely called "the things of the mind," that is, deep reasonings upon abstract truths, such as are the delight of the practised philosopher. There are many who have no sympathy with such things; who regard effort spent upon them as idleness and waste of time; who consider all "philosophizing" as silly vaporizing in a world of unreality. It is remarkable that this should be, since the philosopher, above all others, is most thoroughly and exclusively concerned with reality. It is remarkable, but it is so. But the point we make here is that even those who regard professed philosophers as fools who wear out their minds (and their readers and hearers) in meaningless discussions of "the whichness of what" and "the whatness of which,"—even those scoffers to whom there is no important reality beyond machines and microscopes and bread and sport, even these are seekers after facts with their causes and reasons, their how's and their why's. Your "practical" person, full of scorn for philosophy, is none the less an ardent admirer of the man who knows his job; it is his own proudest boast that in his special sphere of interest and activity he "knows all the answers." So even this "practical" person is proof sufficient of our assertion that the human mind wants knowledge, and wants the how's and why's of what it knows.

But we have no need to pause and argue with the inept, the lazy, the incurious. Our statement that the human mind is naturally philosophical in its effort is manifestly true of the mind at its unspoiled best. That some minds are ill-directed and spend their energies amiss; that some are thwarted by incapacity; that some are quickly weary in the quest of truth,—these facts are in no sense an argument against *the native tendency* of the human mind for ultimate truth. Indeed, they are rather a proof of that tendency. There is an explanation for the fact that many human beings fail to seek out ultimate causes and reasons, fail to realize or to concern themselves about the meaning of existence, and are content with second-best and third-best explanations of the world about them, of life, of duty, of effort. There is an explanation, and only one. It is the fact that something has, in human origins, gone wrong with man; something has hurt his mind, darkening it and making it subject to sudden weariness, willing to surrender its effort under the stress of exacting labor. The name of this fact is Original Sin. And of that we may not pause to speak further in this place.

We come back to our statement that the first root of philosophy is found in man's native tendency to know truths with their evidence. This statement is given with technical accuracy in the following formula: *the first root of philosophy is found in the rational nature of man.*

Now, the nature of a thing is its working essence. And the essence of a thing is that which constitutes it and makes it what it is. Essence regarded as the source of operations is called *nature;* thus we are justified in our description of nature as "working essence." To illustrate: the *essence* of a man (physically considered) is his body and soul; these are the elements which constitute a human being, and *make him what he is* in his fundamental actuality. But the *nature* of a man is the essence looked at as the source and font of human operations. So we say that it is according to man's *nature* that he feels and sees and thinks and wills. Man's essence *works* that way. That is his *mode of operation.* That is his *nature.*

When we say that the nature of man is *rational* we use the term in its original Latin meaning, not in its current meaning of "conscious" or "normal." A *rational* nature means a nature fundamentally equipped for understanding and freely choosing. We do not say that a being of rational nature can think or will at any instant; no, we say that such a being is *fundamentally equipped* for thinking and willing, even though some obstacle should prevent the exercise of these activities. Thus a baby, even a baby yet unborn; a madman; a man unconscious, each of these is *a being of rational nature* as truly as is the alert, mature, and normal man who is consciously exercising his powers of thinking and willing. This is a point of boundless importance for many reasons which lie outside the scope of our present study. But one of these reasons is of such vital character that it must be allowed to obtrude itself even here; we shall pause upon it for a brief paragraph.

One great reason for stressing the true meaning of the phrase "rational nature" lies in the fact that current usage makes the word "rational" practically synonymous with the word "conscious," or the word "lucid," or the word "normal." Thus we speak of one recovered from the stress of high emotion, or of one who has emerged from delirium or coma, or of one who has achieved normality after a temporary lapse into insanity, as one who "is quite rational again." This is a sad, nay a disastrous use of the word. For it has in it the suggestion,—which grew up and grew strong together with the materialistic and pagan view of things which we call "modern" and sometimes "scientific,"—that one who is not "rational" (that is, one who is not in adequate and active awareness and management of himself) is something *less than human.* Especially is this so with reference to the unborn child, the insane, the more benighted sort of criminal, the senile, the immature,—the "unfit," in a word. And out of this evil sense of the term "rational" has come, in a measure far greater than most of us realize, our easy tolerance, our sober acceptance, of "scientific" discussions and justifications of abortion, of sterilization, of euthanasia or "mercy killing." No one would listen for a moment to the proposal, however sober and "scientific," that we should murder or mutilate a great number of perfectly normal men. But many of us will listen patiently, perhaps with half-assent, to the proposal that the abnormal, the subnormal, or the outworn should be eased gently out of life or mutilated and made impotent to propagate. It is, in large measure, our false grasp of the word "rational" that prevents us from seeing that the one proposal is precisely the same as the other. Each is a proposal to maim or murder human beings, every one of whom is *a being of rational nature.*

Here we recall an important Scholastic distinction. A being *fundamentally equipped* for an operation is said to possess *in actu primo* the perfection which that operation indicates or bestows. A being that *exercises* the operation is said to possess its perfection *in actu secundo.* Literally, the Latin phrases mean, respectively, "in first actuality" and "in second actuality"; we may, however, translate them freely as "in basic fact" and "in actual exercise." Thus a baby is a thinking and a walking being *in actu primo* or in basic fact, because it is fundamentally equipped for the operations of thinking and walking, even though lack of experience and of development balks the actual exercise of these operations. After a time, the child will both think and walk, and, in exercising these operations, it will be a thinking and a walking being *in actu secundo* or in actual exercise. It will think and walk *in the second place,* given the existence of the basic equipment for thinking and walking *in the first place.* Now, the point here to remember is that every rational creature is rational by reason of the fact that it possesses *in actu primo* the powers of understanding and free choice.

That every human being is a being of rational nature is a truth discussed in the department of philosophy called *psychology.* For the present, we merely notice the fact that man is rational, that he has the natural equipment and tendency to think, to apprehend, to understand, to think things out, to correlate and integrate his findings and to bring them into unity. In all this man shows himself to be cast in the image of God who knows all things in the unity of eternal understanding. And this connatural human power and tendency for understanding, reasoning, unifying,—this *rational nature* of man,—is the first root of philosophy.

It must be noticed that a rational nature is more than a *knowing* nature. All animals have a knowing nature, but man alone, of all animals, is rational. Animals are equipped for sense-knowledge; man is equipped for intellectual knowledge, that is, for rising from the individual findings of the senses to the suprasensible and universal grasp of reality and for will-acts in the light of this superior knowledge.

Sense-knowledge is knowledge of concrete and individual things; mental or intellectual knowledge is knowledge of essences (expressed in the mind as concepts or ideas) and of the relations of essences (expressed in the mind as judgments and reasonings). The sense of sight, for example, beholds individual objects, say a tree or a group of trees. But the mind, taking the findings of sight, rises from these data to an *understanding* of what *tree* means, not this tree or these trees only, but any tree and every tree. Further, the mind rises to concepts or ideas of things which the senses cannot possibly grasp,—things such as substance, or symmetry, or beauty.

Inevitably, out of its findings and their unions, their comparisons, their relations, their connections, the mind becomes aware of truths which it enunciates within itself as *judgments* and expresses outwardly as *propositions*. And out of judgments, aligned in their proper relations, the mind will draw *conclusions* or further judgments. Thus does the mind *reason* or *think things out*.

Among reasoned conclusions of the mind there are, by natural necessity, certain clearly recognized truths involving duty, obligation, rightness or wrongness; in a word, *morality*.

The fact that a man can define a reality, that he can discuss things in a general way, that he can do a sum in arithmetic or prove a theorem in geometry; the fact that he is aware of duty and recognizes the need of law and order,—all these facts are proof inescapable that man is a being of rational nature, and, by that same token, that he is by nature *philosophical*. Philosophy exists because, first of all, man has a nature that makes him pursue the philosophical quest. Such is the meaning of the declaration that the first root of philosophy is *the rational nature of man*.

b) Primitive Revelation and Tradition

The fact that man is of rational nature, and therefore fundamentally philosophical, does not mean that all human beings are actively interested in the deep and determined process of thinking things out which we call *philosophical speculation*. No, all we may say, and must say, is that man is equipped by nature for such speculation. It is to be expected, however, that man's natural equipment for speculation would manifest itself in the formation of some system of thought about reality. Special tastes and talents, together with favoring circumstances, must have come into play, sometimes in man's history, to put him to the task of using his natural equipment in the developing of philosophy.

None the less, the fact of philosophy in the world is not entirely explained in terms of rational nature, tastes, talents, and circumstances. There is ample evidence in the history of human thought that all men, from the earliest times, have had *some common store of knowledge* to draw upon. The ancients, despite wide variations in their cultures, had many notions in common. They all had some knowledge of the emerging of the earth out of a chaos of waters. They all believed that man was made, directly or indirectly, out of the clay of the earth. They all held that man is meant to serve God. They all were convinced that the human race had somehow gone wrong in its very origins, and that mankind had suffered a fall. They all felt that the business of life involves some sort of cleansing and refining of self, and the attainment of a more perfect state here or hereafter. They all taught that man is, in one way or another, to work for reunion with his Primal Source. Further, all the ancients had the story of a destructive flood of waters which laid waste the world, and the story of the dispersion of human tribes. We must conclude that mankind came to a knowledge of these things through the medium of some *primitive revelation.*

Christians find this conclusion consonant with their belief that God instructed our first parents; that He spoke with them familiarly; that He doubtlessly gave them information about their material origins even as He imparted knowledge of the creation and inbreathing of their spiritual souls which gave them their perfected being as images of God. This primitive revelation of man's nature, dignity, duty, and destiny, together with the earliest and most striking experiences of the human race, must have been a matter of common discussion. All these facts must have been narrated again and again by the human voice as the story was handed on from generation to generation. In a word, the primitive revelation and the first great experiences of mankind must have been perpetuated through early times by *human tradition.*

Now, tradition, unless it is divinely protected and conserved (as is the case with Sacred Tradition which is a source of Divine Revelation), is a stream that inevitably gathers alien matters as it flows along. Man is imaginative, and his fancy tends to dress fact with such abundance of adornment that the fact itself is sometimes obscured and even forgotten. For this reason, modern man, driven by the same imaginative impulse, is too ready to dismiss old traditions as "mere folk-lore." But there is always a reason for folk-lore; there is always a living truth in the wrappings of fanciful detail; there is no such thing as *mere* folk-lore. And so, while it is undoubted that the primitive revelation and the earliest events of human history have come down the stream of human tradition in an imperfect and progressively obscured condition, we are none the less on solid historical ground in our conclusion that these two things (primitive revelation and remembered events of early history) are factual and not fanciful. The *primitive revelation* and *human tradition* come together to constitute a true source of philosophical concepts and speculation. They may justly be regarded as the second root of philosophy.

Summary of the Article

In this Article we have discerned the fact that the first root of philosophy is the rational nature of man. We have defined *nature* as "essence viewed dynamically," that is, essence regarded as the font of operations. And *rational nature* means nature equipped *in actu primo* (or "in basic fact") for understanding and free self-directive choice. We have noticed the fact that man has some common original storehouse of knowledge which can be accounted for only by a *primitive revelation* and an esssentially reliable *human tradition;* these two agencies constitute the second root of philosophy.

Our study thus far has given us the meaning of certain philosophical terms, such as: *essence, nature, sensation* (i.e., *sense-knowledge*), *intellection* (i.e., *intellectual knowledge*), *concept, judgment, proposition, reasoning, actus primus, actus secundus.*

Article 2. The Emergence of Philosophy

a) First Efforts; b) The Ancient Orientals; c) The Early Greeks.

a) First Efforts

Since man is by nature philosophical, it is inevitable that the earliest records of his thinking should manifest something of that human *quest of ultimate causes* and that human *effort to make a deep unification of knowledge* which we call by the name *philosophy.* As soon as man begins to think he begins to think things out; he begins to speculate or reason deeply; he begins to philosophize. As soon as he records his thinking, philosophy begins, however imperfectly, to take form. Philosophy emerges the moment the mind comes to grips with reality and begins to draw conclusions and unify findings.

Some writers speak of a period of human history and of human thinking as "pre-philosophic." With all reverence for great learning, we dare to reject this term as inaccurate. It is true that the earliest records of man's thinking offer us no rounded and systematized interpretation of "all things knowable." But it is equally true that these records show a real approach to the realm of knowables. Such an approach is not pre-philosophical, but simply philosophical. There is no warrant for cramping the meaning of the word *philosophical* to exclude all early reasoning on the subjects of God and duty. For theology and ethics (that is, the philosophy of God, and the philosophy of duty) are as truly philosophical as cosmology (the philosophy of the bodily world) or metaphysics (the philosophy of reality as such). Hence we need not apologize for applying the high name of *philosophy* to the religious and moral conclusions of the ancient oriental peoples who have left us the earliest records of human thinking.

The philosophical efforts of man, from earliest to most recent, are efforts to find the true answers to one or other of certain fundamental questions. These questions may be listed as seven:

(*1*) *The Logical Question,* that is, the question of correct procedure in reasoning, in thinking things out;

(*2*) *The Critical Question,* that is, the question of the extent and reliability of human knowledge; the question of the possibility and method of achieving truth and certitude;

(*3*) *The Cosmological Question,* that is, the question of the ultimate constitution of bodies, and of their nature and properties;

(*4*) *The Psychological Question,* that is, the question of the meaning of life, especially human life, and of the nature and powers of the human life-principle or soul;

(*5*) *The Theological Question,* that is, the question of the existence, nature, operations, and perfections of God;

(*6*) *The Ontological Question* (or, if one prefer, *The Metaphysical Question*), that is, the question of the meaning and properties of *being* as such;

(*7*) *The Ethical Question,* that is, the question of morality in human conduct, of right and wrong, of human duty and human destiny.

These seven questions delineate the field of philosophy. They frame the discussion of "all things knowable."

b) The Ancient Orientals

The ancient oriental peoples were the Hebrews, the Chaldeans, the Egyptians, the Chinese, the Hindoos, the Persians. To the records of these early peoples we turn to discern the emergence of philosophy.

1. The Hebrews, whose name is probably a derivation from Heber who was one of the ancestors of Abraham, had, from their earliest recorded times, a belief in one God (*monotheism*). They believed in the immortality of the human soul, and in a life to come which involves retribution for the good or evil practised in this earthly existence. Evidence for these statements is found in the most ancient books of Holy Scripture. After the 6 century B.C., distinct groups of religious philosophers appeared among the Hebrews: (*a*) *The Pharisees* held the doctrines already mentioned (one God; immortality of the soul; rewards and punishments of a life to come), and they claimed to be the only authorized interpreters of the moral and ceremonial law. (*b*) *The Sadducees* denied the existence of anything spiritual (*materialism*); they acknowledged the existence of God but denied His government and providence in the world (*deism*); they found the true goal of human life in earthly pleasures and enjoyments (*hedonism*). (*c*) *The Essenes* were a cloistered group who held the necessity of self-denial to loose the soul from its body-prison into the happiness of heaven. They taught that the soul existed before it was joined to the body (*pre-existence of souls*), and that it was imprisoned in the body for some fault.

The Hebrew philosophy deserves its name; it must not be brushed aside as pre-philosophical. It deals, however brokenly, with the theological question, the psychological question, and the ethical question. An important point to notice is that this early philosophy had the idea of *one only God;* that is, it held the doctrine of *monotheism.* Here we see that monotheism is a really primitive doctrine, and not the development of cruder beliefs as some materialists and evolutionists of our day would like us to think.

2. The Chaldeans (that is to say, the Babylonians and the Assyrians) at first held by *monotheism;* they believed in one supreme God called *El.* Later they degraded this pure belief into a system of *polytheism,* that is, a theory of a plurality of gods. They held that man exists for the worship and service of divinity; to fulfill his destiny he must practise virtue, he must be a lover of peace, and must be just in his dealings with his fellows.

Again we find *monotheism,* that pure and elevated doctrine, as a really primitive form of belief, indeed of reasoned knowledge. Evolutionists would like to have it that crude and polytheistic beliefs were gradually refined into monotheism, but history has not a single instance of such a refinement. Monotheism precedes polytheism, and, among peoples not divinely protected from the lapse, monotheism degenerates into polytheism. Notice that the Chaldeans dealt with the theological question and the ethical question.

3. The Ancient Egyptians were, at first, monotheists; they lapsed into polytheism at an early period of their history, and deified the elements and parts of the universe. About the 7 century B.C. there was a mighty religious revival among the Egyptians, and the very animals of sacrifice came to be worshipped. But animal worship (*zoölatry*) was unknown to the most ancient Egyptians. The Egyptians believed in the immortality of the soul, and, about the 7 century B.C., they came to believe in the transmigration of souls (*metempsychosis*). They taught the necessity of virtuous living as the means to happiness in a life to come.

Here we find the elements of a philosophy which dealt with the theological question, the psychological question, and the ethical question.

4. The Ancient Chinese believed in one God called *Shang-ti,* a personal deity, distinct from the world, and all powerful. This pure belief quickly degenerated, especially after the 12 century B.C. when ancestor worship came strongly into vogue. Worship of the sun, moon, and stars (*sabaeism*) also appeared. After the 6 century B.C., the Chinese were much influenced in thought and conduct by their philosophers, especially Kun-fu-tse (Confucius) and Lao-tse. Confucius preached faithful observance of ancestral customs; he discouraged the natural tendency of men to pry into causes and reasons; his was a philosophy to kill philosophy. Lao-tse taught the existence of a Supreme Being called Tao (hence his doctrine is called *Taoism*) who produced the world. Tao is ever serene, untroubled; man must model himself on Tao; man must cultivate serenity of mind, caring nothing for riches or honors, or even for learning or for laws; man must follow quietly and unexcitedly his own natural bent.

The ancient Chinese dealt with the theological question, and, in a measure, with the psychological question; their great philosophers were concerned chiefly with the ethical question.

5. *The Ancient Hindoos* had sacred books called *Veda,* that is, *science.* These show traces of an original monotheism, but only traces, however plain. Polytheism came into being among the Hindoos at an early period. The Hindoo philosophy is very vague, but it contains unmistakable evidence of some belief in human immortality, in man's duty to worship divinity and to avoid sin. Between the 8 and the 5 century B.C. certain books (called *Brahmanas* and *Upanishads*) were written to explain the *Vedas.* These hint at a supreme and personal God called *Prajapati,* but this notion is quickly submerged in a welter of polytheistic doctrine. The theory developed in the *Brahmanas* is that the world and all things in it are *maya* or illusion. There is only one reality called *Brahma.* Man must rid himself of the deceiving idea that he exists as an individual; he must strive to merge himself consciously in Brahma with whom all things are really one (*pantheism*). Aligned with this doctrine of Brahma is *Buddhism* which holds the world unreal and illusory and teaches man to seek changelessness and peace in a state of *Nirvana* in which all desire is dead, all emotion extinguished.

The Hindoo philosophy deals slightly with the theological question, largely with the ethical question. Notice that it is *pessimistic* in character; it holds that man's lot is one of deception and pain, and teaches him that his sole ethical effort is to be rid of pain.

6. *The Ancient Persians* were monotheists at the first, but about the 8 century B.C. there appeared a mighty teacher called Zarates or Zarathustra (whom the Greeks called Zoroaster) who taught the existence of two warring gods (*religious dual-*

ism) ; one of these was the Supreme Good, the other the Supreme Evil. The good deity was called *Ahura-Mazda* (the Greeks named him *Ormuzd* or *Ormazd*) ; to him we attribute all good things, fire, light, stars and planets, summer, fertility, the human race. The evil deity was called *Angra-Mainyu* (the Greeks made the name *Ahriman*) ; to him are to be attributed all evil things, darkness, cold, bad spirits, disease, death, poisonous plants, ferocious animals, storms, and all destructive forces. These two divinities wage ceaseless war. One of the followers of Ahura-Mazda is the great spirit *Mithras* who will captain the forces of good to the final defeat of Angra-Mainyu. Perhaps, after the evil divinity and his followers have been hurled into the pit of punishment, Mithras will intercede for them, and they will ultimately be admitted to the paradise of delights in which Ahura-Mazda reigns.—Man was created pure by Ahura-Mazda ; he ate certain forbidden fruits and, in consequence, lost the love of his creator and was numbered with the hosts of Angra-Mainyu. Human nature was thus soiled at its source, and each individual feels within himself the war of good and evil. Man must rid himself of the evil and seek his original perfection. Man's soul is immortal ; it will be brought to purification and happiness either by strong efforts for virtue in this life or by suffering hereafter.

The ancient Persians discussed the theological question and the ethical question with incidental discussion of the psychological question. We notice in their strange mélange of doctrines some vestiges of the primitive revelation in the somewhat distorted account of man's creation and original sin.

c) The Early Greeks

Most accounts of philosophy begin with the speculation (that is, the deep philosophical studies) of the Greeks, dismissing the ancient orientals as pre-philosophic. We have noticed the unfairness of this practice.

The Greeks had a natural liking for things of the mind. They were inclined to dwell upon what they saw in the world about them and to think out causes and reasons. Among the Greeks, far more than among any other pre-Christian people, philosophy was steadily cultivated. It reached a state of rounded development in the Golden Age of Socrates, Plato, and Aristotle.

The earliest Greek philosophers attacked the cosmological question; they sought the explanation of the bodily world. Other questions of philosophy were only incidental to their studies.

For convenience, we group the philosophers of this period into "schools," that is, classifications of philosophers who studied the same matters or held similar views. The "schools" we are to notice are: the Ionians, the Pythagoreans, the Eleatics, the Atomists, and the Sophists.

1. The Ionians, taking up the cosmological question, asked what is the original matter of which the bodily world is made. (*a*) Thales, of the 7 and 6 centuries B.C., taught that the world-stuff is water, for the world is a mixture of solids, liquids, and gases, and water is the only substance which we commonly find in all three forms. (*b*) Anaximander, of the 7 and 6 centuries B.C., thought the original world-stuff is a kind of spray or mist which is an infinite and living substance (he called it "the Boundless"). Out of this substance all bodily things emerge, and, under the action of heat which is inherent in it, they merge into it again, and this process goes on continuously (theory of an *infinite series of worlds*). The earth is a cylinder poised in the center of the universe. All matter is alive (*hylozoism*); plants and animals come by progressive upward stages from the slime of the heated earth (*evolution* or *transformism*). (*c*) Anaximenes, of the 6 century B.C., regarded the original world-stuff as a kind of vapor, infinite and alive, which, by thickening and thinning (condensation and rarefaction) causes different things to emerge; these bodies float in the infinite vapor like leaves in an autumn breeze. (*d*) Heraclitus, of the 6 century B.C., made the primal world-stuff a kind of fire, infinite, alive, intelligent. This fire is not a mass of matter but a kind of all-pervading reason which operates by its inherent power (*dynamism*) to produce bodies;

the production of bodies goes on by blind necessity (*determinism*). (*e*) Empedocles, of the 5 century B.C., held that the world-stuff is a compound of air, earth, water, fire; these *four elements*, by their various comminglings, make up the bodily world and all things in it. Two forces play upon the elements, a unifying force called *love* and a separating and diversifying force called *hate*. The bodily world is alive (*hylozoism*), and has the power of sensing. (*f*) Anaxagoras, of the 5 century B.C., taught that the world-stuff is a mass of particles of every kind of body found in the universe. This mass was motionless and inert; it was put into a whirling movement by the action of a Divine Mind which is no part of the mass of matter. The whirling motion caused different bodies to "separate out." The Divine Mind knows all and rules all.

In general, the Ionians taught a *cosmogony*, or theory of the emergence of the world, rather than a *cosmology*, or theory of the nature of the world; still, they dealt proximately (and not philosophically) with the constitution of the bodily universe, and hence deserve to be called cosmologists. Their doctrine is hylozoistic, dynamistic, evolutionistic, deterministic, and sometimes (as in Heraclitus) pantheistic. Of all the philosophers of this school Anaxagoras is by far the most notable, for he alone achieved the idea of an independent Divine Mind as the original mover and ruler of the world.

2. The Pythagoreans (called so from their leader Pythagoras who lived in the 6 century B.C.) were of mathematical mind; they were charmed by the *order* and *harmony* of the universe, by its *regularity* and *proportion*. They felt that the world is not only expressible in mathematical terms, but that it is mathematical in nature. They taught that all things are *numbers*, and number is expressed in *harmony*. The Pythagoreans believed in an all-pervading divinity. They taught that man's soul (which is a number) is imprisoned in the flesh for some primordial sin; unless it be purified by virtuous living, it will pass, when a man dies, into another body, and into another and another, until purification is attained or the soul is found hopelessly vile. Here we have the first appearance among the Greeks of *metempsychosis* or the transmigration of souls.

The Pythagoreans are a step higher than the Ionians. The Ionians achieved a *physical* idea to explain the world; the Pythagoreans a *mathematical* idea. This idea is very vague, but it is more abstract than that of the Ionians, and hence more suitable to serve as a focussing-point for a philosophy of the world. Philosophy could not come into its own, however, until man had achieved a *metaphysical* idea (the idea of *being as such*); this was first set forth and satisfactorily discussed by Aristotle in the 4 century B.C.

3. The Eleatics (called so from the city of Elea where notable members of this group lived and taught) were impressed by the variety and changeability of the world. They concluded that change is incompatible with substantial reality. Hence they taught that there really is no change; all change is illusion. "All *is;* nothing *becomes.*" All bodies are of the same essential nature.

The Eleatics (important among whom were Xenophanes, Parmenides, Zeno of Elea, Melissus of Samos, of the 6 to 4 century B.C.) were *monists,* that is, they taught that there is only one kind of bodily substance. By implication they were *pantheists,* for they made the matter of the world self-explaining, hence necessary and eternal, and therefore divine.

4. The Atomists thought of the world-stuff as a great mass of particles like a dust storm. All the particles have the same nature (*monism*); they differ only in shape, size, and weight. The particles do not cling together; they are held apart by vacuoles or intervals of vacuum. They are eternal, and have been in motion from eternity. Out of their motion come various arrangements of differently shaped atoms which we know as bodies. Man has knowledge of *sense* and of *thought.* The atom-constituted bodies throw off images of themselves, like shells, and these somehow enter man's senses and produce sense-knowledge. This knowledge is not trustworthy. The knowledge of *thought* is reliable. Man must find his true good in tranquillity of soul; he is to obtain this by cultivating pure thought and by using all material things with great moderation.

The atomists were *materialists* for they acknowledged no reality but the bodily world. They were *monists* for they taught that matter is "all of a piece." They were *mechanicists* (or *mechanists*) for they explained the variety and multiplicity of the world by mechanical movement of atoms. By implication, they were *pantheists,* for if matter is all, then matter is self-existing and divine. In addition to the cosmological question, the Atomists discussed the critical question (nature and reliability of man's knowledge), and the ethical question (man's purpose in existing, the means he is to use). Notable Atomists were Leucippus, whose times are doubtful, and Democritus who lived in the 5 century B.C.

5. *The Sophists* (in Greek, *sophoi* or "the wise ones") took up the critical question. They concluded that no one can know anything with certainty (*skepticism*). (*a*) Protagoras, of the 5 century B.C., said that everything is in a state of *becoming;* there is no stable *being*. Man's knowledge is never absolute; it is relative to the subject, that is, the person who possesses it (*relativism* and *subjectivism*), so that what is regarded as true for one person at one time may be false to another person or to the same person at another time. The individual man is thus *the measure of truth;* "man is the measure of things." (*b*) Gorgias, of the 5 century B.C., declared that nothing exists, and if anything did exist it could not be known with certitude (*nihilism* and *skepticism*).

The sophists were skeptics, and their influence degraded the philosophical effort. They have to their credit, however, that they raised the critical question.

Summary of the Article

In this Article we have investigated the earliest records of human thinking to discover the sources of philosophy. We have noticed the doctrines,—inaccurately called pre-philosophic,—of the ancient Hebrews, Chaldeans, Egyptians, Chinese, Hindoos, Persians. In the records of all these people we have discovered one constant note—*monotheism.* Thus we see that the evolutionists are wrong when they try to persuade us that the pure idea of one supreme God is a progressive development and growth out of cruder notions. Monotheism definitely came first; polytheism and other debased religious philosophies came later as a lapse and retrogression due to man's original fall and the consequent darkening of the human mind.—We have noticed various groups or schools of early Greek thinkers among whom philosophy began to take more perfect form. We have discussed the Ionians, the Pythagoreans, the Eleatics, the Atomists, the Sophists. We have seen that the chief interest of the early Greeks centered on the world about us; their main discussion turned upon the cosmological question.

Incidentally, we have learned many valuable terms used in every treatise on philosophy: *speculation, monotheism, polytheism, materialism, hedonism, deism, pre-existence of souls, metempsychosis, zoölatry, sabaeism, pantheism, pessimism, religious dualism, hylozoism, infinite-series-of-worlds, determinism, a physical idea, a mathematical idea, a metaphysical idea, monism, skepticism, relativism, nihilism, subjectivism.*

CHAPTER II

THE DEVELOPMENT OF PHILOSOPHY

The present Chapter studies the growth of philosophy after its emergence in the early Greek schools, and traces the development of philosophic thought to its relatively full expression in the magnificent synthesis of Aristotle in the 4 century B.C. The Chapter also discusses the retrogression of philosophy after Aristotle. These matters are studied in three Articles:

Article 1. The Philosophy of Socrates and Plato
Article 2. The Philosophy of Aristotle
Article 3. The Course of Philosophy after Aristotle

Article 1. The Philosophy of Socrates and Plato

a) The Essential Question; b) Theories of Socrates; c) Theories of Plato.

a) The Essential Question

It is useless to employ human reason in the quest of truth unless it can be known beyond doubt or quibble that the mind is capable of attaining truth and holding it with certitude. Man cannot attain to *all* truth, for the scope of the intellect, while tremendous, is not infinite. But there is a vast domain of truth which man is competent to investigate and within which his natural mental powers can bring him to unwavering certitude. If this fact be not recognized at the outset, no development of philosophy is possible. Without a recognition of *human power capable of knowing things with certitude,* philosophy becomes silly vaporizing and the baseless fabrication of a dream. Therefore, the essential question of philosophy is *the critical question,* that is, the question of the value and extent of the human knowing-power; the question of knowledge, truth, and certitude as available to man's connatural and unaided efforts.

When Socrates came upon the scene, in the 5 century B.C., the ability of man to know things *for certain* was being cast into doubt by the Sophists. The doctrine of these teachers was *skepticism,* that is, the doctrine that man cannot be certain of anything and that all his knowledge is valueless or, at best, of dubious value.

It is, of course, impossible to formulate a direct proof by reason for the reliability of reason. Such a proof would involve the fallacy of "begging the question," that is, assuming at the outset the point to be established by the proof. Nor is a proof necessary. A proof is always a careful and methodical unfolding of a thing which is complicated; it is a simplifying; it is a bringing to light and evidence what is not evident in itself. But when a thing is simple to begin with, no simplifying is called for. When a thing is uncomplicated, no unfolding of complications is possible. When a thing is self-evident, external evidence is not needed. One does not need a lighted lamp to discover the noonday sun. One does not demand proof that the eyes can see. One simply beholds the sunlight and uses one's eyes. That a man can think, and think things out by putting two and two together, is as direct and evident an experience as seeing with the bodily eyes in daylight. Proof is neither possible nor necessary.

Still it is possible to formulate an *indirect* proof of the self-evident truths of man's existence and man's ability to think and by thinking to arrive at certitude and reliable knowledge. Such proof is found in the impossible and self-contradictory character of the opposed doctrine called *skepticism.* For skepticism is the total paralysis of philosophy; it is, as G. K. Chesterton once remarked, "the suicide of thought." Like suicide, is it an insane thing. Skepticism asserts that it is certain that nothing is certain. It uses reason to show that there is no use using reason. The skeptic cannot speak without affirming his own existence as a certain fact, without affirming certain meaning in the words he utters, without affirming the certain existence of those to whom he speaks, without affirming the truth of his own theory that no truth of theory is possible. Therefore, the skeptic cannot open his mouth without contradicting himself and denying his own philosophy even as he states it. The skeptic has no recourse but to remain forever silent.

Socrates did not pause to analyze the error of the skeptical Sophists. To their doubts and denials he opposed a human and manly acceptance of the power of man's mind to attain truth and to hold it with certitude. This he took for granted, as every sane man must. Starting with this premise, he developed his philosophy of *the critical question,* giving his theory of knowledge, its character, its value, its purpose. He tied in his studies of the critical question with *the ethical question,* and, to some extent, with *the psychological question* and *the theological question.* But the main mark and characteristic of Socrates' philosophy is that it is *critical* and *ethical;* it deals with human knowing and with virtue, and indeed it brings these two things together in one. In much this theory is erroneous, but it marked a splendid step forward in the development of true philosophy (or true *speculation*), and it was a needed brake upon the ruinous course of the Sophists.

b) Theories of Socrates

Socrates lived from 469 to 399 B.C. He has left us no writings, and it is likely that he wrote nothing to leave. He taught only orally, and his teachings have come down to us through the writings of his pupils, Plato and Xenophon. Thus our "sources" are *secondary,* since only a man's own writings are *primary* sources of his teachings. But these secondary sources are, in the present case, reliable.

Socrates felt a divine call to teach and to improve the lives of men. Teaching was for him a religious duty. He recognized the fact that no improvement in men's lives and morals is possible without a solid philosophy of knowledge. For why speak of duties to men who cannot be sure of anything, and hence cannot certainly know that they have duties at all? Why talk of morals if there is no reliable knowledge that morals exist or are desirable? So intimate indeed is the relation of knowledge to right living that Socrates declared that knowledge *is* virtue. He maintained that to know thoroughly what is right is to make the doing of wrong impossible.

Now, Socrates must have known very well that we often act in contradiction to our knowledge. With the poet Ovid, he must have had experience of "seeing and approving the better things, yet doing the worse." Nor did he excuse sin and crime as the product of sheer ignorance. No, he held that *when a man knows thoroughly and realizes all the implications of what he knows* he cannot act in such a way as to make practical denial of his knowledge.

Yet Socrates stressed the knowing-power too strongly. He should have stressed free-will as well. Man's mind is not like the all-embracing daylight. What a person knows, in full setting, with all implications clearly evident, is not present to the casual mental glance as a wide and varied landscape is present to the glance of the eye. The human mind is, in its action, rather like a narrowly focussed spotlight which throws its light on one small space and leaves many available areas in darkness. And the hand behind the spotlight, turning it this way or that, to take in this consideration or to omit that other, is the free-will. Whatever proposed course of action is illuminated by the spotlight of the mind has aspects of attractiveness and aspects of unattractiveness, and the mind dwells on whichever of these two things the will decides it shall consider. No matter how good an object of consideration may be, the will can focus the mind on features of it that are unattractive and repellant. And no matter how bad an object may be, the will may turn the light of the mind upon some real or apparent phases of it that are attractive. Hence, sin is possible, even when the sinner "knows better." To put this technically: "Man is capable of objectively indifferent judgments."

Perhaps Socrates stressed knowledge so strongly because he earnestly wished to root out the pernicious error of the Sophists who made knowledge of no value at all. At all events, he did make knowledge the one thing necessary for man's mental and moral well-being. And he held that of all knowledge *knowledge of self* is the core and the essence. "Know thyself!" was the summary of his teaching.

Why should a person strive to know himself? Because, said Socrates, all knowledge is *in* him as planted seeds are in the earth. He must labor, as the gardener labors with hoe and water-pot, to bring this germinal knowledge to birth, growth, fruitfulness.

Is this latent knowledge *inborn* in the mind? It is not certain that Socrates held this doctrine (*innatism*). If he did, he was utterly wrong, for all our natural knowledge is *acquired;* it begins with the action of the senses on the bodily world around us; from sense-findings the mind or intellect arises to knowledge that is quite beyond the reach of the senses, and forms ideas or concepts, judgments, and reasonings. But perhaps Socrates did not teach innatism. He may have taught that the seed-knowledge with which the mind is endowed was implanted by the action of the senses upon the material and sensible universe. Whatever he taught about the origin of knowledge, it is clear that he held that the finished product is to be worked out of the mind itself.

How shall a person set to work to bring to fruitfulness,—that is, to clear, certain, scientific understanding,—the seed-knowledge of the mind? By following *the Socratic Method.* This method consists of two processes, the *ironic* and the *maieutic.*—(*a*) When a youth came to Socrates for instruction, the great teacher would receive him with every mark of respect, and would ask him questions, seeming to be himself a pupil rather than a teacher. Invariably the newcomer would grow expansive under this treatment, and presently he would begin to "show off." Now, the questions of Socrates seemed innocent, but they were most shrewdly put. Sooner or later the over-confident newcomer would involve himself in contradictory answers. Again and again he would be led into conflicting and impossible statements. Socrates would gently point out this distressing state of affairs, and before long the poor victim would be forced to make shamefaced admission that he did not know what he was talking about. This was what Socrates was working for. The *confession of ignorance* is, he taught, the first essential step in the work of achieving knowledge of self. Thus far *the Socratic irony*. It cleared and loosened the mental soil.—(*b*) Then came *the maieutic process,* that is, the process of "bringing to birth" the ideas and judgments of the mind. This process amounted to study and discussion,—"dialogue," it was called. If, for example, the question, "What is virtue?" was posed for his students, Socrates would use,—if necessary,—the ironic process to disabuse the pupils' minds of hazy, inept, inadequate preconceptions. Then he would call for examples of virtue. He would require a pupil to explain why he had named each example *virtue*. He would institute comparison of example with example, noting similarities and differences. At length, the pupils would be prepared to formulate a clear and precise *definition* of virtue. Now, once a person can clearly define a thing, he *knows* that thing. Thus, by the maieutic process, is knowledge "brought to birth."

This method of working out a concept by studying various instances or examples is known as *the inductive method* or simply as *induction*. Socrates is rightly regarded as "the father of induction."

The concepts or ideas worked out by the maieutic process are used by the mind in forming *judgments* and arriving at conclusions by *reasoning*. Such judgments and reasonings, said Socrates, are unchangeably *true;* they constitute *science;* they are known with *certitude*. Thus did Socrates contradict the doubts and denials of the Sophists with a ringing assertion of the possibility of achieving truth, certitude, science.

We see, in all this, that Socrates was concerned with the critical question; we also notice that this question is intimately bound up in the Socratic system with the ethical question, since Socrates held that *knowledge is virtue*. Dealing directly with the ethical question, Socrates says that man is made for happiness, and that happiness is the fruit of goodness, that is, of virtuous living. And, since knowledge is virtue, and is to be attained by striving to develop the contents of the mind, man's great moral effort must be directed to knowledge, especially self-knowledge. *"Gnothi s'auton,* Know thyself!" was the constant cry of Socrates.

As to the theological question, it is fairly clear that Socrates believed in one supreme God. But for the sake of avoiding political troubles,—which came upon him notwithstanding,—he conformed to the polytheistic practices of his times.

On the cosmological question, it is likely that Socrates taught the production of this world out of *eternal matter,* and that he regarded the world as the best that could possibly be made (*cosmological optimism*). On both scores he was wrong. He did not identify the world with God (*pantheism*), but held that God is present everywhere in the world, ruling it in all things (*divine providence and government*).

Discussing the psychological question, Socrates held that man has a soul which is distinct from the body. The human soul, he taught, is like God inasmuch as it is *simple* (that is, not made of parts), *immortal,* and *endowed with understanding and memory.* It seems, however, that Socrates failed to realize that the cause of the soul's immortality is its *spirituality*. It will be noticed, too, that Socrates failed to mention *free-will* as a faculty of the soul, and one that makes it like to God. And he mentions understanding and memory as though they were two faculties, whereas they are one; the intellectual memory is but one function or service of the understanding (i.e., the intellect) itself.

What Socrates taught about the union of soul and body in man, is not clear. He may have held, as did Plato later, that the soul is *in* the body as a hand is in a glove; that is, he may have taught a merely *accidental* union of soul and body. The truth is that soul and body in man are *substantially* united; soul and body constitute a single substance, *the human substance.*

Such in briefest outline were the teachings of Socrates. Despite incompleteness and errors, these theories constitute *a developing philosophy* which is immeasurably superior to anything accomplished by thinkers of preceding ages.

The fame of Socrates as a teacher and his widening influence over minds, especially the minds of the young, brought him to the unfavorable notice of the politicians. These fine gentlemen managed to have him condemned to death. He drank the deadly hemlock in the year 399 B.C.

In passing, we must contradict the sentimental opinion that the suicide of Socrates was a noble deed. If it were not for the artistic and touching account of it we have from the pen of Plato, we should probably never think of it as something fine and full of dignity. Suicide is never noble. It is, in itself, a contemptible and a cowardly deed. Of course, Socrates, despite his magnificent mind, was under the sway of pagan opinion and custom; without doubt he regarded the taking of his life as a thing justified and even necessary in the circumstances. We make no attempt to fix his personal guilt. We simply point out the truth of sane ethics that a man may never take his life by direct means. No man may justly be compelled to be his own executioner. Even if he be willing to spare the hangman an ugly job, he may not kill himself. For it is manifestly an unnatural thing (and hence contrary to the natural law) for a man to take his own life, even if that life be forfeit.

One final word. While Socrates was wrong in identifying knowledge and virtue, he deserves the highest praise for his efforts to put ethics on a reasoned basis, and to show that many things are good or bad in themselves. He made moral science more than a set of rules of etiquette, or a programme of whims, or a code of fads, or a list of likes and dislikes. A great many of our modern intellectuals would do well to ponder and to imitate this notable Socratic effort.

c) Theories of Plato

The name *Plato* is familiar to everyone, even to Macaulay's schoolboy. But many are unaware that the word *Plato* is a nickname. The real name of this philosopher was Aristocles. It is said that he was of stocky build, and that his broad shoulders earned him the nickname *Plato,* for *platos* is Greek for *breadth.* Perhaps the famous name *Plato* was the invention of some companion who fixed it upon the young Aristocles as a schoolboy of our day labels a comrade by reason of physical appearance and knows him thenceforth as "Shorty" or "Stumpy" or "Slim."

Plato was of noble descent. He was a splendidly gifted man, and he used his gifts with studious diligence. He was a poet, a playwright, an observant traveller, a philosopher, and,—most important of all,—a literary stylist of the first rank. Plato destroyed his plays and poems, but he retained his splendid style, and this fact (together with the other fact that many of his works survive intact to our day) has a great deal to do with his enduring fame. Many of his theories are exalted and attractive, but it may be questioned whether his essential philosophy would have lived if it had been clothed in less artistic expression. Does anyone doubt that a masterly style can be so effective as to "put a man over"? Let such a person consider Renan. Let him consider Pascal. Let him even consider Will Durant. Then let him consider Plato.

Plato (427–347 B.C.) studied under the philosopher Cratylus and then for eight years he was the pupil of Socrates. His own period of teaching was a long and notable intellectual reign. He died in Athens at the ripe age of eighty.

We have thirty-five dialogues attributed to Plato. Many of these are unquestionably genuine; some are spurious; some are of doubtful authenticity. Among the important ones commonly accepted as genuine are: *Gorgias, The Banquet, Phaedo, Phaedrus, The Republic, Timaeus, Laws, Theaetetus,* and most of his *Letters.*

Like Socrates, Plato was interested, first and foremost, in the critical question, but this question was, for him, intertwined with the psychological question rather than with the ethical question as in the Socratic system. The basic and unifying doctrine of Plato's philosophy is his *theory of knowledge.* This is a famous theory, and it served Plato well in his efforts to bring into a harmonious system the notable teachings of his predecessors and contemporaries. But, for all that, it is a false and futile theory.

Plato taught that each man was originally a soul. He was a spirit living in a world of things-in-themselves; a world of substantial universal ideals or forms.

The world about us is a world of individual things. We see individual trees, we speak to individual men, we hear individual sounds, we notice individual instances or expressions of beauty. And yet our intellectual knowledge is not individual; it is universal. The eye can see only individual trees, but the mind or intellect knows what *tree* means. We have knowledge of tree-in-itself or tree-as-such. We can write the definition of tree, and it defines each and every tree that has ever existed, or exists now, or will exist, or can exist. For we know and define *an essence;* we are not confined to the sense-knowledge of individual things that have that essence. How can it be that, in a world made up exclusively of *individual* things, we have this *universal* knowledge of essences in the abstract?

Aristotle was presently to give the right answer to this important question. He was to teach that the mind has the power of peering beneath the trappings of individuality and getting at the essences of things. This *abstractive power of the human intellect* was something that Plato neither recognized nor suspected. Plato thought that the only explanation of the universal ideas in our minds is found in the fact that those minds once confronted universal things. So he taught that we have had a previous existence in a spiritual realm (*pre-existence of souls*). There we confronted and beheld not trees, but tree-in-itself; there we saw, not a beautiful object or scene, but beauty-subsisting-in-itself; there we knew, not something good, but substantial goodness itself.

Now man, the soul, somehow sinned. The spirit that dwelt in the world of things-as-they-are, or things-substantially-subsisting-in-themselves, was somehow contaminated, and this by its own fault. For this offense, the soul was imprisoned in a body and put here on the earth. As the soul was thrust into its body-prison, it forgot all its splendid knowledge. But the body is equipped with channels of knowledge; we call them *the senses.* These can deal only with the externals of individual things, but still they do give us knowledge. And this individual knowledge garnered by the senses stirs the soul, prods it to recall what once it knew. And so, stirred by the objects of sense, a man dimly and imperfectly remembers what things are. *To know is to remember.*

Here we see that Plato taught these things: (*1*) the pre-existence of souls; (*2*) the innate or inborn character of knowledge; (*3*) the purely accidental (that is, non-substantial) union of soul and body; (*4*) the existence of a supernal realm where things exist in universal and not as individuals; (*5*) by implication, he denied the abstractive power of the human mind or intellect. And in all five teachings Plato was calamitously wrong.

The previous existence of souls (or pre-existence, as it is technically called) is both philosophically untenable and theologically reprobated. The moment that God creates the soul (and God immediately and directly creates each human soul) He joins it substantially with its body, though the body be but a microscopic reality in the bosom of a mother. One identical instant, unbroken, undivided, is the instant of the *creation* and the *substantial uniting* (or *infusion*) of the soul. The very first moment in which a human soul exists without its body is the moment that comes immediately after a man's death. There is no such moment before conception or birth.

Innatism or the doctrine of inborn knowledge is a theory wholly indefensible, as philosophers of all ages have shown, from Aristotle to Locke. We *acquire* our knowledge. Starting with the experiences of the senses which bring us knowledge of things in their concrete and material individuality, we rise, by the abstractive power of the mind, to the recognition of what *kind* of things we sense; we recognize *essences;* we form universal ideas or concepts. And these are the elements of our intellectual knowledge.

As we have seen in discussing the theories of Socrates, the union of soul and body in man is a substantial union, not an accidental one. The soul is not merely *in* the body. Soul and body are so united as to form one single, if compound, substance. Man is not a body alone, nor a soul alone; neither is he merely a soul-in-a-body. Plato said that the soul is in the body controlling it as a rower is in a boat moving it at will by his efforts at the oars. This is wholly false. Man is an animated body, a soul-infused body, a *soul-and-body compound.* Union of soul and body is not accidental but *substantial.* The soul is indeed the most important part or element of a man; it is what the Scholastics call the substantial form of the living body; yet it is not the whole man. And while the soul, which is a spirit, can exist alone, and does exist alone when it leaves the body at death, it has a kind of connatural need for the body because it cannot exercise *all* the functions of which it is the natural principle or source unless it be joined in substance with its body. Hence we see that sane philosophy finds entirely acceptable the Christian truth of the ultimate resurrection of the body.

Plato's notion of a supernal realm where things exist as universal substances is a fanciful conception, highly poetic, pleasingly imaginative, but it is a wholly gratuitous assumption and is in no sense a philosophical truth. Indeed, reason cannot admit the possibility of any finite thing existing in universal. Plato's vague theory seems to imply the notion that all the subsisting universal forms or ideals are unified and identified in the Subsistent Ideal of The Good. A sympathetic interpreter could, with a bit of straining, bring this theory into some agreement with the majestic truth that the Infinite Goodness, God Himself, is the only Being which exists eternally and necessarily, and that in Him, identified with His Undivided Essence, are the archetypal ideas or forms of all things creatable. But, could such an interpretation of Plato's theory of ideas (or ideals) have been suggested to him four hundred years before Christ when he walked the groves of Academe, it would doubtlessly have been to him the occasion of no little astonishment.

Of the abstractive power of the human intellect which Plato implicitly denies without having heard of it or thought of it, we have already spoken briefly and we shall have occasion to speak again in a later Article.

Plato's theory of knowledge supports, however vainly and shallowly, the important doctrines of the *changelessness of truth, the possibility of man's achieving certitude,* and *the possibility of science.* Like Socrates, Plato, despite his purpose of harmonizing and unifying all notable theories of philosophers, turned his face steadily against the destructive and self-contradictory skepticism of the Sophists.

In discussing the cosmological question, Plato teaches that the bodily universe and all the bodily things in it are ultimately made of some primordial world-stuff which has the elemental forms of air, earth, fire, and water. Thus Plato borrows from the Ionians, particularly from Empedocles. We must ever remember that he was a harmonizer; he had the avowed purpose of bringing all acceptable philosophies into unity and system. The primordial world-stuff (which first appears as air, earth, fire, water) is sometimes called *the Platonian prime matter.* This term is apt to be misleading, for Plato's world-stuff was a definite *kind* of matter, and hence was not *primary* but *secondary.* We shall discuss the true meaning of "prime matter" in our study of Aristotle's cosmology.

Plato believed, with Socrates, that the world is the best of all possible worlds (*cosmological optimism*) since God could make nothing inferior. And, since life is superior to non-life, the world must be alive (*hylozoism*).

God,—the Subsistent Idea or Ideal of The Good,—created the world. As Creator, God is called *Demiurge*. Before the bodily universe was made, God created certain spirits; to these He committed the work of creating the bodily world. Yet He reserved to Himself the creation of man's soul.

Plato's cosmology is full of errors. Neither his primal matter (which turns out to be secondary and not primal) nor his elements are ultimate explanations of bodies. Both are bodies themselves, and hence offer the same problem to the philosopher as the universe taken at face value. As for his cosmological optimism, the world is not the *absolutely* best world, else the inexhaustible power of the Creator would be exhausted in its making; it is *relatively* the best inasmuch as it is most admirably suited for its purpose. Nor is anything to be called inferior or imperfect which fits into its place and service for the achieving of purpose. Hence Plato's argument for optimism and for hylozoism are gratuitous and valueless.

As we have seen, much psychological doctrine is bound up with Plato's fundamental philosophy, his famous Theory of Knowledge. Coming directly to the psychological question, Plato teaches that man's soul (directly created by God) is spiritual, rational, self-moving, immortal. The body-prison in which the soul is enclosed was originally a male body. From this was drawn a female body and also the bodies of animals. Once produced, living bodies proceeded to multiply by the process of generation. In addition to the spiritual soul, man has a sensing-soul and a soul which is the source of courage. Only the spiritual soul is immortal. If a man properly purifies himself in this life and casts off the guilt of the offense that led to the imprisonment of his soul in the body, the soul will return at his death to the realm of substantial ideals or forms from which its primal fault banished it. If, however, a man have lived ill, his soul will pass at his death into a female body (*transmigration of souls* or *metempsychosis*). If the female existence be badly spent, the soul will next appear in an animal, and eventually, if evil endures, in a plant. Hopelessly incorrigible souls will be put in a place of torment. At times Plato speaks of this hell as eternal; again he seems to suggest that all souls will eventually be purified and sent to the heaven of substantial ideals.

The idea of a primal fall of man is common to all the ancients and can be explained only as a surviving remnant of the Primitive Revelation. All the world remembers Original Sin, and that, as Mr. Chesterton points out, is one reason why so many modern intellectuals are anxious to deny it. Plato's theory of three souls in man is fantastic; perhaps we might interpret this doctrine to mean that man's soul has three notable modes of action. The doctrine of a spiritual, immortal, rational soul in man is true, and is demonstrated in the department of philosophy called Rational Psychology. The notion of transmigration of souls is oriental rather than Grecian, yet it had won the approval of those Greeks who followed Pythagorean doctrine, and so Plato puts it into his harmonized system. It is utterly false, however, and lacks every vestige of scientific or philosophical proof. The notion that existing females are only reincarnations of unworthy males should scarcely endear Plato to the devout female sex. The Platonian doctrine of heaven and hell falls short of reality but suggests it. Plato shrinks from the bald assertion of the eternity of hell as many persons do today under the mistaken impression that they are being fair and merciful. Anything short of an *eternal* sanction for the moral law cannot satisfy reason, nor can it meet the requirements of sane feeling. The eternity of hell is not only a fact, but a truly sane fact, a merciful fact, not a cruel conception involving mere revenge.

In discussing the ethical question, Plato holds that sin is inevitable because of the dullness of the mind which guides the will. But, says Plato, the inevitable sin is to be laid to man's charge; he is responsible for it *in cause,* inasmuch as he freely committed the primal sin which brought imprisonment in the body and consequent dullness of mind. The ultimate goal of human effort is happiness. Man does not find happiness in things that serve his earthly use (*utilitarianism*), nor in things which flatter the senses (*hedonism*), but in the steady effort to live virtuously and to know The Good, that is, God. Earthly man is meant for life with his fellows, and human society takes on a necessary form in *the State.* The individual is necessarily a citizen. As such he exists for the State. The civil power (that is, the State) must take control of each child early in life; it must discover the child's special aptitudes and train him in accordance with them, so that the State may be a harmonious and smoothly functioning organism. The best form of government is that in which a few wise men hold the place of control (*aristocracy* or *sophocracy*). The next best form of government is military rule (*timocracy*). Less desirable and even bad forms of government are: *oligarchy* or the rule of certain families; *democracy* or the rule of the rank and file of common people; and *tyranny* or the rule of an absolute sovereign who lacks wisdom, foresight, and kindness.

Plato rightly declares that the goal of human conduct is happiness, and, surprisingly enough for a man unenlightened by Christian Revelation, he is right in teaching that happiness is to be sought in the knowledge of God and the practice of virtue. That man sins inevitably, at least venially, sometimes in life (unless he be kept from it by a special Providence) is true; it is not true, however, that man cannot avoid mortal sin if he uses the grace of God which is made available to all without exception. Of course, it would be unfair to expect Plato to know this truth for it is a matter of the Christian Faith. Plato is entirely wrong in his theory that the citizen exists for the State. Strictly speaking, the State exists for the citizen. And while the State must control the citizen in many things and exact obedience to its laws, it does so in the interest of the body of citizens, not in its own interest as though it were a thing independent of the citizens and superior to them. For, while the State is *a natural society* and not an artificial one founded on some compact or agreement of men (as Hobbes, Rousseau, and others were to teach later in their theories of *Social Compact* or *Social Contract*), it is not the owner of its citizens but their servant; it is not their superior but their inferior. Of course, it is not for the individual man to say that, since the State is his servant, he may order it about as he chooses; the State is not his personal servant, but the servant of all citizens together. And, while the individual man is *the* important thing (since he, not the State, not society, is the image of God), he must remember that there are many other individuals with rights equal to his own and of the same sort as his own. Hence the individual must be prepared to make willing personal sacrifice, to endure inconvenience, to curb anti-social impulses; he must obey civil laws, and must expect and accept punishment for the violation of these laws,—which really means the violation of other men's rights. Sane ethics thus avoids two evil extremes which actually meet in their enslavement of the individual: it avoids *exaggerated individualism* (with its inevitable enslavement of the many in the interest of the few who happen to have power), and it avoids *totalitarianism* or *State absolutism* (with its inevitable enslavement of the citizens in the interest of civil power, or, more precisely, in the interest of evil politicians who manipulate the civil power). The root of Plato's calamitously mistaken doctrine of State absolutism is found in his view of the State as an organism of which the citizen is but a cell, that is, a thing dependent, inferior, existing only for the well-being of the larger organism of which it is but a tiny part. This view (which was later to be developed by Herbert Spencer, who taught that all humanity is one organism) is full of damage to the human race. One type of such damage appears in the cry for State control of education,—a thing which Plato himself openly favored. It must be kept steadily and clearly in mind that *parents* have the right and the duty of educating their children. And the aim of true education is the producing of good men and women, not the producing of good citizens. Of course, good men and women will be good citizens, but that is incidental to their character as good men and women. The function of the State in education is to guard the rights of parents in the matter, to supply opportunity for the realization of this right, and to help in various ways in its actual exercise. But State control of education is an unqualified evil; it works always to the ruin of sound government and peaceful social life; inevitably so, since it is a contradiction of the natural law.

Summary of the Article

In this Article we have noticed that the first and fundamental question of all philosophy is *the critical question,* that is, the question of the extent and reliability of human knowledge. We have seen that the truth that man can know, can reason, can have certitude, is a self-evident truth which neither requires nor admits direct proof. We have studied, in brief outline, the doctrines taught by Socrates and by Plato, finding in them both truth and falsity, sometimes strangely commingled, but discerning in them a new and penetrating philosophical effort, a more thorough and complete speculation, than the pagan world had yet known. In a word, we find in these two sets of theories *a developing philosophy;* we find that here the true and perennial philosophy begins to take form.

Our vocabulary of philosophical terms and phrases has been enriched as we learned the meaning of: *the Socratic Method* (with *ironic* and *maieutic* processes); *induction; optimism; innatism; sensation; intellection; substantial union; accidental union; simplicity; Platonic subsistent universal ideas, or ideals, or forms; essence; Platonic prime matter; utilitarianism; individualism; totalitarianism; State; State absolutism; Social Contract Theory* (or *Le Contrat Social*).

Article 2. The Philosophy of Aristotle

a) Aristotle; b) Logic; c) Physics; d) Metaphysics; e) Ethics.

a) Aristotle

Aristotle was born in 384 B.C. at Stagira (and hence he is called "The Stagirite") in ancient Chalcis. His was perhaps the finest mind, in natural gifts, that the world has ever known. For twenty years he was a pupil of Plato, carrying on meanwhile his private researches in philosophy and in physical science. He had an interest in biological study, and it is likely that he did some dissecting under the eye of his father, Nichomachus, who was court-physician to the king of Macedon. Aristotle spent some time in travel, and afterwards he was tutor to the young Alexander whom the world was to know as "the Great." Then he set up as a teacher at Athens. His pupils about him, he lectured as they all walked slowly up and down the shaded walks of the Lyceum of Apollo. And thus his school came to be known as "the peripatetics," a name derived from the Greek *peripatein* "to walk about." After a dozen years of teaching, Aristotle incurred the displeasure of the politicians, for he had acquired far too much influence with the young men of Athens to be a safe person to have about. He quietly slipped away, and died a natural death in Euboea in 322 B.C. when he was sixty-two years of age.

We have some of Aristotle's writings, although certain critics think these are but notes taken by his more gifted pupils. No such masterful style appears in these works as graces the writings of Plato. If Aristotle really wrote them, he did not take time to edit them and set them in finished order. Yet, for all that, these writings are among the most precious pages that the world possesses.

We group the writings of Aristotle under four heads: Logic (the *Organon,* or, as he called it, *Analytic*); Physics; Metaphysics; Ethics.

b) Logic

Logic is the science of *correctness* in the human knowing-process. For thinking must be *correct* if it is to lead one securely to knowledge that is *true* and *certain.* Today we distinguish in Logic a twofold science: one, the science of correct thinking, of legitimate procedure in reasoning; we call this Formal Logic or Dialectics; the other, the science of truth and certitude as achievable by thinking, that is, by reasoning; we call this Major Logic or Criteriology. Aristotle, with perfect scientific acumen, assigned the study of truth and certitude to metaphysics.

Aristotle invented the science of Formal Logic or Analytic, and he developed it into a rounded and relatively perfect thing. Of few men and of few achievements may such a statement be made.

The mind has three major operations: it directly *knows things* (that is, it grasps essences in an abstract manner); it compares its findings and *judges* their agreements and disagreements (that is, it pronounces upon what it knows); finally, it works out further judgments by *reasoning* upon judgments already formed. The first of these operations is called *apprehending;* the second, *judging;* the third, *reasoning.* The purpose of Formal Logic or Dialectics (or of Analytic) is to discern the mode of procedure which the mind must follow to insure a reliable result; it is to discern the "laws of thinking"; it is to know how and wherein the three operations, and especially the last (i.e., *reasoning*), are legitimate and justified.

Aristotle analyzed the mental processes with enlightened accuracy. Discerning the fact that the mind, by its native power, rises from the findings of the senses to reality that lies beyond sense-grasp, and *abstracts from* the individual character of sense-objects to know things *in universal,* he goes on to set forth and prove the existence of three grades of mental abstraction, the *physical,* the *mathematical,* the *metaphysical.* These three grades or degrees of mental abstraction are important in themselves and also as the proper bases of the classification of the sciences which deal with extramental reality.

Apprehending supplies the mind with elemental knowledge, that is, *ideas* or *concepts* which are the mental representations of *essences*. Then the mind goes to its proper work of *judging*, pronouncing, recognizing truths, connecting subject-idea and predicate-idea. Judging is the fundamental thought-process. The operation called reasoning is but a series of judgings, connected, related, leading to a final act of judging and pronouncing some *agreement*,—that is, bringing together some subject and some predicate,—or *disagreement*,—that is, denying some predicate of some subject. In a word, reasoning is a roundabout way of arriving at a judgment which is not immediately manifest to the mind. Judging is the basic, the essential process of thinking.

Now, in judging, the mind pronounces on the agreement or disagreement of ideas or concepts; the mind associates or dissevers a predicate-idea and a subject-idea; the mind affirms or denies a predicate of a subject. Thus judging is *predicating*. Aristotle discerns five ways in which predicating takes place; every judgment is necessarily made according to one of these five ways. The Five Modes of Predicating are called *the predicables* (in Greek, *categoremata*). These are: Genus, Species, Difference, Property or Attribute, and Accident. To explain and illustrate:

(*a*) *Genus*—When the mind predicates one idea of another (applies predicate-idea to subject-idea) in such wise that the predicate expresses that part of the essence of the subject which the subject has in common with other things from which it is none the less essentially distinguished, the predicate-idea is called *the genus* of the subject-idea, and the judging or predicating is called *generic*. Thus, in the judgment, "Man is animal," the predicate-idea "animal" expresses part of the essence "man," but not all of that essence for man is more than animal; the predicate-idea expresses that part of the essence "man" which man has in common with other things, namely, non-rational animal beings.

(*b*) *Species*—When the mind predicates one idea of another (i.e., predicate of subject) in such wise that the predicate expresses or defines the entire essence of the subject perfectly and exclusively, the predicate-idea is *the species* of the subject-idea, and the judging or predicating is called *specific*. Thus, in the judgment, "Man is rational animal," the predicate-idea expresses completely, perfectly, and exclusively the essence of the subject-idea. This predicate applies to no other subject. The predicate is an essential definition of the subject. The predicate is *the species* of the subject.

(*c*) *Difference*—When the mind applies predicate-idea to subject-idea in such wise that the predicate expresses that part of the essence of the subject which marks the subject off from other things with which it has a common genus, the predicate is called *the difference* (or *the ultimate difference* or *the specific difference*) of the subject. Thus, in the judgment "Man is rational," the predicate-idea expresses what distinguishes the subject-idea from another idea which has with it a common genus, that is, from non-rational animal. The judging or predicating here is called *differential.*

(*d*) *Property* or *Attribute*—When the mind applies predicate-idea to subject-idea in such wise that the predicate expresses what belongs to the subject by natural necessity but is no constituent element or part of its essence, the predicate is called *the property* or *the attribute* of the subject, and the judging or predicating is called *proper*. Thus, in the judgment, "Man is a-being-that-can-laugh" the predicate-idea expresses what belongs by nature to the subject although it is no part of the essence of the subject.

(*e*) *Accident*—When the mind applies predicate-idea to subject-idea in such wise that the predicate expresses what *may* belong to the subject, although this is no part of the essence of the subject, nor does it follow naturally upon the nature of the subject by any necessity, the predicate is called *the accident* of the subject, and the judging or predicating is called *accidental.*

Thus, in the judgment, "Man is a-being-that-can-read" the predicate-idea expresses what may *happen* to be true of the subject, but is not necessarily so.

Notice carefully that *the predicables* are *modes of judging in the mind.* They are in no wise classifications of things. Nor are they, strictly speaking, classifications of ideas. They are modes or ways in which one idea may apply to, or be predicated of, another.

Now, the things or realities which are represented in the mind by ideas, are classified, according to their intelligibility or reference to the mind, under ten heads called *the predicamentals* or *the categories* (in Greek, *categoriai*). Aristotle resolved all knowable things into these ten supreme genera or master classes. There are, indeed, certain points of fact that the mind can consider which do not directly fall under any of the categories or predicamentals; these things are called pre-predicamentals and post-predicamentals. Yet, indirectly, or analogously, everything to which the mind of man can turn its attention is ascribable to one of the ten categories. Literally, they are classifications of understandable *finite* being; yet, by analogy, even the infinite Being is viewed as pertaining to the first of the categories or predicamentals. To determine these classes, and so to construct a workable plan for the philosopher whose task is the deep investigation of reality, Aristotle reasoned out a list of the basic questions that the mind must ask in its effort to know all that can be known of anything. These questions are ten and only ten. Two thousand years and more of incessant testing have proved beyond quibble that none of the questions is superfluous and that no additional questions need be asked, or, indeed, can be asked. The answers to the ten fundamental questions are *the categories* or *the predicamentals.* Notice carefully that the predicamentals are not merely a list of things, but a list of the supreme classes of things as understandable. Questions and categories are these:

QUESTIONS	THE CATEGORIES or PREDICAMENTALS
1. What (is the thing itself)?	1. *Substance* or *one of Nine Accidents*
2. How much?	2. Accident of *Quantity*
3. What sort?	3. Accident of *Quality*
4. In what comparison or reference?	4. Accident of *Relation*
5. What doing?	5. Accident of *Action*
6. What undergoing?	6. Accident of *Passion*
7. Where?	7. Accident of *Place*
8. When?	8. Accident of *Time*
9. In what position or attitude?	9. Accident of *Posture* or *Position*
10. With what externals or vesture?	10. Accident of *Habit*

As we have seen, judging is the basic thought-process. But judgment is very often balked by insufficient clarity of knowledge (or, more precisely, of ideas or concepts), and it becomes necessary *to reason out* the judgment. Two ideas may not, in themselves, be so clear in the mind that it can say that they are in agreement or in disagreement. In this case, the mind uses a third idea which is known in its reference to the original two, and through the medium of *this common third idea* the relation (of agreement or disagreement) of the original two ideas may be recognized. Such is the process of reasoning. And its expression (in the mind, or outwardly in speech or writing or other sign) takes the shape of what is called *a syllogism.*

A judgment is expressed (mentally or verbally) in *a proposition.* A syllogism consists of three propositions or expressed judgments. The first two (which express the relations of two ideas to a common third) are called *premisses.* The last (which expresses the relation of the original two ideas, known by their relations to the common third idea) is called *the conclusion.* Here we have a syllogism:

First or major premiss: Every tree is a plant
Second or minor premiss: The oak is a tree
Conclusion or consequent: Therefore, the oak is a plant

Reasoning is the syllogism and the syllogism is reasoning. Those shallow critics who scoff at the syllogism, are forced to express their scoffing in syllogisms. For this is the way the mind works, and there can be no quarrel with it. This is its nature. This is its fixed mode of action. There is no other way to think things out. A man might as well quarrel with the structure and action of his feet, and expect them to hear or speak, as to find fault with the "mental triangulation," that is, the syllogism, by which the mind works out truths that are not immediately evident.

Reasoning is either *deductive* or *inductive.* When (as in the example just given) the reasoning process or syllogism proceeds from a general or universal truth to a particular or individual application or expression of it, the process is *deductive reasoning* or simply *deduction.* The principle (i.e., the basic guiding truth) of deduction is this: Whatever is true of all members of a class is true of each member; whatever is to be denied of all is to be denied of each. When the reasoning process or syllogism proceeds from individual instances to general or universal conclusion, the process is *inductive reasoning* or simply *induction.* The principle of induction is this: Whatever is true of each member of a class is true of all members; whatever is to be denied of each is to be denied of all. Deduction and induction are complementary, not opposed, methods of reasoning. The nature of the investigation and the state of the mind's information to begin with, indicate which method is to be used.

Since induction is the only instrument available to the laboratory scientist, it has come to be called "the scientific method." Yet the whole purpose and drive of this method is to arrive at general or universal truths which will enable the investigator to *deduce* conclusions. If induction is used to determine the nature of water, and it is discovered that water is H^2O, then deduction is thereafter used to determine that if the stuff under consideration is water it is necessarily H^2O.

Students whose knowledge of the history of philosophy is inadequate have hit upon Roger Bacon, a philosopher of the 13 century, as the inaugurator of the inductive method, especially when it is smugly called "the scientific method." Yet Aristotle made notable use of the inductive method.

c) Physics

The term "physics" means, as a department of philosophy, the philosophical science of mobile or changeable being. It is not to be confused with the experimental science of physics which the name usually indicates in our day. Physics here is a department of philosophy; it seeks *ultimate* causes and reasons. It is the philosophy of the universe of bodily things around us. It is Natural Philosophy.

Aristotle accepts the reality of change or "becoming." Thus he opposes the fantastic and unreal theory of the Eleatics (*see Chap. I, Art. 2, b. 3*). Now, the most manifest sort of change or movement is found in the bodily world around us, of which we are a part. Thus Aristotle's physics deals primarily with *the cosmological question,* the question of the root-constitution, and the activities, of bodily things. Since man is bodily, despite the fact that his most important element is spiritual, he falls under the consideration of Aristotelian physics; thus we have also here a discussion of *the psychological question,* the question of life and of living bodies.

A body, lifeless or living, is *bodily.* All bodies are at one in this point, no matter how great their essential differences in other respects. And bodies do differ essentially. There is an essential difference between the body called a boy and the body called a dog; between the body called a tree and the body called a rock. As bodies they are at one; each is as truly *body* as the others. But they are not the same *essential kind* of body. Aristotle teaches that the identity of all bodies in *bodiliness* is owing to the fact that all bodies have a substratum of *primal matter*. And each body is constituted in its essential kind, each is made an-existing-body-of-this-specific-sort, by its *substantial form* or substantifying determinateness,—for "form" is not to be taken lightly as a word meaning mere shape or outline or something accidental; it is here *substantial* form. An existing body is ultimately (i.e., philosophically) explained as *the substantial union* of *primal matter* with *substantial form*. This doctrine came to be known as *hylemorphism* (sometimes spelled *hylomorphism*), a term which derives from the Greek *hyle* "matter," and *morphe* "form."

Primal matter (or, as it is more commonly called, prime matter) is the wholly passive substantial substrate of all existing bodies. It has no proper existence of its own. It exists only in existing bodies, that is, in bodies in-formed by substantial form. Prime matter is a substance, but not a complete substance; it requires the co-substance called substantial form to give it existence in existing bodies. Prime matter is the most imperfect of things; it has no determinateness at all (for determinateness is a "form," substantial or accidental); it is "form-less" in itself. It might be called the substantial *capacity* for bodily existence, but it is not an independently existing capacity. A body comes into actuality, into real existence, when substantial form in-forms (or is fused with) prime matter. And (after first creation) this prime matter already existed in another body or other bodies before becoming substantially fused with the present substantial form. Thus prime matter is not a *kind* of bodily stuff (for *kind* is a form); it is not an existing mass of matter out of which bodies emerge in determinate individuality under action of the substantial form. It is wholly *potential* (i.e., aptitudinal; a capacity), and it is described as "pure potentiality." This potentiality is actualized (i.e., made an existing body) by substantial form, and the substantial unit of matter-and-form is an existing body. The identity of all bodies in bodiliness is owing to prime matter (not actively but passively); the essential differentiation of bodies is due to their respective substantial forms.

Substantial form is the actuating, substantifying, principle of a body. It is the substantial constituent principle which makes a body exist in its essential kind. Substantial form is a substance,—that is, it is a reality suited to exist itself and not to be merely the mark of something else; it is no mere accident,—that is, a reality unsuited to exist itself and suited to exist as the mark of something else. But substantial form (unless it be spiritual) is not a complete substance; it requires the co-substance called prime matter with which to fuse substantially to constitute an existing body. And yet, it does not stand to prime matter as something separate; for it does not (unless it be spiritual) exist by itself, nor does prime matter exist by itself. The two exist in substantial union; both are partial or incomplete substances; together in substantial fusion or unity they constitute a complete substance, that is, an existing bodily substance.

When a body is substantially changed,—as food, for example, is changed when it is turned into the very substance of the being that digests and absorbs it,—the old substance is not annihilated and a new substance created. Prime matter, in-formed as one body, loses the substantial form of that body, and instantly, without lapse of time, is in-formed by a new substantial form. The instantaneous cessation of the old form is called "corruption"; the simultaneous emergence of the new form is called "generation"; or, more precisely, the former substance ceases to be or "corrupts," and the new substance appears or "is generated." Corruption and generation are but two views of the one instantaneous substantial change: the corruption of one body is the generation of another or others, and the generation of one body is the corruption of another or others.

Unless a substantial form be spiritual, it is said to be "educed from the potentiality of matter" when a body is generated; and it is said to be "reduced to the potentiality of matter" when a body is corrupted. Prime matter is the bridge, so to speak, which supports substantial change. It is "in potentiality" (or has the capacity) for union with any substantial form that can make it an existing body; when this potentiality is actualized, the form is said to emerge or *to be educed* from the potentiality of matter. And when a body "corrupts," that is, loses its substantial form to gain another or others, the ceasing substantial form falls back, so to speak, into the aptitude of matter to have such a form; it is "reduced to the potentiality of matter."

Prime matter and substantial form are *ultimate* constituent principles of bodies. Bodies, said Aristotle, are *proximately* reduced (or analyzed into) certain *elements;* these are four: air, earth, water, fire. These proximate elements of bodies, by their varied unions, make up the different kinds of bodies we find about us here on earth. But the elements (air, earth, fire, water) are themselves bodies, and are constituted *ultimately* by prime matter and substantial form. Aristotle's "elements" are, of course, now known to be inadequate. But the discovery of such proximate elements is the task of laboratory science, not of philosophy.

Aristotle thought that the heavenly bodies are made of a purer and superior kind of material than that which enters the constitution of earthly bodies; he thought that the heavenly bodies are naturally incorruptible. The earth, in his opinion, is the most imperfect of bodies, and naturally tends to corrupt, that is, to undergo substantial change. Aristotle held that matter has been produced or caused; it is not self-existent; but he believed it has been produced *from eternity.*

Aristotle taught, and rightly, that the human soul is the substantial form of the living human being. Indeed, the life-principle (or *psyche*) is the substantial form of every living body, plant, animal, man. He discerned the fact that man has the activities of plant, of animal, and of reasoning creature; yet he taught that man has but one soul, and that this is the rational soul. Whether Aristotle held that the soul is truly spiritual and immortal is a matter of dispute. It is certain, however, that he denied the pre-existence of souls.

d) Metaphysics

The word *metaphysics* is not Aristotle's own. It was used by Andronicus of Rhodes (about 70 B.C.) as a label for those works of Aristotle which were arranged *to follow after* his treatises on physics; for the Greek *meta* means "after." Metaphysics deals with reality, not as limited to this nature (*physis*) or that, but as viewed apart from material limitations. Its proper scope includes spiritual being and also *all* being in so far as it can be considered as free from every material determinant and restriction, from all that makes it this or that class or kind. Thus metaphysics does come "after" (or reaches beyond) the more special studies in philosophy which consider (*a*) material being, as physics does, or (*b*) logical being, as logic does, or (*c*) moral being, as ethics does. Metaphysics is the science of non-material *real* being. It is no airy or imaginative philosophizing about abstractions that no one can understand; it is not something "away up in the air"; it is the deepest philosophy of *reality;* it is the very heart of philosophy.

The basic idea of metaphysics is that of *being* (*ens* in Latin; *on* in Greek). In this idea all others are rooted, for every idea is the idea of some *thing,* that is, of some *being.* Anything that can be *thought of as existing in the order of reality,* independently of the creatural mind, is *real* being. Anything that can be thought of as existing in the mind and dependently on the mind (such as, subject, predicate, species—as *predicable*) is *rational* or *logical* being. Anything that can be known in reference to the law which marks the boundary between right and wrong, is *moral* being. Now, logical being and moral being have place and value only in a world of real being. And it is with this world of real being, universally and most penetratingly considered, that metaphysics deals.

The idea of being (and of real being) is *transcendental.* That is, it soars over the fences of classification. For the idea of being is the idea of *being as such,* and knows not *kinds* or *sorts.* Every being is being, and even the distinction that marks off one class of thing from another is being.

Still, the meaning of *being* is not precisely the same in all references. God is a being, man is a being, a tree is a being, the color of a rose is a being, the distinction between man and tree is a being. But God is infinite, self-existent, necessary being. Creatures are not necessary beings; they are *contingent* beings, that is they are *produced* beings and as such are dependent or contingent upon their causes. Of contingent beings, some are *substantial* (man, tree, rose); some are *accidental* (color of a rose). Hence, while all things are beings (and *real* beings in so far as they are *existible* in the extramental universe) all things are not identical in possessing every implication of the term *being.* The philosopher expresses this truth in some such way as this: The transcendental idea of *being* does not apply to its inferiors or subjects (that is, to the things it designates or denotes) in a *univocal* manner (that is, in precisely the same sense in each case), nor in an *equivocal* manner (that is, in a manner utterly different and unrelated in any two cases), but in an *analogous* manner (that is, in a manner partly identical and partly different in various cases). In a word, while all conceivable things are *beings,* there are classifications of beings on the score of necessity, contingency, substantiality, accidence.

Out of the root-idea of *being* Aristotle draws certain self-evident truths or "first principles." The truly *first* "first principle" in the order of all thought and knowledge is called *the principle of contradiction.* Now, a principle is a source, in any sense; and a source of knowledge and thought is *a guiding truth.* The basic guiding truth is this: that a thing cannot be, at one and the same time and under the same aspect, both existent and non-existent. This is the principle of contradiction. It emerges from the idea of *being* when it is considered as *something* which cannot simultaneously be *nothing.* Unless this principle be acknowledged (and it is perforce acknowledged even by those who try to doubt or deny it), all thought and all expression of thought become impossible. For if this principle be fallacious, the very word "fallacious" might also mean "true."

Out of the principle of contradiction come other self-evident principles, such as *the principle of identity and difference* ("What is, is; what is not, is not"), and *the principle of the excluded middle state* ("A thing either is or is not; there is nothing midway or neutral between being and non-being").

In his metaphysics Aristotle also considers being *as cause,* being *as effect,* being *as one* or in unity; being *as true;* being *as good;* being *as predicamental* (i.e., as classified in the categories); being *as actual* (or *existing*); being *as potential* (i.e., capable or apt for existing).

Being as *actual* (or being *in actu*) is existing being. Being as *potential* (or being *in potentia*) is existible being. A thing is *actually* what it is; a thing is *potentially* what it may become. The potentiality of a being is either sheer possibility, and then the being is *objectively* potential; or the potentiality is the capacity of an existing thing to realize its capabilities which actually exist, and then we have *subjective* potentiality. A boy is actually a boy; potentially he is a grown man, and this potentiality resides in the boy as in its *subject;* here we have subjective potentiality. Again, the boy is potentially President of the United States; this is objective potentiality or sheer possibility, for there is not in the boy any natural or arranged direction or drive tending towards such an end.

The more actuality a thing has, the more perfect it is. For the more it is *actual* the more it *is,* and the more, so to speak, it *has.* In other words, the greater the actuality of a thing, the less is its capacity for being perfected. Still more briefly, the greater the actuality, the less the potentiality. Now, as reason sees, there must be a First Being that is *entirely* actual, with no perfectibility or potentiality about It. Thus *Pure Actuality* is a name and a definition of God.—At the other end of the scale of perfection is unmixed potentiality or *pure potentiality;* this is a definition of prime matter.

Aristotle indicates that God is *the final cause* of the universe (that is, the end or goal of all things), and he uses this truth to show further that God is also the first effecting or producing cause of things. Aristotle mentions creatural causes (or *secondary causes*), and notable among these are certain "separate intelligences" (which we might call spirits or angels) who have charge of the heavenly bodies.

Our sketch of Aristotle's metaphysics is a very thin sketch indeed; in the nature of things, it cannot be complete or very detailed even as far as it goes. It is presented merely to give the student a general grasp of the scope and character of the science of metaphysics, and to afford him some opportunity of appreciating the notable work achieved by Aristotle in rounding that science into acceptable form.

e) Ethics

The Greek word *ethos* which gives us the term *ethics* is the same in meaning as the Latin *mos* (stem *mor-*) which gives us the term *morals.* It means *that which is characteristic of man.* Now, the real characteristic of man, his hall-mark so to say, is found in the fact that he can act freely, self-directingly, and responsibly. In a word, the distinctive mark of human activity is this: *it comes from a free-will.* Thus ethics is the science of "free-will actions."

Now, free-will actions will lie in line with reason or will conflict with reason; they will, in other words, fit harmoniously with the purpose for which man exists, and for which free-will is given to him, or they will clash with that purpose. Accordingly, such actions will be *right* and *good,* or they will be *wrong* and *evil.* Ethics, therefore, deals with the *morality* of freely-willed human conduct.

The end and purpose of man's existence, and the end and purpose to which all his deliberate action ought to be directed, is *the good,* that is, the boundless good. In the achieving of that good, man is to find the completion of himself, the filling up of every rational tendency and appetency; and this will be his beatitude, his happiness. For the achieving of the boundless good (the *summum bonum*) and beatitude man must seek to know and love truth and to act in conformity with it. In particular, man must rightly know and appreciate his own character and place and duty as *man.* An important item in this knowledge is the fact that man is by nature a *social* being; he lives with others of his kind and has rights and duties in their regard. Man is inclined towards conjugal society or marriage; he requires civil society or the State. As to the form of government in the State, times, circumstances, and temperaments will be the determinants. There is also a master-and-slave society which is useful (and perhaps necessary, Aristotle seems to say) but which does not involve slave-ownership. Master and slave should be friends; slaves must never be subjected to cruel treatment.

Aristotle's ethics is not a perfect moral science. He omits the necessary *eternal sanctions* for the moral law. He wrongly supposes that the mastery of slaves is a good, and perhaps a naturally necessary thing. But he is worlds ahead of Plato in his clear discernment that the State is the instrument of the citizens, not their owner. He rightly holds that some civil rule (i.e., the State) is naturally required by men living in society, but that its *form* is for the citizens to determine.

Summary of the Article

We have outlined, in this Article, the philosophy of Aristotle, prince of philosophers. We have seen that Aristotle is the inventor of Logic and have noticed that he also rounded this science into completeness.—In Physics, we have seen the matter-and-form doctrine, known as hylomorphism, as Aristotle's philosophy of the bodily world. No more acceptable theory of matter (that is, cosmology) has as yet been formulated. Aristotle was, of course, very deficient in point of experimental physics. His times did not afford the opportunities and the instruments for accurate physical and chemical research. He assumed as his hypothesis in the matter of experimental science the doctrine of Empedocles on the "four elements," and so did all philosophers and scientists up to the Middle Ages. Still, Aristotle's philosophy of matter is not to be undervalued because of his inadequate knowledge of experimental physics; philosophy does not depend upon the laboratory, even though it uses the findings of science for telling illustration and for direction in its investigations. Aristotle was not, after all, directly or deeply concerned with the proximate principles of bodies; his was a philosophic quest; he sought ultimate principles. And the Aristotelian cosmology, while often challenged and questioned, has managed to outlive all objections and objectors; it has held its own for over two thousand years. Hylomorphism may not be the last word in the philosophy of bodies; it may come to suffer modification and even essential change. It leaves things to explain, it is not without many difficulties; but its difficulties and deficiencies are neither so many nor so baffling as those involved in the several theories of matter which have tried to supplant it.—In metaphysics Aristotle is on undebatable ground; here true philosophy suffers neither doubt nor hesitation. We have seen that metaphysics is the philosophical science of non-material real being. We have noticed the first principles involved in the very concept or idea of being, and we have seen that these principles are the indemonstrable but necessary and indubitable truths upon which all knowledge and all the sciences ultimately depend. We have discussed the doctrine of actuality and potentiality in being.—In our brief consideration of Aristotle's ethics we have noted his doctrine of man's purpose in existence and of the means available for the achievement of that purpose. We have seen that Aristotle taught,—with perfect truth,—that man is, by his very nature, a social being; that he is in natural need of civil society or the State; that the State is not the owner of the citizens nor the end for which they exist. We miss in Aristotle's ethics the all-important *supreme norm of morality* with its *eternal sanctions.*

The Article has supplied us with some new philosophical terms, and has repeated others with which we should now be familiar: *apprehending, judging, reasoning* (or *inference*), *idea, concept, judgment, syllogism, deduction, induction, the predicables* (*genus, species, difference, property, accident*), *the predicamentals* or *categories* (*substance and the nine accidents*), *being, real being, logical being, moral being, inferiors of an idea, transcendental idea, univocal predication, equivocal predication, analogous predication, principle, first principle, actuality, potentiality, matter, form, prime matter, substantial form, hylomorphism.*

Article 3. The Course of Philosophy after Aristotle

a) The Later Greek Schools; b) Greco-Jewish Philosophy; c) Neoplatonism; d) Gnosticism; e) Manicheism; f) Patristic Philosophy.

a) The Later Greek Schools

After Aristotle philosophy suffered a long period of retrogression. Ancient errors were revived. Chief of these were *skepticism,* which denies the ability of man to attain truth and certitude; *materialism,* which asserts that the bodily universe is the whole of reality; *pantheism,* which, in one way or another, identifies God with the material world.

The chief interest of the "schools" or groups of philosophers centered, at this time, upon *the ethical question,* the question of human happiness and the means of attaining it.

The most notable of the "schools" are here to be briefly considered. These were the Stoics, the Epicureans, the Skeptics, and the Eclectics.

1. *The Stoics,*—chief of whom were Zeno of Citium, Cleanthes of Assus, and Chrysippus of Soli,—held that the material

world is the only reality (*cosmological materialism*), and that God is *the soul of the world;* He is a kind of fire, and of this fire the human soul is, so to speak, a spark (*pantheism*). Everything exists and happens by fixed law and necessity; neither God nor man has any freedom (*determinism*). Man's business is to find happiness. But, since man, like everything else, is subject to the sway and buffetings of changeless fate, the only way to happiness is that of stolid and passionless endurance. "Bear and forbear" is the Stoic motto. This motto is capable of a splendid and Christian interpretation, but, as is manifest, the Stoics did not understand it in any such light. Man, said the Stoics, must be apathetic, neither giving way to pleasure in the things of sense nor acknowledging the pressure of sorrow and pain.

2. *The Epicureans,*—named for Epicurus, an Athenian philosopher,—held that man can have no true intellectual knowledge, but only the knowledge that comes through the senses (*sensism*). The action of the senses, that is, *sensation,* is either pleasurable or painful. Man must avoid what is painful and indulge what is pleasurable. Yet man must not wallow in sense-pleasures, for excess is always productive of subsequent pain. Hence man must live with great moderation; he must hold desire in check; he must cast off all worry and all fear. Thus shall he achieve *serenity of mind and heart,* and this is the true pleasure for which man is made.—All this amounts to *hedonism,* or quest of what is sweetly pleasing; and some *pessimism* or the conviction that the best life has to offer is the avoidance of pain. —The Epicureans thought that the bodily world is a kind of cluster of particles, variously united by sheer chance to constitute the different things we see about us. Here we have *materialistic atomism* and *casualism.*

3. *The Skeptics,*—variously classified as the Pyrrhonians, the Neo-Pyrrhonians, the Academians,—held that man cannot attain to certain knowledge of anything; he cannot surely and positively know truth. Some skeptics admit the possibility of attaining probability, and some say that even this is beyond man's

powers. Hence philosophy and science are illusory. And no moral duties exist, for if man can know nothing for certain, how can he know that any duty certainly binds him? The best a man can do is to seek quietness and imperturbability of mind; in this lies his happiness.—It is manifest that the view of the skeptics is *pessimistic, amoral,* and *stoical.*

4. *The Eclectics,*—named from the Greek *eklegein* which means "to choose out,"—thought that true philosophy is scattered piecemeal throughout all existing theories, and it is the business of the philosopher to sift it out. The "test" for the authentic philosophy is, according to the Greek Eclectics, a person's direct experience plus a kind of "inner voice" or instinct which proclaims truth or indicates its presence.

It is manifest that these later Greek schools worked a damage to philosophy. They represent a "throw back" to crass materialism and pantheism. Despite the doctrine of moderation which they generally recommend, they represent a surrender to sensualism. Their ignoring or denial of philosophical certitude is the suicide of thought; they make all science and all philosophy utterly impossible.

There is a dead and pessimistic sameness in these schools. This is due to the fact that their ethical theory is wholly divorced from reality. Ethics, as a human science, is the fruit of the sound philosophy of reality, indeed of true metaphysics. When it is severed from this true source or principle, ethics becomes a subjective theory of flabby sentimentalism and invariably degenerates (as history shows) into dull and dreary pessimism.

b) Greco-Jewish Philosophy

The so-called Greco-Jewish philosophy was the result of an attempt to draw into a harmonious system the Greek philosophy (especially that of Plato) and the Old Testament Scriptures. The effort was made by certain Jews of Alexandria in Egypt, chiefly by Aristobulus (2 century B.C.) and Philo (born about 25 B.C.).

Aristobulus is notable as the inaugurator of the system. Philo is the one great name associated with this syncretizing or amalgamating effort.

Philo was a contemporary of Our Lord. He was known as an eminent scholar with an unbounded love for the philosophy of Pythagoras and of Plato. Like Aristobulus, Philo was convinced of two things: first, that Holy Scripture is the source of *all* truth; true philosophy derives from Scripture, and therefore the function of the philosopher is the interpreting of Holy Writ; second, the Greek philosophy is the best that man has done in his quest for wisdom; it is the true philosophy; therefore, it must be fundamentally at one with Scripture and indeed, rightly understood, must be seen as something derived from Scripture. Philo sets to work to harmonize and unify philosophy and revelation.

Philo teaches that God is an inexpressibly perfect Being. God begets the Logos or Word which contains in Itself patterns of all creatable things as well as the power to produce them and to interpenetrate them as their soul. The Logos does Its work by impressing *forms* upon matter. Matter is wholly imperfect; it exists eternally; it is independent of God. The souls of men existed before their bodies, and were imprisoned in bodies in consequence of some offense. Release from the body-prison is achieved by conquest of fleshly tendencies and cultivation of serene contemplation of God. Unless a man take the one means of release, his soul passes from body to body in a continuous transmigration which is the only hell. The study of philosophy is a splendid aid in quelling passion and setting up the spirit of contemplation.

Philo is manifestly *eclectic* in tendency, for he "picks and chooses" the elements of his doctrine from Greek philosophy and Holy Writ. He is, in many points, Platonic: thus he holds to the subsistent forms of things resident in the Logos; to the pre-existence of human souls; to the transmigration of souls (although his transmigration is ever from one human body to another and never downward through animals to plants, as in Plato); to the merely accidental union of man's soul and body. We notice, too, that Philo adopts the Stoical idea of a world-soul. And he borrows (as the Greeks had borrowed before him) the ancient oriental notion of rapt contemplation or ecstatic absorption in God.

Like the later Greek schools just discussed, Philo represents a retrogression in philosophy, not an advance. His system is more Greek than biblical. It contains deeply erroneous doctrines on *the theological question, the psychological question, the cosmological question,* and *the ethical question.* Based as it is on the gratuitous assumption of Scripture as the only source of knowledge, it also errs on *the critical question.* Throughout, Philo makes Scripture conform to his conception of Greek philosophy; he seldom, if ever, puts pressure on his philosophy to bring it into line with Scripture. His system is, among other things, materialistic, pantheistic, and pessimistic.

c) Neoplatonism

Neoplatonism, like the Greco-Jewish philosophy, is an attempt at "blending." It is an amalgam of Plato's philosophy and ancient oriental doctrines; with these are mingled some almost forgotten doctrines of the earliest Greeks. Neoplatonism is not a single or clear-cut system; various Neoplatonist theories were taught at Alexandria, at Athens, and in Syria. The Athenian "school" of Neoplatonism was the most worthy of note because it had the one philosopher of importance whose name is associated with this syncretizing and eclectic movement. This was Plotinus (204–269).

Plotinus taught that there is a formless Supreme Being. This being he calls *The One.* From this Being emerges mind or intelligence; that is, *Nous.* From Nous comes *The World-Soul.* Here we have indubitably a pagan's mistaken interpretation of the

Christian doctrine of The Blessed Trinity.—The human soul, while radically identified with The One, with Nous, and with World-Soul, is nevertheless a sort of individual; it existed before it had a body, in which it is unhappily and unnaturally enmeshed; it is immortal. The soul must struggle to be free of the trammels of the flesh and to rise to contemplation of The One in conscious union with Nous and World-Soul. Perfect attainment of this glorious contemplation (which is one of direct or intuitive vision) is only to be attained in the life to come. Souls that fail to free themselves of subjection to the body will have to endure a succession of transmigrations until they have finally attained to purification.

Plotinus borrows from strangely assorted sources. From the Christian faith he takes (and distorts) the notion of the Trinity, and the doctrine of the Beatific Vision. From Pythagoras (and Plato) he takes transmigration, and from Plato he takes the pre-existence of human souls. From the old Ionians he borrows the notion of a living world (for the World-Soul, or Demiurge, makes the world a living thing); and the notion of a world-soul itself is borrowed from the Stoics.

Plotinus is pantheistic, hylozoistic, and materialistic. It is interesting to note in passing that Henri Bergson (1859–1940), a French Jew who came to recognize the truth of the Catholic religion although he did not enter the Church, considered his appreciation of Christianity to be the fruit of his devoted study of Plotinus. Divine Providence leads sincere minds to truth from the most unlikely beginnings.

d) Gnosticism

Certain heretics of early Christian times called themselves by the Greek name of *gnostikoi* or "the enlightened ones." These folk are known in history as the Gnostics, and their doctrine is Gnosticism.

The Gnostics claimed to have a special divine illumination (or *gnosis* "knowledge" or "enlightenment") which is denied to ordinary men. By aid of the *gnosis* they claimed to understand all fundamental truths. Their doctrine is a sad mixture of Neoplatonism, badly twisted Christian doctrine, and plain paganism.

The Gnostics taught that God cannot come into contact with matter, for matter is wholly vile and God is all-perfect. God created spiritual beings; these created others less perfect than themselves; these created others still less perfect, and so on until *the least perfect spiritual beings* created the bodily world.

Matter, or bodiliness, is the source of all evil. The human body is the source of evil in man. Man must free the soul from the influence of the body which imprisons it so that death may restore it to its pure and pristine state.

Among the spiritual beings that intervene between God and the material world is one called *Christ*. Another is *Jesus*. These are two beings, not one. Jesus assumed an apparent human body and Christ was united with Him at the baptism by John in the Jordan. Jesus and Christ, in union, worked for the deliverance of mankind from pains. At the Crucifixion, Christ withdrew from Jesus, and Jesus suffered pain and death in His apparent human body.

Gnosticism is an example of what prideful ignorance can do. As philosophy it is meaningless, for it is wholly gratuitous, baseless, and grotesque. It died quickly; by the end of the 3 century it was extinct. But something like Gnosticism is always recurring in the world, and notably in times of intellectual exhaustion or decadence. In our own day such vagaries as Theosophy and Rosicrucianism, and other quackeries which promise to "unleash the divine power within each man" suggest the Gnostic error.

Valentinus, Marcion of Sinope, and Basilides of Alexandria, —all of the 2 century,—were notable Gnostics.

e) MANICHEISM

Manes or Mani,—whose name is Latinized as *Manichaeus,*—was a Persian reformer of the 3 century. He taught a mixture of doctrines taken from Zoroaster, the Neoplatonists, the Gnostics, and the Christians.

Manicheism holds the theory of two first principles, one of goodness and light, the other of evil and darkness. These are God and Satan. Each produced creatures of his own, and the world is made up of these; hence the world is a mixture of good and evil. Each human being is also a mixture of good and evil. Man must seek to make the good in him triumph over the evil that is there. He achieves this victory by contemplation of the truth and by bodily austerities. Still, since the average man is very weak and consequently unable to wage the constant exacting warfare against evil, he need not concern himself too much about the effort.

Manicheism, like all decadent philosophies, is full of a great weariness together with a wistful longing for ideals and a pathetic half-attempt to set forth a system of guiding truths.

f) Patristic Philosophy

The Fathers of the Church (that is, *Patres Ecclesiae,* whence comes the adjective *Patristic*) were those holy and learned men of the first Christian centuries who wrote notable treatises in explanation or defense of the Catholic Faith. In their work of uprooting heresy and planting true doctrine, the Fathers came constantly upon false philosophical theories which had to be met and answered on philosophical grounds. Thus many of the Fathers were, perforce, philosophers, and some of them filled the office with eminence. Among these we must mention St. Clement of Alexandria (2–3 century); Origen (3 century); Minucius Felix (2 century); Tertullian (2–3 century); Lactantius (3 century); Arnobius (4 century). We must mention also the great Greek and Latin Fathers who flourished after the Council of Nice (A.D. 325). The "Big Four" among the Greek Fathers were Saints John Chrysostom, Athanasius, Gregory of Nazianzen, and Basil. Among the Latin Fathers, the "Big Four" were Saints Jerome, Ambrose, Gregory the Great, and Augustine. Of all the Fathers, by far the most notable in philosophy was the illustrious African, Aurelius Augustinus, whom we know as St. Augustine of Hippo.

St. Augustine (354–430) was not only a great philosopher; he was one of the very greatest that the world has ever known. To a genius approaching, if not equalling, that of Plato or even that of Aristotle, he joined the light of knowledge that comes with the Christian Faith. In the cast of his philosophy he is Platonian rather than Aristotelian, for in his day Plato was universally regarded as the king of philosophers. Aristotle was not recognized at his true worth until a much later day, although he was always held in reverent esteem. It was left for two great Dominicans, William of Moerbeke and St. Thomas Aquinas,—the former by a pure translation and the latter by his interpretation and application of Aristotelian philosophy,—to bring Aristotle to his true place as far and away the greatest philosopher of ancient times, and indeed of all times.

St. Augustine taught that the mind of man is adequate to attain to truth with certitude; he held that the mind is much aided in its work by endeavoring to have as clear an idea of God as it is possible to achieve; for to know God is to have some concomitant knowledge of God's creatures and of all knowable things.

St. Augustine proves the existence of God from the contingency of the world; from the nature of the human soul; and from the character of human knowledge. He shows that God is infinite, eternal, changeless, and absolutely free; that God creates in goodness, unimpelled by any stress or necessity. He says that, in the beginning, God made all living bodily creatures (excepting man) in *germ;* that is, God gave to certain particles of matter a kind of seed-force (or *ratio seminalis*) to develop into determinate plants and animals at a time set beforehand by God. Man, however, is not explained by this theory of *rationes seminales.*

Man's soul is a spiritual and immortal substance, wholly present in every part of the living human body. As to the origin of the soul, St. Augustine felt that the inheritance of Original Sin indicates the fact that the soul is somehow drawn from the souls of parents (*traducianism*). In this he is wrong. Each soul is immediately created by Almighty God at the moment it is joined with its body in the bosom of the mother (*creationism*). The doctrine of Original Sin does not necessitate the traducianist theory. We take our *nature* (that is, our complete working essence), under God, from our parents, although we do not take our *souls* from them; and it is *human nature* that is infected in its source by Original Sin; it is our individual *human nature* that incurs this evil heritage.

Man, says St. Augustine, is endowed with free-will. He tends of necessity towards beatitude or happiness, but he freely chooses the means whereby he seeks to attain this beatitude. Man's freedom of choice is in no way hindered or hampered by God's foreknowledge of human acts. The object that will perfectly fill up man's capacity for happiness is God alone; St. Augustine cites and interprets Plato in proof of this truth. God is to be known, loved, and served in this life, and He is to be possessed in heaven by an immediate intuition or direct vision of the Divine Essence (*the Beatific Vision*).

The law or norm of morality for man is the Eternal Law. The Eternal Law is God Himself inasmuch as He ordains the order He has set up in nature to be conserved and forbids it to be disturbed (*the natural law*). Man's normal and natural grasp of the natural law is effected by *reason,* that is, by the thinking mind, and in this service reason is sometimes called *conscience.*

God is in no sense the cause of moral evil or sin. Sin is possible because of the abuse of free-will by man, and God, having bestowed free-will, does not take it away again even when it is abused. In His loving Providence, God draws good out of evil, even of moral evil. God may be called the cause *per accidens* (that is, *the accidental cause*) of physical evils in the world; yet these evils, rightly undergone, prove to be blessings to man.

Summary of the Article

In this Article we have briefly discussed the more notable expressions of the philosophy of times following the Golden Age of Greek achievement. The Later Greek Schools, and the syncretizing systems (Greco-Jewish philosophy, Neoplatonism, Gnosticism, and Manicheism) have nothing whatever in the way of solid or original thought to offer; their borrowings from many sources are, for the most part, set forth as gratuitous assertions. The decadence of philosophy represented in these schools and systems was checked at last by the emergence of the perennial philosophy as developed by Christian minds, most notable of which was that of the illustrious St. Augustine.

The Article has furnished us with some new philosophical terms and has made use of some already familiar: *skepticism; materialism; pantheism; cosmological materialism; soul-of-the-world theory; Stoicism; Epicureanism; Eclecticism; determinism; sensism; materialistic atomism; casualism; hedonism; Manicheism; Gnosticism; Neoplatonism; traducianism; creationism* (with reference to the soul); *theory of "rationes seminales"; the natural law; the Eternal Law; the Beatific Vision; reason; conscience; cause per accidens.*

CHAPTER III

THE PERFECTING OF PHILOSOPHY

This Chapter discusses the rounding of philosophy into full and relatively complete form in the Scholastic System, the best synthesis that man has been able to achieve. This is the *philosophia perennis* in mature form, ready to serve man in his studies and investigations, to guide his thinking into rich and profitable fields, and to assure the sane advance of true science. The Chapter looks into the forces and influences that made for the perfecting of philosophy and outlines the work of the more notable philosophers of the Period of Perfection. These matters are presented in two Articles:

Article 1. The Factors of Perfection in Philosophy
Article 2. Some Great Philosophers of the Age of Perfection

Article 1. The Factors of Perfection in Philosophy

a) Factors; b) Atmosphere; c) Themes; d) Equipment; e) Movements.

a) Factors

By the "factors" of the perfecting of philosophy we mean those facts and circumstances which proved to be strong influences upon the thinking of scholarly men, stirring them to philosophic effort. Of all such factors,—and there must have been a rather large number of them,—we choose for mention and brief discussion only three; these we deem the most important of all. They are, first, the intellectual atmosphere in which men of genius went to work; second, the questions that engaged their special attention; third, the equipment with which they undertook their task

Of course, the men themselves, the thinkers, the philosophers, were the greatest "factors" in the progress they made. But it seems somewhat inaccurate to call them by that name, as though they were but an element in a kind of mechanical process that worked inevitably and automatically. We dare not degrade great gifts of mind, great patience, and tireless labors, by naming them so harshly. Therefore, we shall understand "factors" in the sense explained in the preceding paragraph, not as men or as the gifts of men's minds and spirits, but as the things that helped to stir men of great mind and great diligence to the task of bringing philosophy to a perfected state.

b) Atmosphere

By the "atmosphere" we mean what may be called the spirit of the times, the interests and the temperaments of people. Now, beginning in the late 8 century, and extending through a period of about six hundred years, there was current in Europe a spirit, —always strong and often widespread, although never, of course, universal,—for deep study, for living with "the things of the mind"; in a word, for philosophy. Without such an atmosphere, philosophy could not have matured. As a plant requires suitable soil and climate, with a proper amount of light, heat, and moisture, so philosophy,—considered objectively,—requires a suitable intellectual climate or atmosphere in which to attain its growth.

In the 8 century a new spirit appeared in Europe; a spirit for learning. This fact was first made manifest in the multiplication and the enlargement of schools, especially of the *parish schools* and the *cathedral schools*. The spirit of learning was fostered by Charlemagne who brought to the continent from the British Isles the learned Alcuin and a staff of teachers to take charge of the *palace school* (the Palatine School) and to make it a proper model for the others. Through the centuries a zeal for learning grew among the people. The 14 century found the European world furnished with many great *universities*,—Cracow, Rome, Bologna, Paris, Cologne, Oxford, Cambridge, and others. All of these were *Catholic,* for European civilization was Catholic; all were fostered and furthered by ecclesiastical power.

In passing, we must not fail to notice the fact,—admitted by every honest historian,—that the spirit of study and the zeal for learning are regularly manifest where the Catholic Faith has been established and when the turbulances of an uprooted paganism have been stilled. The Catholic Church has ever been the true mother of education, of philosophy, and of solid science.

c) THEMES

One of the most important themes of discussion in the age of which we now speak was that of the nature and value of knowledge. This metaphysical question, basic in philosophy, was focussed upon the elements of human knowledge, our *ideas.* Now, ideas are, in themselves, *universal ideas,* and the realities which they represent in our minds are represented there in a *universal* manner. When, for example, we have the idea or concept of *tree,* we have knowledge of what tree means; we can write the definition of tree as such; the definition is applicable to each and every possible tree, regardless of size, location, botanical class. For, we know *an essence,* and we know it as abstracted from the circumstances and limitations that mark the individual things which have that essence in the world of things outside the mind. This is what we mean by saying that ideas are universal ideas, and that we know things in universal.

Now, there is no question that the thing known in an idea or concept is present to the mind in an abstract and universal way. But there can be question about the way in which that essence actually exists in the things that have it. How, for example, does the essence *tree,*—which is the *object* or "thing known" in the idea *tree,*—exist in the actual trees which exist or can exist in the world of reality outside our minds? Does this essence exist *universally* in each individual tree? Or does each tree merely reflect this objectively existing essence as each of a thousand mirrors reflect the same sun?

Our ideas (as we learned in studying *the predicables* or *categoremata* of Aristotle) are applicable to things, or are predicable of things, as constituting their essence or as indicating what must be or may be associated with their essence. Of the five modes called *the predicables,* the most notable are *genus* and *species.* If the idea *body* is predicated of trees, grass, flowers, weeds, moss, vines, and stones, it is predicated as their *genus,* that is, as an essence which is in each of the things named, and yet is not their *entire* essence; for the plants are more than bodies, they are alive. If, of the first six items mentioned, we predicate the idea *plant,* this is their *species,* for it expresses their entire essence; the points in which the various plants differ are non-essential or accidental. Now, the question arises: how does the universal *body* (that is, the essence *body,* known in universal) exist in all these things, and in all others called *body?* Do genera and species have actual existence in things outside the mind, and if so, what is the character of this existence? This is the famous "Question of Universals" which was hotly debated for more than four centuries, and indeed is sometimes debated among non-Scholastics even today.

The idea is *a universal idea.* The object of a universal idea (that is, the objective essence known in the idea) is called "the universal." What are universals? What are genera and species? These questions are identical in meaning, and they pose the "question of universals."

There are four doctrines possible in the matter of universals. Three of these are fallacious; one is correct and true. It required the genius of the 13 century to establish the true doctrine, which we list here as the fourth, that is, Moderate Realism.

1. *Extreme Realism* (called *Ultra-Realism* and sometimes simply *Realism*) holds that there are universal essences in the world of reality outside our minds. There is, for example, a universal essence of man, and of this essence individual men either have only a part or share, or each individual reflects the entire essence as a little mirror reflects the whole sun. This doctrine

which comes flatly in conflict with both reason and experience is to be rejected.

2. *Conceptualism* says that the human mind is built to form ideas, and these have no knowable corresponding reality in the world outside the mind. Individual human minds are like so many Ford motors, all alike, all working the same way. Therefore, universals are really nothing in themselves, they are merely modes of the mind's working. This doctrine which destroys the value of all knowledge and plunges us into the insane contradictions of skepticism is to be wholly rejected.

3. *Nominalism* says that the mind, faced by a vast and complicated world of individual things, finds it convenient to make groups of these things and to affix a name or label to each group. The basis of the grouping is a "similarity" in things. The names or labels are our ideas. Thus ideas are not representations of essences; they are merely group-names. There are no truly universal ideas; hence there are no universals. Nominalism is destructive of all knowledge, of all reasoning; it renders science and philosophy impossible; it is full of the contradictions of skepticism, as, for instance, when it affirms a universal grasp of "similarity" even in its denial of the universal grasp of anything. Therefore, nominalism is to be rejected.

4. *Moderate Realism* (called also *Qualified Realism*) says that outside the mind only individual things exist. There are no universal essences in the world of creatures. Creatures cannot exist universally, but only individually. But the mind, in forming its universal ideas, follows no mere inner drive of its nature wholly divorced from the things known (as Conceptualism maintains), nor does it merely apply names to groups of "similar" things (as Nominalism teaches). The mind is able to see wherein a plurality of things are *at one.* The mind sees, for example, that all trees are trees. It can form the universal idea *tree,* and the idea truly represents the reality which makes *any* tree a tree. In a word, the idea tree represents the essence tree. Only what is present to each tree

individually is represented in the mind universally, that is, in a manner abstracted from, or prescinding from, the individual limitations (size, location, botanical kind, number of leaves, etc.) which make a tree *this individual tree*. The mind knows things *really,* according to the *reality* which is their essence, but the mind knows in a mode or manner which is its own. Now, the mind's mode of knowing is the mode called *universality*. Hence, the universality of our ideas is in the mind and from the mind, but it is based upon reality inasmuch as the essence which the mind knows universally is actually verified individually in each and every thing which has that essence. Here we see the reason for calling this true doctrine on universals *realism,* and at the same time *qualified* or *moderate* realism. For our ideas represent essences *really,* yet we do not assert that the object of an idea (that is, the essence represented; the "universal") exists as a universal essence outside the mind.

The Question of Universals was not the only theme discussed by the philosophers of the age of the perfecting of philosophy. Far from it. But this is a question of outstanding importance, and it brings with it the study of nearly every important question of metaphysics. For, as we have seen, the critical question (which has to do with the nature, value, and extent of human knowledge) is the fundamental question of all philosophy; and the question of universals is the very focus and point of the critical question. Penetrating study of the critical question, and, in special, of the question of universals, could not fail, and did not fail, to bring with it deep interest and active discussion of all other important philosophical questions.

The themes discussed in the Period of Perfection were, therefore, fundamental and all-important themes. They constituted a notable "factor" in making the age what it was, a time of bringing philosophy to rounded completeness.

d) Equipment

The great philosophers of the age of the perfecting of philosophy brought to their task no certified list of credits from some collegiate agency. Nor had they at ready disposal endless libraries of printed books, in most of which, to steal a phrase from Mr. C. E. M. Joad, each author thinks it interesting to present the reasons which have led him to formulate his particular brand of error. The limitations of the time were, in some sense, a benefit. The philosophers had great writings; they had such a library as their times could boast; it was a library that could be known and mastered, and was worth the effort that mastering required. It was not a babble of voices confusing issues and overwhelming the mind with unlimited digression and unrestrained ineptitude.

From the late 8 century there were available for the studious mind the works of Plato and of Aristotle at least in part (although until the 13 century Aristotle was known in Europe in very defective and even falsified translations). There were also the works of Porphyry, Boethius, Victorinus, Macrobius, Apuleius, Cassiodorus, Trismegistus, Hippocrates, Lucretius, Seneca, Cicero, Galen, Martian Capella, St. Augustine, Origen, St. Clement of Alexandria, Lactantius, St. Ambrose, St. Gregory of Nyssa, Nemesius, Pseudo-Dionysius, St. John Damascene.

e) Movements

Matthew Arnold says that great creative epochs in literature result from the happy concurrence of two notable powers,—the power of the man and the power of the moment. It may be truly said that the age of the perfecting of philosophy came from a similar union of powers.

Although we refuse to list the men of the period as mere "factors" of philosophical achievement, we must notice the fact that the age was one of great and gifted teachers. Among these we mention Alcuin, Roscelin, Anselm, William of Champeaux, Abelard, Bernard of Clairvaux, the doctors of the schools of Chartres and St. Victor, William of Auvergne, Alexander of Hales, Bonaventure, Roger Bacon, Albert the Great, Thomas of Aquin, Henry of Ghent, John Duns Scotus, Raymond Lully,

William of Ockham. In addition to these Christian teachers the Arabians Averroes and Avicenna, and the Jewish philosopher Moses Maimonides, lent their learning and energy to the philosophical effort of the times.

As for the power of the moment, four items may be mentioned. First, philosophy, ripened by five centuries of intense study, was ready for expression in an orderly and complete synthesis at the opening of the 13 century. Second, the works of oriental philosophers were spread, in Latin translation, through western Europe; these aroused both sympathy and strong controversy, and so proved to be a force in the intellectual movement of the age. Third, great universities were multiplied and their influence was a strong and steady force for philosophical achievement. Fourth, the religious orders of St. Francis and St. Dominic carried to the common people not only the better knowledge of the Catholic Religion but also a great deal of philosophical knowledge; for members of these religious families went everywhere and were often forced to meet on philosophical grounds the thinkers of non-Christian persuasions.

Summary of the Article

In this Article we have noticed some telling influences which helped to make the Middle Ages the period of the perfecting of philosophy. We have listed such influences as *atmosphere, themes, equipment,* and *movements.* We have taken special note of the theme of *universals.*

Our philosophical vocabulary has been enriched, in the Article, by some new terms and by the recollection of others seen before: *universal, universal idea, predicables, genera and species, abstractive power of the mind, Exaggerated Realism, Conceptualism, Nominalism, Moderate Realism.*

Article 2. Some Great Philosophers of the Age of Perfection

a) Anselm; b) Abelard; c) The Arabians; d) Albert; e) Aquinas; f) Scotus; g) Ockham.

a) Anselm

St. Anselm of Lombardy (1033–1109), Abbot of the Benedictine Monastery of Bec in Normandy, and later Archbishop of Canterbury in England, was the foremost philosopher of the 11 century.

One of his chief interests,—which led to only partial success in the efforts it engendered,—was the distinction between theology and philosophy. St. Anselm disagreed with those philosophers (such as Erigena) who held that these are really one science. But it was left for St. Thomas Aquinas, in the 13 century, to show with scientific exactness that there is a clear line of demarcation between them, and that theology (that is, supernatural theology) is one science and philosophy another.

St. Anselm offered reasoned proofs for the existence of God and for the Divine Attributes. He argued cogently in evidence of the truth that the human soul is spiritual and immortal. Although he rightly taught that the soul acquires intellectual knowledge by abstracting ideas or concepts from sense-findings, and using these in judging and in reasoning, he inclined to the Platonic doctrine that soul and body are united accidentally and not substantially; in this, of course, he was quite wrong.

The heretics of St. Anselm's day were fond of dialectics,—that is, of fine logical reasoning; theirs was rather an abuse, than a proper use of logic. Nevertheless, many pious and learned men were led to see in dialectics a kind of snide trickery, and even a devilish device for the spread of error and the confusing of minds. St. Anselm stood sanely and firmly against this mistaken view of logic. He employed it himself with telling effect, and so routed the heretics with their own weapon. Thus he saved the good name and the splendid service of dialectics for Christian scholars; he justified for all time the use of sheer reasoning and philosophical argument in the exposition and defense of the Christian Faith. Yet he clearly declared that the Christian has no need to *rationalize* his Faith; possessing the Faith, reason can serve to show its truth and glory, and so attract those who have it not. The motto of St. Anselm was *"Credo ut intelligam,"* that is, "I believe that I may understand": "I find in my Faith a great light which aids me in understanding other things; I do not need to philosophize about creatures to justify myself in believing." Another motto of St. Anselm was *"Fides quaerens intellectum,"* "Faith seeking to understand": that is, "If you have the Faith to begin with, you have a head-start in the work of philosophy; you need not philosophize yourself into an acceptance of the Faith."

Perhaps St. Anselm is best remembered in our times for his famous "ontological argument" for the existence of God. This argument is not a valid one, but it has intrigued the minds of thinkers for nearly a thousand years. Descartes, Leibnitz, and Spinoza were among famous men to study it, reshape it, and present it. Despite its attractiveness it fails to make conclusive proof. Of course, it is in no wise required. The inescapable force of the *a posteriori* arguments for the existence and attributes of Almighty God make other arguments superfluous. But St. Anselm, like many another since his day, thought that an *a priori* argument (or rather an argument *a simultaneo*) could be developed from the fact that man inevitably has some notion of Deity. The famous argument ran thus:

All men, even unbelievers, have an idea of God; it is the idea of the most perfect Being thinkable;

Now, the idea of the most perfect Being thinkable is the idea of an *existing* Being (for, if it lack existence, it lacks a most notable perfection and hence is *not* the most perfect Being thinkable);

Therefore, God really exists.

The fallacy in this argument lies in the fact that it "jumps" from the realm of thought (called *the logical order*) to the realm of reality outside the mind (called *the ontological order*), and thus leaves a gap in the reasoning. If we restate the argument, observing the strict rules of logic, we shall see that the conclusion is quite different:

God is the most perfect Being that can be thought of;
Now, the most perfect Being that can be thought of must be thought of as existing;
Therefore, God must be thought of as existing.

This argument is perfectly legitimate. But the fact that God must be *thought of* as existing cannot be used as a proof that God *actually does exist.*

Gaunilo, a critic of St. Anselm's argument, tried to reduce it to absurdity in some such fashion as this:

I have an idea of a most beautiful and perfect floating island;
Now, unless it exists, it is not most beautiful and perfect;
Therefore, this floating island exists.

This nonsense merely proved the fact that Gaunilo did not understand St. Anselm's argument. For the Saint was speaking of the First, the Infinite, the Necessary Being, not of a creatural and limited thing like a floating island. No limited thing can be limitless in perfection. No creature can be envisioned as *most perfect.* The very concept of a creature is the concept of a thing perfectible. St. Anselm spoke only of that Being which we cannot help thinking of (and which even atheists cannot help thinking of; for they must have an idea of what they are denying when they deny God) as *absolutely perfect,* as *limitless in perfection,* as *infinite.* No one *needs* to think of a floating island or of any limited reality. But the idea of *the absolute* is inevitable to normal and mature minds. Indeed, if the ontological argument did not unwarrantedly assume *a priori* the objective validity of thought, it would be a cogent and irrefutable proof of God's existence.

b) ABELARD

Peter Abelard or Abaelard (1079–1142), a native of Brittany, became in early manhood the outstanding teacher of his age. He was universally regarded by his contemporaries as the greatest of living philosophers. In this opinion Peter Abelard wholeheartedly concurred. He was a fiery teacher and speaker, a clever dialectician, a man too intent on triumph in debate. There were few questions of philosophy upon which he failed to touch; there were few to which he gave thorough and complete treatment. His great service to philosophy is that he stirred up the thinkers; he awoke enthusiasm. Even his errors, championed so earnestly, aroused opposition that led to the clear exposition of many a truth that had been only half understood or but murkily explained.

Abelard rightly maintained that the use of reason is of the greatest value in setting forth the truths of Faith. Yet, despite his tendency to run to extremes, he did not declare that reason is all-sufficient (*rationalism*) for the full understanding of every truth. Hence is is not just to call Abelard a Rationalist, as too many have done.

In the matter of universals Abelard came near the right doctrine of Moderate Realism. In his day the terminology of this question had not been finally formulated, and hence there is some obscurity in his position.

Abelard says that God is so far above expression that all our speech about Him is figurative. Here he is wrong. God is infinite, and our minds and our mode of speech are finite. But, for all that, we can have a knowledge of God that is *literally* true knowledge, not figurative knowledge, even though it is never exhaustive. All that we know of as absolute perfection (that is, pure or *unmixed* perfection) we attribute to God *literally,* though in a transcendent or *eminent* way.

Abelard mistakenly thought that God is compelled by His goodness to create, and to create the best of all possible worlds (*theological necessitarianism* and *cosmological optimism*). Now, compulsion in God is unthinkable, since He is infinite and supremely independent, and, being the Source of all reality, there is nothing outside God which could conceivably work an independent influence upon Him. Nor is there anything within God to compel creation. All that God has, He is. God's Goodness is God Himself eternally subsisting. Hence the idea of compulsion in or upon God is a self-contradictory notion. God is not obliged in any way to create, nor, freely choosing to create, is He obliged to create the best of all possible worlds. As we have seen in another place, it is sufficient that His work be worthy of Him; that it be splendidly suitable for achieving the end for which it is made.

In his studies upon the ethical question, Abelard rightly holds that God is the Supreme Good towards Which man of necessity tends. God is the ultimate end of man in all human acts. And the possession and enjoyment of this *objective End* is the *subjective* last end of man: that is, beatitude in the possession of the Supreme Good.—In trying to fix *the norm of morality,* Abelard hesitates, and finally sets down two opinions, neither of which is correct. He thinks that the law or line which marks off good from evil (the norm of morality) is either God's will alone, or man's intention. Now, the true norm of morality is *God as Eternal Law,* that is, God as Divine Understanding and Will, not God as Will alone. God's will is, humanly speaking, consequent upon His knowledge of what is in line, and what is out of line, with Himself. Man's intention cannot be the *norm* of morality. It is a determinant of morality in so far as a bad intention can spoil a good act and make it evil; but a good intention cannot save a bad act and make it good. The norm of morality is The Eternal Law; it is applied by human reason judging on the objective right or wrong of a situation here and now to be decided; in this service, human reason is called *conscience.*

c) The Arabians

Two notable philosophers among the Mohammedan Arabs of the Middle Ages must be mentioned here. These are Ibn-Sina (more commonly called by the Latinized form of his name *Avicenna*) and Ibn-Roschd (usually called *Averroes*).

Avicenna (980–1037) was a native of Bokhara; his parents were Persian-born Arabians. He was a man of intellectual gifts. A physician of renown as well as a philosopher, he is forever memorable for his book, *The Canons of Medicine,* which served for many years as the standard texbook for students of medical science.

Averroes (d.1198) was a Spanish-born Arab. He was a notable commentator on Aristotle as well as a distinguished thinker in his own right.

The fact that the question of universals was of burning importance in the Middle Ages explains the enduring of these Arab names. For the Arabians were deeply interested in *the origin of ideas,* and their theories touched the very heart of the controversy on universals.

The true doctrine on ideas may be summed up thus: there are no inborn ideas; man *acquires* all his knowledge. Ideas result in man's intellect from the action of the mind on the findings of sense. From these ideas others may be worked out by a further process of abstraction. So the mind rises from those ideas immediately formed upon sense-action (*physical ideas*) to concepts of pure quantity (*mathematical ideas*) and concepts of *being* considered apart from all the limitations of materiality (*metaphysical ideas*). In a word, ideas have their origin in the native power of the human mind or intellect to abstract understandable essences (called *intelligible species*) from sense-findings, and to hold these within itself as representations of reality. Each human being has a mind or intellect. The intellect, in so far as it *abstracts* ideas (or intelligible species) from sense-findings (and from ideas already formed) is called the *intellectus agens* or active intellect;

in so far as it expresses within itself the abstracted essences or intelligible species and holds these as representations of reality (thus *knowing* reality), it is called the *intellectus possibilis* or understanding intellect.

Now, the Arabians who followed Avicenna held the strange doctrine that there is a common *intellectus agens* for all men, just as there is one sun in the sky to lend light to all eyes. Averroes and his followers went further; they taught that the intellect, both *agens* and *possibilis,* is a common possession, a reality outside all individual men. Individual man has no intellect at all. His knowing-power is merely that of the senses. And, since the senses are organic (that is, dependent on bodily members), there is no justification for the conclusion that man has a spiritual element in his make-up. Therefore, man has no spiritual soul; when he dies he perishes utterly. So far Averroes the philosopher.

But Averroes the theologian, holding fast to the Koran, teaches that man has an immortal soul. Here we have the beginning of that most disastrous of all doctrines, against which the mighty St. Thomas Aquinas was to rise in towering strength: the doctrine of *a twofold truth.* This pernicious doctrine holds that what is true in philosophy may be false in theology, and vice versa. The twofold-truth doctrine was taught in the 13 century by Peter d'Abano and John of Jandun in Italy, and by Siger of Brabant in the University of Paris. The doctrine is wholly indefensible, and it leads directly into the insane self-contradiction of skepticism. It is ruinous of all knowledge, of all science, of all philosophy.

The doctrine of twofold-truth is no longer defended by theorists; St. Thomas put an enduring end to all discussion of the matter. But it endures *in practice,* especially in the form of a twofold morality. Thus there are people who will justify sharp practice and open savagery by quoting as sound principles the silly clichés, "Business is business" and "All's fair in war,"—as though the business man and the soldier had a set of moral laws for office hours or term of service, and another set for private life. The modern "mercy killers" exemplify the same satanic doctrine of a twofold morality, as do the birth-controllers, the sterilizers, and the advocates of concubinage under the name of trial-marriage. These people would have us believe that there is a moral law for ordinary people, and another moral law for the aged, the emotional, and other exceptional persons. Again, we find this evil doctrine in the writings of those who maintain (as Professor Dowden does in his biography of Shelley) that a "genius" is not bound by the ordinary laws of morality which regulate the conduct of persons of more common clay. Against the twofold-truth theory,—and its offshoot, the theory of a twofold morality,—we must take a firm stand. Truth is one, constant, consistent. One truth cannot come in conflict with another truth. And the truth of morality is like all other truths. There can be no such thing as a diversity of moral codes to suit diversity of persons or circumstances.

d) Albert

St. Albert the Great, known to his contemporaries as Albert of Cologne, and frequently called by the Latin form of his name, Albertus Magnus, was born in Swabia, part of present Germany, in the last years of the 12 century or the first years of the 13. He died in 1280. Albert was a member of the Order of St. Dominic; he was made Bishop of Ratisbon in 1260. Pre-eminently a student and teacher, he resigned his bishop's see after three years of office. Most of his teaching was done at the universities of Paris and Cologne.

St. Albert is called "The Universal Doctor," and the name is justified, for he was a man of enormous capacity for learning and of tireless diligence in study and research. His works are many, and they cover wide and various fields,—philosophy, theology, Scripture, natural science. His genius was analytical; he worked out an amazing amount of scientific knowledge. The synthetical power which collates, integrates, focusses, and refines the fruits of analysis, was not so marked a gift of St. Albert, although he certainly possessed it in good measure.

Albert was an Aristotelian. He purified the translations of Aristotle of much Arabian interpolation. In his treatise on Aristotle's *Physics,* as well as in his own studies and experiments, Albert contributed more to the development of physical science than did the much lauded Roger Bacon.

St. Albert's work was notable and it was nobly done. It stands upon its own merits. But, looking upon it in retrospect, we must judge that Albert's greatest service to philosophy was the fact that he prepared the ground, so to speak. for the work of his illustrious pupil, St. Thomas Aquinas.

e) Aquinas

St. Thomas of Aquin,—more commonly called St. Thomas Aquinas, or simply Aquinas,—was born during the young manhood of St. Albert and died before him. Yet it seems natural for us to think of St. Thomas appearing on the intellectual scene after St. Albert had departed. He was a pupil of St. Albert, and this enlightened teacher recognized his genius in early student days when fellow-pupils considered Thomas only a dreamy lad of no particular talent.

Thomas was born between 1224 and 1226 in Roccasecca in Italy. He died March 7, 1274, while on his way to attend the Council of Lyons. Thus he lived, at most, but fifty years. Yet the accomplishments of his comparatively short lifetime were enough, one might suppose, for twenty men of twice his span of years. If we except Aristotle, and perhaps Augustine, the history of philosophy has no name to offer that deserves to stand in the same line with that of St. Thomas Aquinas. It may be unfair to compare Thomas with Aristotle, for Aristotle worked in the night of pagan antiquity while Thomas labored in the daylight of Christianity. Perhaps it is but just to say that, in point of natural gifts, Aristotle stands alone, and that, in point of natural and supernatural gifts combined, Aquinas far surpasses Aristotle.

St. Thomas produced a veritable library of valuable writings. These are remarkable for their scope, their completeness, their clarity. No taint of pride, no vain show of erudition for its own sake, soils any page he wrote. No man ever knew more thoroughly, and more sympathetically, the significant writings of all his predecessors in philosophy, theology, Scripture, and physical science. Thoroughly equipped with an easy mastery of the world's worthwhile knowledge, St. Thomas brought to bear upon every question the light of his own mighty and original mind. In him the power of analysis and the power of synthesis seem equal.

Following the lead of St. Albert, St. Thomas purified many doctrines attributed to Aristotle of their Mohammedan accretions, and he induced his friend and fellow-Dominican, William of Moerbeke, an able linguist, to make a Latin translation of Aristotle from the original Greek.

St. Thomas settled the perplexing question of the distinction between philosophy and theology by justifying the principle: *Sciences are distinguished one from another by their respective formal objects, and ultimately by the "formal object quo."* We have explained this point in the Introduction (*cf. Intro. 4*).

In the matter of universals, St. Thomas offers compelling proof for the truth of the Aristotelian doctrine of Moderate Realism. He devotes full and detailed study to the basic concept or idea of *being*. This concept is the first idea in every order,—the order of time (*chronological order*), the order of knowledge (*logical order*), and the order of understandable reality (*metaphysical order*). For the very first idea or concept acquired in life (since we are born without any equipment of ideas) is the idea of some *thing,* that is, of some *being,* and the notion of *some* being involves, implicitly, the notion or idea of *being as such.* Further, the analysis of every concept takes the mind back to the fundamental notion of *being.* And, finally, every reality that can be thought of as existing is necessarily understood as some *thing,* that is, as *being.*—The idea of *being* is truly *transcendental* (*cf.*

Chap. II, Art. 2, d). Other transcendental ideas which extend or specially apply the idea of *being* are distinct from the idea of *being* by only a distinction of reason (i.e., a logical distinction) not a real distinction. These ideas are: *thing, something, reality, the one, the good, the true.* Together with *being,* these are called "the transcendentals."

St. Thomas holds the sane Aristotelian doctrine that *all* human knowledge takes its beginning in the action of the senses on the bodily world around us. He rejects the Augustinian theory (favored by the Franciscan tradition) that a special divine illumination is required for certain kinds of knowledge,—such as knowledge of first principles, or knowledge of spiritual realities. Our natural knowledge, says St. Thomas, is due to the fact that the mind is equipped with a power of abstraction which it employs first upon the findings of the senses, and then upon ideas themselves for their further refinement or elaboration. Thus, as we have noticed elsewhere, the mind arises from the *physical* order, through the *mathematical* order, to the *metaphysical* order of concepts or ideas. Thus there are three *grades* of abstraction. These are truly grades or degrees; they are not merely kinds; they are like steps in one stairway. St. Thomas takes the three grades of abstraction as the basis for the general classification of sciences.

In point of *physical* philosophy, St. Thomas holds with Aristotle that all physical being (that is, all being subject to change) is compounded of actuality and potentiality (*actus et potentia*). Further, all bodily being (all *ens mobile*) is composed of *matter* and *form,* and, fundamentally, of *prime matter* and *substantial form.*—St. Thomas teaches that, at any given moment, only one substantial form can in-form or actualize the same prime matter; in this point, he differs from the view (Scotistic and Franciscan) of those philosophers who defend the "plurality-of-substantial-forms theory." Spiritual substances are pure forms. *The principle of specification,* by which one essential kind of substance is distinguished from every other kind, is *substantial form. The principle of individuation,* by which individual substances of the same species or kind are distinguished from one another, is *in-formed prime matter as quantified.* St. Thomas holds that the human soul is, in each man, the substantial form of the living body. The soul does not exist before its union with the body. At one and the same instant each soul is *created* and *infused* (i.e., substantially united with the body) by Almighty God.—St. Thomas rejects the Arabian doctrine of a separate and common intellect serving all men, and offers proofs for the existence of intellect as a faculty of each human individual. He shows that man has free-will, that is, that the human will is endowed with freedom of *choice of means* to the necessary (and *not* free) ultimate end, the Supreme Good.

In point of *metaphysical* philosophy, St. Thomas treats of *being* in itself, of *being* as it is in the mind (that is, truth and certitude).—He asserts a *real* distinction (not merely a rational or *logical* distinction) between the essence and the existence of an existing creature.—He extends Aristotle's doctrine of causes, and deals most profoundly with the effecting or efficient cause, and with its subsidiary, the instrumental cause. He shows that God is First Effecting Cause, that the divine "effectingness," as act and as power, is identified with the Divine Substance. In creatures "effectingness" (or efficiency) as act and power is something really distinct from their substance; it is something they have, not something which they are; hence, *faculties* are things really distinct from the creatural substance which possesses and exercises them.—St. Thomas shows that God, the Necessary and Self-Subsistent First Being, is the Effecting, the Final, and the Exemplar Cause of all perfection, that is, of all positive being. He shows how God *concurs* with creatures in their connatural activities, and he maintains that the divine concurrence is not only *simultaneous* with the actions of creatures, but *antecedent* to such action; yet such antecedent concurrence (called *physical premotion*) in no wise destroys the nature of the acting creature; even if the creature be *free,* its freedom is not destroyed or in any sense hindered, for "God moves every being in a manner consonant with its nature."

In point of *moral* philosophy or *ethics,* St. Thomas shows that man, in every *human act* (that is in every thought, word, deed, or omission which is done knowingly and freely), tends towards the Supreme Good, the possession of which will constitute man in the state of perfect beatitude. Even the sinner, perversely choosing evil, chooses it under the guise of good, that is, of something that will *satisfy.* Man is made for God and endless perfect happiness. This end cannot be achieved perfectly this side of heaven, but it can be approximated here on earth by living for God, by knowing, loving, serving God. Since God has made man for Himself and happiness, He has a plan, an arrangement, a law which man must follow to attain His end. In other words, the Divine Reason (that is, God as Intellect and Will) has established the law which directs all things to their last goal or end. This law is The Eternal Law. Man, when he comes to the use and practice of his mental powers, inevitably becomes aware of "an order in things" which he must not disturb but must conserve; man's awareness of The Eternal Law is "the natural law." And man, in all his human acts, inevitably sees them in their relation to the natural law, and mentally pronounces upon their agreement or disagreement with the natural law. Such a pronouncement is called a judgment of *conscience.* And thus we notice that the *norm of morality* is The Eternal Law as applied by conscience.

St. Thomas has been called, and with justice, the prince of philosophers and of theologians. His works merit the earnest study of every thoughtful mind.

f) Scotus

John Duns Scotus (1266/74–1308), a member of the Franciscan Order, was a philosopher of extraordinary gifts and of wondrous accomplishment. He studied at Oxford, and later taught there and at the University of Paris. He wrote commentaries on Aristotle and on other philosophers, and he produced a notable treatise on theology. He also wrote *Quaestiones Quodlibetales,* a discussion of a variety of questions. Many other works are attributed to Scotus. The scholarly researches of the Franciscan Friars in our own day have shown beyond doubt or question that some of these works are spurious, and that some theories long attributed to Scotus are not truly his.

Scotus is known as "the Subtle Doctor." He had a mind of marvelous acuteness, and an untiring zeal for intricacies of discussion in which none but the keenest and most devoted students could keep pace with him. In some points he disagrees with St. Thomas. For instance, he has small reliance on the unaided human reason as the basis of certitude, and requires Faith and Revelation for the solution of some problems of philosophy. He does not agree with Thomas in point of "the principle of individuation" which he holds to be, not *quantified matter,* but a positive reality added to a being fully constituted in its specific nature; he calls this positive individuating reality by the name of *haecceitas,* which might be clumsily translated as the "thisness" of the being in question. Again, Scotus teaches that in a created being there is not a *real* distinction between existence and essence, nor is there merely a *rational* or *logical* distinction; the distinction in this instance is *an actual formal distinction arising from the nature of the reality* in which the distinction is found. This distinction (usually called "the Scotistic formal distinction") is, therefore, something less than *real* distinction, and something more than *logical* distinction. Again, in point of universals, Scotus accepts Moderate Realism, but his expression is involved, and some critics interpret him in such wise as to make him an Ultra-Realist. Again, Scotus defends the "plurality-of-forms theory"; he holds that in man, in addition to the spiritual soul which is the substantial form of living man, there is a substantial body-form or "a form of corporeity." Scotus holds that man is not moved, in his free-will acts, by the ultimate practical judgment of the mind (the *ultimum judicium practicum*), but that this judgment is only *a condition* requisite for the will's uninfluenced action. Scotus holds with unwavering certitude to the spirituality and immortality of the human soul, yet he teaches that its immortality is proved by an appeal to Revelation, and not by unaided reason.

A man of the highest gifts, Scotus has had, and has today, a mighty influence among Scholastic philosophers. He was the great luminary of the Franciscans as St. Thomas was the light and oracle of the Dominicans. The *Thomist* and the *Scotist* schools are in lively existence at the present time, especially in the realm of speculative theology.

Scotus was a man of most holy life; we may soon read his name in the list of the canonized saints.

g) Ockham

William of Ockham was a notable Franciscan philosopher of the 14 century. He was born about 1280 and died in 1348. The name by which this philosopher is most commonly known is that of his home town, Ockham or Ockam, of Surrey in England.

William was of impulsive and even stormy temperament, and his life was not without troubles. He wrote commentaries on the philosophy of Aristotle, on the famous "Sentences" (that is, doctrines) of Peter the Lombard, and on the writings of Porphyry.

His contemporaries hailed William as "the Venerable Inceptor" of a theory of knowledge called *Terminism*. But this was really no new theory; it was merely Nominalism in a new dress and with a new name.

William of Ockham is memorable for one valuable rule for philosophers, *Entia non sunt multiplicanda sine necessitate,* which, translated literally, means, "Things are not to be multiplied without need"; the force of the rule might be given in this fashion, "Explanations are to be made in the simplest and most direct fashion which the facts allow, without needless complications and distinctions." This dictum came to be known as "Ockham's Razor," for it was formulated to cut away wasted verbiage and needless involvement of reasoning. It is a good rule, but William himself used it without nice discernment of when "multiplication of things" is actually necessary. He sometimes used the "razor," not only to remove extraneous matters, but to level off the features of his subject. Like all impatient men who want to make complicated matters simple, he sometimes turned simplification into falsification. This note of impatience, this eagerness to make the deepest and most complicated questions as simple as A-B-C, was,—as is always the case when it appears in the works of men of influence,—a sign of decadence in philosophy. For any impatience with multitudinous detail indicates a loss of the philosophic temper which must be tirelessly patient. Ockham is the symbol and mark of a turning-point in philosophy. He is the last great figure in the age of perfection; some make him the first great figure in the age of transition, even when they try to hide the fact that the transition was also a retrogression. The cord of strong philosophic thought which had begun to fray under the friction of Thomistic-Scotistic argument, snapped asunder under the impatient dicta of William of Ockham. It was literally cut by "Ockham's Razor."

Summary of the Article

In this Article we have outlined some notable points in the philosophy of the more important medieval pre-Scholastics, St. Anselm, Peter Abelard, Averroes, Avicenna. We have sketched the work of the great Scholastics, St. Albert the Great, St. Thomas Aquinas, John Duns Scotus. We have mentioned the *Terminism* of William of Ockham.

The Article has extended our vocabulary of philosophical terms, and has recalled some formerly learned: *a priori; a simultaneo; a posteriori; the ontological argument; the logical order; the ontological order; pure perfection; mixed perfection; eminent perfection; the norm of morality; The Eternal Law; conscience; abstraction* (*physical, mathematical, metaphysical*); *species (sensible, intelligible); intellectus agens; intellectus possibilis; theory of twofold truth (and twofold morality); being; transcendental idea; distinction (real, logical); grades of abstraction; principle of individuation; principle of specification; essence; existence; actuality; potentiality; divine concurrence; physical premotion; the Scotistic formal distinction; plurality-of-forms theory; Thomism; Scotism; Terminism; Ockham's Razor.*

CHAPTER IV

THE COURSE OF PHILOSOPHY TO OUR TIMES

This Chapter discusses the progress, and the retrogressions, of philosophy during the last six centuries. The 14, 15, and 16 centuries are often called *the period of transition* from the age of Scholasticism to the philosophy of modern times. The student may be astonished to know that the modern period begins with the 17 century; this fact must come as a shock to a generation that has been taught, by every agency from radio to university, that even so recent a time as the last decade of the 19 century is fogged in a remote and ridiculous antiquity. The modern period of philosophy, extending through three and one-half centuries to our own day, is conveniently divided into two parts, the first of which discusses the period of transition, and the second, the philosophers and systems of note since the 16 century. The Chapter is accordingly divided into two Articles:

Article 1. Transition from Medieval to Modern Philosophy
Article 2. The Philosophy of the Last Three Centuries

Article 1. Transition from Medieval to Modern Philosophy

a) The Fading of Scholasticism; b) Revivalist Philosophies; c) Philosophy and Natural Science; d) Philosophy and Social Science.

a) The Fading of Scholasticism

It is usual to speak of the *decline* of Scholasticism during the 14 and following centuries. The word is unfortunate. For to decline is to suffer from an inner weakness, to undergo an essential disintegration, in a word, to decay. Now, Scholastic philosophy is a body of truths; it is the best system of philosophical principles that the human mind has been able to discover and integrate in more than twenty-five hundred years. Such a thing does not decline; it does not decay. It may lose favor with men; it may lose popularity; it may fade into the background. But there is no inner weakening or essential disintegration. It remains as true as always, no matter how it may be treated or regarded. Thus we speak of the *fading* of Scholasticism rather than of its decline.

Beyond all question, Scholasticism faded, and that with astonishing rapidity. There was a time when it had the field of philosophy practically to itself. This does not mean that all Scholastics were in full agreement on the solution of every problem, or that all followed the same course in solving problems. Scholasticism is one philosophy, but it admits of a variety of incidental treatments within its essential boundaries. It is a roomy household with ample space for a large family wherein tastes and temperaments may give rise to various and even conflicting opinions and modes of expression. As long as a member of this great family remains loyal to the home, supports the family honor, and holds to its essential ideals, he retains his place and rank in it. Scholasticism has unity in essentials, variety in modes and stresses. It has claim not alone to the title of true philosophy, but to the name of a human and even beautiful institution, for beauty is sometimes,—albeit imperfectly,—described as "unity amid variety."

Scholasticism once had its field to itself. No rival system of importance stood opposed to it in the 13 or three following centuries. Yet it faded from favor, and that suddenly, in the 14 century. The age of the giants was abruptly over when the giants died. As the Golden Age of Greek philosophy came to a sudden end with the death of Aristotle, the Golden Age of Scholasticism closed definitely with the death of the great masters of the 13 century. Neither Greek philosophy at its best, nor Scholasticism in its perfection, gave place to a stronger opposed system. There was no stronger opposed system. There was hardly an opposed system at all. Scholasticism faded; it was not driven from the scene. It faded for no want of perfection in itself, but for want of ability and of interest on the part of men. And inability and lack of interest came in turn from many causes which may be loosely summed up as distraction, ineptitude, mental weariness, the misdirection born of the Scotist-Thomist debates, and laxity in the methods and programmes of educational institutions, especially the great universities.

People with pretensions to scholarship sometimes write with deliberate pen that Scholasticism faded because the Scholastics of the later time were so deeply engaged in finicky quibbles, in thin eristic reasonings, in the endless fretting out of distinctions and subdistinctions, that they lost the respect of all learned and studious men. This is a half-truth and its unqualified allegation is more damaging and libellous than a whole falsehood. It is partially true, and entirely misleading. It paints a picture of silly Scholastics splitting hairs and of solidly learned men looking upon the process with disdain. Now, a great number of the later Scholastics did unquestionably split hairs and waste their time. But if they lost the respect of solid men, it was not Scholasticism itself which lost, or deserved to lose, that respect; yet the picture we speak of suggests precisely this. Again, the picture presents a splendid body of scholars scorning the Scholastic quibbles. One wonders just who those splendid fellows were. And, if they were of such solidity in scholarship, how comes it that they lacked penetration to recognize the fact that a system of philosophy is not to be judged by unworthy and inadequate representatives?

We hear until we are weary the mildewed story about Scholastic philosophers arguing endlessly on the question of how many angels might dance on the point of a needle. This story is offered by countless critics and historians who propose it as typical of the later Scholastic debates. But the story rather illustrates a type of mind in critics and historians than a type of Scholastic argument. For if this story is typical of the philosophic effort, it seems to be the only story of its type. It is an illustration that illustrates only itself. Certainly, it is not typical of Scholasticism, early or late, nor is it typical of the veriest dolt who had the remotest claim to knowledge of Scholastic philosophy. To take the silly thing seriously for a moment, it is obvious that any Scholastic philosopher, even a poor Scholastic philosopher, even the poorest Scholastic philosopher among the Scholastics of that later day when the glory and the great popularity had passed, would have instantly pointed out to the inept inquirer that there could be no discussion of such a question at all, much less an endless discussion. Such a question could not possibly arise among Scholastics who were well aware that a needle-point is material and has quantity whereas an angel is a spirit that cannot be quantified or considered as taking up any material space at all.

The true explanation of the fading of Scholasticism is not to be found in the silly fable of the debate about angels and the point of a needle. As has been indicated, it goes to a greater depth than that probed by a needle, and spreads over an area wider than that of the points of all needles.

"Rem acu tetigisti!" cried the ancients when a person had made a clear point in argument: "You've touched the thing with a needle; you've hit the nail on the head!" We cannot salute the angels-and-needle-point fabulist with such a praiseful cry. For the fabulist has not touched the character of the later Scholasticism with his needle; he has not hit the nail on the head. He has lost the needle in a haystack of misinformation; he has failed to see the nail or to come within striking distance of it.

For the whole point of this story about dancing angels and a needle-point is that it is a joke. The fabulist has confused the point of a needle with the point of a joke; and he hasn't seen the joke. That is why he is petulant, and why he petulantly calls the later Scholastics fools who made philosophy ridiculous. The man who can't see a joke is usually half-conscious of his own ineptitude; he grows surly or petulant about it; he comforts himself with the thought that the joker is an ass.

There may come a day when fabulists, petulantly arrogant, may dismiss with contempt some sacredly esteemed institution of our times,—say, for instance, the American system of education. In that remote day, serious writers will declare that the Americans of the twentieth century had such a foolish opinion of the nature of education that they lost the respect of all learned men. For, they will say, an American schoolmaster of the age in question was once heard propounding to another American schoolmaster the absurd problem, "When is a door not a door?" When (it will be tediously explained) leaders in education came to frittering away their time and their mental efforts on such nonsense, it is manifest that education was in a bad way. And so will arise a new myth about new Dark Ages and all the rest of the tiresome drivel that passes for information about a time half-known and half-forgotten and wholly misunderstood. And all because heavy critics and stolid historians lack wit to see a joke. The modern fabulist is stuck on the point of a medieval needle. The fabulist of the future will run headlong into a solid American door. No jar will suffice to make his inadequate faculties take hold of the fact that the door is ajar.

But, quite apart from all the fabulist's serious nonsense, it must be admitted that the later Scholastics wasted their time on meticulous inconsequentialities. There were no intellectual giants among them, but that fact is irrelevant. A long succession of men of genius cannot be expected. The world's work, intellectual as well as physical, must, in the main, be carried on by ordinary plodding folk of the kind snobbishly called mediocre. The dazzling achievements of genius must be recognized, esteemed, and preserved by the interest and effort of common men. This was the task of the later Scholastics. This task the later Scholastics failed to perform. There was among them a slackening of interest, a lack of well-directed effort, a let-down in consistent mental application of the type we now love to call "constructive." And why did this lamentable falling off occur? Well, as we have said before, a great many intellectual leaders of the time were distracted and wearied, especially by the Thomist-Scotist arguments. And why did they succumb to such weakness? Because men are children of a fallen sire; men always tend to grow lazy and slipshod. And when they have once given way to intellectual laziness and have begun to suffer from the ill equipment that comes of it, men resent guidance, they fret at the exactions of study, they begin to wonder whether, after all, the laborious ancients and the lauded masters were not making much ado about nothing, or at least about a very little. Now, the very soul of such resentful fretting is pride. When pride takes hold of the mind, real scholarship dies. For humility is not alone the basic and essential moral virtue; it is the basic and essential intellectual virtue as well.

Pride,—born of laziness, incompetence, injured self-respect,—is the real root reason for the fading of Scholasticism. Indeed, this spirit of pride was abroad in the world in the 14 and following centuries. Humility faded with the fading of the Faith. The works of pride which supplanted humility are, as the Apostle says, manifest: Liberalism, the pagan Renaissance, the Protestant Reformation, naturalistic philosophies, Humanism, Sociology. Among such things truth cannot live; it is pushed to the background; it inevitably fades.

Scholasticism faded in the 14 century. Yet by the middle of the 15 century there was a notable movement afoot to restore it to its rightful place. The Dominicans and, later, the newly established Society of Jesus, did much good service in that direction during the 15 and 16 centuries, and we come upon notable names among the Scholastics of the time: Cajetan, Francis de Ferrara, Francis de Vittoria, Melchior Canus, Bannez, John of St. Thomas, Fonseca, Vasquez, Molina, Suarez. But, despite the splendid efforts of these champions, Scholasticism was increasingly regarded as a system outmoded, a religious philosophy suited only for the Catholic whose Faith was now scorned by the majority of men. Scholastic philosophy failed to secure a place of prominence in the eyes of the non-Catholic world until late in the 19 century.

b) Revivalist Philosophies

The human mind, as Karl Adam aptly says, cannot live upon denial; it is made for thesis and affirmation. With the fading of Scholasticism men turned to other doctrines.

The impatience of the post-medievals with the authority of the masters of Scholasticism was only a phase of a general and increasing impatience with all authority, notably religious authority, and even divine authority. The ideals of the Cross, of self-discipline, of life in obedience and docility under the guidance of God's Church, were unacceptable to the mood of the time. Men were caught in the shackles of half-education and baseless self-esteem. They forgot the lesson of wisdom that it is truth which makes men free. They sought what they called a larger freedom, which was but a mirage of freedom, in the things of man and time rather than in the things of God and eternity. Scorning the masters of immediately preceding times, they shifted their allegiance to ages long past. They found something new and exhilarating in the works of the ancients, the achievements of the old pagans in language and letters, in arts and philosophy. Interest and enthusiasm grew for sheerly human achievement. Thus was *humanism* born into the world.

Plato and Aristotle, recaptured for Europe in acceptable translation, won many admirers. The Stoics and the Epicureans had followers too. Some revived the doctrines of Averroes as the final philosophy, but most turned to teachers more ancient. In all this stir of humanistic study there was something of the thin enthusiasm which accompanies the promotion of a fad. And the fad died, leaving no valuable fruits. Of course, the flight from authority never really made a start; all that the Liberals of the time accomplished was a shift of authority, a substitution of the dubious authority of half-grasped ancient theories for the truly liberating authority of sound philosophy.

No really eminent names are encountered in the lists of philosophers of the revivalist movement in the 15 and 16 centuries. Among Platonists of the 15 century we may mention: Pletho, Ficino, Bessarion, Giovanni della Mirandola. Among Aristotelians (falsely so called, for they were materialists and not true Aristotelians at all) were: Theodore of Gaza, Achellini, Pomponazzi, and, in the 16 century, Andreas Caesalpinus, Joest Lips, and Peter Gassendi.

c) Philosophy and Natural Science

The newly developing experimental sciences of the 15 and 16 centuries offered themselves as a substitute for philosophy to men who had cast aside,—for the most part without examining it,—the ordered system of Scholasticism. *Naturalistic* philosophies made their appearance. And the name *natural philosophy* was given to what we should now call experimental physics.

The naturalistic philosophers were in tune with the humanistic mood of the time. *Man* was doing things; man was discovering what makes the universe tick. "Glory to man in the highest," (as Swinburne was later to sing) "for man is the master of things." The swift formulation of philosophies from the findings of incipient physical science helped humanism to do its work,—that is, it helped dehumanize mankind. In the older and spiritual philosophies man was regarded indeed as the clay of the earth, but clay infused and in-formed by spirit, and cast in the image of God. In the naturalistic and humanist philosophy man was soon regarded as animal merely, the product of a blind clash of physical forces in a wholly material universe; man was, as Homer had called him, "only the saddest of the beasts of the field."

The student is cautioned here not to confuse the genuine scientists of this time with the mistaken and absurd philosophers of science. Sometimes indeed a real scientist overstepped the bounds of his province and turned philosopher. It is a thing even the best intentioned scientists are forever trying to do. But others attended, in the main, to their own business; they accomplished a great deal for the advancement of true scientific knowledge. We appreciate the achievements of a Copernicus (1473–1543) and a Kepler (1571–1631); we deprecate the foul ineptitude of an unspeakable Girodano Bruno (1548–1600). The Church as well as true philosophy recognizes the findings of true science, esteems the genuine scientist and furthers and fosters his work. But the Church and true philosophy also recognize the sham scientist. They see in him the enemy of truth, and they condemn him as such. Yet out of this sane procedure a muddle-headed minority takes occasion for charging the Church and Scholastic philosophy with opposition to science. The student must be prepared for this. When he hears the silly phrase about "the conflict of science and religion," let him be ready to show, with enduring patience, that there never was, never is, never can be, a conflict between the true religion of the Catholic Church and genuine science.

The whole history of science and of the Catholic Church is evidence of the fact that truth never contradicts truth. Time after time, over-enthusiastic scientists, as well as the foggy-minded fellows who call themselves Liberals and Progressives, have sought the unqualified approbation of the Church for their seemingly well-founded theories. And, failing, they have turned on the Church as decadent, outmoded, fogyish, doomed to general contempt as a hopeless reactionary and stick-in-the-mud. But each time the scientists and the sciolists and the Liberals and the Progressives have had to change their tune and their theories. Meanwhile the Church, secure and serene, remained the sane guardian of truth. Sometimes even Catholics, like Lord Acton in 1854, have been so dismayed and provoked by the attitude of the Church towards "progressive culture" that they have broken out in petulant complaint. But time proved the Church right and the Progressives wrong. This sort of thing has happened so often and so invariably, that one might suppose that the Progressives, the Liberals, the Dawnists, and the materialists of every stripe would proceed with some caution in their judgments upon the stand of the Church. But Progressives never progress; they are proof against learning anything. The Church has been in vital existence for two thousand years; the scientific effort (since man's genius has supplied it with laboratory instruments and the means for controlling the conditions of investigation and experiment) has a history of four or five hundred years at the most. In this long course of time, in pre-scientific and in scientific ages, the Church has steadily vindicated her character as the promoter and guardian of truth. At the same time she has risked name and reputation a hundred times to stand squarely against some suddenly popular theory which all the world regarded as scientific fact. Time has always justified the Church. For the Church has never run with the mood of the hour; she has never cared a fig about being in the fashion; she has never flinched under the angry charges that she is obstructionist and reactionary. She has cared for truth, and she has neither feared to protect it at the cost of popularity or to promote it in the face of mistaken opposition. And in all this, the Scholastic philosophy parallels the Church. This is not due to the fact that Scholasticism is "Catholic philosophy," but to the fact that both the Church and Scholasticism are eminently sane.

Those who dislike the Church and Scholasticism are eager to have these institutions seen in any unfavorable light. They like to talk of "the quarrel of science and religion" and of "the conflict of the Church with scientific progress." Such phrases are wholly false and unwarranted; the man who uses them confesses the essentially defective character of his education. When confronted by what appears to him an amazing denial, such a man will murmur something about Galileo. And that "sizes" the gentleman once and for all. For if anything were needed to show that the Church is the defender of true science, the case of Galileo would meet all requirements. No matter what a few churchmen had to say, the Church had no condemnation for the scientific teachings of Galileo; Copernicus had taught these in a work dedicated to the Pope, and Copernicus, a faithful son of the Church and perhaps an ecclesiastic, had been dead twenty years when Galileo was born. What the Church,—and even local Church authority,—condemned in Galileo was his attack on Holy Scripture, and in this the Church was manifestly right and Galileo was wrong. The so-called imprisonment of Galileo (referred to sometimes as "a martyrdom in the sacred cause of science") was an enforced residence for a short period in the palatial home of a friend. This imprisonment was a disciplinary measure imposed, according to the procedure of the time, upon a recalcitrant Catholic; it had nothing whatever to do with his scientific teachings. Further, the scientific data propounded by Galileo were based upon unscientific grounds. The Church would not approve the deducing of even true conclusions from false premises. Nor would she allow the scientific world to be deceived by the theory of Galileo that there is a contradiction between scientific fact and the revealed word of God. In a word, the Church stood for science as opposed to scientism, for truth as opposed to falsity.

There is no conflict between the Church and science; quite the contrary. But there is, and must be, a conflict between the Church (with Scholastic philosophy) and sham science.

d) Philosophy and Social Science

The humanistic interest in everything that *man* has achieved turned, in the 16 century, to the matter of laws and the management of civil society. The emergence of "the principle of nationality" lent emphasis to the interest in social science and helped to make it a substitute for philosophy and even for religion.

St. Thomas More (1480–1535), the glorious English martyr, wrote a book called *Utopia* (a name coined from two Greek words which mean "not a place" or "nowhere") in which he described the life of a people living on an imaginary island. Their government was that of a republic. Laws were administered most wisely;

absolute equality was insured to all citizens; all enjoyed continued peace and happiness. Now, St. Thomas More was an able statesman; he knew well how governments are run. His picture of the ideal island republic may be a whimsy to express "wishful thinking," or (and more likely) it may be a satire on the new voices that were crying wildly for social legislation as the one means of salvation; the "heaven on earth" people; the "make the world a better place to live in" crowd.

Hugo de Groot (commonly called *Grotius,* a Latinized form of his name) was a studious Protestant divine who wrote well and learnedly on *The Right of War and Peace.* He failed, however, to recognize the fact that man is *by nature* a social being. He thought that civil society (or *The State*) is somehow the product of a kind of arrangement and agreement among men, an artifiicial and not a natural institution. This *social contract theory* (taught later by Rousseau and by Hobbes) is untenable; it has long been recognized on all hands as fallacious, and it holds a place in the history of human thinking only as a philosophical curiosity. De Groot died in 1645.

A name familiar in the ears of modern men, especially when there is question,—as there is such painful question today,—of the rights of governments over citizens, is that of Nicholas Machiavelli (1469–1527). His famous book *Il Principe* ("The Prince" or "The Ruler") sets forth a theory of government which may well be called diabolical. Machiavelli held that the whole purpose of man's existence and efforts is the glorification of the State. The State is supreme. The State owns the citizen. Nothing whatever is wrong or unlawful if it helps to establish or maintain the supremacy of the State. The ruler, therefore, must have no qualms about devising measures, however crafty, and enforcing edicts, however cruel or oppressive, so long as these things serve to make the power of the State absolute. It is manifest that this doctrine is not *a philosophy* of State supremacy, but *a religion* of State worship. As a religion it is necessarily opposed to the true and divinely established religion. Machiavelli renounced and denounced Christianity, as every heretic has done since the founding of the Church. For centuries civilized peoples have considered the very name of Machiavelli a term of reproach. The adjective "Machiavellian" is used to describe what (on the part of rulers or racketeers) is mean, sly, crafty, heartless, inhuman, and filthy. But we have lived to see a day, and that in a century that is forever advertising itself as "enlightened," when the base ideals of Machiavelli are not only adopted, but actually achieved, in the greater part of what was once Christian Europe. And the crawling infection of this loathsome thing threatens to spread over all the earth.

Summary of the Article

In this Article we have noticed some philosophical trends of the 14, 15, and 16 centuries, *the period of transition* from the Golden Age of Scholasticism to the vague conflicts of modern philosophy. We have seen how Scholasticism faded from favor and from the knowledge of men. We have noted the reasons which account for its recession, and we have rejected the cheap explanation which puts the entire blame for the submerging of the doctrines of the Schoolmen upon the Scholastics themselves, although we have seen that a good deal of the blame actually attaches to them. We have noted the rise of humanism, that soul of the Renaissance, and the revival of pagan philosophies which it brought briefly into vogue. We have noticed the infiltration of the humanistic spirit into physical science and the arts of law and government,—as well as into what we now call sociology,—and we have seen how it emerged in philosophies of naturalism which tend to deny or ignore God and Christianity and the true purpose of human life.

Among philosophical terms which we shall meet in later studies and serious readings, we have met and mastered the following: *humanism, naturalism, liberalism, the State, the Social Contract Theory, Machiavellianism.*

Article 2. The Philosophy of the Last Three Centuries

a) The Seventeenth Century; b) The Eighteenth and Nineteenth Centuries.

a) The Seventeenth Century

The period of transition ended with the 16 century. In the 17, there appeared more or less rounded systems of non-Scholastic and anti-Scholastic philosophy. The most notable philosophers of this time were Francis Bacon, John Locke, and René Descartes. A common note in the philosophies of these three, a note common to all the philosophies of the last three centuries and right down to our own day, is the confusing of the realms of sense-knowledge and intellectual knowledge. Bacon, Locke, and Descartes are at one in another point: the mistaken effort to remodel and rebuild the whole structure of philosophy. Now, the man who is confused on the proper spheres of sensation and intellection, and who, notwithstanding, blandly assumes that he knows enough to discard as useless all the achievements of his predecessors, is not only guilty of mountainous pride; he is deliberately destructive of that bond of continuity and endurance which is at once the test and the guarantee of true philosophy.

We shall here make a short and sketchy study of the chief doctrines of Bacon, Locke, and Descartes, and we shall glance briefly at the teachings of four other 17 century philosophers, Hobbes, Malebranche, Spinoza, and Leibniz.

1. Francis Bacon, Lord Verulam, Viscount St. Albans (1561–1626) was a native of London; he was educated at Cambridge. He was a lawyer, a politician, a statesman of sorts, and a philosopher. Such are the parts which history assigns him. Rumor imputes to him two others: that of a dipper into public funds for personal profit, and that of the writing of the plays commonly ascribed to Shakespeare. We are interested in Bacon solely as philosopher.

Bacon's *Instauratio Magna* or *Great Reconstruction* was a book which proposed to rebuild the entire edifice of philosophy. Bacon would first clear away, then build. To clear away, he would have man banish prejudices (that is, pre-judgments, long accepted notions) because these are merely idols in the temple of the mind. There are four types of such idols. First, there are *idols of the den,* which are prejudices that come of one's own natural bent or bias and of one's own dullness. Secondly, there are *idols of the tribe,* or prejudices inherited, or born of early environment and education. Thirdly, there are *idols of the market-place,* or prejudices acquired from the spirit of the times or from local influences. Fourthly, there are *idols of the theatre,* or prejudices that come of reading and esteeming the pre-Baconian philosophers, especially the old Scholastics.

The clearing away process demanded by Bacon recalls the Socratic "confession of ignorance," but any resemblance in the two processes is superficial. Socrates was essentially a humble man; his clearing away of the self-esteem of the pupil was a lesson in the docility required for learning anything. All sound teachers commend the process. Huxley, who failed to follow his own prescription, enunciated it well when he said that a sincere student or scientist must "sit down before fact like a little child." But Bacon was, whether consciously or unconsciously, a proud man; his clearing away of "idols" was a snub to all thinkers who had lived before his time. Socrates said in effect, "Let us labor to rid our minds of faulty notions, especially the notion that we are wise and well informed." Bacon said in effect, "Now I'll take charge. Please rid your minds of the things I dislike very much."

Having cleared out the idols, Bacon would build. He would use the one and only *scientific method,* that is *induction.* He held deductive reasoning useless; he rejected metaphysics. The first thing of all that the builder must do is the arranging of subjects of study, the "line-up" of sciences. The Scholastics, following Aristotle, had made this *subordinatio scientiarum* an objective thing; they were guided by the *objects* studied; in this they were realistic and sane. Bacon made his arrangement of sciences subjective; he based it upon the powers or faculties of the investigator: memory, imagination, reason.

Having made out the list or schedule of sciences, Bacon would attack each with the most careful *observation* and *experiment*. He would draw up lists, and follow tables of (*a*) essence or presence, (*b*) deviation or absence-in-proximity, (*c*) comparison, and (*d*) absence or rejection. If, for example, the investigator were trying to find the nature of heat, he would list all objects and activities in which heat is always present (Table of Presence); then he would make a list of things that lack heat but appear to bear in themselves no opposition to it (Table of Deviation or Absence-in-Proximity); next he would list heat-bearing things to show variations in degree (Table of Comparison); finally, he would list things incompatible with heat (Table of Absence or Rejection). Out of such slow and elaborate effort the investigator would learn at last the true cause of heat, and through its cause he would arrive at a knowledge of its nature.

Bacon was neither a great philosopher nor a notable scientist; he was a literary theorist about philosophy and science. His ambitious and impossible intention of making philosophy over foredoomed him to futility and failure. Three particular weaknesses marked his effort: first, a false *subordinatio scientiarum;* second, an inordinate stressing of induction; third, a constant confusion of sentient with intellectual knowledge. The second and third of these points still endure in modern philosophy, and they rob it of effectiveness and solid achievement. Bacon has gone into history as the originator of modern *empiricism,* that is, the system of those who place all faith in observation and experiment, playing up the role of the senses and minimizing the place of reasoning in the attaining of truth. Empiricism is sometimes called (with partial accuracy) by the name of *sensism.*

2. John Locke (1632–1704) was another notable exponent of empiricism. He was a native of Wrington in Somersetshire, England, and was educated at Oxford. His most notable piece of writing is *An Essay Concerning the Human Understanding.*

Locke had the characteristics of most of the articulate university men of his day: a petulant rejection of Scholasticism without understanding it; a self-confident notion of doing philosophy all over again from the ground up; a readiness to speak with an air of finality upon subjects imperfectly mastered.

Now, the desire to see philosophical doctrines so clearly expressed and proved that none may doubt them is human and natural and even admirable. But the assumption that all philosophy can be reduced to the clarity of A-B-C is fantastic. And the further assumption that all philosophers of past times have been woolly-minded blunderers is ignorance and intolerable "cheek." The old impatience, the old want of humility, which brought in Humanism, the Renaissance, the Reformation, and all the other thin veneerings which have tried to pass for truth are evident in Locke as they are evident in Bacon, Descartes, and nearly all non-Scholastic philosophers from the 14 century to the present moment.

Locke had doubtlessly in mind the recasting of philosophy, for he was not wholly pleased with Bacon's plan. Still, he seems to have had no detailed plan of his own. Indeed, he did not feel the need of any plan. He was convinced that, once the human mind had learned to grasp things clearly, once it knew its own powers and recognized its true limitations, once it was sure of the nature and extent of its knowledge, the developing of philosophy would be a sheerly natural growth. Thus, Locke's special interest was *the critical question,* and he wrote of it in his famous Essay.

Keen as he was on clarity of knowledge, Locke did not escape the fatal confounding of sense-knowledge with intellectual knowledge. And so he proceeded to make confusion more confounded, so that one may take not only different, but opposite, doctrines from the premises his theories afford. Follow him in one set of principles and develop these to the end; you find yourself in *ideal-*

ism, the dream-philosophy which turns reality into shadow. Follow him in another set of thoughts, and you will be involved in *sensism* and *positivism* which takes the reality around us as the only thing there is, and denies value to the intellect and to reasoning (even to the reasoning by which you have reached this dull conclusion).

This impossible agglomeration of conflicting theories was proposed, explicitly or implicitly, by a man of undoubted mental gifts who was thwarted at the outset by his muddling of the basic question of all philosophy, the critical question. It is pathetic to realize that he *knew* it was the basic question. Inevitably, Locke went wrong in his ethical doctrine, especially in point of the norm or rule of morality; for out of a man's philosophy of reality and knowledge comes his theory of morals, and Locke's philosophy of reality and knowledge was wrong philosophy. Locke admitted the existence of a divine law, but it plays little part in his practical conclusions. His moral theory comes to this: our deliberate conduct is good and praiseworthy if it conforms to public opinion of what such conduct should be; otherwise it is evil and blameworthy. This is not only a cheap and futile theory, but it is impossible to apply, for public opinion is the most fluid and changeable of things, and what is a virtue at one moment might well be a vice at another. This theory of *moral relativism* is utterly false and destructive.

Locke is remembered for his distinguishing of *primary* and *secondary* sense-qualities in bodily things. In his study upon the nature of knowledge, he had constantly to face such questions as: are sense-objects really what they appear to be; is the grass really green; is the whirling wheel actually in motion; is the stone truly solid? Locke decided that there are certain qualities common to all bodies (impenetrability, extension, shape, rest, motion) and these are *primary* qualities which exist as objective things. He said that there are also other qualities not found in *all* bodies alike (color, sound, taste, odor, temperature, resistance) and these are *secondary* qualities which are largely *subjective,* that is, not so much objective things as the perceivings or feelings of the person who senses them. Locke's distinction of sense-qualities as primary and secondary may serve us as a mere convenient list. But his theory of their objective reality cannot stand. For we are wholly unaware of the primary qualities except through the medium of the secondary. And if the secondary be unreliable (being largely subjective) we have no reason to put any trust in the actuality of the primary qualities. Locke's theory on sense-qualities points the way to the self-contradiction of complete skepticism.

One thing Locke did in a masterly way. He refuted *innatism,* the theory that our knowledge is inborn, and that it advances in us, not by the acquiring of anything from without, but by its inward growth or development. Apart from his refutation of innatism, Locke's contribution to philosophy is negligible; indeed he is a confusing and a destructive force.

3. René Descartes (1596–1650) has been called the father of modern philosophy, a title which would have more meaning if "modern philosophy" had any sort of consistency or would stand still long enough to be identified. For all that, the title is justified. For "modern philosophy," although it is composed of wildly variant theories, is one in its tentativeness, its hesitancy, its dubious tenure. And the man who injected the note of doubt as *a positive element* into human thinking was a delicate little French mathematician named René Descartes. Descartes,—whose Latinized name *Cartesius* explains the fact that his theories are called *the Cartesian philosophy,*—will be gratefully remembered by all schoolboys as the inventor of analytical geometry.

Descartes had a great mind, but he had the mental shortcomings of his time: the contempt for old Scholasticism (which he took no trouble to understand); the lack of careful distinguishing between the essentially different types of human knowledge, that of sense and that of intellect; and, above all, the consuming desire "to shatter philosophy to bits and then remold it nearer to the heart's desire."

Descartes was a mathematician. He wished to make philosophy a kind of mathematical science; at least, he wished to express it with mathematical clarity. As geometry begins with self-evident truths called axioms, philosophy must begin with some basic truth which is so evident, so inevitable, that it cannot be doubted even by a fictitious doubt of the mind. Descartes found that we may doubt, or pretend to doubt, everything except *ourselves doubting*. In other words, I can doubt everything by an effort of mind; but I cannot doubt that *I* am *making an effort of mind*. That I exist as a thinking individual is the primal and indubitable truth. Descartes formulated it thus: *"Cogito ergo sum"* (*Je pense donc je suis; I think therefore I am*). But the *ergo* (or the *donc* or the *therefore*) has not the implication of a reasoned conclusion. No, the two facts of existence and thought are simultaneously and inevitably recognized. Upon the fact of *the thinking existence,* as upon the one fundamental certitude, all philosophy must be built up.

Upon this foundation Descartes proceeds to build accordingly. *I think.* My thoughts are reduced to elements: ideas and judgments and feelings. Ideas and feelings are what they are; they are true *in themselves.* But when I make judgment upon thoughts and feelings I may go wrong. I am only safe in judging upon such ideas as I recognize to be wholly objective, not my own making or devising. Now, I find that I have an idea of absolute perfection, of absolute actuality. I could not have made up this idea, for its perfection is beyond my powers. Therefore this idea must have been impressed upon me by the existing reality which is absolute perfection. Such a being exists. Thus am I aware, with full certitude, of the existence of God. Now God, the all-perfect, would not, in fact, be all-perfect if He were in any sense a deceiver. Therefore, He has given me reliable, and not deceiving, knowing-powers. These, of course, are limited, for I am limited myself. My senses and my mind may not present reality to me perfectly, but what they present is reality. Of the bodily world I can be sure, at the least, that it actually exists as an extended or bodily reality.

The human mind, says Descartes, is essentially *thought.* A bodily being is, in its essence, *extension.* Plants and brutes are not truly alive; they have no life-principle or soul; they are splendid automata, fine pieces of machinery which the Creator works. Man has the only type of soul there is: it is a thinking, a reasoning soul.

Descartes is wholly wrong, despite the fact that his intellectual powers were splendid. He starts wrong, and the farther he proceeds along the way of his theory, the farther off he veers from the straight line of truth. Such is the tragedy of a logical mind after a false start. Descartes finds the thinking individual the indubitable reality. But is thought more immediate and sure than feeling? Besides, if I am sure only of *myself thinking,* I can develop no philosophy; for I have no self-evident certitude (in the Cartesian sense) of the *value* of my thinking. I cannot argue, as does Descartes, that the inevitable thought of an infinite being proves the existence of such a being as the *cause* of the thought; for, according to Descartes, the principle of causality is subject to doubt. Nor can I argue that God's existence is proved by my knowing-faculties, and then prove my knowing-faculties reliable because God would not deceive me; this is reasoning in a circle, proving A by B and B by A.

In nearly every point, the philosophy of Descartes is misleading, and in most points it is plainly false. Yet this philosophy, or welter of theories, has had a tremendous influence upon human thinking for nearly three hundred years.

4. Thomas Hobbes (1588–1679), English politician and philosopher, was, in the main, a follower of Bacon. He insists on the distinction between sense-knowledge and intellectual knowledge, and then immediately mixes them up confusedly, to the extent that he attributes a sort of intellect to brute animals. In political theory, he holds that man is not naturally a social being, but that civil society (i.e., the State) is the result of a social contract or social compact. He teaches State absolutism, and declares that the civil power must regulate all our activities, even those of religion. In his theory of knowledge, Hobbes is a nominalist; in physical philosophy, he is a materialist.

5. *Nicholas Malebranche* (1638–1715), Parisian philosopher and ecclesiastic, thought it impious to say that a creature is the cause of its activities, since God alone is to be regarded as the source of all action. Creatures furnish *the occasion* ("the stage setting") for God to intervene and cause them to act or operate. This quite fanciful and fallacious theory is called *occasionalism.* Further, Malebranche taught that our knowledge (in its elements, that is, *ideas*) comes from *the inborn idea of God,* in the light of which other things are understood. For the logical order (that is, the order of thinking or knowing) must follow the ontological order (that is, the order of things). As God is first in the ontological order, He is first in the logical order. This doctrine is known as *ontologism.*

6. *Baruch Spinoza* (1632–1677), a Dutch Jew, followed Descartes in an attempt to set forth philosophy in a mathematical fashion. His philosophy amounts to *pantheism* which is involved in his definition of *substance* as a reality which does not require the idea of any other thing in order to be understood. Spinoza inconsistently insists on the existence of the individual soul and its immortality, together with its obligation to practise virtue. Spinoza is a pathetic figure. Ousted by the Synagogue, unacceptable to the Gentiles, he shrank from public notice and was content with the humble employment of a polisher of lenses, a trade which returned him what sufficed for his simple requirements and gave him many hours of freedom for the study of philosophy. Spinoza has the appeal of a genius misunderstood and maltreated.

He has a particular attraction for the dilettanti and the parlor-philosophers. But with all regard for the man's sincerity, and with proper commiseration for him as the butt of meanness and persecution, we must recognize his teachings as false and pernicious.

7. *Gottfried Wilhelm von Leibniz* (1648–1716) has been described as "the most extraordinary example of versatile scholarship on record." He was a mathematician, and the inventor of differential calculus. He was a linguist, a historian, a theologian, a philosopher. Yet for all his splendid mind and great learning, he was wrong in his fundamental philosophical theories. He taught that the world is a composite of material and spiritual things, all of which are made up of unextended elements called *monads.* Each monad is independent of the others, yet each, by *the law of pre-established harmony,* reflects in itself all the modifications or changes that occur in every other. Soul and body in man are like two clocks, each keeping perfect time (by *the law of pre-established harmony*) but without any real influence upon each other. The soul is a monad; it reflects in itself, as do all monads, the entire cosmos, not by the influence of other things upon it, for such influence does not exist, but by being the sufficient setting or occasion for such reflection through the operation of the law of harmony. The soul is unaware of most of the things reflected in it; time and experience, however, bring it a clear and usable knowledge of some of the images, and these are its *ideas.* Thus Leibniz taught a sort of *innatism.* God's pre-established harmony moves man's will to determinate action, yet in such wise that man remains free (*physical premotion*).—Leibniz offers cogent proofs for the existence and the perfections of God, arguing from the contingency of the world of creatures to the necessary existence of Self-Subsistent Power and Infinite Intelligence. Leibniz also acknowledges and reshapes the "ontological argument" of St. Anselm, and reasons that if a Self-Subsistent Being is possible, it must be actual. Leibniz holds that God, by reason

of His complete and boundless perfection, has made this world the best world possible (*cosmological optimism*).—Leibniz's doctrine on the constitution of the world is called *monadology*. It is a theory in conflict with both reason and experience. Yet it intrigues unwary minds, particularly because the doctrine of pre-established harmony cuts many difficulties from the path of physicist and philosopher. But it is a doctrine of unreality. Monads are unextended, non-bodily, and hence the universe has no true existence as an extended reality; it becomes illusory, a dream-world. Thus Leibniz is but a step removed from *idealism* which denies value to the findings of the senses and reduces the world to a set of mental images. The philosophers of the next generation took that step.

b) The Eighteenth and Nineteenth Centuries

The philosophers of the 18 and 19 centuries carried forward, in the main, the theories of Bacon, Locke, Descartes, Spinoza, and Leibniz, and tried to reason the world out of existence. Existence is reduced to thoughts or ideas, to will-force or *élan*. This is nothing new, nor was it new in the 18 or 19 century. It is the core of the old Eleatic philosophy, and it is latent in every sophist, skeptic, and relativist theory of things and thoughts.

We shall discuss very briefly the doctrines of Berkeley, Hume, Kant, Hegel, Schopenhauer, Nietzsche, Comte, Spencer, James, and Bergson, with incidental mention of Fichte, von Schelling, Mill, and Dewey. We shall notice the revival of Scholasticism.

1. George Berkeley (1685–1753), Kilkenny born, and Protestant Bishop of Cloyne in Ireland, was idealist in philosophy, but not in such matter of fact things as money. He worked hard to secure a grant from the English Government for the purpose of founding in Bermuda a great college to train missionaries for the conversion of America. Indeed, he had the promise of £20,000, and, on the strength of it, he went to Rhode Island to secure the interest and help of New Englanders. But the politicians failed him; the promised money was not voted. Perhaps his experience with practical politics helped turn him into an utter idealist,—but no, attractive as the thought remains, it cannot be so; for Berkeley's significant writing was all done by 1715, and he did not visit America until 1728. His chief philosophical work was a treatise on *The Principles of Human Understanding.* Notice how steadily the basic question,—that is, the critical question,—held the attention of all philosophers during the centuries of the early modern era. And still that question was not sanely treated nor brought to full answer. Despite their constant cry for clarity in knowledge, the philosophers of this time succeeded only in making knowledge more misty and valueless.

Berkeley goes confidently to work to explain the human mind and its relation to reality. He says that if anything exists at all, it exists *as knowable,* and there exists a mind capable of knowing it. Further, each man's *knowing* is what *gives* him the world he knows. The very *being* of things is, for each person who knows them, the *perceiving* of them: *esse est percipi,* "to exist is to be perceived." Now, there is ultimate reality in the Divine Mind. Each human mind somehow *shares* the creative perceiving of the Divine Mind. Thus while Berkeley is idealist, he is not utter subjectivist. He once wrote, "I question not the existence of anything we perceive by our senses." But he should have added that "existence" means to him "existence in the mind," and basically in the Divine Mind.

2. *David Hume* (1711–1776), native of Edinburgh and a product of its university, denied the existence of all substantial reality, material or spiritual. In his *Treatise on Human Nature* he declares that man's mind is only a collection of perceptions. These perceptions are either *impressions* or *ideas.* Impressions are sensations of pleasure, pain, awareness of qualities and relations. Ideas are but the faintly remembered images of impressions formerly experienced. This vague philosophy has a very modern sound: a collection of impressions collected nowhere;

contents of a mind which is not a container. Here we have the smug unintelligibility of the modern neo-realist's definition of mind as "a cross-section of the environment." Hume does not deny God, but he denies the value of the customary proofs for God's existence, since these are based upon a reality which he does not accept. He is inconsistent, however, for in his *Natural History of Religion* he writes, "The whole frame of nature bespeaks an intelligent Author." In morals, Hume set up *the public good* as the standard of right and wrong, and assigns to feelings rather than to reason the task of applying this ethical norm. —Summing up: Hume holds that the only thing that can be said, with full certainty, to exist is our perceptions (impressions and ideas). In and among these perceptions there is no causal connection; indeed, there is no knowable causality anywhere. If things outside us really do exist, there is no proof of their existence available to us.

3. Over in Germany, in his native city of Koenigsberg, a professor named *Immanuel Kant* (1724–1804) read Hume's arguments with dismay, and finally tossed them aside with contempt as "dogmatic dreams." Hume takes away all grounds of certitude; the best a man might have of him is a thin probability, and this, as Kant noticed, is not usable knowledge at all. What a man needs, said Kant, and what he can have is *truly scientific knowledge,* that is, knowledge that is universally and necessarily true and reliable. The experiences of the senses is individual, and, no matter how consistently and for how long a time the senses find a fact solid, there is always the possibility that the next experience will show it to vary. So far Kant agrees with Hume: sense-experience cannot give the mind more than probability. But, said Kant, there is another element in knowledge, an *a priori* and *subjective* element which is anterior to sense-experience and in no wise dependent on it. This is the element which enables us to have true and certain knowledge and to add item to item with complete security in building up the edifice of science.

We pause here to settle the meaning of important terms. Knowledge that we obtain through experience is *a posteriori* knowledge, that is, it comes *after* experience and is dependent upon it. Now, as we have seen, it is Aristotelian and Scholastic doctrine that *all* human knowledge is of this type; no knowledge is born in us; no item of knowledge exists in man except such as has been *acquired*. Kant, however, insisted on the existence of certain "forms" or items of knowledge (space and time, certain regulative judgments, and certain master-ideas) as inborn and *a priori*. Of course, there is a legitimate use of the terms *a priori* and *a posteriori* (literally "from beforehand" and "from afterwards") in describing types of argument. But there is no legitimate use of *a priori* as a term descriptive of knowledge itself. Kant uses the term so, and he follows the despised Hume so far as to make the knowledge described by this term a very part of the mind of man, an element of its *being* and not merely an element of its *equipment*.

To answer the basic question, "What can I know with scientific certitude?" Kant wrote his book *The Critique of Pure Reason*. In this work, Kant assigns to man a threefold knowing-power: sensibility, intellect, reason. Knowable things, on the other hand, are of two classes: appearances of things or *phenomena,* and essences of things or *noumena.*—Man, by sensibility (that is, by his senses) takes in the phenomena of the world about him. Somehow, we know not how, the phenomena set his sense-power to work; we dare not say that the senses perceive even the phenomena as these exist in nature; we may only say that somehow phenomena stir the senses to act. Now the formal constituent, the essential element, of the sensing-power or sensibility (that is, its character or "shape") is the twofold determinant of *space-and-time*. Man has sense-experiences "here" and "now," and he recalls them as "there" and "then." But this conditioning of phenomena by *space* and *time* is man's own contribution to the knowledge-act. Space and time in no wise represent things, nor are they things; they are the inborn *a priori* element of the sensing-power. Just as a curiously shaped bottle will take in liquid or powder and conform the mass of the substance taken in *to its own shape,* so the sensing-power, which has the shape of *space-and-time,* takes in the action of phenomena on the senses and shapes these phenomena accordingly. The result (that is, phenomena-conditioned-by-space-and-time) is called *empirical intuition.*—Now, just as phenomena stir the sensibility to act, so the finished products of sensation (that is, empirical intuitions) stir the next knowing power, *the intellect,* to act. The intellect takes in the empirical intuitions and conforms them to *its* shape, its own inborn *a priori* forms. These forms are four sets of triple judgments, called the twelve *categories.* These are like grooves or moulds into which the molten metal of empirical intuitions is poured, and the resultant piece of knowledge is, in each case, *a judgment.* The four master categories (each of which has three branches) are: *quantity, quality, relation,* and *modality.* Thus the judgment "A comes from B as effect from cause" is not the objective knowing by the mind of a state of fact; it is merely the result of the action of *intellect* turning the sense-findings (or empirical intuitions) of A and B through the groove (or category) of *relation,* and through that branch of relation called *cause-effect.* —Once more, just as the finished products of sensibility (that is, empirical intuitions) stir the intellect to the act of judging, so the judgments of the intellect stir *the reason* to its action. The innate *a priori* shape of reason is determined by *three master-ideas:* the idea of *the self,* the idea of *the not-self,* the idea of *the super-self.* In other words, the three regulative ideas of reason are the ideas of self, the world, and God. The judgments of intellect are poured through the threefold mould of reason, and the result is *reasoned knowledge.*

Now, the essential thing about knowledge, when we attempt to fix its value on the score of truth and certitude, centers in *judgments.* After all, reason merely handles judgments and learns from them. Upon judgments we must fix our attention. There are two types of judgment, *a priori* and *a posteriori.* Looked at in another way, there are two other types: *synthetic* and *analytic*. We already know the meaning of *a priori* and *a posteriori,* and indeed, according to Kant, all judgments are *a priori.* We must look at the other terms. A judgment is rightly called *synthetic* when it is "put together," for that is precisely what the word *synthetic* means. If I make the judgment, "John is sick," I have a synthetic judgment; the predicate does not necessarily belong to the subject, but I *put* it with the subject because I have learned from John or from his doctor that it *happens* to belong there. But if I make the judgment, "A circle is round," I have an *analytic* judgment; for by analyzing the subject, by studying it and knowing just what it is, I learn that the predicate used *belongs* there, since a circle to be a circle *must* be round.

Kant held that the only judgment which can give absolute certitude must be *a priori,* since, indeed, he admits no other type. But, he maintains, an *a priori* judgment that is *analytic* marks no advance in knowledge. To build up science, there must be growth, development, advancement. Hence there must be *synthetic* judgments which are also *a priori.* The *synthetic a priori judgment* may be called the heart of Kant's philosophy. And we may say now in passing that *the synthetic a priori* judgment is a contradiction in terms and in thought; it is an impossibility. The examples offered by Kant are either (in our terminology) *a posteriori* judgments, or they are *analytic* judgments. For instance, Kant says that the judgment "five plus seven equals twelve" is *a synthetic a priori* judgment. It is nothing of the kind. It is a simple analytic judgment. Replace the words or the figures for five and seven and twelve by an equivalent number of dots or strokes; you will have exactly the same thing on either side of the equals-mark. The judgment is as plainly analytic as "A is A."

Let us cast back a moment, and make a summing up of the Kantian theory of human knowing: Phenomena of bodily things somehow stir man's sensibility to action, and sense takes in phenomena in its own way, shaping and conditioning them by its innate forms of space-and-time, thus producing empirical intuitions. The empirical intuitions somehow stir man's intellect to take them in and run them through its forms or categories, thus producing judgments, the truly certain and valuable judgment always being *synthetic a priori.* Finally, the judgments of intellect somehow stir the reason to take them in and view them in the light of its regulative ideas of self, the world, and God. Notice that the sole point of connection of man's knowledge with reality outside the mind is the vague influence of phenomena on the sensing-power. From that point on, the whole process of knowing, and its products, are man's own. Here is *idealism,* here is *subjectivism* with a vengeance. And Kant plainly asserts that the *noumena* or essences of things cannot be known by man. The phenomenon is not strictly knowable, but it moves the senses to act; the noumenon is not knowable at all. The noumenon (*Das Ding an sich*) lies outside the reach of mortal man.

So Kant is as subjectivistic as Hume ever dared be. And yet this is the man who threw Hume's book aside with the sneer, "Dogmatic dreams!" What singular smugness could have made Kant suppose that he was dealing with the problem of knowledge *critically* and not dogmatically? Yet he calls his system "transcendental criticism."

Since we cannot know noumena, the science of metaphysics, the very heart of philosophy as the Greeks and Scholastics understand it, becomes illusory and impossible. Is it not strange that a man of Kant's undoubted intellectual gifts did not notice here an absurd contradiction? Why, he has just finished explaining to us, in great detail, the whole nature of the human mind; and now he concludes that we cannot know the nature of anything! And his reasoning,—more than "slightly foxed" as the booksellers say,—about the character of the mind, and about the nature of phenomena and noumena, is actually interwoven with terms and thoughts metaphysical; yet he says that metaphysics is illusory and impossible!

So far, Kant's *Critique of Pure Reason.* It will be noticed that the doctrine contained in this work opens the way to complete skepticism, and therewith it opens the way to a denial of moral obligation and of purpose in human existence. For if nothing can be known with certitude, as skepticism maintains, then there are no certainties in the realm of morals, religion, or social duties; then there is no certainty that man is made for a purpose at all, or even that man exists. Whether Kant noticed this fact, and, as a Lutheran, deplored it, or whether (as has been said) his Emperor summoned him and demanded that he furnish a philosophical basis for morals and religion, cannot be said. But Kant wrote a second book to supply the defects mentioned. He said that *pure reason* is not enough for man; he must live by *practical reason* as well. In his first book, Kant sought the answer to the question, "What can man know with certitude?" The answer was, "He can have true certitude by his *synthetic a priori judgments.*" But this is mere statement. The real answer to which Kant's work inclines the thinking mind is, "Man can know nothing with certitude." Kant's second book, *The Critique of Practical Reason,* answered the question, "Are there certitudes, outside the reach of pure reason, that I must recognize and act upon?" Kant answers with an emphatic, "There are." These truths are known with certitude by *practical* reason. First, a man is aware of *duty.* He knows with clear certitude that murder and stealing are wrong, and that he has the indispensable duty of avoiding such things. He knows that there are certain loyalties which indicate things that he is in duty bound to observe and do. By his practical reason, man is aware of the inner command, "Thou shalt" and "Thou shalt not." This command is *categorical,* that is, it is unconditional; it is not, "Do this, if you please," "Avoid that when convenient"; it is a matter of simple "Do" and "Avoid." Kant calls this inner voice *The Categorical Imperative.* A Christian would call it conscience, and would explain that it is the voice of reason (the same reason with which we work out a theorem in geometry) pronouncing on the agreement or disagreement of a situation (here and now to be decided) with the norm or law of morality. Kant's *Categorical Imperative* is like conscience in its clear decision and unequivocal command; it is entirely unlike conscience in its blindly unreasoning assumption of authority.

First, then, man's awareness of duty is a certitude; it is a certitude because of The Categorical Imperative. Now, this Categorical Imperative is *a law*. But a law must come from a law-maker. Neither I myself have set up my Categorical Imperative (for it often orders me to do what I should like to avoid, and to shun what I would willingly do) nor has it come from any earthly king, court, or senate, for it speaks with an authority that is absolute and not one supported by temporal sanctions of fine or imprisonment. It is a supreme law; it is an absolute law. It must come then from the Supreme and Absolute Being. That is, it must come from God. Therefore, God exists.—Further, the Categorical Imperative makes a man aware, not only of duty, but of the fact that he must freely embrace the performance of duty. He is aware that he can disregard, although he cannot be ignorant of, this law of conduct. In a word, he is aware, and with true certitude, that he is *a free and responsible being*.—Again, man, a free and responsible being, is aware that by freely acting in accordance with the commands of the Categorical Imperative *he perfects himself*. And he is aware that this self-perfecting may go on through the longest life without reaching the limits of its capability. Therefore, he concludes, he can go on becoming more and more perfect *forever*. In other words, man is aware of endless existence before him; he knows *he has an immortal soul*. Thus out of the cunning device of *The Categorical Imperative* Kant draws the doctrines that satisfy his Lutheranism (or his Emperor), although his basic philosophy of "transcendental criticism" knows nothing of these doctrines. He sets forth, in orthodox fashion, the *practical* truths of the existence of God, the fact of moral duty, the immortality of the soul, the freedom of the human will.

Kant wrote a third book, *The Critique of the Faculty of Aes-*

thetic Judgment in which he brings out the attractiveness of moral goodness in a manner more striking than that of *The Critique of Practical Reason.*

Despite errors, absurdities, and contradictions, Kant's philosophy,—notably that of *The Critique of Pure Reason,*—has exercised a tremendous influence upon human thinking for a century and a half. It exhibits the roots of those weaknesses we have come to regard as characteristic of what is loosely called "the German philosophy." It refuses to face reality (witness the wholly subjectivistic character of knowledge); it unduly stresses the *ego* (witness the inner and autonomous character of knowledge and morality); it proclaims the perfectibility of *the will,* upon which the followers of Kant were soon to harp most strongly—and from Nietzsche to Hitler we are to hear of "the will to power," the will which makes "the superman" and "the master race."

A final word on Kant. In offering and defending his low estimate of pure reason as incapable of achieving certitude (apart from the mysterious judgments which are *synthetic a priori*) Kant appeals to his so-called "antimonies" or "contradictions." He holds that when pure reason tries to apply the categories in the abstract realm of logical inference (whereas its business is to pour findings through fixed moulds) it gets beyond itself and comes a cropper. It finds that it can prove, with equal facility, things directly opposed. Thus, he says, it can prove that space is finite, and also infinite; it can prove matter divisible and indivisible; it can prove human freedom existent and non-existent; it can prove that God is necessary and also non-necessary. In all this, and in the examples offered in proof of it, Kant is entirely gratuitous and sophistical. Besides, he stands self-condemned in using logical reasoning to establish the fact that logical reasoning is useless. We merely mention the "antimonies" because we discern in them an element of *materialism* in the heart of an *idealistic* theory. This materialism was to appear in full form in later philosophies which took inspiration, at least in part, from the doctrines of Immanuel Kant.

4. Two followers of Kant, *Johann Gottlieb Fichte* (1762–1814) and *Friedrich Wilhelm von Schelling* (1775–1854) taught that the mysterious noumenon of Kant is the projection of an *Absolute Ego*. This Ego sets up Self as against the background of Not-Self and then realizes that after all Self and Not-Self are truly One. Technically, we have the *thesis,* the *antithesis* and the *synthesis* of the Absolute Ego. The final *synthesis* in which the Ego "composits the Self and the Not-Self" is the developing and perfecting of *Will.*—But by far the most important among the immediate followers of Kant was *Georg Wilhelm Friedrich Hegel* (1770–1831). To Hegel the synthesizing element which merges Self and Not-Self is universal awareness, absolute reason. Individual men have reason, but the human reason is but a gleam of the Absolute Light. The world is merely *phenomenal,* it is an external expression of Absolute Reason; it is a series of flashes and shadows cast by the Cosmic Light of Reason. Towards the perfect harmony of Absolute Reason everything (as history proves) works upward, not sweepingly, but step by step, each more perfectly harmonizing and purifying than the preceding. In the civil State, this drive towards Reason shows itself under the aspect of *Will.* As one nation conquers another, and then is conquered in turn, we note the purifying and harmonizing drive towards Reason. Such successive steps towards the ideal were, first, the oriental State, then the Roman State, and, last and best expression of progress, the German State. Progress must go by conflict and through the conquest of contradictions.

5. *Arthur Schopenhauer* (1788–1860) is a name popularly known as almost synonymous with "pessimism." He denied the existence of happiness for man, and felt that the best man could hope for was an occasional relief from pain: "life is a path of red-hot coals, with a cool spot here and there." Schopenhauer declared that *will* is the very essence of things. This will is not a force guided by intelligence or reason; it is a blind, irresistible drive. It is not a striving for something as a goal; it is a drive that exists for itself. This is a world-will. It is manifest everywhere, in the force of gravitation and in the most sublime tendencies of men towards their ideals. The apparent world is *phenomenal;* it is our conception of things; it is *idea* which we explain sufficiently for our needs as space, time, causality. But there is a real world too, a *noumenal* world, which is not idea but *will*. The world-will is active in us; it is very hard upon us; it makes us strive ceaselessly for what we can never find, that is, peace, rest, and enduring satisfaction. Thus it is a source of pain. Man may find a partial and temporary relief from this pain by contemplating works of art. But a more lasting relief comes from resisting will; from the effort to kill within oneself the desire for continued life, health, property, comfort, friends; from refusing the work of seeking to attain such goals as eternal rest, heaven, moral ideals.—Schopenhauer is of the later German school in his doctrine of all embracing will, but he is alone among German philosophers in ascribing to the efforts of universal will no goal, no good, no improvement.

6. Schopenhauer was saddened by the pain that men must endure through the harsh and profitless drive of world-will. But *Friedrich Wilhelm Nietzsche* (1844–1900) was gladdened by it. For, said Nietzsche, the pain and strife of existence are meant to harden us, to strengthen us, to develop us so that we may ultimately produce *superman*. We should therefore be ruthless, hard, unsympathetic; we should refuse to indulge self or others; we should sternly cultivate *the will to power*. Christianity, said Nietzsche, with its doctrines of obedience, resignation, loving kindness, is not the guide we require; it proclaims *a slave morality*. We need no God, no supernatural aim. The aim of true ethics is the development of the great, the strong, the ruthless blond beast, *the superman*.—We need not pause upon the absurdity of this doctrine of Nietzsche, which, as Chesterton points out, is not a philosophy of strong muscles but of weak nerves. Indeed,

Nietzsche was himself a man of such weak nerves as to be hardly sane. It is interesting to note that the philosophy of *ruthless will to power* still finds expression in the ideals and the warlike actions of many of Nietzsche's countrymen.

7. The ethics of Nietzsche are a crude and brutal *naturalism,* that is, a theory that man needs no power but his own, and no aim beyond this world. Naturalism is one form of *materialism* which denies or disregards everything spiritual and supernatural. Naturalistic ethics appear in the mistaken philosophies of all ages, proclaiming men naturally good, naturally directed upwards and onwards, and urging that he be left unhindered and undirected so that through fullest self-expression he may come to perfection. The Christian remembers, however, that man's nature is a fallen nature, and that, since the Fall, no man can be merely natural and remain decent. A man, says Chesterton, must be supernatural or he will be unnatural. Nietzsche set up a naturalistic doctrine in crude and harsh terms. The same type of doctrine was presented more subtly by *Auguste Comte* (1798–1857), *John Stuart Mill* (1806–1873), and *Herbert Spencer* (1820–1903).

Comte says that man has passed naturally through three intellectual stages: *the theological stage* in which he referred power and control to Deity; *the metaphysical stage* in which he sought to understand things in the general abstractions of philosophy; and finally the true and perfect *positive stage* in which he finds all knowledge in the mathematical and experimental sciences, chief of which is *sociology,* the science of humanity. Humanity is the only God.

Mill declares that man must be guided in his actions by *utility.* Actions are good or evil in so far as they preserve us from pain or subject us to pain (*moral utilitarianism*). Utility or usefulness is not to be judged selfishly; it is to be sought in the greatest pleasure of the greatest number of men. We learn, for the most part, by the method of "trial and error" in what courses of action such utility is to be found.

Spencer discards the "trial and error" method. He says we must study nature and adjust ourselves to it so that we may act for the greatest pleasure of the greatest number. We are helped in our effort by *natural evolution* which tends to level out differences among men. All nature is marked by a steady progress "from the homogeneous to the heterogeneous" and we must not get ahead of this process or we shall have trouble and pain and the world will be filled with unrest. Nor must we be eager for absolute truth either in science or in religion. Truth is for us always *relative,* for the ultimate always eludes our grasp. Science must be content with the positive data which fall under observation of the senses (*sensism and positivism*), and religion (or theology) must be content to make rules for practical conduct, leaving aside all doctrinal or dogmatic statements about the Great Unknown (*agnosticism*).—Spencer is full of self-contradiction. He professes to know the absolute truth that absolute truth is unknowable. He is dogmatic in his assertion that dogmatic assertion is unseemly. He limits science to positive sense-data, and this very theory is not capable of either expression or proof in terms of sense-data, and hence is, by his own standard, a wholly unscientific theory. His doctrine of natural evolution is a hypothesis which he proposes as absolute truth. Indeed, Spencer makes mankind *a single organism* which is growing steadily more diversified and perfect by the process of evolution.

8. The sensism and positivism of Spencer, together with the agnostic and relativist theory, were advanced by *John Dewey* (1859–), an American philosopher. Dewey thinks that philosophy must concern itself with the discovery of practical rules to keep men in accord with the march of events. Philosophy is but a guide for action. *True* and *false* are to be understood in the light of social experience; what has proved beneficial to man is true and good; what has been found socially harmful is evil and false. This doctrine is usually called *pragmatism* from the Greek *pragma,* a deed, work, or action.

9. William James (1842–1910) is usually regarded as "the father of pragmatism." James teaches that the working or workability of a thing (for man's benefit or hurt) is the test of its good or evil, its truth or falsity. Besides the test of workability, two others are to be applied: any new idea, to be true, must be in harmony with ideas already tested and proved true; secondly, the new idea must not conflict with accepted *ideals,* especially those that are religious or moral. James says that man's mind requires certitude in many matters in which his mental power is not adequate to attain it. Where the mind fails, the will must step in and make a decision. Indeed, a man cannot avoid such intervention of the will. If he says, "I cannot decide; I must remain in doubt," he is actually willing not to decide; he is, in fact, *deciding* not to decide. Now, a decision to leave important matters unsettled is less valuable to man, less practical, less useful, less workable, than a straightforward affirmation or denial. Since decision must be made in any case, it is better to have a clear decision than a muddled one. Therefore, a man should have "the will to believe" either one or other of the contradictory answers to important questions. Thus is the will invoked in the philosophic pursuit of truth.

10. James calls upon the will to help man interpret (indeed to *create*) truth. But *Henri Bergson* (1859–1940), a French Jew, calls rather upon man's *feeling.* He calls for a sympathetic effort after truth, not a cold analysis. He says that to know truth we must sympathetically enter into things and know them from within. Thus we must seek truth by intuition, by direct, sympathetic, non-rationalized grasp. It is thus that we are aware of *self,* and of self as part of a living and pulsating *nature of things,* the inner force of which (or *élan vital*) is a continuously creative power. Bergson was much influenced by the teachings of Plotinus. In the last years of his life, leaving the sterile philosophy of *élan vital,* he recognized the truth of the Catholic religion, which he called "the complete fulfillment of Judaism." Yet he failed to enter the Church, lest his conversion seem one of convenience to escape the hardships of impending anti-Semitism. He asked that a Catholic priest be present to pray at his funeral.

11. The philosophies of the last three centuries have been, in the main, futile vagaries, born of a fundamental misconception of the nature of human knowledge. *The critical question* has been the chief point of interest, and out of the mistaken solution of this question have come, as a natural consequence, mistaken doctrines in the realms of cosmology, psychology, and ethics.

The 19 century saw a notable revival, which continues to develop vigorously to the present moment, of the ancient sanity known as the Scholastic philosophy. This noble system which alone has historical and factual claim to the name of the true philosophy suffered an almost total eclipse from the late 14 to the early 19 century. Then Catholic philosophers, strongly sponsored in their efforts by the great Pontiff Pius IX, made their voices heard in the world of thought. The Jesuit, Matthew Liberatore (1810–1872), and Cajetan Sanseverino (1811–1865) did truly significant work for the reviving of Scholasticism. And when Pope Leo XIII issued, in 1879, his Encyclical *Aeterni Patris* which prescribes the teaching of Scholastic and Thomistic philosophy in Catholic colleges and seminaries, the revival quickly assumed full force and form. Among many notable proponents of Scholasticism, from the time of the Encyclical to this present, we may mention Zigliara, Billot, Mercier, Lépicier, Garrigou-Lagrange, Gredt, Maritain, DeWulf, Gilson, Nys; and, in our own country, Shahan, Turner, Pace, Poland, Coppens, Brother Chrysostom, Sheen. The Scholasticism of our times is often called Neo-Scholasticism. The name does not mean that the *philosophia perennis* is made "new" in itself, but that its wondrous light is employed in studying and interpreting the newest findings of the modern experimental sciences.

Summary of the Article

In this Article we have learned something of the philosophers and the philosophies of the last three centuries. The notable names of the 17 century which fell under our observation were Bacon, Locke, Descartes, Hobbes, Malebranche, Spinoza, and Leibniz. Those of the 18 and 19 centuries were Berkeley, Hume, Kant, Hegel, Schopenhauer, Nietzsche, Comte, Spencer, James, Bergson, Fichte, von Schelling, Mill, Dewey, and certain writers and teachers of the revival of Scholasticism.

We have encountered many philosophical terms and phrases, some of which are now familiar, some new. Among these we list for review: *empiricism; sensism; positivism; idealism; subjectivism; materialism; pessimism; naturalism; occasionalism; ontologism; pragmatism; moral relativism; moral utilitarianism; Bacon's "idols"; Locke's primary and secondary sense-qualities; Descartes' "cogito ergo sum"; State absolutism; Leibniz's "law of pre-established harmony"; monadology; Kant's "phenomena and noumena," "categorical imperative," and "synthetic a priori judgments"; the triad of the Germans, Fichte, von Schelling, Hegel, viz., "thesis-antithesis-synthesis"; "will to power"; élan vital; Neo-Scholasticism.*

PART SECOND

The Questions of Philosophy

Philosophy seeks the deepest evidenced knowledge about all things. Its essential questions are seven: what is the right procedure in reasoning; what gives us certitude that we know truth; what is reality; what is the ultimate truth about this world; about God; about man; what, in view of all this knowledge, is the right way of conducting human life?

This Part of our treatise studies, rather in outline than in detail, these seven basic questions and their answers. The Chapters are the following:

CHAPTER I

THE LOGICAL QUESTION

The Logical Question is the question of correct procedure in thinking things out, that is to say, in *reasoning*. Here we investigate the process of reasoning, not its content. We are not concerned to discover the intimate nature of the process of reasoning; we are interested here solely in the function, the action of reasoning; we study to know what makes this action correct, legitimate, justified. We study and identify the various operations of the mind or intellect; we note their outer expression; and thus we seek to discover and formulate *the laws of thought*. The science thus developed is called *Logic*. More precisely it is *Formal Logic* or *Dialectics*.

This Chapter is divided into the following four Articles:

Article 1. The Operations of the Mind
Article 2. Ideas and Terms
Article 3. Judgments and Propositions
Article 4. Reasoning and Argument

Article 1. The Operations of the Mind

a) The Mind; b) Fundamental Operations of Mind; c) The Grasp of Knowledge.

a) The Mind

The *mind* is man's most perfect knowing power. It is the intellect or understanding. Some modern writers and teachers use the term *the mind* to signify any form of conscious life; we do not. We hold the terms *mind, intellect, understanding* as strict synonyms. Among bodily beings, *man alone has mind*.

Man has bodily knowing powers called *the senses*. There are five external senses: sight, hearing, taste, smell, and feeling or touch. There are four internal senses: imagination, sentient consciousness, sentient memory, and instinct. The senses are bodily powers. But the mind is a spiritual power. The senses lay hold of individual material objects. The mind lays hold of these objects in a suprasensible manner, and it also lays hold of objects which are entirely out of reach of the senses.

By the sense of sight, for example, we lay hold of bodily things that have color. We see individual things,—people, trees, animals, rocks. But by the mind we understand what these things are in themselves. We see this or that tree; but we understand what *tree* is. The tree we see is this one bodily thing. But the mind's knowledge of *tree* enables us to *define* tree, and the definition fits not only this one bodily thing, but each and every tree that ever *was* or *is* or *will be* or *can be*. We know an essence. Therefore philosophers say, "The senses grasp things *in individual;* the mind grasps things *in universal.*" Thus it is apparent that the mind lays hold of things in a suprasensible manner.

The mind also lays hold of things that the senses cannot grasp. By the mind we know what a *spirit* is, or a *soul,* or an *angel,* or *God;* the senses cannot know these objects. Again, by the mind we know what *honor* is, or *liberty,* or *patriotism,* or *unity,* or *truth*. These things are outside the reach of the senses.

The mind is a *spiritual* knowing power or *faculty*. It is a faculty of man's soul. But man is not a soul alone, nor a body alone; man is a single compound of body-and-soul. In this present life, the mind of man cannot come into direct or immediate knowledge of the essences of things; it must get at these essences by working them out from the findings of the senses. For all human knowledge in this world *begins* with the action of the senses, and of the external senses. The mind draws from sense-findings the essential elements which constitute its object.

That the mind is a soul-faculty, and that the soul is a spiritual substance, are truths investigated in the part of philosophy called psychology. We shall take up these truths in the chapter on The Psychological Question.

b) FUNDAMENTAL OPERATIONS OF MIND

The findings of the outer senses are immediately carried inward to the inner senses of imagination and sentient consciousness. Imagination in its first and basic use is not the fancy by which we "make up" images; it is not a cartooning power; first of all it is a faithful reproducing power; it presents inwardly the findings of the outer senses exactly as these are experienced. And sentient consciousness makes us *aware* of the things thus sensed outwardly and represented inwardly in the imagination.

So far the senses serve the mind: they grasp their objects, and these are inwardly reproduced or represented in conscious imagination. Here the mind goes to work on them.

The very first thing the mind does is to *pay attention* to the sense-findings held in imagination. It focusses upon them, finding in them a certain point of interest and inquiry.

Secondly, the attentive mind lays hold of the point of interest and inquiry, and draws it out, so to speak, from the circumstances and limitations with which it is involved or united, and *views it alone*. The mind is thus said to draw out or *abstract* an essence. Thus the second mental act is that of *abstraction*.

To illustrate. Suppose a boy who has no knowledge whatever of what *circle* means is shown three circles of different size drawn in different colors on a blackboard. First, the boy sees the pictures, and at once the seeing is taken inward and recorded in conscious imagination. Then the boy's mind or intellect *attends;* it focusses on a point of inquiry, "What kind of thing is this?" Attention continuing, the boy's mind notices that while all three pictures are different in size, position, and color, they are *all the same* in point of roundness; they are all pictures of *the same thing*. The boy's mind fixes on *this one thing,* drawing it out from the circumstances and limitations of size, position, color, and grasping it alone. In other words, the boy's mind *abstracts from* the non-essential details of size, position, and color, *the thing,* the *essence,* which each of the pictures represents. This grasp or understanding of an essence is called *apprehending* or *apprehension,* and the essence apprehended and possessed by the mind is now held in the mind as *a concept* or *an idea.*

The first operation of the mind is *the forming of ideas.* Ideas are formed (and "formed" does not mean "made up," but "legitimately worked out") by the *abstractive* power of the *attentive* mind working on the findings of the senses, as held inwardly in the imagination. In other words, the forming of ideas, or *apprehension,* is the mind's basic operation, which it exercises by means of *attention* and *abstraction.*

The second operation of the mind is *judging.* When the mind has acquired some ideas or concepts by the first operation of *apprehending,* it tends to compare them, to notice likenesses and differences, and *to pronounce upon its findings.* This pronouncing of the mind on the agreement or disagreement of ideas is the operation called *judging.*

Judging is the basic process of thinking. The fruit of judging is *the judgment,* that is, the pronouncement of the mind on the agreement or disagreement of two ideas. And the judgment is a *thought.* An idea alone is not a thought, for an idea is a simple grasp of an essence,—it is a *simple apprehension,*—in which the mind merely takes in an essence, a root-meaning, without saying anything about it. But when the mind compares its ideas (always two by two) and pronounces upon them, it is *thinking.* Now, the mind in its pronouncing upon two ideas will pronounce truly or falsely. Therefore, truth or falsity is to be found in the judgment, not in single ideas. When the mind judges (that is, pronounces) in such a way as to square with fact, its judgment is true; otherwise its judgment is false.

The third and final operation of the mind is *reasoning* or *inferring.* Reasoning is the process of thinking things out.

When the mind cannot make a judgment on the agreement or disagreement of two ideas, this is because it does not know the ideas clearly or because it cannot behold them distinctly in their relations to each other. In this case, the mind employs a third idea which it does know in relation to each of the others, and, through the mediation of this third idea, the mind thinks out or *reasons out* the relation of the two to each other. Thus if the mind is unable to judge on ideas "A" and "B"; if it cannot judge, "A is B" or "A is not B," because "A" and "B" are not distinctly grasped in themselves or in their relations to each other, then the mind calls in idea "C" which it knows distinctly in itself and in its relations to the other two. And the mind reasons thus:

A is C
C is B
Therefore A is B

or thus:

A is not C
C is B
Therefore A is not B.

Here the mind is able to reach judgment on "A" and "B" through their known relation to "C." Notice that the thing the mind is after in the whole process is a justified *judgment*. Thus it is manifest that the process of reasoning is a roundabout way of arriving at judgment. This fact explains why we have called judging the basic thinking process. A judgment reached by reasoning is said to be *reasoned out* or *inferred;* the process of reaching the judgment in this fashion is called *reasoning* or *inference*. More precisely, this reasoning is called *mediate* inference, because the reasoned judgment is reached through the *medium* of a third idea.

To sum up. There are three notable operations of the mind: apprehending, judging, reasoning. Apprehending is the mind's grasping of an essence; the essence once grasped is held in the mind as a *concept* or *idea*. Judging is the mind's pronouncing on the agreement or disagreement of two ideas; the pronouncement, as a thing accomplished by the mind and in the mind, is called a *judgment*. Reasoning is a roundabout or mediate way of reaching judgment when this cannot be reached directly by the study of the two ideas with which it deals; the result or fruit of the reasoning process is *a piece of reasoning* or *a mediate inference.*)

c) The Grasp of Knowledge

The mind forms ideas, judges upon them, and reasons out inferred judgments as *conclusions* or *consequents.* These items of its possessions the mind holds more or less perfectly, and evokes them on occasion. Thus the mind has the function of retaining and using its knowledge. Inasmuch as the mind keeps what it has learned, it is called *the intellectual memory.*

Notice a contrast here. We have sentient memory (as do many animals less than man) and intellectual memory. The function of sentient memory is *to recognize* sense experiences as having been known before. Sentient memory is not the sentient retaining power; this power is the imagination. But the mind, inasmuch as it *retains and recognizes* meanings,—that is, things *understood* and not merely sensed,—is the intellectual memory.

All knowing, sentient and intellectual, is a kind of grasping, a kind of getting hold of reality and taking it in. When we know an object, we take it into ourselves and possess it; and yet we leave it where it is and as it is. We do not take in known objects physically, but cognitionally. We take them in in a kind of image. And yet the image is not a mere picture, even a moving picture. It is a vital and conscious grasp, whereas a picture, even a cinema projection, is a lifeless and unconscious representation.

When we know a thing we are joined with it, but the joining does not produce a *third* thing as the joining of material objects always does. A signet impressed on wax results in *figured wax;* an image impressed on a photographic film results in a *figured film.* But an object known is impressed on a knowing power or *faculty* without resulting in a figured faculty. A signet impressed on wax shapes and limits the wax; the signet impressed on the faculty of sight does not shape and limit vision. Knowing is a unique grasping process which leaves the object known *in its ob-*

jective otherness even while that object is grasped and possessed. In a word, knowing is not cramped and limited by the material limitations of the thing known. This is true of all knowledge, and eminently true of intellectual knowledge which grasps objects *in universal.* And therefore philosophy declares that the very root of knowing is *non-materiality,* that is, freedom from the limitations of matter. The knowledge-image which is the means of our knowing is not a material or physical image; it is a cognitional image; it is called, in an ancient phrase, an *intentional* image. The term *intentional* is not here suggestive of what is usually meant by *intention;* it does not indicate a purpose of the will. It means *according to the intent, the bent, the tendency* of a knowing power. An *intentional* image is not a physical image, but an image suited to the intent, tendency, or character of knowing and of knowledge. It is a *psychical* image or *species.*

The grasp of knowledge is the laying hold of reality in intentional image.

Summary of the Article

In this Article we have mentioned the chief operations of the mind: apprehending, judging, reasoning, and we have learned a brief explanation of each process. We shall have more detail about these operations in the Articles which follow. We learned that apprehending is accomplished by the abstractive activity of the attentive mind, that is, by attention and abstraction. We have seen that the second operation of the mind, that is, judging, is the basic thought process, and that apprehending is preliminary to judging, while reasoning is only an indirect way of reaching a position in which judging is possible; reasoning itself is accomplished by connected judging, and it consists in the drawing out of one judgment from two others. We have noticed that the fruit of apprehending is the concept or the idea; that the fruit of judging is the judgment; that the fruit of reasoning is a mediate inference. We have learned that, in apprehending, the mind lays hold of a reality by grasping its essence in intentional image, which is an image unaffected by the material limitations of individual things as these exist in nature.

Article 2. Ideas and Terms

a) The Idea; b) The Expression of Ideas; c) The Clarification of Ideas.

a) The Idea

An idea is *the representation of the essence of a thing in the mind.* It is an intellectual intentional image.

By the idea we have intellectual knowledge of an *essence.* This knowledge is *abstracted* by the mind working upon the findings of sense. Certain ideas are formed by a second abstraction from ideas already in the mind, and these are called *abstractive* or *derived* ideas. The ideas of things around us in this bodily world are formed directly by the mind from sense-findings; these are *intuitive* ideas.

When we analyze an idea we find that it is, first of all, a mental representation, or intentional image, or grasp of *something,* that is, of some *thing.* The idea of *thing* (or *being*) is not analyzable; it is a *simple* idea. But all other ideas have this idea of *thing* or *being* as their first element, and to this other ideas are added as further elements. Thus all ideas except the idea of *being* are *compound* ideas.

The analysis of a compound idea is the breaking up of an idea into *the other ideas* that are its elements or *notes.* Now, the sum of the notes of any idea makes what is called its *comprehension* or *connotation.* Thus, for example, the comprehension of the idea *body* consists of three notes, for a body *means* (a) a thing; (b) a subsistent or substantial thing; and (c) a corporeal subsistent thing. The make-up of an idea in itself is, therefore, its comprehension.

Now, the idea is a representation, an image. The *things* which it represents or images come together to constitute the *extension* or *denotation* of the idea. Hence the extension of the idea *body* is the sum or collection of all actual and possible bodies, that is, all lifeless bodies (liquid, solid, gaseous), and all living bodies (plants, animals, men).

The more notes in an idea, the more accurate, definite, and limited is its scope of application. Thus the idea *living body* applies to a far smaller number of things than the idea *body*. Therefore we have an axiom: *the more notes there are in the comprehension of an idea, the fewer items there are in its extension, and vice versa.* This is put more briefly in the following formula: *the greater the comprehension, the less the extension, and vice versa.*

An idea, regarded from the standpoint of its extension, is called *singular* when it represents a single individual, or a single group. Thus the idea of *John Jones,* or of *my father,* or of *this family,* is *a singular idea.*—When the idea represents more than one of the things that belong to its extension, but not all, it is called *particular.* Thus the idea of *some men,* or *a few families,* or *most teachers,* is a particular idea.—When the idea is used to represent its *inferiors* or *subjects* (for so the items of its extension are called) without any sort of limitation it is called *a universal idea.*

Now, an idea *in itself* is always universal. It represents an essence, and so is, in itself, applicable to each and every being that has or can have that essence. A universal idea is made particular or singular *by a restriction* in its use or application.

Even when there is actually only one being which has or can have the essence represented in the idea, the idea is still universal. For the human mind conceives even such a singular essence *as though it could be* found verified in a plurality of things. Thus the idea of *God* is the idea of a Being unique and supreme. But the mind, in its first vague formation of this idea, does not advert to its uniqueness; this knowledge comes later. Therefore we assert that the idea *as such* is universal. That is to say, the first grasp of an essence, the idea upon first formation, is the knowing of an essence *independently of the fact that this essence may be found verified in only one subject or inferior.*

b) The Expression of Ideas

A human being has an inevitable tendency to convey knowledge as well as to acquire it. The normal mind wants to carry its ideas, judgments, reasonings to other minds, or, at any rate, to give them some outer expression for its own benefit or pleasure. There is in man a natural and an inevitable drive towards the outer expression of knowledge.

Now, an idea is expressed outwardly by *a term*. Sometimes the idea itself is called *a mental term*. The outer expression of the idea in speech is called *an oral term*. The oral term has as its extension and equivalent *the written term* and *the gesticular term*.

A term expresses an idea, an understood meaning, an intellectually grasped essence. It is not the expression of feeling. A sob is not a term, nor is a sigh, a yawn, a grunt, or a groan. A term expresses *an idea*.

A term expresses an idea *completely*, whether simply and explicitly or by implication. Every word is not a term, for some words do not express ideas. Such words as prepositions, adjectives, adverbs, are not terms in themselves, although they are fitted to be parts of terms. Nouns are terms, and noun equivalents or substantives. The verb is a term when its subject is expressed or understood and, if it be transitive, when its predicate is also expressed or understood; but this is true only when the verb is used in the present indicative active. A noun expresses an idea explicitly (for example, *man, fire, thought*); a present indicative verb expresses an idea by implication; thus "he lives" expresses the idea *life* by asserting *its presence* in an individual. A term expresses an essence or a rounded essential meaning.

A term, then, is a word or a group of words which completely expresses an idea. A term is the outer *sign* of an idea. It is also the sign of *the thing* which the idea represents.

The actual terms used in any language are arbitrary or conventional signs; they are due to human invention and choice. For while *speech* is natural, the determination of terms in a language is not; otherwise there would be but one language in the world.

A term may have several possible *meanings*. Thus "body" may mean a corpse, a part of an automobile, or a group (such as "a body of citizens"). The *precise* sense or meaning in which a term is taken in any individual use is called its *supposition*.

c) The Clarification of Ideas

When an idea is first formed it may be *obscure*. To know, for instance, that a pomegranate is a fruit is to know something essential of it, but not all. Such knowledge is not clear enough to allow the mind to distinguish this fruit from other fruits. Ideas must pass from obscurity to clarity and distinctness to be of best service to man, and man has a tendency to bring his ideas to their more perfect state. To this end he *analyzes* his ideas and discerns their comprehension; then he sums up his analysis in *a definition* of the essence represented by the idea. Definition is thus a means of clarifying ideas.

Definition is an explanation of three things: of *the idea* in the mind, of *the thing* or reality which the idea represents, and of *the term* which expresses the idea. Thus the definition of *man* tells: (*a*) the meaning of the idea or concept of *man* in the mind; (*b*) what the human essence is as it exists in individual men; (*c*) what the word or term *man* means. It is customary to speak of the definition of *terms*, but this fact must not lead us to lose sight of the full nature of definition as the explanation of the idea, reality, and term.

A definition is a formula (of speech) which clearly expresses the meaning of an idea, reality, and term. It serves to clarify knowledge and to impress it sharply upon the intellectual memory (that is, upon *the mind as memory*). To realize its purpose a definition must be *exact;* it must be *clear;* it must not include the term defined but must express this in other and fuller terms; it must state the general class to which the reality defined belongs, and then mention the precise marks of distinction which make the reality a specific member of that class. A definition which fails to meet any of these requirements may be *a loose definition* or *a description,* but it is not a scientific or philosophical definition. Manifestly, a definition must be positive, not negative.

There are two types of definition, *physical* and *metaphysical.* When a definition tells what a thing is by naming its actual constitution as a thing, it is *a physical definition*. Thus *man* is defined as "a creature composed of body and soul." When, however, a definition tells what a thing is by naming *the points of reality* which make it *understandable,* it is *a metaphysical definition.* Thus man is defined as "a rational animal." In other words, this latter definition sums up the points of reality which the mind grasps in understanding what *man* means, viz., that he is a *thing,* that he is a *subsistent* thing, that he is a *bodily*-subsistent-thing, that he is a *living*-bodily-subsistent-thing, that he is a *sentient*-living-bodily-subsistent-thing (and so far all the points of reality —*thing, subsistent, bodily, living, sentient* define *animal*), that he is a *rational*-sentient-living-bodily-subsistent-thing. All the points of reality by which *man* is grasped by an adequate mind may be summed up as *animal* plus *rational,* and thus the metaphysical definition of *man* is "a rational animal."

Another means of clarifying ideas and terms,—in a word, clarifying knowledge,—is that known as *logical division.* Definition analyzes the comprehension of an idea and states what it finds; logical division takes the extension of an idea and sets the items found there in orderly groups. Logical division is *a classification* of the items or members of the extension of an idea. The technical name for these items or members of extension is *subjects* or *inferiors.* Thus, to illustrate, Tom, Dick, and Harry, as well as Mary and Jane, are *subjects* or *inferiors* of the idea *human being.*

When we classify by logical division we must have, in each instance, a single standpoint, otherwise confusion and not clarification of knowledge will result from our effort. This requirement is expressed in the rule, "There must be, in each use of logical division, only one *principle of division.*" To classify *people* as "college graduates, high school graduates, and Catholics" (as a recent poll actually did) is wholly illogical, for the principle of division shifts from *schooling* to *religion* and so spoils consistency and induces confusion. For the rest, logical division must be *complete,* enumerating all items in proper groups; it must have *no overlapping* of items; it must be *properly arranged* so that larger items are listed with their kind, then the members of these, then the members of these members, keeping each section of the grouping on an even plane. Finally, logical division *must not be too detailed.* Violation of any of these rules would make logical division an instrument of confusion instead of clarification of knowledge.

Thus two notable means of clarifying ideas and terms, and so two means of making knowledge more valuable to man, are *definition* and *logical division.*

Summary of the Article

In this Article we have defined *idea* and have learned what is meant by its *comprehension* and its *extension.* We have noticed that, on the score of comprehension, ideas are *simple* or *compound;* and that, on the score of extension, ideas are *singular, particular,* or *universal.* Yet we have seen that the idea in itself and by its nature is universal. We have learned that the idea is outwardly expressed by *the term,* which is the sign of an idea and of the reality of which the idea is the mental representation. We have studied two important means of clarifying ideas (and terms), viz., *definition* and *logical division.*

Article 3. Judgments and Propositions

a) The Judgment; b) The Proposition; c) Properties of Propositions.

a) The Judgment

Judging is the operation of mind which results in *the judgment*. The judgment is the pronouncement of the mind on the agreement or disagreement of two ideas.

Ideas *agree* in so far as their respective comprehensions are not in conflict, and also in so far as their subjects or inferiors are found in the same field of extension. In so far as their respective comprehensions are not the same, or not compatible, and also in so far as their subjects or inferiors cannot be classed in the same field of extension, they are said to *disagree*.

Thus the judgment "man is mortal" is a pronouncement (made upon the investigation of the comprehension or inner meaning of the ideas *man* and *mortal being*) that *man* is contained in the field of extension of *mortal being*. In other words, it is a pronouncement of the fact that *man* is the subject or inferior of the idea *mortal being*, and consequently it enunciates *mortal being* of *man* as *predicate is enunciated of subject*. This pronouncement is an *affirmative* judgment. The judgment "man is not a spirit" is a *negative* judgment.

We must here briefly recall what we learned in some detail when we studied the logic of Aristotle (*Part First, Chap. II, Art. 2, b*), that is, the doctrine on *the predicables*.

When the mind judges it pronounces, it *predicates;* it declares that a subject-idea (or inferior) is contained or is not contained in the extension of a predicate-idea. Thus in the judgment "man is mortal," the mind pronounces or judges that the things meant by *man* are also in the extension (or field of meaning) of the idea *mortal being*, and that therefore *man* (taken in extension as all actual and possible human beings) is the *subject* or *inferior* of which *mortal being* is a proper predicate.

Now, when the predicate-idea exactly defines the subject-idea (as in the judgment, "man is a rational animal") the predicate-idea is called *the species* of the subject-idea, and the predication is *specific.* When the predicate-idea expresses *part* of the subject-idea and that part which the subject-idea has in common with other ideas, the predicate-idea is called *the genus* of the subject-idea, and the predication is *generic;* for example, "man is an animal." When the predicate-idea means (or expresses within the mind) that *part* of the subject-idea which differentiates it from other ideas with which it has a common genus, the predicate idea is called *the specific difference* of the subject-idea, and the predication is *differential;* for example, "man is rational." When the predicate-idea means no part of the subject-idea but expresses what naturally belongs to the subject-idea, the predicate-idea is called *the property* or *the attribute* of the subject-idea, and the predication is *proper;* for example, "man is risible (that is, a-being-that-can-laugh)." When the predicate-idea expresses or means what may happen to be true of the subject-idea, although it is no part of it nor anything naturally belonging to it, the predicate-idea is called *the accident* of the subject-idea, and the predication is *accidental;* for example, "man is a reading animal."

These then are *the predicables:* species, genus, specific difference, property or attribute, and accident. Note well and remember: the predicables are modes of predication, of judging; they are not modes of being or classes of things.

As we have noticed elsewhere, the judgment is marked by truth or falsity. When the judgment of the mind squares with reality, the judgment has what is called *logical truth.* When the judgment is mistaken; when, as a fact, the predicate-idea is enunciated of a subject-idea with which it is not in agreement, or when the predicate-idea is denied of a subject-idea with which it is in agreement, the judgment has *logical falsity.* Remember: truth and falsity are things to be assigned to *judgment,* not to ideas or concepts.

b) The Proposition

The operation of apprehending produces the idea, and the idea is outwardly expressed by the term. Now, the operation of judging produces the judgment, and the judgment is outwardly expressed by *the proposition.* The proposition is therefore a formula of terms which expresses the agreement or disagreement of a predicate-idea with a subject-idea. The subject-idea is expressed in a term called simply *the subject;* the predicate-idea is expressed in a term called *the predicate;* the pronouncement of agreement or disagreement is expressed in *the copula,* that is, the present tense of the verb *to be,* used affirmatively or negatively.

A proposition is *categorical* if it is a straight affirmation or denial; it is *hypothetical* if it enunciates *a dependency* of one proposition on another without actually affirming or denying either. Thus, "man is an animal" is a categorical proposition; "if man has sentient life, he is an animal" is a hypothetical proposition. A categorical proposition is *simple* if it contains one predication; otherwise it is *compound.* Further, a categorical proposition is *affirmative* or *negative* according as the copula is "is" or "is not." A categorical proposition is *absolute* if it enunciates the agreement or disagreement of subject and predicate and nothing more; if it tells *how* they agree or disagree (that is, possibly, necessarily, contingently, impossibly) it is *modal:* "a circle is round" is an absolute proposition; "a circle is necessarily round" is a modal proposition. Finally, a proposition is *universal* when its subject is in full extension ("All men are mortal"); it is *particular* when its subject is in partial extension ("Some men are foolish"); it is *indefinite* when its subject has no *expressed* extension ("Men are sentimental"); it is *singular* when its subject is a singular term ("This man is angry"; "John is ill"). For convenience in handling propositions without the cumbrous titles, the various types of propositions are reduced to four, and these are labelled by letters. We must say a word in explanation of this.

Since we have mentioned four types of propositions on the

basis of *quantity* or extension (universal, particular, indefinite, and singular) and since what is called the *quality* of a proposition is twofold (affirmative, negative), it seems that the types of categorical and absolute propositions should number twice four or eight. Yet we reduce the total to four in this way: in respect of *quantity,* propositions are really *universal* or *particular;* for the *singular* proposition uses its subject in full extension since it has an extension of only one, and it is thus equivalent to a universal proposition; and the *indefinite* proposition is readily interpreted as either universal or particular. Thus, in the singular proposition "John is ill," the subject *John* is in full extension, and the proposition is equivalent to a universal proposition, since having the subject in full extension is the definition of a universal proposition. And the indefinite propositions, "Man is mortal," "Men are musical" are readily interpreted by the mind to mean, "All men are mortal" (which is a universal proposition) and "Some men are musical" (which is a particular proposition). Therefore, for purposes of logic we declare that there are but four types of categorical absolute propositions, since there are two quantities (universal, particular) and two qualities (affirmative, negative). Thus we have the following propositions:

The universal affirmative, called the A-proposition: "All men are musical";

The universal negative, called the E-proposition: "No men are musical";

The particular affirmative, called the I-proposition: "Some men are musical";

The particular negative, called the O-proposition: "Some men are not musical."

A proposition for the purposes of logic must be *in logical form.* That is, it must be in the present tense, indicative mood, and the verb must be the copula (the verb *to be*). Thus, "John said he liked music as a child" is made to read, "John is a-person-who-said-he-liked-music-as-a-child." The entire phrase "a person who said he liked music as a child" is a single term which serves as the predicate of the proposition. In passing, it is hoped that the student will instantly notice that here the mode of predication is *accidental.*

c) Properties of Propositions

A property of a proposition is something which naturally belongs to a proposition. There are three notable properties of propositions; they are functionable uses or simply functions which the proposition may be made to serve. These functions are useful for they help us to test the full meaning of a proposition, to see all its implications, to make *immediate inference* of points not noticed at first, and they often enable us to indicate at once the fallacy of a mistaken statement. The running of a proposition through the functions called its properties is a kind of shake-up or analysis which may be a great aid to clear and exact thinking.

The three notable properties of propositions are these. (*a*) A proposition may be contrasted with its opposites; (*b*) it may be expressed in equivalent terms; (*c*) it may, under definite conditions, have its subject and predicate change places. These three properties of propositions are called respectively, *opposition, equipollence,* and *conversion.*

(*a*) *Opposition of Propositions.*—Opposition of propositions is that quality of propositions which renders them capable of contrast with their opposites.

The *opposite* of a proposition is another proposition *which has the same subject and the same predicate,* but which differs in *quantity* (extension of subject) or in *quality* (character of copula as affirmative or negative) or in both. There are four types of opposites: *contradictory* propositions, *contrary* propositions, *subcontrary* propositions, *subaltern* propositions.

Contradictory propositions differ in quality (one affirmative, one negative) and also in quantity (one universal, one particular). These propositions are *perfectly* opposed. They exhaust the possibilities, and so *one of them must be true and the other false.* Contradictory propositions are "A—O" and "E—I." For example, "All men are musical—Some men are not musical"; "No men are musical—Some men are musical."

Contrary propositions are two *universal* propositions which differ only in quality. They are "A—E." "All men are musical—No men are musical." *Contraries cannot both be true, but both may be false.*

Subcontrary propositions are two *particular* propositions which differ only in quality. They are "I—O." "Some men are musical—Some men are not musical." *Subcontraries may both be true, but both cannot be false.*

Subaltern propositions are two propositions which differ only in quantity. One is universal and one particular, but both are affirmative or both are negative. They are "A—I" and "E—O." The universal proposition is *the subalternant;* the particular proposition is *the subalternate.* "All men are musical—Some men are musical"; "No men are musical—Some men are not musical." *If the subalternant is true the subalternate is true, but not vice versa; if the subalternate is false the subalternant is false, but not vice versa.*

The opposition of propositions is graphically shown in what is called "The Square of Opposition" or "The Logical Square":

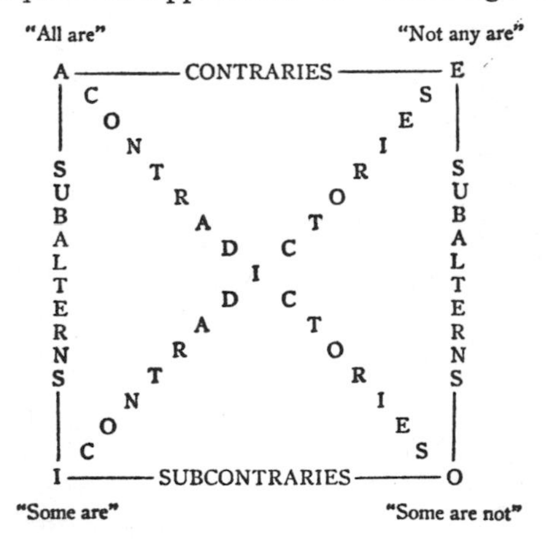

(*b*) *Equipollence of Propositions.*—Equipollence means *equivalence*. It is the property of a proposition which renders it capable of being expressed in equivalent terms. But it has a narrower meaning than this in our present use of it. It means the property of a proposition which makes it *the equivalent of its opposite* by the inserting of *negative particles*.

To make a proposition *the equivalent of its contradictory,* insert a negative before the subject. Thus, "All men are musical—*Not* all men are musical." The second proposition is equivalent to "Some men are not musical."

To make a universal proposition *the equivalent of its contrary,* insert a negative before the predicate. Thus, "All men are musical—All men are *not*-musical." The second proposition is equivalent to "All men are unmusical" or "No men are musical."

To make a particular proposition *the equivalent of its subcontrary,* follow the same rule as with contraries; insert a negative before the predicate. Thus, "Some men are musical—Some men are not musical."

To make a proposition *the equivalent of its subaltern,* insert a negative before the subject and also before the predicate. Thus, "All men are musical—Not all men are not musical." The second proposition is equivalent to "Not all men are unmusical" or "Some men are musical." Similarly, "Some men are musical—Not some (i.e., any) men are not musical." The second proposition is equivalent to "Not any men are unmusical" or "All men are musical."

(*c*) *Conversion of Propositions.*—Conversion is the property of A- E- and I-propositions (*not* of O-propositions) which justifies the mind in putting the subject in the place of the predicate and the predicate in the place of the subject, certain rules being carefully observed.

The rules of conversion are two: *there must be no change of quality:* affirmatives convert to affirmatives, and negatives to negatives; and *there must be no expanding of the extension or denotation of terms.* The second rule means that we are not allowed to say more in the converted proposition (called *the converse*) than is justified by the original proposition (called *the convertend*). We may say *less* in the converse than is said in the convertend, but not *more.* The reason for the two rules is manifest: it consists in the fact that the converse is *taken* from the convertend, and therefore must not express anything *other* or anything *more* than can be found in the convertend.

When a proposition converts to its own type, we have *simple* conversion; when it converts to another type, we have *accidental* conversion. A-propositions convert accidentally; E- and I-propositions convert simply; E-propositions also convert accidentally. As a practical guide, remember the following:

(*1*) *A- converts to I-.* Example: "All men are musical—Some musical beings are men."

(*2*) *E- converts to E-* and *E- converts to O-.* Example: "No men are musical—No musical beings are men"; "No men are musical—Some musical beings are not men."

(*3*) *I- converts to I-.* Example: "Some men are musical—Some musical beings are men."

(*4*) *O- is not convertible.*

An O-proposition cannot be converted without violating the rule which forbids the expanding of terms; therefore, O- is not convertible.

Summary of the Article

In this Article we have studied the second major operation of the mind, that is, *judging,* and *the judgment* which is the product of the operation. We have noted that the basis of the judgment is the comparison and analysis of two ideas. We have also seen that judging means *predicating,* and we have called to mind the five possible modes of predicating, called *The Predicables.* We have studied the expression of the judgment, that is, *the proposition;* we have distinguished various types of propositions, especially from the standpoint of quantity and quality, and we have reduced all absolute categorical propositions to four types known as A-, E-, I-, and O-propositions. We have learned the meaning of *properties of propositions* and have noticed the value and the function of the properties called *opposition, equipollence,* and *conversion.*

Article 4. Reasoning and Argument

a) Reasoning; b) Expression of Reasoning; c) Laws of Argument.

a) Reasoning

Reasoning, the third and most complex of the major operations of the mind, is a roundabout or *mediate* way of reaching a judgment that cannot be made *immediately*. It is an operation of the mind in which the relation of two ideas (as agreeing or disagreeing) is inferred from their respective relation to a common third idea.

The man who realizes that one and one make two does so *immediately*. His comparison of the ideas "one and one" and "two" shows him that these are identical. But the man who proves that the angles of any triangle come to a sum of 180° has reached his final judgment after a long series of connected judgments, each of which was arrived at by comparing two ideas with a common third. He has reached the final conclusion by a process of sustained *reasoning* or *mediate inference* or *discursive thought.*

Each step of the reasoning process by which we "think things out" consists, implicitly or explicitly, of three judgments. In the first of these, one of the two ideas which we seek to bring together in final judgment is compared with a common third; in the second, the other idea is compared with the common third. These two judgments constitute the *antecedent* element of reasoning. The judgment which is latent in the antecedent is explicitly rendered as the *consequent* element of reasoning.

The antecedent thus consists of two judgments called *the premises.* The consequent is a single judgment called *the conclusion.*

Thus the reasoning process proceeds in this fashion:

Antecedent.. { "A is C" —*First or Major Premise*
"C is B" —*Second or Minor Premise*

Consequent... "A is B" —*The Conclusion*

The three judgments are the "matter" of reasoning; the "form" of reasoning is the *logical connection* or *sequence* (known technically as *consequence*) which shows that the final judgment (the conclusion) is inevitably to be drawn from the other two (the premises).

Certain general laws of reasoning are to be noticed: (*a*) *If the antecedent is true the consequent or conclusion must be true.* For, since the conclusion is wholly drawn from the premises, any falsity that appears in the conclusion must have been taken from them. (*b*) *If the antecedent is false, the consequent may be true or false.* For, it is possible that a conclusion should express truth for some other reason than the fact that the conclusion follows upon the premises; hence the conclusion may be true even though the premises be false. (*c*) *For value in the conclusion, it must proceed from certainly known premises.*

Reasoning is *deductive* when its course is from the more general to the less general; it is *inductive* when its course is from the less general to the more general. Deductive reasoning is called *deduction;* inductive reasoning is called *induction.* These are not opposed methods of reasoning; they are supplementary. To argue from the fact that all metals are heavier than water to the fact that this metal or these several metals are heavier than water is deduction. To argue from the fact that this or these metals are heavier than water to the general conclusion that all metals are heavier than water is induction. Pure reasoning, as in most mathematical sciences, is deductive; reasoning based on experiment and observation of data is inductive.

b) Expression of Reasoning

As *apprehending* results in *the idea* which is expressed in *the term;* as *judging* produces *the judgment* which is expressed in *the proposition;* so *reasoning* gives us *a mediate inference* which is expressed in *argument* or *argumentation.*

Argument or argumentation is therefore a formula of terms and propositions which gives outer expression to the reasoning process and its result.

The most perfect form of argument is *the syllogism. The syllogism is an argument consisting of three propositions so connected that when the first two are given the third follows of necessity.* The propositions express the *antecedent* and the *consequent* elements of the reasoning process, and they are known by the same names. The antecedent element of the syllogism consists of two propositions called *the premises* (the first of which is *the major premise,* and the second *the minor premise*); the consequent element consists of a single proposition called *the conclusion.*

There are two main types of the syllogism, the *categorical* syllogism, and the *hypothetical* syllogism. The categorical syllogism consists of three categorical propositions. The hypothetical syllogism consists of one hypothetical proposition and two categorical propositions. Examples:

Categorical syllogism:	Every bodily being is a substance A stone is a bodily being Therefore, a stone is a substance
Hypothetical syllogism:	If a stone is a bodily being, it is a substance A stone is a bodily being Therefore, a stone is a substance

Although fundamentally the laws governing the syllogism are the same for all types, it is a convenience for the student to have definite regulations for the forming and judging of each type, and so we shall presently discuss two sets of laws, one for the categorical syllogism, and one for the hypothetical syllogism.

The material element or "matter" of the syllogism consists of *three propositions,* and ultimately of *three terms* each of which occurs twice. We have already learned that the propositions are called *major premise, minor premise,* and *conclusion.* We must now learn that the terms are called *major term, minor term,* and *middle term.* The major term is the term which serves as the predicate of the conclusion. The minor term serves as the subject of the conclusion. The middle term is that with which the major term and the minor term (called *the extremes*) are compared in the premises; it does not occur in the conclusion. In the first premise, that is, the major premise, one of the extremes is compared with the mean or middle term; in the other premise, that is, the minor premise, the other extreme is compared with the mean or middle term; in the conclusion, the extremes are brought together as subject and predicate of an affirmation or denial. Hence, the middle term (called *the mean* in contrast to *the extremes*) is the term which is found in each premise but not in the conclusion.

The student will identify the major premise, the minor premise, the conclusion, the major term, the minor term, and the middle term in this syllogism:

All books of the Bible are useful reading
Exodus is a book of the Bible
Therefore, Exodus is useful reading

c) The Laws of Argument

The laws of argument are the reasoned rules which must be observed if the syllogism is to be correct and legitimate. Since there are two main types of argument, viz., the categorical syllogism and the hypothetical syllogism, we set forth two sets of laws.

1. The Categorical Syllogism

Here we have eight laws, four of which apply to *the terms* of the categorical syllogism, and four to *the propositions* of the syllogism.

LAWS OF TERMS

1. There must be three terms; neither more nor less.
2. These must not be found in a fuller extension in the conclusion than they are found in the premises; they may be found in lesser extension.
3. The middle term must be used in full extension at least once.
4. The middle term must never be found in the conclusion.

LAWS OF PROPOSITIONS

1. Two affirmative premises cannot lead to a negative conclusion.
2. Two negative premises cannot have any conclusion.
3. Two particular premises cannot have any conclusion.
4. If there is *negation* or *particularity* in either of the premises, it will appear in the conclusion.

The "figure" of the categorical syllogism is determined by *the position of the middle term in the premises.* The middle term may be: (*a*) subject of the major premise, predicate of the minor premise; (*b*) predicate of both premises; (*c*) subject of both premises; (*d*) predicate of the major premise, subject of the minor premise. Hence there are *four figures* of the categorical syllogism. These are called simply the First, Second, Third, and Fourth Figures. If we take M to stand for the middle term, P for the major term, and S for the minor term, we may thus illustrate the four figures:

Fig. I	*Fig. II*	*Fig. III*	*Fig. IV*
M — P	P — M	M — P	P — M
S — M	S — M	M — S	M — S
S — P	S — P	S — P	S — P

The first figure is called the most perfect figure for the reason that in it the necessity of drawing the given conclusion is most plainly evident. Hence logicians have developed an elaborate system of rules for *"reducing* syllogisms of the last three figures," that is, of restating these syllogisms in the shape of the first figure. We shall not pause to discuss this "reduction of syllogisms."

In addition to "figure," each categorical syllogism has "mood." The mood of a syllogism is determined by *the sequence of types of propositions* which compose it. Since categorical syllogisms are made up of propositions of the types A-, E-, I-, O-, the mood of syllogisms is expressed in these letters. A syllogism like that given above ("All books of the Bible, etc.") is called AAA because it consists of three A-propositions; we say its *mood* is AAA. The following syllogism, as the student will notice, is in the mood AII:

All good books are valuable
Some of my books are good books
Therefore, some of my books are valuable.

There are nineteen useful *moods* of categorical syllogisms. Other combinations of types of propositions than these nineteen are useless, for they make up syllogisms which do not square with the laws of terms and propositions already studied; hence they make *invalid* syllogisms. The nineteen useful moods are these:

In the First Figure: AAA, EAE, AII, EIO
In the Second Figure: EAE, AEE, EIO, AOO
In the Third Figure: AAI, EAO, IAI, AII, OAO, EIO
In the Fourth Figure: AAI, EAE, AII, AEO, IEO

2. *The Hypothetical Syllogism*

A hypothetical syllogism is a syllogism which has a hypothetical proposition as its major premise. Now, there are three types of hypothetical proposition: the *conditional,* the *conjunctive,* and the *disjunctive.* The conditional proposition begins with "if." The conjunctive proposition states the impossibility of two things concurring (as "John is not at the same time standing and running"); it is always equivalent to *two conditionals* (thus "If John stands, he is not running"— "If John is running, he is not standing."). The disjunctive proposition enumerates all possibilities, one of which is true and the rest false; it is always equivalent to a series of conditionals. Thus, "It is spring, or summer, or autumn, or winter" means that it *is* one of the seasons (*all* of which are mentioned) and *not* any of the others; this is equivalent to "If it is spring, it is not summer, autumn, or winter; if it is summer, it is not spring, autumn, or winter," and so on. Thus it appears that all types of hypothetical propositions are reducible to the conditional type. Still we distinguish three types of hypothetical syllogism according to the three types of hypothetical propositions, and we express rules for each. The studious pupil will not have great difficulty in thinking out the reasons for these rules; he will find the basis of all of them in the fact that all hypotheticals can be reduced to the conditional type and are ultimately governed by the laws which spring from its nature. Here we briefly discuss: the conditional syllogism, the conjunctive syllogism, and the disjunctive syllogism.

(*a*) *The Conditional Syllogism.*—The first part of the major premise (the conditional proposition in the syllogism) is called *the antecedent,* the second part is *the consequent.* Thus, in the proposition, "If it rains, there will be no game," the antecedent is found in the words "If it rains"; the consequent is found in the words, "there will be no game." The laws upon which the conditional syllogism is based are these: *If the antecedent is true, the consequent is true, but not vice versa;* and, *If the consequent is false, the antecedent is false, but not vice versa.*

Hence, the following is a valid conditional syllogism: "If it rains, there will be no game. It rains. Therefore there will be no game." But this conditional syllogism is invalid: "If it rains, there will be no game. There will be no game. Therefore, it rains." As is evident, the game may be canceled for a variety of reasons other than unsuitable weather, and we cannot conclude from the cancellation of the game that rain is falling.

(*b*) *The Conjunctive Syllogism.*—The parts of a conjunctive or a disjunctive proposition are called *members.* The laws of the conjunctive syllogism are these: *If one member is true, the other is false;* and, *If one member is false, it does not follow that the other is true.* Thus we have a valid syllogism in the following: "John cannot be in New York and Chicago at the same time. He is in Chicago. Therefore, he is not in New York." But the following syllogism violates its laws and is invalid: "John cannot be in Chicago and New York at the same time. But he is not in Chicago. Therefore, he is in New York."

(*c*) *The Disjunctive Syllogism.*—*The major premise must be a complete disjunctive,* omitting no possible member. *The truth of one member means the falsity of all the rest. The falsity of one member means the truth of one of the others.* "It is spring, or summer, or autumn, or winter. But it is, in fact, summer. Therefore, it is neither spring, nor autumn, nor winter." The syllogism would be invalid if the major premise were, for instance, the following: "It is spring, or summer, or autumn," for a possible member has been left out, and the disjunction is incomplete. The syllogism would be valid, as it is in the form first given, if the minor premise were negative, thus: "It is not spring. Therefore, it is summer, or autumn, or winter." Similarly, the syllogism would be valid if two or more members were denied in the minor premise: "It is neither spring nor winter. Therefore, it is either autumn or summer."

By way of postscript to our treatise on syllogisms and their laws of structure and validity, we must mention certain *irregular syllogisms.* The following irregular types are important to notice:

1. The Enthymeme is a shortened syllogism; one premise is omitted as easily understood. Thus: "John is a good boy; he will do his duty" tacitly supposes but does not express the major premise, viz., "Good boys will do their duty."

2. The Epicherema is a lengthened syllogism, for it adds a word of proof or explanation to one or to both of its premises. Thus: "These pupils will study hard, for they are diligent. Those who study hard will pass the examination, for hard study develops capability. Therefore, these students will pass the examination."

3. The Polysyllogism is a connected *series of syllogisms* (two or more) in which the conclusion of one is the major premise of the next succeeding. Thus: "The man of good life avoids sin. He who avoids sin advances in virtue. Therefore, the man of good life advances in virtue. He who advances in virtue is pleasing to God. Therefore, the man of good life is pleasing to God."

4. The Sorites is a connected *series of premises* so arranged that the predicate of one is the subject of the next succeeding; the conclusion combines the subject of the first premise with the predicate of the last. Thus: "A worldly man has many unchecked desires. He who has many unchecked desires feels many wants. He who feels many wants is distressed in mind. He who is distressed in mind is not at peace. He who is not at peace is not happy. Therefore, a worldly man is not happy."

5. The Dilemma or *horned syllogism* offers, in a major disjunctive premise, two alternatives or "horns," and in two conditional premises it catches an opponent on either one horn or the other, and reaches the same conclusion by either alternative. Thus: "The Catholic religion was spread through the world either with the help of miracles or without the help of miracles. If with the help of miracles, it is divine, for miracles are the incontestable mark of divine help and approval. If without miracles, its rapid spread in the face of every worldly obstacle is itself a miracle, and this miracle proves it divine. Therefore, in either case, the Catholic religion is divine." If, in this type of argument, the major disjunctive premise offers three possibilities, the syllogism is called a *trilemma;* if four, it is called a *quadrilemma,* and so forth.

Another postscript must here be added to warn the pupil against tricky arguments which may appear valid but in reality are not so. Such arguments are called *fallacies.* Notable fallacies are the following:

1. Equivocation consists in using a single term in two different meanings, thus making it equivalent to two terms. By equivocation a *fourth* term is introduced into a categorical syllogism, and this renders the argument valueless. Example: "It is wrong to worship others than God. But Catholics worship others than God (for they worship Saints). Therefore Catholics do what is wrong." Here the term "worship" is used in two different meanings. In the major premise it means "pay divine honor to"; in the minor premise it means "give religious reverence to." Hence the argument reaches no justified conclusion.

2. Compounding is the taking of a term or proposition in a *solid* or *compounded* sense when it is meant to be taken in a *divided* or *distinguished* sense. Thus the phrase, "The blind see" is obviously meant to be *divided* and so means, "Those who were once blind, but have been cured of their blindness, are now able to see." The fallacy of compounding ignores this requirement of reason, and uses the term (and proposition) in a solid or compounded sense: "Christ said, 'The blind see.' This man is blind. Therefore, on Christ's word, he sees."

3. Dividing is the taking of a term or proposition in a divided sense when it is meant to be taken in a solid or compounded sense. Thus, "A sick man cannot be well. But John is sick. Therefore, John can't be well (that is, he cannot recover)." The manifest sense of the major premise is a solid, compact, undivided acceptance of "a sick man as such," and means that a sick man cannot be a well man at the same time that he is sick. The fallacy of dividing ignores this compact or compounded sense of the term "sick man" (and of the term "well man" too) and splits the meaning to base one assertion on one part of it, and to draw a conclusion from the other part.

4. Missing the Point or *Ignoring the Issue* is a fallacy which comes from a mistaken (or sly) effort to prove one thing by offering argument for another. Thus many pseudo-scientists have thought that they proved *the evolutionary hypothesis* by arguing that the development of the world as we know it *took a long time.* Another example is found in the effort to disprove the infallibility of the Pope by arguing that it is possible for him to commit sin.

5. Begging the Question is a fallacy which comes from the fact that the very point to be proved is assumed as a fact and used as a basis of argument. A book appeared some twenty years ago which purported to prove the animal descent of man. It began with the fair declaration that the evolutionary hypothesis is truly only a hypothesis. But after less than twenty pages, the *fact of evolution* was constantly adduced *as an argument* to prove the thesis of the book. One type of begging the question is known as *the vicious circle* which consists in proving A by B, and then proving B by A. Descartes was guilty of such a fallacy when he argued that our reasoning power is trustworthy because God would not give us deceiving faculties; then he proceeded to use his reasoning power as a valid instrument to prove the existence of God.

Summary of the Article

In this Article we have defined *reasoning,* and have discussed its *antecedent* and its *consequent* elements. We have distinguished two types of reasoning, *the deductive* and *the inductive.* We have studied the *expression* of reasoning in terms and propositions, and have learned that this is called *argument* or *argumentation,* and that its most perfect form is *the syllogism.* We have noted the two chief types of syllogism, *the categorical* and *the hypothetical,* and have set down the reasoned laws that determine the structure and the value of each type. We have also noted *the figures* and *the moods* of categorical syllogisms. We have noticed certain types of *irregular syllogisms,* and have indicated certain *fallacies* which the careful thinker must avoid.

CHAPTER II

THE CRITICAL QUESTION

The Critical Question is the question of the trustworthiness of human knowledge. In discussing the Logical Question we sought to know what makes the process of reasoning *correct.* In discussing the Critical Question we seek to know what guarantees the same process as fruitful of *true and certain knowledge.* Since this question, like the former, is concerned with the mind and its knowing, it is in the department of Logic. The science which answers the Critical Question is therefore often called *Major Logic,* and sometimes *Material Logic* since it deals with the "matter" rather than with the "forms" of thought. Most often, however, this science is called *Epistemology,* "the science of knowledge," or *Criteriology,* "the science of the criteria," by which we test the truth and certitude of knowledge. We have chosen to take the last name *Criteriology* rather than *Epistemology* as the source of our description of this question of philosophy. Hence we speak of the *critical* question rather than of the *epistemological* question.

The Chapter is divided into the following four Articles:

Article 1. Truth and Certitude.
Article 2. Various Doctrines on Certitude
Article 3. The Sources of Certitude
Article 4. Scientific Certitude and Its Acquisition

Article 1. Truth and Certitude

a) The Nature of Truth; b) Classification of Truth; c) The Mind and Truth.

a) The Nature of Truth

Truth is a *relation;* it exists *between* two things. The two things are *mind* on the one hand, and something judged by the mind, that is, some judged *reality,* on the other.

When the judging mind forms a judgment which accurately squares with the reality about which the judgment is made, *there is truth in the judging mind.* In other words, when we know things accurately and factually, *we have the truth* about them. And since things are knowable, since they can be rightly judged upon by the mind, *there is truth in them* to know. Truth, therefore, is the relation of equality, of squaring-up, of adequation, between the mind and reality. The opposite of truth is *falsity.*

b) Classification of Truth

Since truth is the relation of equality or adequation between the mind and reality, it can be looked at from two standpoints, that of the mind, and that of reality. Inasmuch as the mind can square up to reality by knowing it accurately, the mind can obtain and possess truth. This is *truth in the mind,* or *truth of thought,* or *truth of knowledge.* Its technical name is *logical truth.* Inasmuch as any reality is knowable, inasmuch as it can be rightly known and accurately judged by an adequate mind, truth abides in it. This is *truth in things.* Its technical name is *ontological truth.*

Hence we have two classes or types of truth: the truth of thought and the truth of things. There is a third type of truth which does not concern us here beyond a simple mention: this is the *truth of speech* and it consists in the agreement between the knowledge and the words of a speaker or writer. Truth in its logical and ontological aspects is *verity;* truth of speech is *veracity.* Veracity is called *moral truth.* We shall discuss moral truth when we take up the Ethical Question.

Now, things or realities are what they are. And they are necessarily *knowable* as they are. If a knowing mind does not judge them truly, this is not the fault of things but the inadequacy of the mind or its precipitate use. Hence, things are necessarily true; there is no such thing as the falsity of things; there is no *ontological* falsity. When we call things false as we often do,—for we speak of false teeth, false whiskers, and false friends, to name but a few of a long list of such expressions,—we speak figuratively, not literally. For false teeth, false whiskers, and false friends are not teeth, whiskers, or friends at all; they are things which bear the appearance of teeth, whiskers, and friends, and so an unwary mind may be led to judge that they are really teeth, whiskers, and friends. Thus it is manifest that the falsity touches *the judgment* about things, not the things themselves. It is *logical* falsity, not *real* or *ontological* falsity.

There are, then, three types of truth: ontological truth, logical truth, and moral truth. In other words, we have truth of things, truth of knowledge about things, and truth of utterance or speech. But there are only two types of falsity: logical falsity, which consists in mistaken judgment; and moral falsity, which consists in telling lies.

Strictly speaking, there are no *degrees* of truth. A thing is true of necessity, for it is what it is. A judgment is true or it is false. An utterance is true or it is mendacious. There is, therefore, no comparing of truth and seeing it as *true, truer,* and *truest.* But here again we have a way of speaking as though truth could be parcelled out in degrees. We say, for example, "Your view of this matter seems truer than John's view." But what we mean is, "You seem to know more about this matter than John does," or "Your view is more extensive, more complete than John's." The degrees are in one's knowledge of truth, not in truth itself. We may always learn more about a thing, but our knowledge does not become truer as we advance; it becomes more ample. What we knew at first, if we had logical truth about it, remains true knowledge; our subsequent learning does not make the first truth truer.

There are, however, degrees of falsity. The full-grown tree which casts a shadow does not grow taller or shorter, but the shadow grows longer or deeper with the shifting, or the change of intensity, of light. Falsity is like the shadow; it has degrees of length and depth, but what casts the shadow remains unchanged. For falsity is all in the mind or in speech, whereas truth is based upon adamantine reality. The mind can be more deeply and deviously deceived; the lips can utter more and more details of falsehood. To take a new analogy, there is only one surface of the lake upon which the boat floats safely, but if it sinks, it may sink deeper and still deeper into the water. There are, therefore, degrees of falsity, but no degrees of truth.

c) The Mind and Truth

Philosophers list for us a litany of "states of the mind with reference to truth." Such states are the following:

1. Ignorance is absence of intellectual knowledge in a person. It is a negative state of the mind with reference to truth. Ignorance may be an absence of knowledge which ought to be present, such as ignorance of legal procedure in a judge; and then it is called *privative ignorance,* for it constitutes a *privation,* a hurtful lack, in the person who suffers it. Or ignorance may be the absence of knowledge which we have no right to expect to be present, as ignorance of legal procedure in a farmer who has never studied law; and then it is called *negative ignorance* for it is a simple negation or simple absence of knowledge. The absence of knowledge in beings that could not have it in any case is called *nescience* and not *ignorance.*

2. Doubt is the suspension of the mind between two contradictory judgments, between "It is" and "It isn't." When this indecision is owing to seemingly equal evidence on each side, it is called *positive doubt;* when it is owing to the absence of evidence for either side, it is *negative doubt.* A balance-scale stands even when there is an equal weight in each pan; it also stands even when there is no weight at all in either pan; here we have a telling illustration of positive and negative doubt.

3. Suspicion is the first inclination of the doubting mind to make a decision one way or the other. In doubt, the mind is like a man standing on a fence-top, perfectly erect, inclined to neither side. In suspicion, the mind *begins* to incline towards one judgment and away from its contradictory.

4. Opinion is the decision of a mind not wholly free of doubt. It is a decision; the mind gives judgment; but it is not a wholly confident and unhesitant judgment; there is in the mind some fear that maybe, after all, truth lies on the opposite side. It differs from doubt, for in doubt the mind stands hesitant; it differs from suspicion, for in suspicion the mind is inclined to make judgment but does not make it. Opinion is a clear decision and judgment of the mind, upon evidence that appears sufficient to win its assent, but it is not a judgment made with full and perfect confidence of being in the right.

5. *Certitude or certainty* is found in the mind's unhesitant assent to truth. It is a judgment wholly confident, completely without fear of being wrong. In doubt, a man "doesn't know what to say"; in suspicion, he "inclines to think"; in opinion he "believes it to be thus"; in certitude, he *knows*. But cannot a man be certain of what is not true? Yes, but we have a special technical name for such certitude; we call it *error*. The name *certitude,* strictly used, is reserved for the mind's unwavering assent *to known truth.*

It is manifest that the only knowledge that is worth winning is *certain knowledge of truth.* The human mind naturally wants *truth;* it wants true *knowledge;* it wants to hold true knowledge *with certainty.* Here in a single sentence we have the whole object of the science of criteriology; we may sum up that object in three words out of the sentence: knowledge, truth, certitude. Nay, we may sum it up in one word, *certitude;* for certitude means *certain knowledge of truth.* Hence all our discussion of the Critical Question will focus on *certitude.*

Summary of the Article

In this Article we have defined *truth,* and have distinguished three types of truth: *ontological truth* or *real truth* which is the truth of reality or of things; *logical truth* which is the truth of judgment, of thought, of knowledge; and *moral truth* which is the truth of speech. We have noted that the opposite of truth is *falsity,* which cannot exist in the ontological order (for things are what they are), but can exist in the logical and in the moral order.

We have seen that there are no *degrees* of truth, but that there are degrees of falsity, just as there are no degrees of variance in the straight line that runs from point A to point B, but there are endless degrees of variance of lines that run from point A and *miss* point B. We have listed various states of the mind with reference to truth: *ignorance, doubt, suspicion, opinion, certitude, error.* We have noticed that the Critical Question focusses upon *certain knowledge of truth,* or, in a word, upon *certitude.*

Article 2. Various Doctrines on Certitude

a) Skepticism; b) Idealism; c) Sensism; d) Traditionalism; e) Dogmatism.

a) Skepticism

Skepticism is the doctrine which denies the possibility of achieving certitude. It is called *absolute skepticism* if it denies that man can have even probability, that is, a justified *opinion,* about reality. It is called *qualified skepticism* if it accepts the possibility of attaining knowledge that is *probably* true.

After all, there can be only two fundamental doctrines about the possibility of achieving certitude, that is, about the value or trustworthiness of human knowledge. One of these doctrines holds that certitude is possible, the other holds that it is not possible. Between *skepticism,* on the one hand, and what is called (perhaps regrettably) *dogmatism* on the other, there is no room for new doctrines. Hence, every doctrine on certitude will be either *skeptical* in character or it will be *dogmatic.* We shall advert to this fact when we come to the description of the several doctrines we are to discuss.

Skepticism as a theory of knowledge, or rather as a theory of the non-existence of true knowledge, offers the following arguments:

(*a*) Our faculties,—that is, our knowing-powers,—often deceive us. Experience is proof sufficient of this fact. We may think we see a thing when as a fact we do not see it; we may judge that a distant mountain is ten miles off and then find to our surprise that it is thirty miles off; we may judge a wheel which whirls with great rapidity to be standing still; a child at its first cinema-show thinks the pictures are real persons. Since, then, our faculties are at least sometimes deceiving, we have no assurance in any instance that they are giving us truth. Just as a man who is known to be a liar cannot be trusted in any utterance, even if he be actually telling the truth, so our faculties are never to be trusted. In other words, we never can have *certitude*. Even if our faculties sometimes actually tell the truth, we have no means of *knowing* that this is the case. Therefore, the quest of certitude is vain. Man must be content to remain in ignorance or, at best, in doubt.

(*b*) We cannot know but that we are the creatures of a Power that delights to see us milling about hopelessly in tangles of doubt and error.

(*c*) To know a thing with certitude we must have proof or evidence that the thing is true. But then we must also have proof or evidence that the proof or evidence is reliable. And then we must have proof for this proof. And so we go on endlessly. Now, it is acknowledged on all hands that one cannot build a solid argument on an endless series of proofs. There cannot be a useful "progress unto infinity" in argument. There must be some solid starting-point, some absolute ground on which the whole edifice of evidence rests. But, as we have seen, there can be no such solid ground. Therefore, the mind cannot achieve certitude.

Such are the arguments of skepticism. We must look into them to see whether they are of any value. But, before all, we must notice this fact: the defender of skepticism asks us to accept his doctrine *that it is certain that there is no certitude*. He offers evidence for a doctrine *which denies the value of all evidence*. He uses the mind to work out the argument *that there is no use using the mind*. By his own confession, the skeptic is confounded as well as confuted. We may tell him that, by his own argument, skepticism is not a true and certain doctrine as he professes it to be.

In a word, the skeptic contradicts himself; one part of his doctrine cancels out the other, and the result is zero. A sincere skeptic has no recourse but silence. The minute he speaks to explain his doctrine he makes factual declaration of these things: that he certainly exists, and knows it; that he has certain knowledge of the doctrine he holds; that other people certainly exist to listen to him; that others have minds capable of being certainly influenced by what he has to say; that what he has to say is truth, that is, a thing to be grasped with certitude. Therefore, the skeptic cannot speak; he cannot express his doctrine without denying it; he cannot defend his position without showing it to be false. Only in absolute silence, in which he must doubt the existence of his own doubt, can the skeptic steal away from reality. For if a man has not even certitude of the meaning of his words, how shall he dare to ask us to listen to them?

Since skepticism is thus ruinously self-contradictory, we have no need to investigate its arguments for the purpose of refuting it. But we have need to investigate these arguments for our own enlightenment and to equip ourselves for the charitable task of keeping unwary minds from being taken in by them. Therefore we shall glance at them briefly.

(*a*) Our knowing-powers deceive us, says the skeptic. He is wrong. Our knowing-powers, used rightly, are infallible. When we are deceived, it is because we make a headlong judgment without waiting for our knowing-powers to bring in their evidence. Or we use our knowing-powers for purposes they were not meant to serve. Or (in case of the senses) we fail to make allowance for organic defects or for the conditions under which the knowing-powers should operate, like a color-blind man making decisions on tints and shades or a person matching colors under dim or tinted lights. Our faculties do not deceive us, but we frequently misuse our faculties. The man who "thinks he sees a thing" (as at a magician's trick show) when he does not see it, asks more of his eyes than they were given to report; for, as we shall see in a later part of our study, the sense of sight is for one essential purpose and no other, *the perceiving of colored surfaces.* Similarly, when we judge distances by the eye, we may be wrong, especially if we are in an atmosphere rarer or less rare than that in which our ordinary daily experience is gathered; but distance-judging is not the proper work of the sense of sight. Nor is it the first and proper business of the eye to discern rest and motion, nor to determine at once whether a cinema-image is a picture or a person. In all these cases, the deception is in the judgment of the mind, not in the eye or other senses, and it is there by our fault, not by the fault of the mind itself. We judge rashly, precipitately; we do not wait to test conclusions; we make them headlong. But we *could* wait, we *could* test, *we could find solid evidence and true certitude.* Therefore, the assertion of the skeptic that our knowing-powers deceive us, and the instances offered in proof of the assertion, come to nothing. This argument is manifestly valueless.

(*b*) Perhaps we are the creatures of a Power that delights to see us deceived. The sane answer to one "perhaps" is another "perhaps." We might dismiss this silly assertion by saying, "Perhaps not." But we need not be so abrupt. No normal man can look upon existence as a hopeless confusion, a milling about in toils of error and deception. Nature is constant; the farmer plants wheat in confidence that the crop will not turn out to be pineapples; the child grows into a man and not into a griffin. Our knowing-powers serve us well for business and even for pleasure; we can add up the bill at the grocer's and know when we have been given the correct change for the money we offer in payment. And why should a malign Power go to the bother of furnishing to man sense-organs of most wondrous design and delicacy, admirably adapted to what we call their normal use, if these things were to be utterly meaningless and if man could be plunged into witless miseries and contradictions without them? Besides, reason, as well as experience, convinces us past doubting that our Maker and Ruler is the First and the Supreme Being, who is Infinite

Goodness as well as Infinite Intelligence and Infinite Power; the notion of a malign First Being is absurd.

(*c*) There must be an endless series of proofs to establish certitude. This statement is simply not true. There are certain fundamental truths which need no proof, and which cannot have proof, for they are their own proof. These are *self-evident truths* which it is impossible either to doubt or to deny. These are lightsome truths as the sun is lightsome; and one needs no lantern or searchlight to go in search of the noonday sun or to identify it when it is discovered. These self-evident truths are the basis of all certitude; they give us the ultimate ground for evidence which skepticism mistakenly says we cannot find. In recognizing these truths the mind *by one and the same indivisible act* sees *the truth and the evidence or proof of the truth.* Such fundamental and inevitable truths are: (*1*) *the first fact,* which is the fact of one's own existence; (*2*) *the first condition,* which is the character of reason as capable of knowing truth by thinking it out; and (*3*) *the first principle* or *first guiding truth* (called "the principle of contradiction") which is the truth that a thing cannot be simultaneously existent and non-existent in the same way. These truths cannot be doubted or denied. Try, for example, to deny the fact of your own existence. Say, "I do not exist." Then what right have you to say "I"? What you say amounts to this, "I'm here to say I'm not here." Or try to doubt your existence. Say, "I doubt whether I'm here." Your words mean, "I am certain that I am here and that I am entertaining a doubt about my being here." Thus any attempt at doubt or denial of a self-evident truth results in an affirmation of the truth. Such a truth is inescapable. It is not only a truth which *contains* proof; it *is* its own proof which you cannot evade. Hence the statement of the skeptics that every truth requires a proof *other* than itself is a fallacy, and upon that fallacy the whole case for skepticism is wrecked and forever shattered.

But what of qualified skepticism, the skepticism which admits that man can attain to knowledge that is *probably* true and certain? Well, it hasn't a leg to stand on. For the man who says that the best we can achieve is probability is a man who denies certitude, and thus he is an absolute skeptic in spite of himself. If he cries wildly that he is not, and attempts to explain his position in such way as to give value to what he calls probability, then he is actually a dogmatist and not a skeptic at all. There is no middle ground between the positions described by the contradictory judgments, "We can achieve certitude" and, "We cannot achieve certitude." Since they are contradictories, these judgments exhaust the possibilities. For the rest, there is no conceivable probability which does not rest upon *things certainly known*. The man who says something is probable affirms the fact that something else is absolutely sure, just as the man who thinks it probable that the local politicians are a tricky lot, bases his opinion upon facts which he has certainly observed; the probability is in an interpretation of data which are not merely probable but certain.

b) Idealism

Idealism is a kind of blanket-term for all doctrines (and their name is legion) which in any way minimize reality and tend to turn *things* into *thoughts* or mental images, that is, to make reality a kind of dream in our own minds. Sometimes this sort of doctrine is called *subjectivism* (for the person who knows, or thinks he knows, is called the knowing *subject*), and sometimes it is given a special name by the man who professes it, as, for example, in the case of Kant who called it *criticism*. But all doctrines of whatever name which minimize reality and make things into thoughts or images or ideas in the knowing subject, are *idealistic* or *subjectivistic*. The student of this manual will be able to recall, or at least to page back and identify, many idealistic doctrines among those described in the First Part of the book.

It is manifest that idealistic doctrines are also *skeptical*. For if man's knowledge is subjective and not trans-subjective; if it is a home-product of the mind; if man is walking in a dream-world; then his certitudes about things are really not certitudes at all but errors, and certitude is unobtainable. And here we are back at the untenable position of skepticism.

In whatever form it may appear,—whether in the theories of Hume, Berkeley, Kant, Hegel, von Schelling, Fichte, or in the will-philosophies and power-philosophies of the later Germans from Schopenhauer and Nietzsche to Hitler, or even in the so-called practical doctrines of the pragmatists and the neo-realists, —idealism fails to come to grips with reality. Even sensism or positivism which in one way is the opposite of idealism is like it in another way; it fails to recognize a tremendous primal reality, the reality of mind as well as the reality of what the mind represents.

Idealistic doctrine cuts away its own foundations. For if reality is ultimately reducible to states of the mind, what basis have we for accepting as reliable or real the states of the mind? If the world is all a dream, is not the dreamer a part of the world and therefore a part of his own dream; and have we not then a dream *in the void* without a real dreamer? Surely there can be no more complete skepticism than this. Again, the idealist, like the skeptic, must be forever silent. For if he talks about reality, even to deny it, he affirms reality. The idealist supposes that his words have real meaning, and that his theories deal with something that is there, even as he endeavors to deny that it is there and to assert that it is all in his viewpoint, or all in his mind, or all in an unconscionable image.

There is one type of idealism (rightly called so since it minimizes the reality of common experience) known as *relativism* or the *relativity of truth.* This doctrine refuses to recognize the existence of solid reality as a knowable thing, and makes truth dependent upon "the way you look at it" or "the way you experience it." Relativism holds that what is true for one may not be true for all, or may not be true for one in all circumstances. Thus I may truly say that today is hot; but at the same moment in the far north an Eskimo may truly say that today is cold. All this is mere foolery. For manifestly any statement of concrete fact necessarily takes in the pertinent circumstances of that fact. What I say when I declare that today is hot is that *here and now* it is hot; so the Eskimo in his far abode says that *there and then* it is cold. There is no conflict in these statements; one does not deny the other. Neither I nor the Eskimo spoke for all times and places, but each for his own place and time. And what was said was true and eternally true; for unto eternity it remains true that in one precise place and at one precise time it was hot, and in another precise place at a precise time it was cold. As for truths of the rational order, such as the truth that two and two make four, or the truth that any effect must have an adequate cause or sum of causes, these truths are independent of concrete circumstances and are in no sense relative to place, time, or other material factor.

The student will be on the alert for the pernicious doctrine of relativism, and he will have many opportunities of noticing how prevalent among unthinking men is this idealistic theory. He will hear people talking of "religion suited to the needs of our times," as though religious truth were relative to the progress of centuries or the multiplication of mechanical devices or the tastes of men in employment and amusement. He will hear people say that certain teachers are men of "advanced thinking" as though truth were relative to some kind of foot-rule; he will hear of "liberal views" as though fact depended upon the way it is viewed, and were relative to the viewpoint. All such idealistic theory is tainted with the fundamental insanity of skepticism.

c) Sensism

Sensism (often identified with *Positivism* and *Empiricism*) is the doctrine which relies upon the senses, and minimizes the value of the reasoning mind. Thus, upon the face of things, sensism is the opposite of idealism. But we have seen that sensism is itself idealistic and subjectivistic inasmuch as it minimizes the reality of mind.

Sensism is, as a philosophy, wholly inarticulate. We have seen that the skeptic and idealist *dare* not talk, for they open their mouths only to contradict themselves. But the sensist *cannot* talk, for talk is an expression of reasoned thinking which, for the sensist, has no value.

Our senses are wondrous channels of knowledge. Their value is in no wise to be minimized. Without their service, intellectual knowledge would be unavailable in this life. But sanity demands that we recognize both senses and mind. For if it is only by the service of the senses that the mind can find materials to work upon, it is only by the mind that the value of the senses can be estimated and recognized. A man makes himself a cripple if his philosophy of left-footism denies the existence of the right foot, or if his theory of right-footism denies the existence of the left. The sane man is grateful for two feet, and he uses them both to walk in safety.

A sensist cannot express his doctrine in terms that are entirely of the sense order. For any expression of doctrine is an appeal to the mind, even if it comes through the senses. Hence, sensism is an unacceptable philosophy; it is unacceptable because it is impossible.

The laboratorian who relies upon test-tubes and physical analyses, and says that his task is merely one of observation and experiment; that he amasses data, but reaches no reasoned conclusion upon his findings, is not telling the truth. For one thing, he has some intelligible programme which directs his choice of experiments. For another, he has some rational scheme of collating his findings. It is, indeed, impossible for rational man to live or to experiment in a wholly sentient manner, excluding the mind and the value of its reasonings. For the rest, we are quite well aware that many, if not most, of the wild theories which startle the world every day or so, and are forgotten a day or so later, come bounding out of the laboratory which professes to fight shy of all theorizing or "indoctrination," and to concentrate on the amassing of data.

Of course, the sane laboratorian does not profess to be a philosopher, and happy is he if he can overcome the temptation to philosophize. But his science, to which we owe a great deal that makes for convenience and comfort, and even a great deal that makes for the extension of knowledge and the enlightenment of the mind, is taken by the sensist (who professes to be a philosopher) as an embodiment or expression of the sensist theory. We trust, says the sensist, the positive findings of the senses, and of experimental science; we deny the value of your reasonings, your metaphysics. Well, as we have seen, the sensist must offer reasons for the rejection of reason; he does, and they are inadequate as well as contradictory of his own thesis. The sensist must transcend sense, and even become metaphysical, for the purpose of casting a slur at metaphysics. In all this we observe (in the best scientific manner) the self-contradiction of skepticism, the "suicide of thought," the abandonment of all certitude even as the theory presents itself as certain.

d) Traditionalism

Traditionalism is a theory which asserts the incapacity of individual minds to reach truth with certitude. We must rest upon *the racial reason,* upon the strong reasoning power of the whole human race, and not upon the weak reasoning power of Tommy or Jane. Now, the reasoned certitudes of the race are handed on from age to age by the human *tradition;* hence the name of this theory.

If the minds of individual men were like the threads of a tapestry there might be some value in this theory. But the minds of men of successive generations are rather like the links of a chain; and no chain is stronger than its weakest link. A series of weak links will never make a strong chain. If you cannot rely upon individual reason, and the evidence it can discover and offer, you cannot rely upon an agglomeration of many individual reasons, for the character of the thing in either case is the same.

Even if the minds of men were like threads in a tapestry, you could only have a tapestry if each thread would bear some weight, however slight. But the traditionalist will not admit that the individual reason can achieve any certitude, however slight. You cannot make a tapestry of threads too weak to bear their own weight.

If the individual human mind has a value of zero in the establishing of certitude and in the recognizing of certitude with clear assent, then the agglomerate reasons of all mankind suffer the same defect. A sum of zeros, however large, still comes to zero.

It is true that what many men have recognized by reason as the truth stands so far recommended to the individual minds of people who come after them. Tradition has a value. But not as tradition merely. Its value lies in its recognizable reasonableness. In religion, Divine Tradition rests upon the recognizable authority of God, and gives the mind absolute certitude; but there is not here any question of Divine Tradition. Here we speak of human tradition.

There is a doctrine, allied to traditionalism, which declares that the human mind, as individual or in agglomeration, is incapable of knowing truth with certitude, and asserts that *all* certitude rests upon an original revelation made by God to man, and handed on by human tradition. That such a revelation and such a tradition are facts is plain from the history of human thought. But that *all* certitude, in every department of knowledge, rests on this tradition is not a fact. The theory which reposes all certitude upon the original divine revelation,—and which declares that man's certitude is always a certitude *of faith* in this revelation as given to our knowledge by tradition,—is called *fideism.* This doctrine falls, with traditionalism, under the arguments which show that the minimizing of the natural force and value of human reason below its normal limits is a form of skepticism and is therefore destructive of all value in human knowledge and is self-contradictory.

There is another doctrine, called *agnosticism,* which unwarrantedly limits the field of human knowledge, and declares that, for the rest, we must have human *faith.* The field of human knowledge is indeed limited. But it is not limited except where there is no evidence to work with and to rest upon. Agnosticism arbitrarily limits knowledge even where evidence is available. Some agnostics are idealists and say we cannot have certitude except about our own subjective states; some are sensists and say we cannot be certain of anything that lies beyond the range of the senses. Both sets of agnostics admit that some reality lies beyond these limited spheres, and that we do well to *believe* in it, but that we cannot have *reasoned certitude* about it. Agnosticism falls with idealism and sensism, and ultimately with skepticism. It does not demonstrate its doctrines; it simply declares them.

On the other hand, there is a doctrine that the human mind is capable of knowing all reality thoroughly, and that what cannot be so known is simply not existent. This theory is called *rationalism* and ought to be called *irrationalism.* For the human mind, like the human eye, can take in much and see it clearly, but it cannot take in all. There are *hows* and *whys* that lie outside the range of reason just as there are bodily objects that lie outside the range of vision. Indeed, in every question reason must admit the atmosphere of mystery. But mystery is not fog. It is the reach of fact which cannot be fully *explained* by the human mind.

e) Dogmatism

The word *dogmatism* has a harsh and unwelcome sound in modern ears. But this is merely an accident of speech or rather of the current fashion in the use of words. We here employ the word *dogmatism* in its ancient Greek meaning of *thinking*. And a *dogma,* which literally means "a thought," is here employed to mean a self-evident truth. Dogmatism is the doctrine which holds that the human mind, *recognizing, with certitude, self-evident truths,* can build upon them a body of knowledge that is certainly true.

The critical question, put as an actual interrogation, is this, "Can the mind of man achieve certitude?" Notice, it is not, "Can the mind of man achieve *all* certitude." Sanity compels us to acknowledge the fact of limitation in a nature essentially limited. But can we have certitude; can we attain to true and certain knowledge? The skeptic says we cannot. The idealist, the sensist, the agnostic, the traditionalist, the fideist, all say that we can have a sort of broken or incomplete certitude in certain fields. The dogmatist says, "Yes, the mind can have certitude wherever it discovers solid evidence for its judgments."

Dogmatism is a doctrine which finds the mind capable of *squaring with reality;* in other words, of obtaining logical truth. Dogmatism does not merely assert that certitude is obtainable; it does not even rest on assertion that self-evident truths are known with certitude. It *investigates.* It looks for *evidence.* And it sanely accepts evidence. In the judgments which the mind makes necessarily and spontaneously, dogmatism seeks for evidence and finds it in the judgments themselves; it finds that, as a fact, the subject and the predicate of such a judgment are identical, and that alien proof is therefore neither needed nor available. In other judgments, dogmatism looks for evidence in causes, in explanations, in proofs which it weighs and applies by the strict rules of logic. It thinks, it reasons calmly, clearly, consistently, legitimately. It requires evidence suited to the nature of the facts in each case, and sufficient to establish these facts if they are really facts. And it looks only for that degree of certitude which the nature of the facts indicates as possible. Dogmatism never makes blind assertions. It never makes affirmations or denials which the mind is required to swallow without question or investigation. First and last, dogmatism is *the doctrine of the possibility of certitude as obtainable by the mind through the presence and power of objective evidence.*

Thus dogmatism recommends itself to the mind as eminently sane. It involves no self-contradiction as opposed doctrines do. It rests on no blind assumption. It makes no unwarranted limitations or extensions in the field of knowledge. It attaches no value to mere assertion. It seeks to come into clear alignment with reality. It stands alone among all theories or doctrines on human knowledge in the fact that it offers a rounded and complete treatment of the Critical Question. Therefore, it stands alone in its intrinsic claims for acceptance as the true theory of knowledge.

Now, the certitude which dogmatism shows to be possible, is of three chief *degrees*. There are no degrees in *truth,* but certitude is the mind's hold upon truth, and there are degrees in such a hold. Not in its *firmness;* for the least infirmity in the hold of mind upon truth, the least wavering, would destroy certitude and put the mind into a state of *opinion*. The degrees of certitude are degrees in the compelling force of the evidence upon which certitude rests. As we have said, there are three such degrees. First, the mind's assent may be absolutely compelled because the predicate of a judgment is found to be identified completely or partially with the subject. When once the mind knows what is meant by a circle, and by roundness, the mind judges with certitude and necessity that "a circle is round." There is no possibility, even by a miracle, of a circle being anything but round, for roundness is of the very essence of a circle. When the mind recognizes such a judgment its certitude is called *absolute* or *metaphysical*. When, however, the evidence is not essential and intrinsic, but rests upon something other than the essence of the things judged, the certitude is not absolute but is *relative to the evidence* in the case. Now, relative certitude is of two types, *physical* and *moral*. When the evidence of our certain judgment is the consistency of the physical universe, we have physical certitude; thus I have certitude that the apple tree will bear apples and not (barring an ingrafted branch) plums. But my certitude is not absolute. I recognize the fact that the Creator might intervene to make the tree bear plums. Physical certitude is, therefore, the certitude that such a thing is and must be *unless a miracle intervenes*. Moral certitude is based upon the evidence of normal human conduct. I am certain that a mother loves her child, even though it is possible, without a miracle, than an unnatural mother should detest her child. All these types of certitude,—absolute, physical, moral,—are types of real certitude, not of opinion. In each type we have the wholly unwavering assent of the mind to known truth.

But the evidence by which the truth is known is in one case *metaphysical or absolute* necessity, in the second case, it is *physical* necessity, and in the third case, it is *moral* necessity. I have metaphysical certitude when my certitude is founded upon the essences of things; I have physical certitude when it is founded upon the natural mode of action of things around me in this world; I have moral certitude when it is founded upon the mode of free activity characteristic of normal men. My certitude that a circle is round or that a man is a rational animal is metaphysical or absolute certitude. My certitude that a dead man will not come back to earthly life is physical certitude. My certitude that a man who knows what he is talking about, and who is no liar, is actually telling the truth is a moral certitude. In passing, we may advert to the fact that the truths of the Catholic Faith are known by Catholics with metaphysical or absolute certitude, for they are founded on the very Essence of God. Our certitude of what is known by human faith, however,—such as the facts of history,—is only moral certitude. Dogmatism seeks the degree of certitude which is necessary and sufficient according to the nature of the case. It could not reasonably seek metaphysical certitude for the facts of history, nor physical certitude for the free acts of a man.

Summary of the Article

In this Article we have weighed and criticized various types of doctrine on the possibility of achieving certitude. We have considered *skepticism, idealism, relativism, sensism, traditionalism, fideism, rationalism, agnosticism,* and *dogmatism.* We have found that the one doctrine which meets the requirements of reality and human reason, and which involves no self-contradiction or unwarranted assertion is the Scholastic doctrine known as *dogmatism.* We have studied a brief description of dogmatism, and have seen that it shows the possibility of achieving certitude. We have noticed the various *degrees of certitude.*

Article 3. The Sources of Certitude

a) Evidence; b) Evidence of the Senses; c) Evidence of the Mind; d) Authority.

a) Evidence

Evidence is the light of truth shining into the mind and making it see. It is the *understandable object or thing* as *clearly known.*

Sometimes evidence is *immediate,* that is, sometimes it requires no thinking out, no *medium* of reasoning through which it can be made to appear. It appears at once and directly, even as a blazing light appears at once and directly, and we need no other light with which to seek and find it. An immediately evident truth is called *self*-evident. Thus it is immediately evident to the mind that "a totality is greater than any of its parts." The very meaning of "totality" and "part" necessitates this judgment.

Sometimes truth does not immediately appear and must be sought by other light than that which *manifestly* abides in it. Thus the schoolboy's knowledge that the sum of the angles of a triangle is 180° is not immediately evident, but must be worked out through the *medium* of reasoning. Evidence that must thus be worked out is called *mediate* evidence.

Evidence, to be of value, must be *objective,* or, more accurately, *trans-subjective.* It must not be the mere feeling or the mere viewpoint or the mere taste of the person (called *the subject*) who seeks it or is influenced by it; it must not be *subjective. Objective evidence* is the ultimate criterion of truth, the ultimate basis of certitude. For it is the truth "right there looking at you"; it is reality unfolded before the mind; it is the light shining from reality into the understanding and making the mind see.

b) Evidence of the Senses

The channels of knowledge for man are *the senses* and *the mind.* These bring in their findings; they note and accept *evidence;* they are sources of truth and certitude.

Man's knowing begins with the senses, and with the exterior senses. It does not *end* there, but it necessarily *begins* there. The mind takes the findings of the senses and peers beneath their materiality and their limitations to grasp essences and form ideas, and from ideas to form other ideas, and with ideas to make judgments and reasonings. But it all *begins* with the action of the senses upon this bodily world.

There are two classes of senses, *exterior senses* (commonly listed as five: sight, hearing, smell, taste, touch or feeling) and *interior senses* (listed as four: sense-consciousness, sense-memory, imagination, instinct).

Each sense lays hold of reality in its own way. That is, each sense *has its own object*. The external senses take in bodily reality (in cognitional *image* or *species*) but no one sense takes in all bodily reality.

The object of a sense is *proper* if that one sense alone can perceive this object. It is *common* if two or more senses can grasp it. The sense of sight or vision can perceive actual physical color, or, —if one choose to be more accurate,—the reflection of refracted light from bodily surfaces. No other sense can perceive color. Color (which is fundamentally *light*) is therefore the proper object of the sense of sight. But both the sense of sight and the sense of touch can perceive bodily motion; I can *see* that a wheel is turning, or I can place a hand upon it and *feel* the motion. So also with the shape of a body; I can see that a ball is round, or I can take it in my hands and feel its roundness. Thus shape and local movement are *common* objects of sense.

Both *proper* and *common* objects of sense are perceived *in themselves*. By experience the senses also learn to grasp objects which are not themselves perceivable by the senses employed; these objects are said to be perceived *accidentally*. Thus a man can perceive that an apple is sour by tasting it; he perceives the sourness in itself. But a man who knows apples may be able to *see* that the apple is sour because his experience tells him that apples of that size, color, and kind are sour apples; he sees the sourness, not in itself, for it is not visible; he sees the sourness *accidentally* by reason of its known association with what he sees.

Now, the senses are to be judged, in respect to their reliability, upon their *proper* action; upon the fact that they do or fail to do what they are manifestly framed for doing. When a single sense is used upon a *common* object, or when the senses are used for *accidental* perception, we have surely no right to cry "deceit!" if the judgment founded on such sensings turns out to be false. The senses are wonderfully versatile, and we tend to use them upon other than their proper objects, but we have no right in the world to demand precise and accurate reports from senses so used.

Rightly used, the senses are infallible. And the senses are rightly used when, and *only* when, the following requirements are observed: (*a*) A sense must be employed upon its proper object; (*b*) the sense-organ must be sound, not defective; (*c*) the medium in which the sense is used must be suitable; (*d*) the proper object itself must be so presented to the sense-organ as to lie within the normal range of that organ's activity; (*e*) the sense-organ must be given sufficient time for its normal function.

The assertion that, so used, the senses are infallible is thus established: All human knowledge acquired in this life begins with the action of the external senses, and rests upon sensation (that is, sense-action) as upon its ultimate foundation. If this foundation be insecure, no human knowledge is reliable. And if no human knowledge is reliable, we are at once enmeshed in the insane self-contradictions of skepticism, which is a wholly impossible position. Therefore, we are compelled to acknowledge the reliability of the senses. For the rest, the senses, *rightly used, in accordance with the requirements noted,* are found to square with reality; the test of experience finds in them no deceit, no contradiction, no twist or difficulty. And reason compels us to acknowledge the justice of the five conditions or requirements for the right use of the senses.

The senses therefore *can* be the source of valid evidence; the senses *can* be the remote source of intellectual certitude. The fact that judgment based on sense-findings is sometimes erroneous is owing always to one of two causes: either the findings are not genuine findings (because the conditions requisite for infallible sense-action are not met), or the evidence of the sense-findings is not properly weighed by an attentive mind.

c) Evidence of the Mind

The student is here requested,—nay, implored,—to turn back to the First Part of this manual (*Chap. III, Art. 1, c*) and review the "Question of Universals" there discussed in some detail. This done, he may bravely carry on with the work now in hand.

An *idea* or *concept* is the representation or the re-presence in the mind of the essence of a reality. Ideas or concepts are compared by the mind, and used as the subjects and the predicates of *judgments*. Judgments are thoughts. Judging is thinking. But judgments are not always available upon the simple comparison of a subject-idea and a predicate-idea. Sometimes they must be worked out from other judgments so connected as to lead to them as necessary conclusions. This working out process, this extension of thinking, is called *reasoning*.

The question now before us is this: are judging and reasoning reliable; do these processes present acceptable and even compelling *evidence* to the mind so as to beget *certitude?*

To answer this question we must proceed with great exactness. The judging and the reasoning (that is, the *thinking*) here to be investigated are fundamentally a matter of ideas or concepts. If the ideas are truly representative of reality, then the relations among those ideas are surely capable of supplying evidence for certain judgings and reasonings. Our question comes then to this: are ideas actually representative of reality?

We assert that they are, and for these reasons. (*a*) Ideas are legitimately derived from sense-findings. Now, as we have seen, sense-findings are, when rightly gathered, truly reliable. Therefore, ideas are reliable and can be used in judgments which (again, when rightly formed) express truth with certitude. (*b*)

No doctrine which denies the objectivity or trans-subjectivity of ideas is admissible. For such doctrines, though various in name, come always into two classes: those that proclaim that ideas do not perfectly represent reality, and those that declare that ideas are a home-product of the mind and are turned out of a kind of mental mill without reference to reality. But if the first type of theory be true, then ideas do represent reality, though imperfectly, and the case is ours. If the second type be true, then we must accept *subjectivism* or *idealism,* which we have seen, a few pages back, is an inadmissible theory which involves a fundamental skepticism.

Ideas are valid. In judging, the mind accepts the evidence which the ideas afford. When the mind takes other evidence than that which the ideas themselves afford, it judges by reason of *authority,* of which we have yet to speak. Here we consider only the fact that the mind can find evidence *intrinsic* to ideas. Of course, the mind may make erroneous judgments, but these are made through accidental causes, chief of which are *presumption* which leads the mind to judge upon ideas that are obscure (that is, to judge without really knowing the evidence) and *a headlong impatience* for reaching judgment without due labor (again, without knowing and weighing the evidence). Erroneous judgments come, not from evidence, but from the lack of it or the failure to take it. But when the mind proceeds with caution, prudence, and honest effort, there is no error.

Ideas are built upon evidence gathered from the senses. Judgments are built upon evidence presented in ideas. Reasonings are built upon evidence afforded by judgments. Now, if the first foundation of all this building (that is, sense-action and sense-findings) be secure and solid, as it *can* be secure and solid; if the work of building be legitimately done according to the requirements which the nature of the process indicates, there can be no sane doubt about the security and solidity of the whole edifice. In a word, intellectual evidence, rightly taken, is a valid source of certitude.

d) AUTHORITY

Authority as a source of certitude is *reliable testimony*. It is evidence gathered from the words of a reliable speaker or writer, or from such works of man as reliably express a fact or a doctrine.

Can testimony of this sort be relied upon? Reason declares that it can when it meets certain definite requirements. That the source of testimony (the *witness*, or the thing which embodies an expression of fact or doctrine) be of value, it is required: (*a*) that the testimony be clearly understood; (*b*) that the witness be *thoroughly informed;* and (*c*) that the witness be *truthful.*

In a word, if you understand exactly what a man says and what he means; if you know, or he can show, that he is telling the truth, and that he knows what he is talking about, you reasonably accept his word. You *believe* him; you put *faith* in him. You have the *moral* certitude which is called *the certitude of faith,* although, where there is question of merely human testimony, you cannot have *absolute* or philosophical certitude which is called *the certitude of science.*

Authority offers evidence which recommends itself to reason and which invites the will to issue the command, "Accept this." Human authority cannot compel assent, as *intrinsic* evidence does; human authority is always *extrinsic evidence.* Once you know what a circle is and what roundness is, you cannot refuse to be certain that a circle is round; the evidence is intrinsic; it is right *in* the ideas of "circle" and "roundness." But if a man tells you that a large building is perfectly circular (a thing you cannot safely judge by merely looking at the building) you want to know something about that man before you take his word. You want to know whether he is a liar, or a joker, or a person stating a fact, and you want to know how he knows the building is circular. But if you are satisfied that he *has* knowledge of what he reports, and that he is neither a liar nor a joker, you realize that, while you could stubbornly refuse to believe him, it would be silly to do so. You realize that *in the circumstances* it would be imprudent to cling to doubt. You have here the least and lowest sort of evidence from authority; it is called "the imprudence of doubt." It can give you a true moral certitude, however.

Now, suppose you have knowledge that the man who tells you the building is circular is the architect who designed the building. Suppose, too, you have his word confirmed by the contractor who controlled the work of building, and also by the owner who made the specifications. Suppose, too, you have the word of other men who have measured and tested the building for circularity. You have then *a series* of witnesses to a fact, and these lend increased power to the evidence, not by reason of their number, but by the fact that they check and confirm one another. As a consequence, you are no longer impelled to accept the evidence by a mere imprudence of doubt in the circumstances; you have *positive* evidence which urges you to accept it. You have a much stronger basis for certitude than the simple imprudence of doubt. Still, you could refuse it; for in matters of human faith, in points of moral certitude, the mind assents to evidence only under the orders of the will; for this reason faith is sometimes poetically described as "a genuflection of the will."

In passing, we must notice a valuable contrast between human faith and divine faith, that is, between faith accepted on the word of man and faith accepted on the Word of God. In both types of faith *the will* plays a part, for the will must command, permit, or refuse the mind's consideration of the extrinsic evidence which we call *the motives of credibility*. But once these motives are considered by the mind and judgment is passed, the two types of faith are seen to be quite different. For *once we know that God has spoken and that we have His true word,* we have intrinsic and compelling evidence which begets *metaphysical* certitude. But the evidence of authority in the case of human faith remains extrinsic and non-compelling, and the best it can beget in the mind is *moral* certitude. The reason for this difference lies in the fact that God's very Essence is Truth; God cannot deceive or be deceived. But man's essence is not truth; man can be deceived and man can deceive. Now, certitude that is based upon the essences of things is metaphysical certitude; it is certitude that the thing known or believed must be so and cannot be otherwise even by a miracle.

The most noteworthy expressions or embodiments of testimony are what we are told orally, what is written in history, and what is memorialized in statues, coins, relics, inscriptions, etc. These types of testimony are known as *tradition, history,* and *monuments.* They are valuable in so far as they meet the tests of human authority, that is, in so far as they can be shown to be the testimony of *one who knows,* and of *one who speaks truly,* and of *one who is clearly understood.* When they meet these tests, the three types of human authority or testimony are reliable *objective evidence* and a true source of certitude.

Much if not most of our knowledge is based upon the objective evidence of *authority,* of *testimony.* All historical knowledge is so evidenced, and indeed much scientific knowledge even in the realm of the laboratory. For each experimental scientist cannot spend his life repeating the experiments made by his predecessors. Now, if authority is thus commonly accepted as the source of certitude, if the demands of daily life make it imperative that it be so accepted, if its acceptance does not bring us into conflict with reality but serves us smoothly in our dealings with reality, then it proves itself authentic stuff. It is to be accepted as a reliable source of moral certitude; to reject it stubbornly would be merely silly.

However, much deceit is in the world. Historians can make mistakes; nay, historians can lie, and they sometimes do. Men may speak out of their ignorance or their malice; they may embalm their mistakes and their deceits in lasting works and printed books. Yet all this does not invalidate our argument that human authority *can be* and often *is* the source of true certitude. For we have means of testing the reliability of testimony. What a witness says can be checked and rechecked against other testimony, against the witness of contemporaries, against facts discovered by patient research. And if all truth which relies on human testimony cannot be thus established, at least a great deal of it can be. In the patient and painstaking application of the tests for credibility we can, for instance, know the major facts of history. As to historical *circumstances,* those lesser facts, we are often left hopeless of achieving true certitude.

On the one hand, then, we must not be gullible, and take every statement, especially every printed statement, as proof of the truth of what is stated. On the other hand, we cannot reasonably refuse to accept the tested evidence of tested witnesses.

A final word. We live in a credulous age, and its babyish credulity is large in direct ratio to its smug conviction that it is a learned and an enlightened age. We are too apt to accept unquestioningly any evidence that is offered, especially if it purports to come from "experts," that eerie modern band of soothsayers. We are all too ready to believe firmly in "anything we see in the papers" or anything that is told to us by men who broadcast news by radio. As a consequence, much of what we think is our true and certain knowledge is really opinion, and often very shaky opinion. The cant words, "science," "modern views," "progressive thinking," "experts," "leaders," "reliable sources" and so on, easily deceive us. Although we think ourselves hardheaded and clear-minded, we are in fact the most bewildered and bamboozled generation that the world has ever known. For modern agencies of communication are so multiplied, that from every side, from every angle, come shouting voices that order us about, and plead with us, and make up "propaganda" for us, and offer to "digest" news and literature for us, and urge us, and press us, and bring us under stresses and influences and tendencies. We have need now, as never before, to subject human testimony to rigid and searching inquiry; to know, before we believe, that the testimony is straight, that we understand it in its plain meaning, and that the witness is not a teller of lies or a clever twister of truths.

Summary of the Article

In this Article we have learned the meaning of *evidence.* We have seen that *objective evidence,* which can be *intrinsic,* or *extrinsic,* is *the ultimate source of certitude,* and *the ultimate criterion of truth.* We have investigated the *senses,* the *mind,* and *authority* as fonts of evidence and consequently of certitude. We have tried to establish the value of these fonts. We have noticed some sources of mistaken or falsified evidence which are likely to deceive the unwary mind.

Article 4. Scientific Certitude and its Acquisition

a) Science; b) Method.

a) Science

The Latin word *scientia* which we transliterate as *science* means "true and certain knowledge based on intrinsic evidence."

First and foremost, *science* is *certain knowledge in the mind;* and the reason this knowledge is *certain* is that the mind has a grasp of *how* and *why* the facts that it knows must be so. Further, this *how* and *why* are not furnished by human authority or by direct sense-experience. They are supplied, mediately or immediately, by the searching quest of reason. Science is *"knowledge* that is *certain* because *evidenced* by causes and reasons."

We may be *certain* of a thing we know by direct sense-experience; we may be *certain* of a thing about which a reliable person has informed us; but in these cases, while we have certitude, we have not *science.* Only when we can give some reasoned account of what we know, and of how and why we know it must be so, have we *science.* Thus *science* is another name for *scientific certitude* or *scientific knowledge.* A schoolboy may know that a triangle has angles that add up to 180° because he reasonably accepts the word of his teacher or of the textbook that this is a fact. He has knowledge, and indeed certain knowledge, but not science or scientific knowledge. His certitude is *the certitude of human faith* and not *the certitude of science.* But when the schoolboy has worked out the theorem about the sum of angles; when he has understood the whole problem and every step of its solution, he knows the truth in a new way. For he not only knows *the fact* that the sum of the angles of a triangle is 180°, but he also sees the *reasons* for the fact; he sees *how* it is so, and *why* it must be so. In a word, he now has scientific knowledge or scientific certitude of the fact.

The word *science* is also used *objectively* to indicate the recorded findings of persons who have achieved scientific certitude. Thus when the schoolboy tells us that he is "studying science" we know he means to tell us that he is studying books, or lessons designed by a teacher, in which *certainly evidenced data* are set forth for him to learn. In our day, this objective and general use of the term *science* ordinarily indicates *experimental* science; when the schoolboy says he is "studying science" we think at once of physics, or chemistry, or astronomy, or biology, or a hodge-podge of all these called *general science.* But this accidental employment of a term must not blind us to its fuller meaning. For *science,* in its full objective meaning, is the whole body of ascertained and reasoned truths which human reason has established as truths and has systematized and arranged, no matter what various fields of speculation or experiment such arrangement may entail. And each specific department of that universal body of reasoned and certain knowledge is *a* science. *A science* is, therefore, a body of *related data* set forth *in an orderly manner* which is marked by *completeness* and by *the consistent manifestation of the causes and reasons* which justify each step of its development. In this sense, biology is a science; criteriology is a science; philosophy is a science.

Sciences are of various types. *Speculative* or *theoretical* sciences enrich the mind with truth and certitude, but do not point on to anything that is to be done; *practical* sciences equip the mind with knowledge that points on to action; *experimental* sciences gather their data by laboratory methods; *rational* sciences are developed by the use of reasoned principles; *theological* science is developed according to revealed truth; *physical* sciences deal in some manner with the bodily world; *mathematical* sciences deal with pure quantity; *metaphysical* sciences deal with real but non-material being; *logical* science deals with the mental processes and their fruits or achievements; *moral* science deals with free and responsible human conduct.

Each science has a *material object* and a *formal object.* The material object of a science is the subject-matter of the science, the subject with which it deals or of which it treats. The formal object is the precise aim, point of view, or aspect with which the science treats its material object. The formal object of a science *specifies* it, gives it its character as a distinct science among other sciences in the same general field, that is, among sciences that have the same material object.

b) Method

Method is an English form of the Greek *met'-hodos* which means "a way after." Method is a way after truth, a reasonable and orderly procedure in the attaining of truth and certitude. It is a seemly mode of acquiring truth.

The chief types of method are the *deductive* method and the *inductive* method. The deductive method develops truth by working from general principles to particular instances and applications of these principles. The inductive method works from particular data to build up general principles. These methods are not in opposition. They are supplementary. Some sciences require, by their nature, more of the deductive than the inductive method; other sciences are, by their nature, largely restricted to the use of the inductive method. The fashion of regarding the inductive method as the sole instrument of science is merely silly and impertinent unless the term *science* be unreasonably limited in meaning (as it usually is today) to indicate only experimental or laboratory science. But, with reference to learning in general, the two methods are like the two feet of a pedestrian; he gets on safely, gracefully, and comfortably by the use of *both.*

Different types of sciences have different general requirements, but it is possible to formulate certain inclusive rules governing all methods. Such rules are the following:

1. Proceed from the easy to the difficult; from the simple to the complex; from what is well known to what is less known.

2. The procedure must be continuous, not broken by gaps or jumps; the connection of points and their logical order must be observed and made manifest.

3. The available grade of certitude (moral, physical, absolute) must be sought, and not a higher grade; failure here renders the method inept.

4. The procedure must be clear and not obscured by prolixity, involved language, complicated style; the point of enquiry must be precise and perfectly recognized, and throughout the development of the investigation it must be held steadily in view.

Summary of the Article

In this brief Article we have studied the meaning of *science* as scientific knowledge, and as the body of knowable truths available to man. We have listed various types of sciences. We have indicated the meaning of *the object* of a science. We have discussed *method* or the orderly procedure of mind in the quest of scientific knowledge. We have mentioned *deductive* method and *inductive* method as supplementary types, and we have set down some general laws of method.

CHAPTER III

THE ONTOLOGICAL QUESTION

The Ontological Question is the question of *reality* in its most general, most abstract, most profound meaning. It is the question of *being,* that is, of *being as such,* and not of being as it stands determinate in this nature or that nature or the other nature. It is the question of being or reality stripped of the limitations that come of materiality, that is, of bodiliness or of dependence on bodily things. Hence, it is the question of *non-material real being.* Here we have the heart of metaphysics, and metaphysics is the heart of philosophy. For philosophy is the ultimate science of *all things,* of *all reality,* and here we have all reality drawn into a mighty focus and seen as a single thing, as *being.* The department of philosophy which answers the Ontological Question is known as *Ontology* or *Fundamental Metaphysics.*

This Chapter is divided into the following four Articles:

Article 1. The Nature of Being
Article 2. The Properties of Being
Article 3. The Classification of Being
Article 4. The Emergence of Created Being

Article 1. The Nature of Being

a) Metaphysics; b) Being; c) Determinants of Being.

a) Metaphysics

It is most important that the pupil learn early and learn well the precise meaning of this term *metaphysics.* For there are many, even among the learned, who use the word amiss, and misuse gives us reason to suspect the presence of misunderstanding.

Metaphysics literally means *after-physics*. And *physics* here means no laboratory science of bodies with mass and inertia. It means *natures*. The Greek *physis* is the same as the Latin *natura* or the English *nature,* and it means *a working essence*. Now, the *essence* of a thing is its fundamental make-up, its basic character as such a thing. And when this essence is looked upon as the source and font of activities or operations, it is called a *nature*. Thus, if you want to know the essence of a thing, you look up its definition; its definition tells you what it *is*. But when you know its nature, you know what it *does* or *can do*. The essence of a human being, for instance, is a substantial compound of body and soul. The nature of a human being makes this substantial compound of body and soul the source of all activities that properly belong to a human being: growing, sensing, thinking, willing, etc. We do not say that it is *essential* to man to think; we do say that it is *natural* to man to think. Nature is *essence as the source of operations*.

Now, there are many essences in the world around us,—plants, animals, human beings, lifeless things. Each of these essences has its proper activities, and, in view of these, each essence is a *nature* or *physis*. And, since it is this bodily world that first engages our attention and is the scene of our immediate experience, we speak of the things in this world as belonging to *the physical order*. This, be it understood, is a cramped use of the term *physical,* for *physical,* taken literally, refers to any *physis* (or *nature* or *working essence*) whether it be bodily or non-bodily. But, as we say, the phrase *the physical order* is employed to designate this world of bodily things. Hence any study, any science, of things in this bodily universe is called a physical study, *a physical science*. Now, there are things which the mind notices here in the bodily world which are manifestly not limited to this world but belong to the non-bodily world as well, that is, to the world of spiritual things and to the world as abstractly known. For instance, the term *substance* (which means a reality that is existible as *itself,* and not as a mere mark or qualifier of some other thing) is not necessarily limited to bodies. We can conceive of *spiritual* substance as easily as of *bodily* substance. Again, a thing which is *understood* is transferred, so to speak, into the knowing mind; it is represented there in idea or concept; that is, it is *re-present* there. The *idea itself* is a mental image; we are not talking of the idea itself, however. We are now considering *the thing as it exists* in the knowing mind through the instrumentality of the idea. Manifestly this cognitional existence (or *intentional* existence, as it is called) is not the same as the *physical* existence of a thing known; but it is a *real* existence none the less. My idea of *tree,* as *an idea,* is in and from the mind; it is a *logical* being, not a *real* being. But my knowledge of tree in and through the idea *tree* is knowledge of *reality;* it is *real* knowledge; I know *real being;* and I know it by reason of the fact that *tree* is stripped by mental abstraction of all limitation which makes each tree the one individual bodily thing it is. For my knowledge of *tree* holds good of any tree, of every tree, regardless of size, botanical kind, location, or even actual existence since it holds good of every *possible* tree. In a word, though a tree is bodily in *the physical order* (or the order of bodily things) and though it is sheerly mental in *the logical order* (or order of ideas) it is *real* in the order of *things or realities abstractly known.* Now, the *realities* (and hold hard to that term *realities*) which can be found not only in the bodily world or the physical order, but also in the supra-physical order, whether this be the spiritual order of substances, or the order of realities known in a supra-material way, are said to belong to *the metaphysical order.* And a science of these things is *a metaphysical science.*

Metaphysics, as the name of a science, means the science of *non-material real being.* We have seen that such being is either a spiritual substance, or a bodily thing which is stripped of materiality by abstraction; it may also be any being, substantial or accidental, which exists or has influence in the field of bodies and non-bodies alike and hence is not limited to the material. *Substance* is a metaphysical term; *cause* is a metaphysical term;

such terms also are *essence, accident, relation,* and many, many others. For a substance can be material or it can be spiritual and is still a *substance;* thus substance *is not held exclusively to the material or physical order,* and is, in so far, non-material; and it indicates *reality,* not a mode of being in the mind: hence it is both *non-material* and *real,* and is, in itself, a *metaphysical* term and concept. *Cause* can have place among bodily realities, spiritual realities, and can be traced also in mathematical relations, and in mental relations which are non-mathematical; *cause* can exist among substances, among accidents. It is not held down, therefore, to the order of things material; that is, it is *non-material.* Yet it is *real;* it is conceived as a reality, and where it exists, it exists as a reality. It belongs to the order, not of this *physis,* or of that *physis,* or of the other *physis,* but sweeps up and over and inclusively upon all. It comes *after* the limited *physes;* it is *meta*-physical; it is *metaphysical.* And so with the other examples mentioned. All the terms noted are not so *inclusive* as the term *cause,* but it is clear that all of them are free from the limitations which would hold them exclusively applicable in the realm of bodies; hence we say they are *non-material;* and they indicate *reality;* they are non-material and real, and therefore they are *metaphysical.*

Metaphysics, therefore, is the science of non-material real being. Now, the Greek word *on* (stem, *onto-*) means *being;* and the termination *-logy* suggests *science.* And so the fundamental part of metaphysics, which deals with being *as such,* has been given the name which means "the science of being," that is, the name *ontology.* The other metaphysical parts of philosophy (*theodicy* which studies non-material real Infinite Being, and that part of *criteriology* which studies universals or realities present to real knowledge) belong with *ontology* to the realm of *metaphysics.* The other parts of philosophy (*logic* which deals with mental being; *cosmology* and *psychology* which deal with bodily being, non-living and alive; and *ethics* which deals with moral being) are truly *philosophical* but not *metaphysical.* In *all* departments of philosophy we use terms that are metaphysical, and we apply principles that are metaphysical, but this does not justify the use (far too common even among Scholastic writers and teachers) of the word *metaphysical* as a synonym for *philosophical.*

Our present concern is the Ontological Question, and in discussing it we build up in our minds the science of *ontology,* a truly *metaphysical science.*

b) BEING

The term *being* means *thing, reality.* It means anything that exists or can be thought of as existing.

The Latin term for *being* is the coined word *ens. Ens* has a strength that is lacking in the English term *being.* Perhaps this is because *ens* is coined (for *it would be* the present participle of the Latin verb *esse* "to be," *if that verb had a present participle,* which, as a matter of fact, it has not), and is not a term in constant current use as the English *being* is. *Ens* is used exclusively and precisely in a philosophical sense as a noun, whereas *being* is used in our casual daily speech both as noun and as participle. In the present study, however, we use *being* as a noun to indicate *thing* or *state.* The Latin *ens* is the etymological source of the English *entity.*

The term *being,* like every term, is the expression of an *idea* or *concept.* Now, as we have seen in discussing the Logical Question, an idea has a content or make-up called its *comprehension;* and a field of meaning, of denotation, called its *extension.* We have also seen that ideas, in point of extension, are, in themselves, *universal,* although they may be contracted to the character of *particular* and *singular* ideas. A universal idea expresses in the mind *some one thing,* that is, *some one essence,* which is found in each and every member of the extension of the idea; therefore the universal idea is *predicable* of all and each of these members (called *inferiors* or *subjects* of the idea). There are five possible *modes of predication,* viz., generic, specific, differential, proper, accidental; usually these are called simply *genus, species, difference, property, accident.* Every universal idea will be predicable of its inferiors in one of these five ways. Now, when we regard the idea of *being* as a universal idea, that is, as representing in the mind some one thing, some one essence, that is common to all its inferiors, we find that *there is simply nothing conceivable* which is absent from the scope or extension of the idea *being.* But *how* does it apply to its inferiors; *how* is it predicable of them? Certainly not as accident, property, or difference; and certainly not as species. For these are restricted classifications of *a way or mode of predication,* and, as we have just noted, there is absolutely no restriction in the mode in which *being* is predicated of its inferiors, for it not only applies to all, but to their differences and particularities as well. Everything is a being, every difference of things is a being, every special character is a being, every conceivable *thing* is a being. Is the one classification left, that is, is *genus* the mode of predication proper to *being?* Not precisely. For a genus is, after all, predicable of *a class* of inferiors, and there are boundaries of that class, and things outside those boundaries to which the genus does not apply or of which it is not predicable. This is not the case with *being.* Hence the idea *being* does not apply to its inferiors as a genus. But we have said that *every* universal idea *must* apply to its inferiors in one of the five ways called *the predicables. Being* does not so apply. Therefore *being* is not a universal idea. It is more; it is *a transcendental idea.* It soars above all classifications and is predicable of *everything.* But, since genus is the most *wide* of the modes of predication, we may say that *being,* in its application to inferiors, is closer to genus than to any of the other four predicables. And so, loosely speaking, we say *being* is "a sort of genus" or "a genus by figure of speech"; in short, we say *being* is *a genus by analogy* or that *being* is *an analogical genus.*

What we have said of the idea of *being* is to be said as well of the term *being.* It is a transcendental term, not merely a universal term. It applies to its inferiors (terms that can be used as subject when it is predicate) as an analogical genus.

Being is understood by the mind as contrasted with its opposite, that is, *non-being* or *nothing*. For, as the eye cannot behold a visible object exactly unless it stand against a contrasting background, so the mind cannot see *being* except against the background of *non-being* or nothingness. And the mind sees, even as it grasps *being* as necessarily contradictory to *non-being,* that "a thing cannot *be* and *not-be* at the same time and in the same way." This judgment the mind inevitably pronounces as a self-evident certitude and truth. This is *the fundamental first-principle,* the first of self-evident truths, which serves as root-reason and solid basis for every other judgment. This self-evident truth, this *principle* (that is, this *guiding* truth), is called "The Principle of Contradiction."

Out of the idea of *being* then (which is the very first idea in the order of *time* and in the order of *thinking,* since our first grasp of anything is *as a thing*) comes at once the judgment which is enunciated as the principle of contradiction. Further analysis of the idea *being* makes evident other principles. For, after seeing that a thing cannot *be* and *not-be* in the same way and simultaneously, the mind sees that the classifications of *being* and *non-being* are all inclusive, and it necessarily judges, "Anything either *is* or it *is not;* there is no middle ground between *being* and *non-being.*" This judgment, so enunciated, is "The Principle of the Excluded Middle." Again, the mind, contemplating the idea *being* as contrasted with non-being or nothing, corroborates its finding by asserting the identity of being and the identity of non-being, thus: "Whatever is, *is;* and that which is not, *is not.*" This is "The Principle of Identity." Finally, the mind, dwelling still on the idea of *being* as seen in contrast with its opposite, judges with inevitable and absolute certitude that these opposites are different, thus, *"That which is* is not *that which is not;* nor can *that which is not* be identified with *that which is.*" This is "The Principle of Difference." Thus the mind, studying the idea of *being* and contrasting it with the idea of *non-being,* sees these self-evident truths: that a thing cannot be both of the opposites simultaneously; that the opposites exhaust the possibilities leaving no middle ground which is neither; that each is what it is; that either is not the other. These self-evident truths are primal, basic, fundamental to all thinking; they are the root of every proof, of every sound thinking process and its fruitage. They are called *first principles,* that is, first *intellectual* principles, first *guiding truths.* Their names, to review them, are the principle of contradiction, the principle of the excluded middle, the principle of identity, and the principle of difference. Of these, the *very first* is the principle of contradiction.

c) Determinants of Being

There are no specific kinds of *being as such.* For *anything* is a *thing.* But there are specific kinds of beings, of things, on other bases than the basis of their character as *things* simply. We shall speak of such a classification of things when we come to consider *the categories.* But here, considering being in its most general aspect, we have certain points which we may call *determinants.* Of these we now speak.

1. Real Being—Logical Being.—Anything that is *existible* in the world of realities independently of the creatural mind is *real* being. Anything that depends for its existence on the creatural mind is *logical* being. These types of being are very often called by their Latin names: real being is *ens reale;* logical being is either *ens logicum* or *ens rationis.* Examples of real being: man, hill, fire, soul, spirit, God. Examples of logical being: vacancy, darkness, blindness, death (which are not things but the *absence* or *cessation* of things, and are regarded as things by the mind, thus having their sole objectiveness in and from the mind); fictions of mind like "a square circle"; *modes* and *relations* of mental processes, like genus, species, subject, predicate.

2. Actual Being—Potential Being.—Here we have determinants of *real* being. A real being that exists is *actual* being. A real being that can exist but does not, is *potential* being. In so far as anything exists, it is actual; hence, actuality is a perfection. Insofar as anything existible does not exist, it is potential; hence, potentiality is imperfection; it is unfulfillment. This is why Aristotle defines God, the Infinite Being, as *Pure Actuality*. The transit from potentiality to actuality is called *becoming* or *motion* or *change*. There are four chief types of change: change of substance or *substantial change* (as from living body to dead body; as from lifeless food to living flesh); change *of quantity* (as growth or diminution); change *of quality* (as from hot to cold, from ignorant to learned); change *of place* or local change or local movement. In point of change we see illustrated the axiomatic truth that nothing *becomes,* nothing passes from potential to actual, except under the influence of what is already actual. *Quidquid movetur ab alio movetur.*

Under the head of *actual being* we must consider some types of actuality:

(*a*) *First Actuality—Second Actuality.*—A thing is said to be actual by first actuality or *in actu primo* when it is present in basic fact or in fundamental equipment. Thus a new-born baby is a rational creature and a walking creature. The baby cannot, in fact, *use* its reason or its free-will, nor can it *use* its feet to walk with. But it *has* reason and it *has* feet. Its fundamental equipment for reasoning, willing, and walking is present, is *actual.* But, owing to immaturity and inexperience, this equipment is not yet operative. So we say that the baby is a reasoning, willing, walking creature *in actu primo* or *in first actuality*. Later, the baby will *exercise* the powers of reasoning, willing, and walking. *In such exercise* it will be a reasoning, willing, and walking creature *in actu secundo* or *in second actuality.*

(*b*) *Actuality of Essence—Actuality of Existence.*—About an existing (that is, an *actual*) thing, there are two points of actuality. The thing is what it is in its basic constitution; and, secondly, the thing is *here*. The first point indicates the actuality of *essence;* the second point indicates the actuality of *existence.* There is disagreement among philosophers about *the distinction* between the actual essence and the actual existence of an existing creature. There is no question about the *separability* of these two things, but only about their *distinction.* Some hold that the distinction is *real,* and that the essence of an existing creature is one thing, while its existence is another thing, although these two things are inseparably united in the existing creature. Others hold that these two things,—essence and existence in a creature,—are only one thing looked at in two distinct ways; they maintain, therefore, that the distinction is not *real* but *logical.*

Under the head of *potential being* we must consider some types of potentiality:

(*a*) *Objective Potentiality—Subjective Potentiality.*—A thing looked at as sheerly possible is said to be *objectively* potential. A thing regarded in the causes that may produce it is said to reside in these causes as in its subject, and so is called *subjectively* potential. An open meadow is potentially a field of ripe corn; the thing is possible; corn *could* be planted there and come to ripeness; this is *objective* potentiality. But a field just planted in corn is potentially a field of ripe corn; it is more than sheerly possible, for the causes that tend to produce ripe corn are there and at work; the corn is not yet actual, it is only potential, but the potentiality resides in a subject; here we have *subjective* potentiality.

(*b*) *Active Potentiality—Passive Potentiality.*—Active potentiality is a capacity for *doing.* It is a *fully active* potentiality if it is a capacity for laying hold of something and changing it, as, for example, the digestive power or potentiality which lays hold of food and changes it into flesh and blood. It is an *operative* potentiality if it involves doing without essentially changing what it affects.—Passive potentiality is a capacity for *receiving,* as, for example, the capacity for marble to be shaped into a statue.—

Sometimes our knowing-powers are called *passive* potentialities, for they receive the impression of their objects. But the knowing-powers are also active inasmuch as they *take in* the impression; they *re*-act to the impression. It seems more accurate to call the knowing-powers *operative* rather than *passive*.

Summary of the Article

In this Article we have learned the meaning of the term *metaphysics,* and have clearly determined the parts of philosophy which properly belong under this heading. We have studied the nature of *being*. We have learned that *being* is a *transcendental* concept and term, and that it is predicable of its inferiors in a manner *analogous to that of a genus*. We have studied the *principles* which are immediately derived from the idea of *being* as seen against the background of its opposite, *non-being*. We have learned that these principles are four: the Principle of Contradiction; the Principle of the Excluded Middle; the Principle of Identity; the Principle of Difference. We have noted that the first principle of all is the Principle of Contradiction. These *first principles* are self-evident truths which are fundamental to all thinking and to all certitude in knowledge. We have noted certain determinants of *being:* real, logical; actual, potential. We have seen that actuality is either first actuality or second actuality (*actus primus; actus secundus*); that it is actuality of essence, actuality of existence. We have also learned that potentiality is objective or subjective; active or passive.

Article 2. The Properties of Being

a) Properties; b) Unity; c) Truth; d) Goodness; e) Beauty and Perfection.

a) Properties

A *property* of a thing is what belongs to it by natural necessity because the thing is that specific nature. It is not a *part* of a thing;

it is a quality or characteristic of a thing which is necessarily there because the thing is that sort of thing. It *follows upon* the perfectly constituted nature or working-essence of a thing. Thus, we say that the ability to laugh is a property of man. For when human nature is fully constituted; when nothing (such as immaturity, organic defect, disease, unconsciousness) thwarts the normal functioning of that nature, man will inevitably be able to laugh. Yet the power to laugh is not a part of man's nature; it is something consequent upon that nature when perfectly constituted. A property is sometimes called *an attribute.*

The properties of *being* are of two classes: (*1*) those that belong to *being* as such, and are therefore *transcendental;* (*2*) those that belong to many beings, or even to most, and are therefore *general.*

The transcendental properties of *being* are three: (*1*) unity or oneness; (*2*) truth or trueness; (*3*) goodness. The general properties of *being* are beauty and perfection.

b) The Unity of Being

Every being has *unity* inasmuch as it is *that one thing,* incapable of existing as a multiplication of itself. For unity means *undividedness,* and to say that a thing has unity is to say that it is undivided.

Of course, a thing made of parts can be divided into parts, but the unity of the thing consists in the fact that it is *not* divided, nor can it be divided *and remain that identical thing that it is.* A being as such is incapable of becoming a plurality of itself, a multiplication of itself, a series of repetitions of itself. Other things of the same kind may come from it by generation, but each of these things is *itself* and not the being from which it comes. A bodily thing divided into parts ceases to be that one undivided reality; it has no longer its *being* as that reality. And each part is now that one part; it is a thing with *its* necessary unity.

This necessary unity of *being* does not involve the impossibility of *multiplication of the presence* of a thing. It is conceivable that, by a miracle, one thing, remaining that one thing, should be present in a plurality of places. The five loaves which fed a multitude remained the original five loaves. The "multiplication of the loaves" was the multiplication of the *presence* of the loaves. Each loaf fed many, but it remained that loaf. So in the Holy Eucharist, Our Lord is present in many places, but *He* is not multiplied into many Lords. His *presence* is multiplied.

The unity of a being is called *transcendental* because it is limited to no one class of things, but belongs to *being as such.* Whatever exists, exists in the oneness of its being. Whatever can exist, can exist only inasmuch as it can come into existence as that one thing. Therefore philosophers say *Ens et unum convertuntur,* "Being and unity are interchangeable." Of course, the concept of *being as being* is not precisely the same as the concept of *being as one;* there is *a distinction of reason* between *being* and *unity;* therefore these terms are not perfectly synonymous.

Transcendental unity is of several types or aspects. We call it *concrete unity* when it is the unity of a thing itself, independently of the view of the mind. We call it *abstract unity* (such as unity of genus or of species) when it is the unity of the mind's concept of a thing. Thus John and his dog are each one *concrete* thing; but, in the *abstract* view of the mind these two are one inasmuch as they belong to the one genus, *animal.* Again, transcendental unity is *essential* if it is the oneness necessary to an essence, whether the essence be a substance or an accident; this is unity of *simplicity* in things not composed of parts, and unity of *composition* in things made of parts.

In addition to transcendental unity we may mention here that unity which is proper to bodily things. This is *quantitative unity* or *mathematical unity.* In philosophy we call this type of unity *predicamental unity.*

In considering *substances,* we must inquire what it is that determines the *essential* and *concrete* and *predicamental* unity of each; and we must also inquire what constitutes the thing in its *essential* and *abstract* unity as a specific kind of thing or member of a specific class. In a word, we must inquire what is the source or *principle* of the thing's individuality, and what is the source or *principle* of the thing's species. Now, among bodily substances, *the principle of individuation* is found in its material being, *its quantified material. The principle of specification* is found in that substantial element which makes the bodily substance in question an existing body of this kind; this is called *the substantial form* of the bodily substance. Of *matter and form* we shall speak in some detail in our study of the Cosmological Question which we take up in the next Chapter. Here we must add, however, that when there is question of spiritual substances, these are not individuated, since only a bodily thing is, strictly considered, subject to individuation, that is, to *quantified* identification, to *numbering* as this one, this integer. Complete spiritual substances (and always we mean created and finite spiritual substances) are *pure forms* or *substantial species,* and not *individuals.*

A being, by reason of unity, is that one thing, that *idem ens;* the Latin term gives us the English *identity.* A being has *identity* in or with itself alone, not with other things. It is but looseness of speech that permits us to say, for instance, "These two books are identical." The books are not identical, but alike or similar. We use more accurate speech when we speak of "identifying a person," for then we say who that person is *himself,* not that he is like some other person. A being is identical with *itself,* and this is the effect of its *unity.*

The opposite of identity is *distinction.* Distinction is the absence of identity among two or more things or among two or more ideas of one thing. Distinction among things is *real* distinction; distinction between or among different mental aspects of one thing is *logical* distinction or *distinction of reason.* Logical distinction may be purely rational, lacking a basis in things, or it may have a foundation in reality. The distinction between a man and his weight is a *real* distinction, for the man is one thing and his weight another. The distinction between *animal being* and *rational being* in the one human person is *logical,* for the one identical being is here both animal and rational, and these terms do not indicate *parts* of that being, but different *real aspects* of that which is identical in the undivided person. But this logical distinction *has a basis in reality,* since there are beings which are animal without being rational (beasts) and beings, too, which are rational without being animal (soul after a death; or an angel or archangel). The distinction between the meaning of a term and the meaning of its essential definition (and these two are identical meanings; an equals-mark might be placed between them; the definition is only a fuller statement of what the term means) is a purely logical distinction *without a basis in reality.*

The old Latin terms for logical distinction are these: for logical distinction with a foundation in reality, *distinctio rationis cum fundamento in re* or *distinctio rationis ratiocinatae;* for purely logical distinction without a basis in reality, *distinctio rationis sine fundamento in re* or *distinctio rationis ratiocinantis.*

Among bodily things and their material accidentals, real distinction (which does not necessarily means separation or separability) results in a *multiplicity* or a *multitudo.* Inasmuch as the items of a multiplicity can be measured or counted, they make up *a number.* And *number* is defined as "a multiplicity measured by one," that is, a multiplicity which can be *counted* one by one.

c) THE TRUTH OF BEING

Every being, inasmuch as it *is* a being, is *knowable* by an adequate mind. And inasmuch as it is knowable, a being is the basis of the truth which exists or can exist in the mind which is adequate to know it. And this constitutes what we call the *truth* or *trueness* of *being.*

The truth we speak of here is *ontological truth,* or *truth of things,* or *truth of being,* which we discussed in our study of the Critical Question (*Part II of this manual, Chapter II, Art. 1*).

Truth involves *mind.* A thing or being is what it is. And it is *knowable as such* by an adequate mind. In this its truth consists. Indeed, mind comes first, for created being *depends for its possi-*

bility upon the knowledge of it in the Creator's mind *before* it had any existence. Increate Being is Infinite Truth Itself, identified in perfect simplicity with Infinite Mind.

Every being is true; every true thing is being. *Omne ens est verum; ens et verum convertuntur.* Being regarded as *being* is distinct *by a logical distinction* from being regarded as *what is true;* but between *being* and *truth* (that is, being and true being) there is no *real* distinction. Hence, there is no transcendental or ontological *falsity.* Of logical and moral falsity we have spoken in the Chapter and Article referred to above.

d) The Goodness of Being

Goodness is desirability or appetizability. A thing is *good* inasmuch as it can be the object of a tendency, appetite, or desire. Now *being* as such is capable of having the character of the goal or object of appetite. Therefore, *being as such is good.* We can say here, as we said when speaking of the unity and the truth of being, "Every being is good; every good thing is a being," *Omne ens est bonum; ens et bonum convertuntur.* There is a logical distinction between being as *being* and being as *what is good,* but not a real distinction.

The goodness of which we speak here is *ontological* goodness. It is the goodness of things, of reality, of being. It is *transcendental* goodness, for it is coextensive with *being* which is transcendental. It consists in the fact that being as such (that is, *anything* positively existible) can be the aim, object, purpose, or goal of an appetency or desire.

There are two other basic types of goodness, physical goodness and moral goodness. (*1*) *Physical goodness* is the goodness of a *physis* or created nature. It consists in the fact that the nature or "working essence" *lacks nothing* that should be found in it according to the aim, plan, desire, appetency of its maker. Thus, for example, a man's health is good, *by physical goodness,* in so far as the man's bodily organs and functions are what they ought to be, and lack nothing of what they ought to be. Thus, bread is good bread in so far as it has what bread should have in point of ingredients and preparation, and lacks none of these elements; in other terms, the bread is good inasmuch as it fulfills the seemly aim, desire, appetency, purpose, of the honest baker. (*2*) *Moral goodness* consists in the agreement of human acts (that is, deliberate thoughts, words, deeds, desires, omissions) with the standard or rule of what such acts ought to be. Agreement with this standard is the aim, purpose, desire, or appetency of God, who wills that man keep His law; it is also the fundamental thing which the human will wants and desires. Thus we notice that both physical goodness and moral goodness fit in with our general description of goodness as *desirability* or *appetizability*.

The opposite of goodness is *evil* or *badness*. Evil is not being, but absence, lack, or defect of being. Inasmuch as positive being exists it is necessarily good by ontological or transcendental goodness. There is no ontological evil. But there is physical evil, and there is moral evil. (*1*) *Physical evil* is the lack or absence in a creature of some element, item, or quality that should be there. In so far as a created *physis* (that is, nature or "working essence") suffers such a lack or absence, it is not good, "no good," physically evil, or physically bad. Thus, of a watch which lacks but a tiny hair-spring, we say that it is "no good." Thus, of bread that lacks any one ingredient, or the proper proportion of ingredients, or any of the qualities that should come from suitable mixing and baking, we say that it is "not good" or "bad." Thus, of a man who suffers from but one organic lesion or disease, we say that his health is bad. The evil exampled here is physical evil. (*2*) *Moral evil* is the lack or absence of agreement between a human act and the rule of what it ought to be. Moral evil is *sin*. In so far as a human acts lacks agreement with the moral law in any point (in itself, in its purpose, in its circumstances) it is morally evil or sinful. We can readily see from all this what is meant by the axiom *Bonum ex integra causa, malum ex quocumque defectu,* "For a thing to be (physically or morally) good, it must be *wholly* good; it is made evil by any deficiency or lack." We do not say that a thing is necessarily *entirely bad* because of one lack or defect, but it is *in so far* bad, and if the lack be of great importance it may be wholly bad, as in the case of the watch which lacks but a hair-spring and is wholly useless for purposes of recording time. And, on the other hand, a thing, *in so far* as it approaches the full character of what it ought to be, is good. Thus we may say of bread that it is of good flavor but poor (or bad) texture.

e) Beauty and Perfection of Being

Unity, truth, goodness, are *transcendental* properties of being, for they are coextensive with being; they are really (though not logically) identified with being itself. Along with *being,* these three properties are sometimes listed as "the transcendentals." The properties we are now to mention, that is *beauty* and *perfection* of being, are not transcendental, for, while they are properties of most beings, they are not properties of all; that is, they are not properties of *being as such.*

(*1*) *Beauty* is the property which makes a being pleasing to behold. For a thing or being to be beautiful it must have a certain *integrity* or *completeness,* a certain *fulness* or *richness,* a certain *variety* of pleasing aspects, a certain *unity* or *harmony* which comes of order and balance and proportion, a certain *shining splendor* which crowns all the other elements and gives them effectiveness. These are the objective constituents of beauty in a thing. The subjective element is the *pleasurable beholding* of the beautiful thing, whether by the mind alone, or by the senses and the mind together, with the approbation (or *enjoyment*) of the will alone, or of the will and sense-appetency together. Beauty finds notable expression in *the fine arts:* architecture, painting, sculpture, poetry, music, and allied arts such as that of the actor, that of the orator, that of the writer of artistic prose, that of the producer of fine needlework. The science of things beautiful is called *Esthetics.*

(*2*) *Perfection* is the rounded completeness of a created nature. It is the fulness of being required by a reality to be at its best. Perfection may be *entire* or *partial;* thus perfect health is an entire perfection; perfect eyesight is a partial perfection. Perfection may be *pure* or *mixed,* inasmuch as it is perfection simply or has imperfection mingled with it; thus, life is a pure perfection; the power of thinking things out (that is, of reasoning) is a mixed perfection, for while it is a wondrous power it is indicative of our imperfection in not knowing things at once without the labor of thinking them out. A perfection present *as such* is *formally* present; a perfection present in effect or equivalently is *virtually* present; a perfection present in a manner which transcends creatural experience is *eminently* present. Since God is Infinite Being, and not creatural, we do not predicate perfections of Him literally. Yet we must speak even of the Infinite in the best of such terms as we have, despite their limitations. And so we say that in God there are present all *pure* perfections *formally,* and the noblest mixed perfections *virtually,* and all these *eminently* and in infinite degree, and that all God's perfections are absolutely identified with His simple and undivided Essence. The perfections of creatures are finite, temporal, contingent, composed, mutable. The perfections of God, on the contrary, are infinite, eternal, necessary, simple, and changeless.

Summary of the Article

In this Article we have defined *property* or *attribute,* and have indicated the meaning of *transcendental* property and of *general* property of being. We have defined and classified *the unity of being,* and have determined *the principle of individuation* and *the principle of specification* of creatural being. We have studied *identity* and *distinction.* We have learned what is meant by *the truth of being* and by *the goodness of being.* We have seen that the transcendental properties of being are *coextensive with being itself,* and distinct from being by only a logical distinction. Incidental to our discussion of transcendental unity, goodness, truth, was some account of multiplicity, of physical and moral evil, and of logical and moral falsity. We have briefly described the ***beauty*** of being, and have listed its objective and its subjective elements. We have mentioned the expression of beauty in the fine arts. We have defined *perfection* and have mentioned various types, phases, and degrees in which it appears.

Article 3. The Classification of Being

a) The Categories in General; **b)** The Categories Taken Singly; **c)** Subsistence.

a) The Categories in General

A *category* is *an ultimate classification of things as knowable.* Webster rightly defines category as "one of the highest classes to which the objects of thought can be reduced, and by which they can be arranged in a system."

The categories, as classifications of things (or "the objects of knowledge"), are the philosopher's map, his guide, his plan of work. Indeed, no man, even the least philosophical, can do without a fundamental classification of realities. For we live in such a complex world, we are surrounded by such a multitude and variety of things, that we must have some system and order, some scheme of *unifying* things, if we are to think of them and speak of them at all.

The categories we are to propose and discuss are the *ten categories* or the *ten predicamentals* listed by Aristotle. Founded, as all sane categories must be, on human experience with this thought-provoking and speech-inviting world around us. these ten have stood the test of more than two thousand years and thev have not proved fallacious or defective. They have justified their claim as valid classifications "of the objects of thought and knowledge."

In determining these supreme classes of things as understandable, Aristotle set forth a twofold general division of things, that is, "of the objects of thought and knowledge." He considered that a knowable thing, a reality, is either such a thing as may exist *itself,* may, so to speak, stand on its own feet, or it is such a thing as regularly requires some other thing in which to exist. The first class of things is *substance;* the second class is *accident* or *accidental.* These are the two master-categories.

Substance is a reality which is suited to exist as itself, and not as the mark, determinant, or characteristic of some other thing. Thus, a man is a substance, an angel is a substance, an apple is a substance, an automobile is an artificial union of a number of substances.

Accident or *accidental* is a reality which is regularly not suited to exist as itself, but to exist as the mark, determinant, modification, or characteristic of some other thing, and ultimately of a substance. Thus, the size of a man is an accident or accidental; the color of an apple is an accident.

Accidents are said to *inhere* in the other reality to which they belong. This other reality in which accidents inhere is called *the subject of inherence* or simply *the subject.* One accident may inhere in another accident as in its subject, but at the bottom of all inherence is a substance. Thus the motion of a bullet has a certain rate of velocity and this velocity is an accident of motion which in itself is an accident of the bullet; the bullet is a substance.

It is not accurate to classify understandable reality simply as "Substance and Accident." For there is no general accident; there is only this determinate accident or that determinate accident. The proper way of speaking of the categories is "Substance and the Nine Accidents."

The nine accidents are: *quantity, quality, relation, action, passion, place, time, posture, habit.* These together with *substance* make up *the ten categories* or *the ten predicamentals.*

For a reality to be classified under any of these ten heads it must be a *single, real, finite* being. It must be a single being; *man* is a substance, but *good man* falls under two categories: *man,* substance, *goodness,* quality. It must be a real being, not a logical being (or *ens rationis*), for the categories are supreme classifications of understandable *reality*. It must be a finite being, for the Infinite Being is not to be listed, labelled, or classified; such things are limits and bounds, and the Infinite Being is without limits and bounds.

Still, by analogy, even the Infinite Being is classified under the category of *substance*. But we must be careful to notice that the Infinite Substance, unlike creatural substances, is not capable of being marked by accidents or accidentals.

b) THE CATEGORIES TAKEN SINGLY

(*1*) *Substance* is a reality, bodily or spiritual, suited to exist as itself. The name substance is from the Latin *sub stans* or "standing under," for a creatural substance is capable of "standing under" the accidents of which it is the subject. It supports accidents in being.

(*2*) *Quantity* is an accident proper to bodies; it is the extension of bodies in space. To say a thing is big or little is not to speak of quantity, for quantity deals with measurements. Big and little indicate qualities. If we say a man is six feet tall we indicate quantity; so also we indicate quantity when we say "forty cents," or "a nine by twelve rug," or "a mile walk," or "a two quart bottle."

(*3*) *Quality* is an accident which determines the sort or kind of a thing. Nearly all adjectives indicate qualities. Quality is a very broad and inclusive category. Thus it indicates: (*a*) *dispositions and habits* such as prudence, industriousness, strength, weakness, gullibility; (*b*) *abilities or capacities* such as capability, keen-sightedness, quick-mindedness; (*c*) *passive characteristics* such as color, the state of being esteemed, age, temperature (age and temperature can also be *quantities* when expressed in definite numbers; that is, they can be quantities by analogy); (*d*) *outlines or figures* such as roundness, squareness, angularity.

(*4*) *Relation* is an accident which determines a thing in its standing to or towards another. It is unique among accidents because it involves two realities and does not really exist in either but *between* them. Examples of relation are: equality, similarity, unlikeness, paternity, loyalty, servitude.

(*5*) *Action* is an accident which determines a reality as doing something, as producing an effect. Examples: talking, writing, speeding, striking, painting.

(*6*) *Passion* is an accident which determines a reality as undergoing something, as affected by some action. Examples: being talked to, being written, being struck. As action is expressed by the active voice of verbs, passion is expressed by the passive voice.

(*7*) *Place* is an accident which determines a reality as to position with reference to other realities. Place is an accident which, strictly speaking, is proper to bodily substances only. Place finds expression in such terms as: in the room, at the corner of Main Street, in this county, on the surface of the earth, in that chair.

(*8*) *Time* is an accident which determines a reality in its position with reference to *before* and *after*. Examples: at midday, this evening, at five o'clock, next Tuesday, in 1492, before midnight, after supper.

(*9*) *Posture* is an accident proper to bodies which determines its subject with reference to the arrangement or disposition of its own parts. Examples: sprawled, sitting, standing, lying down, huddled up, erect, prone, cross-kneed, outstretched.

(*10*) *Habit* is an accident proper to bodies which determines its subject with reference to its clothing or external accoutrements or adjuncts. Examples: well-dressed, armored, moss-covered, ivy-hung, bearded, swaddled. In one aspect, habit is also *quality*. Mental and moral habits are always qualities merely. *Habit* as a predicamental or category means some kind of bodily *dress* or bodily adornment or bodily swathing.

c) Subsistence

A thing which is existible as itself and not as the mark of something else is a substance. But sometimes a substance is a *substantial part* of a larger substance, as, for instance, a hand or an arm is part of the human substance. Now, a substance that has rounded completeness in itself, and its own way of acting, is said to be *subsistent*. Substances that are parts of other and greater substances are non-subsistent substances.

A subsistent substance has its own mode of activity; its operations are referred to *it*. A man's actions are referred to the *man*, for a man is a subsistent substance. But the acts of a man's hand are not ascribed ultimately to the hand, but to the man. The man rightly says, "*I* wrote a letter"; he does not say, "My hand wrote a letter." The man is a substance; the hand is a substance; but the man is a subsistent substance and the hand is not.

That which gives a substance its rounded completeness, its crowning perfection, as a thing with its own activities, and a thing to which the activities of its parts are ultimately ascribed, is *subsistence*.

A subsistent substance, that is, a substance that has subsistence, is called a *suppositum* or a *supposit* or a *hypostasis*. If such a substance is of the rational order (that is, if it be basically equipped for understanding and willing) it is *a person*.

We must notice a philosophical axiom: *actiones sunt suppositorum,* "actions are to be ascribed to supposits." The pitcher throws the ball, not merely the pitcher's arm and hand; the horse kicks the hostler, not the horse's hoof and leg.

In passing, Christian students will notice why the Incarnation, the coming of the Son of God in human flesh, is called "The Hypostatic Union." For this Union is in the *Hypostasis* or *Person* of the Son, the Second Person of the Blessed Trinity. In consequence, Our Lord is *one Person* in Whom *two natures are united* substantially,—the nature of God and the nature of man,—so that Christ is true God and true man.

Summary of the Article

In this Article we have defined *category,* and have set down as master-categories *substance* and *accident*. *Substance* has a definite meaning of its own, and whatever falls under this category is a substance, material or spiritual. But whatever falls under the category of accident is a *special* accident; it is one of nine accidents. Therefore, we have learned not to say "substance and accident" when asked for the categories, but "substance and the nine accidents." We must contrast the categorical or predicamental *accident* discussed in the present Article with the categorematical or predicable *accident* discussed in the Chapter on The Logical Question (*Chap. I, Art. 3, a*). We have listed, defined, and exemplified the ten categories. We have added an important word on the meaning of *subsistence*.

Article 4. The Emergence of Created Being

a) Becoming; b) Intrinsic Causes; c) Extrinsic Causes.

a) Becoming

A created being, that is, *a creature,* emerges into being, comes into being. The Increate Being always was and always will be, or, more accurately, always *is*. The created *substance* has, as its name indicates, its first origin in *creation*. Creation is an action proper to Infinite Power alone, which produces a thing in its entirety out of nothing. The first beginning of all creatures is found in creation.

Spiritual creatures have no possible origin except *creation in each case*. Bodily substances, by the process of *generation* (whether vital generation or non-vital generation) come from other bodily substances, following a first creation. Bodily substances have their root-origin in creation, their proximate origin in generation. Accidents come into being along with the substances which they mark or affect. Substances are created or generated; accidents are co-created or co-generated.

The emergence of being is called *becoming*. Emergence of being by generation or co-generation is also *motion* or *change*. But creation is not motion or change. A created being in its root-emergence by creation is not changed from a former state, or moved from a former condition; it *had* no former state or condition, and hence in being created is not *changed*. For change requires a point or state *from which* to start, as well as a point or state *towards which* to tend and *in which* to find its completion or terminus. Similarly, annihilation, were it to occur, would be a total reduction of a thing to nothingness, and nothingness is not a state or a condition or a terminus; it is *nothing;* therefore, annihilation would not be *change* or *motion* since it would lack the terminus or positive goal which change or motion demands. Hence in motion or change (that is, in the *becoming* of creatures after their first creation) there must be *a term from which* (called *terminus a quo*), a *term to which* (called *terminus ad quem*) and *a going over from the one to the other* (called *transitus*). The actual *change* or *motion* or *becoming* is the *transitus,* but the *transitus* cannot take place without the terms. Further, motion or change requires *a mover other than the thing changed,* and, in case of bodily change or *becoming,* it requires *some underlying support,* some bridge, so to speak, over which the change or transit moves, and this bridge remains unchanged. We shall stress the last mentioned fact when we come, in our study of The Cosmological Question, to discuss substantial change in bodies and the substantial constitution of bodies.

Becoming, looked at in itself and statically, is a combination of the accidents called *action* and *passion.* When we speak of substantial change or substantial becoming we mean that *the things changed* are substances, and that one ceases to be while another emerges; we do not mean that *the process* of change is a substance. The process as such is an accident; a kind of composite or cooperative accident of *action-passion.*

Becoming or *action-passion,* considered in its termini, is a process of *cause and effect.* Beings that emerge by creation are *caused* beings, and are themselves the *effects* of creation. Beings which *become* by reason of change or motion are also *caused beings* and are themselves the *effects* of the generation or co-generation which makes them emerge. The study, therefore, of the emergence of created being is the study of *causes* of which created beings are *effects.*

A *cause* is anything that contributes in any manner to the producing or the maintaining of a reality. That which is *within* the being caused, that which is in it to constitute it and to hold it in being as such a thing, in its substance or its accidents, is *an intrinsic cause* or *a sum of intrinsic causes.* That which is not thus within the created thing, but which lends an influence or activity to the producing or maintaining of that thing is *an extrinsic cause* or *sum of extrinsic causes.* We shall next speak of these two types of cause.

b) Intrinsic Causes

Consider a carved wooden statue. Without some *stuff* (in this case, wood) of which it is made, this bodily thing could not exist. The stuff or material out of which a bodily creature is made is therefore a contributing factor to its being; it is *a cause.* We call it *the material cause.* This cause is *intrinsic,* for it is *right in* the finished effect. Only bodily realities have material causes; spiriual substances are not made of any material.

The wooden statue is *wood,* before, during, and after the carving which made it a statue. For the carving has only changed the shape of the wood; it has not changed the wood substantially, but accidentally. Yet it has given the wood a certain *determinateness* as a statue,—an accidental determinateness. Now any *determining* factor is called, in the language of philosophy, *a form.* The carving has given the wood *an accidental form.* And the form constitutes or determines a thing as a reality; hence a form is *a cause.* An accidental form is *an accidental formal cause.* The statue has many accidental points of determinateness; it is of a certain height, a certain weight, a certain color, a certain temperature (at any given moment), and so on. Each of these *determinations,* down to the last and least, though it be but a quarter-inch scratch on the statue, contributes *something* to the making of the statue the precise thing it is in all particulars. Each of these determinations is an accidental form, and *an accidental formal cause.* It is manifest, then, that the accidental formal causes of a reality may be many and various.

But there is an underlying *form* and *formal cause* in the statue which makes it a statue of *wood.* This is *the substantial form of wood,* the substantial principle which makes wood *wood* and not any other substance, such as silver or marble. This substantial form is *the substantial formal cause* of the wood and of the statue made of the wood. There can be in any given unit of substance only *one* substantial form, only one substantial formal cause.

The formal causes (accidental and substantial) are *right in* the effect; hence we call them *intrinsic* causes.

The intrinsic causes are, therefore, *the material cause* (for bodily realities), *the substantial formal cause* (for substances, bodily or spiritual), and *the accidental formal cause.*

c) Extrinsic Causes

The wooden statue was produced by some *activity.* Now, that which *by its activity* produces an effect is called *the effecting cause* of the effect. Sometimes the effecting cause is called *the efficient cause.* In our example, the effecting cause is the man who carved the statue. He is not the effecting cause of the wood of which the statue is made; this is to be found in parent-trees and in the vital activity of the tree itself from which the wood of the statue was taken. But the man is the effecting cause of the *statue,* that is, of this *accidental shaping* of wood. It is evident that the effecting cause is not *in* the effect; we therefore call it an *extrinsic* cause.

The effecting cause is often served by tools or instruments. Each of these, inasmuch as it *channels the effectiveness of the effecting cause into the effect* is called *an instrumental cause.* An instrument used by an effecting cause is itself *a subordinate effecting cause;* the person who uses the instrument is *the principal effecting cause.* The instrumental cause must have in itself *a fitness* for the producing of the effect for which it is used, but it has no virtue or power of its own; it acts by virtue of the principal cause. The man carving the statue is the principal cause of the statue; the tools are the instrumental causes. Yet the whole effect comes from each cause. The statue in its entirety comes from the carver; it also comes, in its entirety, from the carving tools or instruments. But it comes from the carver as *principal effecting cause,* and from the tools as subordinate or *instrumental effecting causes*. An instrumental cause is *extrinsic*.

The effecting cause is sometimes served by a pattern or model which guides the effective activity, and thus contributes something to the effect itself. Such a model or pattern is called *an exemplar-cause*. The wind and rain which wear down the rough rock and make it smooth are effecting causes; they employ no instruments, they need no exemplars or models. But a human effecting cause needs a model. The man who carved the statue had some image before him (person, picture, plan, other statue) or at least in his imagination, even if, to start with, it were a very vague image. While the exemplar cause is more or less accurately reproduced or expressed in the effect, the exemplar or model itself is not *in* the effect. Hence the exemplar cause, like the instrumental causes, is an *extrinsic* cause. The *reproduction or expression of the exemplar or model* in the effect constitutes therein an intrinsic accidental *formal* cause.

All creatural effecting causes are *secondary* causes. Only the First and Infinite Cause is *Primary Cause*.

In addition to the effecting cause, there is another extrinsic cause called *the final cause*. This is the end or the object or the goal or the purpose which the effecting cause tends to attain. The tree tends *naturally* towards fullness of growth and fruitfulness; thus it exhibits *finality* or tendency towards an end. In the tree this tendency is *intrinsic,* but the goal itself is not intrinsic; the full mature tree is not *in* the sapling; it is itself an extrinsic final cause. Man in many of his activities can choose or determine the end towards which his efforts are directed. The carver of the statue had *some end-in-view* which led him to the effecting activity which produced the statue. Perhaps he wished to express his devotion; perhaps he merely wished to have pleasure in doing something he could do skillfully; perhaps he wished to sell the statue for money. In any case he had some *end or purpose,* and this constitutes *the final cause* of the statue. The final cause may be multiple; the man may have carved this statue to glorify the Saint whose image it is, and also to make his bread and butter, and also to please his customer. But the point we note is that the effect is owing to *final causality,* without which the effecting cause would not expend effecting activity. Among creatures, and most evidently among men in their freely chosen activities, the final cause *invites* or *motivates* the effecting cause to use *materials* and impose *forms* by its *activity;* thus the final cause is often called "the cause of causes."

Ends or final causes run in chains or series. Thus we may say that the sculptor made the statue for money, he wished money to buy food, he wished food to live, he wished to live because life is desirable in view of everlasting Good. All chains or series of final causes run at last towards the Supreme Good or God, and the possession of the Supreme Good in endless beatitude. Even the sinner in his crime is looking,—albeit mistakenly and perversely,—for good, and for the Supreme Good; he is, however, looking in the wrong place.

To sum up the theory of causes. Causes are of these types:

- Cause . . .
  - Intrinsic
    - material
    - formal . . .
      - substantial
      - accidental
  - Extrinsic
    - efficient . . *served by* . . .
      - instrumental
      - exemplar
    - final

Summary of the Article

In this Article we have considered the *emergence* of created being, substantial and accidental, by first *creation* and by subsequent *generation*. The emergence of being is called *becoming*. Creation is *absolute* becoming without *change* or *motion*. Generation is *qualified* becoming and consists of change or motion or process of *cause and effect*. We have studied causes, intrinsic and extrinsic, naming their most important types.

CHAPTER IV

THE COSMOLOGICAL QUESTION

The Cosmological Question is the question of the philosophy of the *cosmos* or bodily universe. It is, in a word, the question of *bodies*. It raises the following points for study: the nature of bodily substance, its ultimate constitution, its first origin, its development and goal. The answer to The Cosmological Question makes up that department of philosophy called *cosmology*. This science is part of natural philosophy, not of metaphysics. For, as we have learned, metaphysics is the science of non-material real being; cosmology is a science of material real being. Cosmology is philosophical physics, not metaphysics. Cosmology does not make distinction of bodies as living and lifeless, but studies bodies *as such*. The question of life and living bodies, as distinct from lifeless bodies, is The Psychological Question which we shall undertake in the following Chapter.

The present Chapter is divided into these three Articles:

Article 1. The Nature of the Bodily World
Article 2. The Origin and Development of the Bodily World
Article 3. The Fact of Finality in the Bodily World

Article 1. The Nature of the Bodily World

a) Bodies; b) Quantity; c) Activity of Bodies; d) Constitution of Bodies.

a) Bodies

A *body* is a material substance which normally has extension in space by the three dimensions of length, width, and thickness.

We accept as sane men must, and for compelling reasons which we have considered in studying The Critical Question, the actuality of the bodily world in which we live. We find this world a vast complexity of *natural* bodies, among which we ourselves are numbered. Man, by his inventive activity, has made many *artificial* bodies, from bricks to chronometers, but these are only various arrangements, unions, and treatments of bodies that are found naturally existing in this world. Our present study is concerned with natural bodies, that is, with physical bodies as they exist or are existible in the material world, unchanged by human art or industry.

The bodily world and the bodies that make it up have the following characteristics: composition, changeability, contingency, limitation.

(*1*) *Composition.*—All bodies are compounded or composed. Large bodies are made of smaller bodies, and, as the chemist and physicist will explain, their ultimate physical division (for laboratory science) is a matter of molecules and atoms, and of atomic parts called protons and electrons. But this splitting of bodies into smaller and smaller *parts* cannot be an endless process; there is no material division that can run on to infinity. Physical partition, or division into parts, rests upon another sort of composition as its ultimate basis, and this composition is (as we shall explain hereafter) the composition of *primal matter* and *substantial form.* The point we make at present is simply this: bodies are necessarily *composed.* Composedness or composition is a property of bodies.

(*2*) *Changeability.*—Anything put together can be conceivably taken apart. Anything composed can be decomposed. In a word, anything compounded or composed is subject to *change.* Now, as we have seen, bodies are compounded or composed; hence they are subject to change. Changeability is a property of bodies. Change is called *substantial* when one substance ceases to be and another emerges. Substantial change is an *instantaneous* thing, which, looked at in one way, is the *ceasing* of one substance, and, regarded in another way, is the *emergence* of a new substance. The ceasing of a substance is called *corruption;* the simultaneous emergence of a new substance is called *generation.* The generation of one substance *is* the corruption of another or others, and vice versa. An example of substantial change is found in the process of nutrition by which lifeless food becomes living flesh. Change is called *accidental* when a substance, remaining itself, undergoes a shift in accidentals, as when water which is cold becomes hot. The most notable types of accidental change are *change of quantity* and *change of quality.* Change of quantity is either *increase* or *diminution,* as, for example, the change in the weight of a child from seventy to eighty pounds, or the change made in the contents of the sugar-bowl by taking out a spoonful for your coffee. Change of quality, called *alteration,* is a change in almost any accidental other than quantity; such, for instance, is the change from hot to cold, from young to old, from ignorant to learned, from sinfulness to grace. A change from "fat to thin" is at once a change in quantity and in quality. Our chief concern at this moment is to stress the truth that bodies are properly subject to change.

(3) *Contingency.*—A being which is so perfect that existence is of its very essence is called a *necessary* being; it is a thing that *must* exist and cannot be non-existent. A non-necessary being is called *contingent.* The word "contingent" means "dependent," for a contingent thing depends on its causes to produce it and maintain it; it has in itself no absolute *requirement* for existing. A contingent being *can* exist, but it does not *have* to exist, and it *would not* exist if definite causes, which are prior to it, did not operate to give it existence. It is manifest that bodies are contingent. For we see them emerge, and we see them disappear. Each birth and death, each spring and autumn, each dawn and dusk, is a plain proof of the *contingency* of bodies. For a thing which can *change* has no *necessity* in its being. And what has no necessity in its being is contingent. Now, we have seen that bodies are changeable; it follows that they are contingent.

(4) *Limitation.*—A thing which is absolutely unlimited is

called *infinite*. It is such a being as cannot be increased or decreased in any way; for an increase supposes a point or line or limit where the addition takes effect, and decrease is always a shrinking in of lines. Now, it is manifest that bodies are capable of increase and diminishment, whether literally in point of quantity or analogously in point of quality. Hence, bodies are not infinite, but finite or limited. Bodies, too, are capable of undergoing substantial change, and substantial change (generation-corruption) is a process of loss and gain which, like increase and diminishment, is incompatible with infinity. Therefore, we conclude that bodies as such are limited. Limitation is a property of bodies.

To sum up: a *body* is a material substance, normally extended by three dimensions, and marked by composition, changeability, contingency, and limitation.

b) Quantity

Quantity is that property of bodily substance which *extends* it, spreads out its parts; first, with reference to the bodily substance itself; second, with reference to the place that the bodily substance normally occupies.

Quantity therefore is *extension*. And, as the definition indicates, there are two types of extension. The first and essential type is *internal extension*. A normal effect of internal extension is *external* or *local extension*. A body must be extended *in itself* before it can be extended in space, that is before it can have *place*. And it is conceivable that a body should have the essential type of extension (that is, internal extension) without actually occupying space or being localized within external dimensions. We have no example of such a thing in the natural bodily world, but we have an example in the supernatural order: the actual Body of Christ is present in the Holy Eucharist without external extension.

Internal extension is a property of bodies, that is, it is a characteristic which belongs by natural necessity to bodies. External extension is a secondary effect of quantity (or of internal extension).

A body is not to be identified with its extension any more than a man is to be identified with his size. Just as the man *has* size, the body *has* extension; it is not true that the man *is* his size, nor is it true that a body *is* its extension. A body is a substance; quantity or extension is an accident, albeit a *proper* accident or *property*. A bodily substance is in itself independent of extension or quantity, although extension is *a required condition* for the normal existence of bodily substance in this material world.

The effects of quantity in an existing natural body are these: (*a*) the external extension and localization of the body; (*b*) the impenetrability of the body which renders naturally (but not supernaturally) impossible the compenetration of bodies; (*c*) divisibility of the body into an indefinite number of parts; (*d*) mensurability of the body, which renders it expressible in units of dimension or numberings of parts.

Quantity when unbroken is called *continuous quantity,* and a body of unbroken quantity is called *a continuum,* whether this be *perfect* or *imperfect,* that is, whether the continuum has absolute continuity without pores or interstices, or has, in fact, such "holes" which it surrounds as water surrounds islands. Quantity that is broken up in pieces (like a pound of sugar, or a heap of bits of broken glass) is called *discrete quantity.* Each item of a discrete quantity is a continuum. A discrete quantity is called *contiguous* if its parts or items touch one another (as in a spoonful of salt); it is called *separate* if the parts do not touch (as in a dozen eggs spread widely on a table). *The basis of quantity in bodies is perfectly continuous matter,* at least in its basic physical parts; and perfectly continuous matter can only exist in virtue of a unifying *form* or principle which *determines* the matter as an existing reality of an essential kind. Our bodily world is a great *contiguous quantity* (or *contiguum*) which is made of substances that are, in their essential existing elements, *true continua.*

The extension of the whole bodily universe,—that is, its natural external extension,—fills up *what we think of* as a kind of capacity or container, the name of which is *real space.* The position of each body in space is called its *place.* Our mental image of space as a container of bodies is a mental image and no more; it is an *ens rationis;* it is logical being, not real being. For space is only *thought of* as a container. As a fact, space *is* the actual extension of existing bodies in the universe.

In passing, it is to be noted that philosophy has no quarrel with science on the question of space or that of place. But some scientists, misunderstanding their own field, propound philosophies of space which are in conflict with sound reason. But with physics or mathematics as such, philosophy cannot come into contact or conflict. Professor Einstein's theory of the relativity of space or the curvedness of space does not concern us. This is not properly a theory of space but of *distance* and *measurement,* that is, of partial space and its interpretation in terms of numbering.

Since real space is the actual extension of existing bodies, and since bodies are limited, as we have learned, it follows that real space is limited. The universe may be expanding, it may be contracting, it may be doing neither. But whatever it is doing, at any given instant, it has its definite limits. The fact that man has no instruments to enable him to tell just where these limits lie, does not change the basic fact that the limits are there. Real space is finite.

In addition to real space we may mention *ideal space* (or *the idea of space*) which is the mind's concept of all possible space. So also we may mention *imaginary space* which is the envisioning by fancy or imagination of the visible reaches of space stretching on and on into the void. Ideal and imaginary space are indefinite; real space is definitely limited.

Bodies with quantity are subject to *change.* Change is movement or motion, for "change is a transit, a going-over, a movement from one state of being to another." Now, movement or motion is a matter of "now this—then that"; it is a matter of "before and after." And motion or change, under the aspect of before-and-after, is the basis of *real time*. Time in itself is described as a continuous and numerable series of motions under the aspect of before-and-after. Man conceives of time as *a measure,* just as he conceives of space as *a container*. But just as space in its reality is the real extension of bodies, so time in its reality is the continuous numerable succession of bodily movements. Time *as a measure* is logical being, not real being. Its serves man's uses to note some regular and reliable movement (of sun, of stars, of moon) and to use this as a standard of comparison with other and less regular motions. Thus we have solar time, sidereal time, lunar time. And man's inventiveness,—which is to say, his mind or intellect at grips with material problems,—has enabled him to devise mechanical instruments with regular movements that can be recorded, and to indicate these recordings as intervals of solar time, sidereal time, or lunar time. Thus we have chronometers, watches, clocks. Besides real time, we have *ideal time* which is the mind's concept of all possible numerable and continuous movement; and we have *imaginary time* which is the fanciful envisioning of real time indefinitely extended. Real time is necessarily *finite,* for it is finite motion in a finite world of finite bodies. Ideal time and imaginary time are *indefinite* or *potentially infinite,* but never actually infinite. Thoughtless people sometimes confuse ideal or imaginary time with *eternity*. But eternity is, strictly speaking, the opposite of time. It is an endless "now"; it has nothing of "before and after" which is of the essence of time. Eternity in its strict meaning belongs only to the Infinite Being, to God. Angels and men's separated souls (and men's bodies after the resurrection) have "eviternity" or endless duration without the vicissitudes of time.

c) Activity of Bodies

Activity is a doing, an operating, or at least a co-operating, a responding. All bodily substances are *active* if it were only in holding their parts together by cohesion, or in responding to the thing called gravitation, which is really the effect of the activity of body on body.

Bodily activity is *immanent* or *vital* when its chief effect is in the *agent,* that is, in the thing which is active. Growing, for example, is first of all in the growing body. A tree's growth has an outer effect; the tree casts a larger shade as it grows taller and fuller; it may so grow as to block the view from a window; but the *main effect* of growing is in the growing tree. Such activity is therefore called *immanent,* that is, "indwelling." Non-immanent activity is called *transient,* that is, "passing over" and having its effect outside the agent. The activity of the growing tree in blocking the window, or in throwing a shadow, is transient. Growth is *immanent;* these outer and alien consequences of growth are transient. Truly immanent activity is always *life-activity* or, as it is usually called, *vital* activity.

Transient activity is called *mechanical* when it consists of *local movement.* Such is the activity of the rolling stone, the turning wheel, the expanding balloon, the rising steam, the drive of the tennis-racquet against the ball. Transient activity is called *physical* when it consists of change or motion in quality. Such is the activity of a light which continuously sends out its rays, the activity of a sounding body, the activity of an electrical charge. It will be noticed that physical activity is normally *accompanied by mechanical activity,* for some local movement is to be discerned in every qualitative change or movement; but physical activity as such does not *consist* of these local movements. The man who says that heat is movement (meaning local or mechanical movement) is not thinking clearly or observing well; he should say that heat is *produced* by mechanical movement and is *accompanied by* mechanical movement; he has no right to assert that heat *is* mechanical movement. Transient activity is called *chemical* when it affects a body in its substantial being, and usually changes it into another substance or other substances. Such is the activity which resolves water into hydrogen and oxygen. Chemical activity is usually accompanied by both mechanical and physical activity.

Bodily activity is something which the bodily substance *does;* it is not what the bodily substance *is*. Each body is equipped by its nature with certain powers for activity. No body is *immediately* active, but it is active *mediately,* that is through the *medium* of real powers which it possesses. These powers, in themselves, are accidentals of the bodily substance; they are among its *qualities*.

A false philosophy (that is, a false cosmology) called *mechanistic materialism* teaches that the world consists of *matter and motion*. But this theory is so much a simplification that it is a falsification. It does not explain the origin of motion which is never self-originating; it does not explain the transference of motion; it does not explain the conserving of motion. Another false cosmology (called *energeticism*) explains the bodily world as a complexity of kinetic and potential energies which act according to the laws of conservation, intensity, and entropy. Now these "laws" may be at work in the world but they do not explain the world. Energy requires a source, a sustaining power, a transferring power. To speak of energies, and waves of power, and electrical charges, and so on, without reference to actual substantial bodies exercising such powers by true bodily activity, is like speaking of the tides while denying the existence of the ocean. The truth is that bodily activity exists as the product of bodily substance equipped with powers for exercising such activity.

d) Constitution of Bodies

The question here raised is that of the *ultimate* constitution of bodily substance. We seek to know what makes a body *a body,* and what makes any body an existing reality of the essential or specific kind that it actually is. Thus our investigation probes far more deeply into reality than that of the physicist and the chemist who wish to know the *proximate* constitution of the bodies they handle in their laboratories. Ours is a *philosophical* inquiry; theirs is an *experimental* investigation. The physicist who explains to us that a body is made up of atoms and atomic parts, leaves us, philosophically speaking, exactly where we were before he explained. For the smallest atomic part is *a body.* And our inquiry is, "What makes a body a body?" To tell us that a body is made of smaller bodies is to tell us precisely nothing; our inquiry is about the smallest body as well as about the largest.

The theories about the constitution of bodies may be reduced to four: monism, atomism, dynamism, hylemorphism.

(*1*) *Monism,* a name derived from the Greek *monos* "alone" or "single," means the theory that this bodily world is all one kind of reality; that there are no substantial or essential differences among bodies. Monism is of two types. (*a*) *Materialistic monism* makes the world a vast lump of homogeneous matter of which all bodies,—lifeless, living, plants, animals, men, earth, air, stars,—are different shapings, like differently shaped biscuits from one pan of dough. (*b*) *Idealistic monism* denies the reality of bodily substances as our senses present them to knowledge, and makes them various "appearances" or "expressions" of thought, of will, of "the unconscious," of "the Absolute," of "the Unknowable." The pupil will take benefit here if he will cast back to the First Part of this manual and read again what has been said of the philosophies of Spinoza, Fichte, von Schelling, Hegel, Schopenhauer, Spencer. Both types of monism are *pantheistic,* for if only one reality exists, this must be self-existent reality, and self-existent reality is Infinite Being or God.

Monism is inept and inadmissible. It is inept inasmuch as it offers itself as a philosophy of bodies and then refuses to explain bodies. For it is no explanation of the essence of bodies to say that there is only one body, or that bodies are only apparent. Monism is inadmissible because it involves self-contradiction and thus conflicts with reason, and because it disagrees with normal sense experience which is the basis of all certitude. Both types of monism involve self-contradiction. Materialistic monism makes bodily substance self-existent and hence infinite, whereas bodily substance is (as we have seen) necessarily limited; thus monism preaches "a finite infinity" or "an infinite finiteness." Idealistic monism says there are no bodies, and then tries to explain them as bodily expressions of something else. Both types of monism are manifestly in conflict with normal sense experience, for it is one of the clearest facts of immediate experience that we are living in an actual universe of different bodies.

(2) *Atomism* here means *the atomist philosophy*. It does not mean *the atomic theory* which is generally accepted among scientists. With the atomic theory we have no concern and certainly no quarrel. The case is otherwise with the atomist philosophy. The atomic theory is like an explanation of a log as a thing made up of grains of wood, a perfectly sound doctrine as far as it goes. The atomist philosophy is like an explanation of a log in terms of its grains alone, denying all reference to a tree; and this is an utterly unsound theory.

Atomist philosophy has two notable forms. (*a*) *Mechanistic atomism* says that the bodily world is made up of minimum-particles (or *atoms*) of homogeneous matter, which have different shapes and sizes, and are kept in motion by some outside force. (*b*) *Dynamistic atomism* says that the minimum-particles of homogeneous matter are endowed with their own power of motion. Both forms of atomism explain bodies as the clusterings of differently shaped, differently sized, and variously moved atoms. There is, therefore, no real difference among bodies, and no individual body is truly a substantial unity. Most atomists hold that the atom-clusters called bodies are the result of a chance meeting of these minimum-particles of matter.

We reject the atomist theory as inadequate. It proposes itself as a philosophy of bodies, and ends precisely where it starts—with bodies. To say that bodies are clusters of smaller bodies is still to leave bodies unexplained. Further, the atomist theory unwarrantedly rejects the notion of true substantial unity, and therewith it upsets the possibility of achieving certitude. For, if we cannot trust our knowledge of the substantial character of individual bodies, we cannot trust knowledge at all, and must lapse into the insane position of the skeptic. Finally, atomism is unacceptable because it ignorantly proposes chance as a cause. Chance is never a cause. Chance is a circumstance which belongs to an unpredictable *effect*.

(*3*) *Dynamism,* a name derived from the Greek *dynamis* "force" or "power," means the theory that what we call substantial bodies are collections of "points of force" which have no extension (that is, no quantity), and which attract one another up to a certain distance and then hold one another off. Thus, though unextended, they constitute extended matter by marking, so to speak, extended intervals. The power-points are changeless; hence there is no such thing as substantial change in the world, or even substantial difference of bodies.

It will be noticed that dynamism, like atomism, is radically monistic. All three of the doctrines so far considered have this in common: they reduce the world to a single thing which is either a mass of homogeneous particles, or a series of expressions of a single non-bodily substance, or a complexity of indestructible power-points which are all of the same nature.

We reject dynamism as self-contradictory and inadequate. If dynamism recognizes the actual extension of bodies, it does so by the self-contradictory process of adding a series of zeros and reaching a positive sum. For unextended power-point plus unextended power-point results in inextension, not actual extension. Even if the points are separated by intervals of distance, there is pure vacancy between and among them, and the result of their addition must still be zero. Thus the form of dynamism which affirms the actual extension of bodies also denies the actual extension of bodies. If we consider the form of dynamism which frankly denies the actuality of bodies and makes the universe a dream-world of mere appearances, we find that the theory cannot explain the appearances or interpret the dream. For unextended power-points in motion are invisible and cannot create the illusion of a visible world. Indeed, no illusion of a solid universe could be excited in a mind which had no experience of real solidity to begin with. Dynamism cannot explain what we call solidity, it cannot explain substance, it cannot explain the organic unity of a living body. It invokes the activity of power-points across a void (that is, *actio in distans*), a thing which philosophy finds, at best, of very dubious possibility, and which science has never discovered in any experiment.

The electrical theory of matter and even the electrical theory of life are dynamistic. While that extremely mysterious thing called electricity is everywhere at work in the world, it is a thing which affects bodies but does not wholly constitute bodies. Too many inadequate scientists of our day like to talk in abstract terms of what is really concrete; they say that protons and electrons are "charges" of electricity (that is, "points of power"). What they mean, of course, is that protons and electrons are *particles of bodily substance* charged with electricity.

(4) *Hylemorphism,* a term made up of two Greek words, *hyle* "matter" and *morphe* "form," is the name of the Scholastic doctrine on the ultimate constitution of bodies. This doctrine holds that a body is composed of *primal matter* and *substantial form.* It is the doctrine first explained by Aristotle, four centuries before Christ, and we may say without boasting that it stands miles above any alternative doctrine proposed since. For it meets the full problem it seeks to solve, and it offers a full solution. The doctrine of hylemorphism is not revealed; it is not a doctrine that can claim divine authority. But it is a doctrine which, despite difficulties, has weathered the intellectual and experimental

storms of nearly twenty-five hundred years, and is still the only rounded explanation of the nature of bodies that we possess. It has thus a sound claim upon the attention of our minds. It has a very strong case. Yet there has been, among non-Scholastic philosophers, a marked tendency to contemn this doctrine without investigating it, and even some Scholastics have learned to speak of it with something of a cold and aloof manner. Even men who, in most of their philosophical work, merit our respect, stoop to the indecency and the dishonesty of condemning or ridiculing hylemorphism without having the slightest conception of what it actually teaches, or rather, with a totally wrong conception of what it teaches. For example, Mr. C. E. M. Joad, in his *Guide to Philosophy* propounds, jocosely, a certain series of comments of the "jugginess" of jugs; for this, when he comes to understand hylemorphism he will some day sit in sackcloth and ashes, for he has not shown up hylemorphism; he has only shown that it is possible for a really learned man to air abysmal ignorance.

Now, there are two facts about any actual bodily substance that a philosophy of bodies must face and explain. First, the bodily substance is *a body*. But it is more than that, for it is quite impossible for a body to exist without a specific determinant. We cannot say that a bodily substance *actually exists* as a body and nothing more; that it is no *kind* of bodily substance, but just pure *body*. The second thing, therefore, about an actual body is that it is a determinate *specific* or *essential* kind of body. In a word, some substantial principle must explain the *bodiliness* of a body; and some substantial principle, fused into substantial unity with the first, must explain the *existing specific character* of a body. Hylemorphism calls the first of these principles *primal matter* (or *prime matter*) and the second of these principles *substantial form.*

Let us envision the favorite figure of the old-fashioned novelist. Let us contemplate "the solitary horseman" riding between rows of trees along a rocky road. We shall not pause upon the romantic suggestions of the picture. We shall coldly reduce it to its elements for purposes of philosophical illustration. We shall consider these four things: the man, the horse, the trees, the rocks. Here we have four examples of bodily substance. And the first truth about them is that they are all *bodies,* one as much as another, one as truly and completely as another. Yet, since we are not monists, we face the further fact that, although all these bodies are bodies, they are essentially or specifically different *kinds* of bodies. Each is a bodily *substance;* there is no mere *accidental* in their true bodiliness. Nor is there any mere accidental in their difference as bodily substances. For a substance that is living, like the tree, is *substantially* different from the substance which lacks life, like the rock. And a substance that has sentiency, like the horse, is substantially different from a non-sentient substance, like the tree. And, finally, a substance which has understanding and will (that is, *rational life*), is substantially different from a substance which lacks these perfections; so that the man and the horse are different by no mere accidental difference, but by a substantial difference. The four bodies are all bodily *substance,* yet the four bodies differ from one another *as substances.* There must be, therefore, *a dual substantial principle,* or, more accurately, *two substantially fused substantial principles* in each of these bodies. For the four things are in agreement, they are *at one* as bodily substances, and, at the same time, they are not *the same* substance at all, but are *substantially different.* There must be a substantial principle in each of the four which is the basis of its bodiliness; there must be a substantial principle in each of the four which is the substantial determinant of the kind of substance that it is. The first of these principles is *prime matter;* the second is *substantial form.*

Prime matter or *materia prima* is the substantial principle found in all bodies. It is *common* to all bodies. It is the *common substrate* of all bodies. In point of prime matter, all bodies are *at one.* So far, monism is right; but monism goes calamitously wrong when it stops here. Prime matter is wholly without determinateness in itself. It cannot *exist* itself, for, as we have noticed, it is impossible for an existing body to be just a body and no more, that is, just a body, and not any *kind* of body. Prime matter is substantial, but it is an *incomplete* substance; it requires another substantial thing to exist with it, or rather to give it existence in a determinate body. And this other substantial principle (unless it be a spiritual principle) requires prime matter to determine and make exist as a body; this other substantial principle (always remembering the exception in favor of a spiritual substance) is also an *incomplete* substance. Each leans on each, although the one (prime matter) is the *determinable* element, and the other (the substantial form) is the *determining* element. A crude, and in many ways misleading, illustration of this twofold incompleteness which constitutes a single completeness may be found in the two beams which come together to make the sturdy support of a gable roof. Neither beam can lean at its angle and support the roof without the other. Each renders an incomplete service. But *together* the beams render a complete service. So with the basic elements of bodies.

Prime matter is called "pure potentiality," that is, pure capacity for existence as a body. It is a capacity which must be filled up, determined, made into the only existible body (that is a specific *kind* of *existing* body) by a substantial principle other than itself. And, since the result of the union of this determining principle with prime matter is *a single bodily substance,* the union itself must be *a substantial union,* the substantial fusing of two substantial principles into an actuality which is *a third thing,* and not prime matter alone, not substantial form alone, but *an existing body of a specific kind.*

Prime matter then cannot exist itself, *unformed.* It does exist, but not alone. It exists as the common substrate of all existing bodies. It is that which *makes* any body a body; not *actively,* but by *passively* receiving the impress and union of the substantial form. For the whole character of prime matter is its passivity, its inertness, its indifference (or lack of tendency) to become this kind of body rather than another, in a word, its *potentiality*.

Substantial form, however, is active, determining. It makes the body *actual* (that is, an *existing* body) in a definite *specific kind* of actual bodiliness. The result of the substantial union of substantial form with prime matter is called *second matter* or *materia secunda;* and, of course, *materia secunda* means an existing bodily substance. Substantial form is the root and source of bodily actuality, of substantial determinateness, of activity. Prime matter is wholly potential, indeterminate, inactive or inert.

The doctrine of hylemorphism is not a mere clever invention. It is an explanation based upon the facts of a case. And the test of its value is the fact that it stands up. It has faced many difficulties. There are cases that seem to upset it. But careful investigation has always justified it.

The progress of experimental science, the splitting of the atom, the place and apparent power of one electron more or less in the constitution of a definite substance,—each of these facts, and others of like character, have seemed to some philosophers and to many scientists to be in conflict with the hylemorphic doctrine. But it is not so. There is no value in an argument of this sort: "If I knock out an electron of an atom of substance-A and find that I now have substance-B, it seems that these were basically one substance to start with." The answer is that it seems nothing of the sort. The difference is not a mere difference of accidental character because a number of like particles is an accidental thing in itself. For, although substances act upon one another through powers which are *in themselves* accidental, the activity is truly *of substance upon substance*. And if an electron more, or an electron less, should induce change, this may well be a substantial change. It may well be a change of structure unsuited to the enduring of a certain substantial form, which disappears in consequence; and the new structure receives simultaneously that substantial form which it is suited to support. You change the substance of coal into a variety of substances loosely called "ashes and smoke" by applying the substance of fire. Yet this substantial change is affected by *powers* and *capacities* of the substances concerned, and these capacities and powers are, in themselves, as accidental as a mere numerical sum or numerical arrangement of electrons. The splitting of the atom, or the discovery of the character and function of electrons, is no more a new difficulty to the philosopher of bodily actuality than is the shovelling of coal on the furnace fire.

Indeed, if we short-sightedly declare that true substantial change does not occur, that all substances are the same determinate substance, we still must identify that substance as *bodily* (that is, as having prime matter) and as *determinate in its kind* of bodiliness (that is, as having substantial form). So hylemorphism stands in any case.

But to make all substances one substance is to fall into a self-contradictory theory called monism. It is to destroy the value of the doctrine itself which is proposed as true and certain, for if monism were true, human certitude would be bankrupt. By their fruits you shall know them; a doctrine which leads logically to skepticism or to monism or to both, is a doctrine that bears the evil fruits of falsity. The fact that there is an apparent difficulty on the side of sanity is surely no excuse for going insane. It is rather a strong challenge to the champions of sanity to study its resources more completely and apply its powers more thoroughly and astutely.

For, argue as you will, experiment as you choose, the fact remains and will ever remain that any bodily substance is *bodily* and is a certain specific *kind*. Any body has, of plain necessity, matter and form. If you consider the *terms* old-fashioned, you are privileged to invent more pleasing ones. But you cannot change facts by changing names.

There are persons indeed who say that there is no substantial change. Yet these persons would have a hard time proving their assertion, and the proof lies with them because they make the claim in the face of common human experience and of common human certitude. They have to prove a universal negative experimentally; any logician will be pleased to point out to them the difficulties of their situation.

The change from a living body to a corpse is indubitably a substantial change. For everything by which we identify the organic unity and the substantial character of the living body is not only changed by the thing called death, but all the processes once in possession and in operation are actually *reversed*. Instead of organic unity, we have (immediately upon death) a strong tendency to disunity and diversity; instead of a unified drive or tendency to vital function, we have the tendency to rest and equilibrium. In a word, by all the tests which distinguish one kind of body from another, the corpse is a radically different kind of thing from the living body. Substantial change is a fact. Another interesting example of substantial change is the change of bread and butter into the living flesh of the diner.

Now, if substantial change is a fact, it is an inexplicable fact unless two things are acknowledged: the substances concerned (the substance changed, and the substance which is the result of change) and some substantial actuality which supports the change. When food is digested, it is not a mere preliminary process which *annihilates* the food, a meaningless process which is unaccountably accompanied by the *creation* of blood cells. The ceasing of the food to be food *is* the emerging of the blood cells which came from the change of food. There is no *annihilation* (an abrupt and complete cessation of being) and a simultaneous *creation* (an abrupt and entire production out of nothing of a new being wholly unrelated to the other). No; there is a substantial *change* of food into blood. Now, a change is a transit, a going-over. And a going-over requires a support which does not go over, but which is determined in bodily being first by one determinant, and, this giving way, by a new determinant which instantly takes the place of that which gives way. The support of substantial change is itself a substantial thing, and a substantial element of each of the two substantial bodily beings in turn. This support of substantial change is called *prime matter;* the substantial determinant which makes it one kind of body, and then the new substantial determinant which makes it another substantial body, is called, each in its turn, *substantial form.* Again, you may not like the terms *matter* and *form,* but you cannot deny the facts for which they stand. Substantial change is inexplicable without hylemorphism, although, as we say, you might like it under a more modern name, such as precipitation, or galvinization, or the etiology of substantial emergence.

We have truly said that there are four, and only four, doctrines which propose themselves as fundamental philosophies of bodies, although three of them are not fundamental at all. *All* philosophies of bodies must, in last analysis, be resolved into one or other of these four forms. Now, we have found that three of these four doctrines are unacceptable, for they conflict with experience and are in themselves self-contradictory. Therefore, by exclusion, we prove the one acceptable doctrine to be the true doctrine. This doctrine is hylemorphism.

We stand, therefore, by the doctrine of hylemorphism. We defend it, not as partisans "taking sides," but as lovers of truth. We refuse to leave what is manifestly reasonable, although sometimes difficult of application, in favor of what is manifestly unreasonable and often impossible of application. Hence our acceptance of hylemorphism is right and reasonable; it is worlds away from the stubborn business of taking sides in free debate. In a word, we accept hylemorphism on evidence. Most of those who reject it do so by reason of mood, or temperament, or prejudice, or the desire to keep pace with the current scientistic fashion. It is not difficult to decide which of the parties stands on the more solid ground.

Summary of the Article

In this Article we have defined *body,* and have learned that a bodily substance is, by its nature, *composed, changeable, contingent,* and *limited.* We have investigated the proper accident of bodily substance known as *quantity* or *extension.* We have described *internal extension* and *external extension,* and have noticed that external extension is a secondary effect of true quantity. We have noticed the effects of quantity on a natural body: *external extension, impenetrability, divisibility, mensurability.* We have defined a *continuum,* a *contiguum,* and *discrete quantity,* and have found that the basis of quantity in bodies is perfectly continuous matter. We have investigated briefly the quantities known as *space* and *time.* We have seen that natural bodies are truly the source of *activity,* and we have distinguished activity or action as *immanent* (or *vital*) and *transient.* We have noticed the essential flaw in the cosmologies of "matter and motion" as an explanation of the bodily world. We have studied the ultimate constitution of bodies, listing the four types of doctrine (*monism, atomism, dynamism, hylemorphism*) and have found that hylemorphism alone is without self-contradiction, without conflict with experience, and is in itself a doctrine that squares with the facts it purports to explain.

Article 2. The Origin and Development of the Bodily World

a) First Beginning of Bodies; b) The Age of the World; c) Development of the World.

a) First Beginning of Bodies

That bodies come from other bodies by a process of substantial change called *generation* is a matter of common knowledge and common experience. That the egg comes from the hen, the fruit from the tree, and that, subsequently, a hen comes from an egg, and a tree from the seed of its fruit, are matters that need no proof beyond the mere mention of the known fact. Nor do we need to prove that coal has a vegetal origin, or that water can become hydrogen and oxygen. Our present concern is not, therefore, the origin of bodies by substantial generation, whether this be vital or non-vital. Nor are we concerned with the interesting game of guessing which came first, the hen or the egg. We are interested solely in the fact that there necessarily was a first coming of bodies, and we seek to know by what means this first coming was effected.

Before we take up the question directly, we must reply to the mistaken persons who deny our assertion that a first coming of bodies is a necessity. These people say that bodily substance is *eternal,* that it had no beginning, that it always was and always will be. Some of the defenders of the eternity of matter declare that matter is self-existent and self-sufficient; that it needs no power other than itself to account for its present multiplicity and diversity, or for its marvellous arrangement in various individual bodies, notably in living bodies. This is the doctrine of *atheistic materialism.* Other defenders of the eternity of matter acknowledge some existing power outside matter, some God in fact, who arranges and manages the material world, and gets it on in a seemly sort of development. This is the doctrine of *theistic materialism.* There is yet another type of materialism in connection with the existence and development of matter (for the term *materialism* is very wide in scope and very vague in its general meaning). This is *agnostic materialism* which artfully dodges the issue of God's existence, neither affirming nor denying it. Agnostic materialism simply regards matter (that is, bodily substance or *materia secunda*) as eternal, and suggests that it exists by chance, or by some inner unknown law of its being, or by the operation of an infinite series of causes which make it *evolve* in a certain way,—an infinite series of chicken-and-egg activity, so to speak, in which neither the chicken nor the egg came first. Now, the point to dwell upon is this: all types of materialism of this cosmological sort stress the assertion that matter is *unproduced.* There are philosophers who contend that matter has been *created from eternity,* but these are not the materialists of whom we are now speaking. The materialists do not admit that matter was ever created, even from eternity; they claim that matter is *unproduced,* not created at all, not *caused;* it's just *here.* Yet it is an accepted truth that anything which exists must have an explanation of its existence. If the explanation is in the existing thing itself, then that thing must be so perfect that it *requires* existence; existence is of its *essence;* it is *necessary being,* and, by that fact, it is *infinite* being, *changeless* being, simple or *uncomposed* being. If the explanation of an existing thing is not to be found in itself, it must necessarily be found *in its causes.* Now, the materialists who affirm the eternity of matter deny that it has any causes. Therefore, they hold that matter is in itself necessary, infinite, changeless, uncomposed. But we have seen that matter is precisely the opposite of all this. We have seen that bodies (that is *materia secunda*) are not necessary but *contingent,* not infinite but *finite* or *limited,* not changeless but *changeable* and indeed constantly *changing,* not simple but *composed* or *compounded.* Thus we reject the materialistic theory of the eternity of matter because it is in conflict with plain facts. Further, it contradicts itself; for to speak of unproduced matter is simply to speak of an unproduced production.

Another preliminary problem must be disposed of here. It is raised by the *materialistic pantheists* who identify God and the bodily universe. Like the materialist defenders of the eternity of matter, these pantheists propound a flatly self-contradictory doctrine. For to conceive of God is inevitably to conceive of the Necessary Being, and, by that token, of the Being that is Infinite, Changeless, Simple. But, as we have repeatedly seen, the world is contingent, finite, changeable, and composed. We need not labor the point further; pantheism falls with the materialistic theory of the eternity of unproduced matter.

There is only one other conceivable explanation of the world. It is the explanation which acknowledges the world as *caused,* as *produced,* and this means that it had an absolute and a First Cause, a First Producer, who brought it into being without using any materials at all, who in fact *created* it. This doctrine is called *creationism,* and it is the true explanation of the first origin of the world. This fact is already proved by exclusion. For if three possibilities can be considered, and two of them are found to be illusory and no possibilities at all, the third must stand. And stand it does, not only because all other explanations fail, but because it actually meets the facts in the case and actually explains them to the satisfaction of both reason and experience.

We assert then that the first origin of bodies is found in the act of *creation* by which Almighty God produced them out of nothing. Creation is defined as *the producing of a thing in its entirety out of nothing.* Such a producing is an act of infinite power, and is proper to God alone, and indeed so proper to God that no creature could serve Him, even as an instrumental cause, in the activity of creating. The boundless power of God which can call up *being* and set it in *existence* can also endow bodily being with the tendency and power to develop, to reproduce, to carry on substantial change. We are, as we have said, familiar with this productive process; our only problem was the finding of the *first origin* of the world. This first origin is *creation.*

b) The Age of the World

We have noticed that there are philosophers who think that the world was created from eternity. These persons hold rightly that matter was *produced.* But they assert that God, who exists eternally and certainly can act eternally (and, indeed, does act eternally) has *created* from eternity, so that the world, while produced, had no *beginning in time,* but only a beginning in its nature.

Now, it is true that God acts from eternity, or acts eternally. With God, the Infinite Being, "to will is to accomplish," and no *delay* (as we should phrase it) *in the creatural effect* can have any influence upon the eternal decree which destined the effect or set it in being. But it must be remembered, too, that creation does involve the creature as well as the Creator. The question is not, "Can God create from eternity?" for He is unlimited in power. The question is, "Can a creature *receive* eternal existence, in the sense of beginningless creation?" There is no question of limitation in God; there is great question of capacity in the creature. To say that you cannot take the Atlantic ocean into a teacup is not to say anything about the limits of the ocean; it is to state the limitations of the teacup. Similarly, to state that creation from eternity is impossible is not to limit the limitless God, or say that *here* is a thing He cannot do. It is merely to say that a creature,—and, in our case, a bodily creature,—has not the capacity for receiving eternal or beginningless creation.

We may not declare that creation (in effect) from eternity is absolutely impossible. But it surely looks impossible. God's *decree* to create is as eternal as God; but it seems that this decree, as regards bodies at least, is *an eternal decree to create in time.* And the reasons that make the creation of the world from eternity look impossible are briefly these:

(*1*) *Bodies are changeable* and indeed they are undergoing constant accidental change, and they also undergo substantial change. They experience a series of changes, movements, events. But such a series is actually the essential basis of *time.* Such a series is necessarily a series *with a beginning* as an *event* or *first time-element.* It cannot be an infinite series, since an infinite series of finite things is impossible.

(*2*) *The existence and the record or history of bodies* is a matter measurable by a series of instants or moments, and these are normally the marks of *time.* Tracing back the record by moments, we are compelled to find a *first* moment, that is a first point of *time.*

It appears then that bodies were created in time and not from eternity. Of course, as Christians, we know that creation did take place in time. We have the Scriptural record that God created "in the *beginning";* and the Fourth Lateran Council declared that God "from the beginning *of time,* made out of nothing the creature, both bodily and spiritual." We offer these citations merely to show how reason and Revelation are in agreement on a point. We do not propose either Scripture or the authority of the teaching Church as argument, for such argument is not available to philosophy.

For the rest, there is no need to insist upon creation from eternity as an explanation of the bodily world. And, as St. Thomas Aquinas points out, creation in time is better calculated to impress us with the absolute necessity of a Creator than is creation from eternity.

As to the actual age of the world in terms of *years since the creation,* we can only guess. Scientists seem to prefer guessing in millions and billions of years. Mark Twain said a sagacious thing, and not a merely flip thing, when he declared that some scientists delight in furnishing us "with a spoonful of fact and a carload of conjecture."

The "days of creation" mentioned in Scripture cannot, by force of the word "day," mean periods of twenty-four hours; for the sun, the basis of the twenty-four hour calculation, was not created until the fourth day. These six days (the periods called *the hexahemeron*) may have been tremendous stretches of time. Long or short, there could be no difference to God who is eternal and outside time. But geology, for the earth, and astronomy, for the cosmos in general, seem to indicate that the days of creation were periods of many thousands or even many millions of years. This question, however, is negligible for philosophy.

c) Development of the World

It is known that this earth of ours, which is a very small part of what is called the cosmos or the world, was not always as it is now. It has gone through a series of changes; it has undergone a development. Time was when the earth could not support life; later, plant life appeared, later still came animal life. It is likely that our solar system, and the countless other solar systems of the cosmos or universe of bodies, have also developed and undergone notable changes since the day of the first creation.

The part of cosmology which studies world-development is called *cosmogony.* Our special sciences of geology, zoology, botany, biology, and others, investigate the development of the earth and of living things on the earth. These special sciences, of course, are not philosophy, nor has philosophy any direct concern with their findings. Indirectly, however, the findings must fall under the light of philosophical truths.

The theory that the world was slowly developed out of a mass of primordial matter created for the purpose of such development, and guided and supported in the development by Almighty God, seems very likely true. We may call the development of the world a process of *inorganic evolution,* that is, a development of lifeless bodies by graded stages. As to the development of *life on earth* by a process of *organic evolution,* there is as yet no certainty and perhaps certainty in the matter is unattainable. Philosophy has no quarrel with the hypothesis, nor has religion, except that *human evolution* is in conflict with divine revelation as well as with the findings of solid science. The hypothesis of human evolution, which has intrigued the minds of men since the days of Anaximander in ancient Greece, was a kind of Victorian religion but, like most things Victorian, it has largely faded in our own day. Most scientists of ability and repute are quite ready to agree with Virchow that science knows nothing of any ancestors of man. A point for constant remembrance is this: any process of world-development, or of earth-development, or of the development of plant-life and animal-life, absolutely requires a first Creator who endowed matter with the fitness for development, and with powers for development, and who supports the developing creatures in existence and concurs with their developing activity. No form of evolution or transformism, even the crudest, can get rid of the idea of God the Creator, God the Conserver, and God the Concurrer.

Summary of the Article

In this Article we have seen the necessity of assigning *a first beginning* to account for the existence of bodies. We have considered the hypothesis of *uncaused eternal matter* and have found it wholly unacceptable because it involves a flat self-contradiction. For similar reasons we have rejected *materialistic pantheism.* We have been forced to the conclusion that the only explanation of the existence of bodies is to be found in the fact of *a first creation.* We have defined *creation,* and have contrasted it with *generation* or the substantial emergence of bodies subsequent to creation. We have studied the question of world-development, and of earth-development, mentioning hypotheses and theories proposed to explain the world and the earth as these now exist.

Article 3. The Fact of Finality in the Bodily World

a) Finality; b) The Ultimate End of the World; c) Nature; d) Miracles.

a) Finality

Finality is *final tendency* or *teleological tendency;* it is tendency towards an end, a purpose, a goal.

That bodies exercise such tendency is manifest. Bodies tend to hold on to existence, each in its own nature and order, and existence is surrendered only to compelling forces of destruction which come from other bodies. Among living bodies, the tendency to grow, to attain a rounded maturity and fruitfulness, is evident to anyone who ever planted a garden or noticed the development of animals or of children. No one denies that things in this bodily world tend to proper and proportionate ends. But some persons deny that this tendency is the manifestation of *a purpose,* of *a design;* they deny that this tendency is something *intended* by the Creator, and that it points on to an *ultimate* end. Against these we assert the doctrine of *full finality,* of *end intended,* of *an ultimate end of the world.*

b) The Ultimate End of the World

By the word "end," in its present use, we mean no simple termination, no *finishing* and nothing more. We mean purpose, goal, end-in-view. The phrase "the ultimate end of the world" means the final purpose for which the world is *made* and for which it *exists* and towards the fulfillment of which it constantly *tends*. That there is such an end can be shown by establishing the fact of *design* or *plan* in the world of bodies; for design or plan is a rational means of reaching an end, a purpose, and, in last analysis, an *ultimate* purpose or end.

In this world, natural bodies exhibit a true intrinsic finality, for they cling to their being and their nature, and they manifest activity that is consistent, constant, uniformly proportionate to the active nature of the body in each case. The intrinsic finality or tendency of bodies is for *what is good for them:* self-preservation, quest of food, permanence of their kind through generation or reproduction. In a secondary way, bodies tend towards *what is good for other bodies,* as by the abundance of fruits and seeds, few of which can cause reproduction but which serve as food for plants, animals, and men, and which impress reasoning creatures (that is, in the bodily world, human beings) with the great generosity of the Giver of good gifts. Now, this intrinsic finality of bodies is certainly the result of a plan, and of a plan which comes of intelligence, and ultimately of Supreme Intelligence.

The finality of natural bodies, and their magnificent structure which fits them admirably for their connatural activities, are incontrovertible evidence of *design* and of ultimate Intelligence, and so of Ultimate End. Nor can *imperfections* in bodies be alleged as an argument against design or finality. For imperfections cannot be recognized as such unless by a mind which has the grasp of a standard, by a mind which knows what *perfection* in the case means; for an imperfection is a falling short of *a recognized perfection,* that is, of a recognized design, plan, and purpose. You cannot know what imperfect eyesight is unless you have knowledge of what perfect eyesight is. Imperfections are a proof of perfection, that is *of the standard.* When a person objects that such or such a body falls short of perfection, he acknowledges the existence of the standard of perfection and the normal tendency of a body to attain it.

There is, then, in this world of bodies a finality, a drive towards a certain perfection, a tendency towards a goal or end. Now, ends are often like steps in a stairway, one is subordinate to another. But none of the steps has any meaning at all except in view of the *last* step. It is the *ultimate* end which gives meaning to all subordinate ends. Wherever there is a series of connected ends, there is an ultimate end.

The ultimate end of the world must be the end established by the Creator; it must be the Creator's purpose in creating. And since *end* means *good*, the ultimate end must be the ultimate good, the complete fulfillment of every tendency to good. It must be the Limitless and Necessary Good Itself. In a word, it must be Almighty God. The words of Holy Writ may serve us as a scientific statement of fact, "The Lord hath made all things for himself."

Notice another conclusive argument for the truth that God is the ultimate end of all creatures. God is infinite Wisdom; He therefore acts for a most worthy end. But *before* creation (to speak in imperfect human terms) there is no actuality except God alone; there is nothing that could serve as an end except God Himself. Therefore God creates all creatures for Himself; God is their ultimate end.

How shall things serve their last end; how shall bodies serve the purpose of the Creator who made them for Himself? *By manifesting His goodness,* and thus *procuring His external formal and objective glory.*

All bodily creatures, man excepted, tend *by necessity* to their ultimate end, and necessarily attain it. Man has free-choice, and he may abuse it, he may sin. But his sin cannot defeat the purpose of his existence, except for himself personally. *He* may come to utter ruin and everlasting pain; but his existence as an image of God is a manifestation of God's loving kindness, of His power, of His wisdom. And even in hell, man will render testimony by his intelligence to the *justice* of God just as truly as souls in heaven will render intelligent testimony (or *formal glory*) to the *mercy* of God. And God is *one;* in God justice and mercy are substantially one, and are identified with God Himself. Hence, all bodily creation, man included, will inevitably attain its ultimate end. If man misses his own endless felicity, he has missed *the secondary end* of his existence, not its primary or ultimate end.

c) Nature

The *nature* of a thing means its working essence. But in our present use of this term we mean *general nature,* we mean all bodily substances (since cosmology speaks only of bodies) inasmuch as these produce or undergo effects. We mean the active world around us: the air, the clouds, the running streams, the minerals, the growing plants, the singing birds, the thinking men. We mean *all bodily substances as active.*

Each natural body has its normal structure and its normal type of activity. All bodies,—man (in his moral or responsible conduct) excepted,—act as they do by necessity. Observing bodies and their structure and activity, we notice their constancy and consistency. We find that water runs downhill, that bodies tend towards the center of the earth, that plants tend to grow to maturity and fruitfulness, that fire burns dry wood, that water is H^2O. Such facts and occurrences are not random or occasional, but invariable when bodies are left in their normal condition. We make a record of our constant experience of what bodies are and of what they normally do. We set down such records in physical and chemical formulas. We call them *physical laws.* What we really mean in calling our record of constant experience by the name of *law* is this: God the Creator, in creating bodies, has manifestly imposed upon them, with their physical structure, a definite range of activity; He has given to natural bodies *the law of their being and their doing.*

The constant mode of action of the universe in its larger parts (interplanetary attraction, coherency of solar systems, activities in interstellar space such as cosmic radiation) is expressed in formulas called *cosmic laws*. The constant mode of being and of action of earthly bodies is expressed in formulas called *physical laws*. Both cosmic laws and physical laws are called *natural laws* or *laws of nature*. The pupil will be very careful to make a clean distinction between *natural laws* and *the natural law;* for *the natural law* (always with the article) means the Eternal Law for human conduct inasmuch as this is knowable to sound human reason without divine revelation. In a word, *the natural law* is *the naturally knowable moral law.* On the other hand, *natural laws* (or *laws of nature*) are *cosmic laws* and *physical laws* which necessitate (inasmuch as they are ordinances of the Creator) the activity of bodies as such, but have no concern with the free-will acts of man.

The harmony of nature so charmed the ancient Greeks that some of them,—notably the Pythagoreans,—considered it the very essential of bodily reality, and so declared that the one suitable name for the bodily world is *cosmos* or "the beautiful" or "the well ordered." This harmony is noticed in individual natures too, in the complexity and balance of their parts, in their remarkable fitness for their proper activities. But it is in the larger sense that we consider the harmony of nature; we take it as a suitable arrangement of bodies in the material world for their seemly mutual activities in view of their common ultimate end. This world-harmony we call *the order of nature.* The working out of the order of nature, or the actual exercise of natural laws, we call *the course of nature.*

d) Miracles

A *miracle* is a wondrous event in the sensible or bodily order, out of the course of nature, produced, directly or through the instrumentality of a creature, by Almighty God.

Some scientists and philosophers mistakenly regard the laws

of nature as laws binding upon the Author of nature. They say, —as did the smug Victorians,—"Miracles simply do not happen." They assert that miracles are impossible.

Now, if miracles be impossible, the impossibility must come from one of three causes, viz., (*1*) they involve self-contradiction; (*2*) God is unable to produce them; (*3*) they are unworthy of God. But we can prove by sound reasoning that none of these causes is actual.

(*1*) Miracles do not involve self-contradiction. They do involve a contradiction to our experience, but, after all, our experience is not in control of the world; it is merely a record of what we ordinarily find in the world. If a miracle were something like a "square circle" it would be utterly impossible, for a square circle is a contradiction in thought and in terms; it consists of two elements that cancel each other and leave nothing. But a miracle, like the raising of Lazarus, or the preservation of the young men in the fiery furnace, or the curing of the man born blind, is no such contradiction. Lazarus was raised from the dead; he was not made a "dead living man"; *that* would be a contradiction and an impossibility, or rather a *nothing*. That nature does not give life to a corpse does not mean that God cannot restore life to what once had life. The laws of nature are necessitating forces on nature, not on God. There is no obligation on the Giver of life to give it always in precisely the same way.

(*2*) God is able to produce miracles. The objectors say that God would contradict Himself in working miracles, since He made the laws of nature, and, by a miracle, would suspend them. Such suspension amounts to a reversal of His decree which set the laws of nature in being. It is a sort of confession of a mistake in the original plan which has now abruptly to be corrected. And since Almighty God makes no mistakes, He can make no corrections. Hence He cannot perform miracles. The answer to this little difficulty is simply that a miracle is no suspension of the laws of nature, no correction of a mistake in the original plans. A miracle is, to our time-bound view, *an exception* to the laws of nature, but the exception is an integral part of God's eternal plan for the universe; it is no exception to God, but part of the original plan. God has no "before and after"; a miracle does not mean that God made natures with their laws and *afterwards* discovered a situation in which these laws should not apply. What we call the exception is as everlasting as the law or rule. The resurrection of Lazarus is as eternally decreed by God as the law of nature which requires (as we inaccurately say) dead men to stay dead until the day of general resurrection.

(*3*) There is nothing unworthy of God in a miracle. On the contrary, God in His pity for our weakness and stubborn ignorance, sometimes startles us into a recognition of essential truths. A miracle is an admirable means to attain this purpose. If miracles were a kind of magician-show for the entertainment of men, they would be unworthy of God. But miracles are not for our entertainment but for our instruction unto salvation. The raising of Lazarus, the cure of the man born blind, the feeding of the multitude in the desert,—in fact, all the miracles of Christ, and all the authenticated miracles in the history of the Church, have had, as their manifest purpose, the enlightening of minds, the winning of wills, and the saving of souls.

Miracles, then, involve no contradiction, no impossibility, no unworthiness. There is consequently no basis for the assertion that miracles cannot happen. But there are objectors who say that although miracles can happen *we cannot identify them as true miracles*. We may know well enough that a wonderful thing has happened, but how can we tell that this wonder is beyond the powers of nature? Laws of nature hitherto hidden to us may be in operation to produce the wonder. And even if it could be known that a wonderful event is outside the range or course of nature, how can we know that God produced it? It might be the doing of evil spirits. In a word, say these objectors, we can know *the historical truth* of miracles (that is, we can recognize them as wondrous events) but we cannot know *their philosophical truth* (that is, we cannot identify them as true miracles).

We answer that it is possible to identify miracles historically and philosophically. Dr. Alexis Carrel, speaking of the miracles he witnessed at Lourdes, said that he believed in them because he had to trust the testimony of his own senses. People who witness miracles are aware that something wonderful has happened. We can surely know so much. And we can identify miracles philosophically by careful investigation and sound reasoning. We may not know all the laws of nature; some of these may be hidden to us; but we do know that nature is *constant* and *consistent,* that nature does not deal in contradictions. Hence, if a wondrous event is found upon careful investigation (not on snap judgment made upon half-sensed appearances) to be flatly against the ordinary course of nature, it is silly to say that it may be due to the course of nature. We may ask, "Can nature do *this thing?";* if the answer is (as it would be in the case of the young men in the fiery furnace), "No, for nature tends to do the exact opposite"; then the wondrous event is *contrary to nature.* We may inquire, "Can nature do this thing *to such a subject?";* if the answer is (as in the case of the resurrection of Lazarus or the widow's son), "No, for while nature can give life, it cannot give life to a corpse"; then the wondrous event is *beyond nature* and *above nature.* We may inquire finally, "Can nature do this thing to this subject *in this way?";* if the answer is (as in the case of an instantaneous healing of a gaping wound), "No, for while nature can heal a wound, it requires the co-operation of much time"; then the wondrous event is still *beyond* and *above* nature. If the three wondrous events are proved to be true miracles, they are called, respectively, *miracle of fact, miracle of subject,* and *miracle of mode.* But even before they are proved to be true miracles, we can know that they are events not to be explained by hidden powers of nature, for they are *contrary to nature,* or *above nature,* or *beyond nature.* To prove them true miracles, it remains to show that they are in very fact the works of Almighty God. The test here is, "By their fruits you shall know them." Consider to what end the wondrous event is performed; what effect it exercises on its subject and those who behold it; what is the nature of the doctrine it is performed to establish; what is the character of the person used as the instrumental cause of the event; what circumstances mark its performance. Out of the careful investigation of all these matters will emerge the knowledge that the work is of God or that it is not of God. A miracle is usually not identified suddenly; it must stand up under most careful and scientific scrutiny. The Catholic Church, which sanely recognizes two things about miracles,—that they *can* happen, and that they *have* happened,—is most careful to investigate a wondrous event in itself and in all its circumstances before acknowledging it officially as a true miracle.

Summary of the Article

In this Article we have discussed the meaning of *finality* or *final tendency,* and have indicated the fact of finality in the bodily world. We have justified this as true finality, born of *design,* and *intended* by the Creator. We have seen that the end towards which anything tends is *good,* and that the ultimate end of all creatures is the Boundless Good (the *Summum Bonum*) which we call God. We have learned the meaning of *nature* in a general sense, and have discussed *the laws of nature,* whether these be *cosmic laws* or *physical laws;* we have learned not to confuse these terms with *the natural law* which is the naturally knowable moral law for human conduct. We have defined *the order of nature* and *the course of nature.* We have discussed *miracles* and have seen that miracles are possible, and that they can be identified as true miracles both *historically* and *philosophically.*

CHAPTER V

THE PSYCHOLOGICAL QUESTION

The Psychological Question is the question of life and living bodies. The department of philosophy which answers this question is called *philosophical psychology* or *rational psychology*. In our day, the simple name *psychology* usually suggests the great mass of laboratory sciences which bear that general name. These are not the concern of philosophy, although their findings, like the findings of all the special sciences, must ultimately fall under the light of philosophy and take form under its principles. The name *psychology* is Greek for "the science of the soul" or "the science of the life-principle," although, in many a modern book labelled as psychology you will find no mention of the soul and precious little about a substantial principle of life, where you do not find the frank denial of such a principle. The philosophical science of psychology attempts to set forth in an ultimate manner the truth about life and living bodies. Sometimes this science is presented in two parts, called respectively *minor* and *major* psychology, which deal first with life in plants and brute animals, and then with life in human beings. The two Articles of this present Chapter follow this division:

Article 1. Life in Plants and Animals
Article 2. Life in Human Beings

Article 1. Life in Plants and Animals

a) Life; b) Vegetal Life; c) Sentient Life; d) Species of Living Things.

a) LIFE

Life as it appears in living bodies (and we have no means, in a natural science, of discovering and investigating the life of pure spirits like the angels) is sometimes described as *the capacity for self-perfective movement or activity.* Sometimes this brief description is further shortened, and it is said that life is *self-motion.*

In discussing The Ontological Question we have learned that anything moved is moved by something other than itself. It would seem at first glance that self-motion is a contradiction and an impossibility. But the phrase does not mean that the living body moves itself into existence, or sustains itself there, or equips itself for its activity. Like other creatures, it depends for its being and its activity upon Creator, Preserver, and Concurrer. But, granted that it is created, preserved, and sustained in function, the living body tends by its activity to express, develop, or perfect *itself.* In this the living body is distinct from the non-living body, all activity of which is transient. Perhaps it would be a just revision of the brief description of life given above, to say that life, in living bodies, is *a capacity for immanent activity.*

Life in living bodies is *a capacity* for activity, and *an exercise* of this activity. As a capacity it is called *life in actu primo,* that is, life in first actuality, or life in basic fact. As the exercise of life-functions, it is *life in actu secundo,* that is, life in second actuality, or life in actual exercise.

Now, the capacity for life-functions or *vital operations* is entirely due, in living bodies, to the presence of a substantial principle, a life-principle, a soul, a psyche. Indeed, it is accurate to say that life *in actu primo* or in basic fact is the soul. For the soul is that actuality whereby the body is alive and can exercise vital operations. The soul or psyche or life-principle is a substance (*incomplete* in lesser bodily beings than man) which is substantially joined to the body-substance. Indeed, the soul is *the substantial form* of the body, and is therefore the substantial principle which makes the body *exist* as a *living body* of its *specific kind.* The soul is substantially united with the body in such a way that the result is *a single living thing,* a single if compound substance.

Life is *essentially* different from non-life. A living body is not merely a more complex thing than a non-living body; it is *an essentially different kind of thing.* Note the following points of difference between living bodies and non-living bodies: (*1*) *Origin:* Living bodies come from parent-bodies, immediately or mediately; they are of the same nature as the parent-bodies. Non-living bodies come by physical addition or partition, or by chemical fusion, from other bodies, but not by vital generation; and often (as in water generated from hydrogen and oxygen) the generated body is not of the same nature and essence as the generating bodies. (*2*) *Growth and Decline:* A living body *grows* by multiplication of cells into a determinate kind of organism, and to this end it exercises the operation of true *nutrition.* Non-living bodies have no true immanent growth, but "grow" by accretion or addition of elements laid on outside (as in crystalline growth or the growth of a snowdrift). Living bodies run their course and then break down and decay, losing all their capacity for vital operation. Non-living bodies tend to remain stable and in equilibrium, and when they are worn down and dissolved this is due to outer agencies, not to the break-down of an inner substantial principle. (*3*) *Structure and Operation:* A living body is cellular in structure. Cells are built up, by an inner drive, into most varied parts or organs which cooperate in the marvellous unity of an organism. Non-living bodies are not cellular, nor are their activities immanent; they are built up of homogeneous parts without interdependence or organic unity. —Now it is manifest that bodies which exhibit such fundamental differences in origin, development, decline, structure, operation, are not mere varieties of one kind of thing. They are *things essentially different;* since they are essentially different substances, they are *substantially* different. And this is proof sufficient that *life cannot originate in non-life* through an added complexity of structure to a non-living body by mechanical, physical, or chemical activity. *Life comes from life* and *a living body comes from living bodies* and ultimately from the First Cause or Creator of life and living bodies. This is the conclusion of sane physical science as well as of philosophy.

Life in living bodies manifests a *scale* or *gradation.* There are three types of such life, and these stand related, not like steps in the same stairway, but like three sets of parallel stairs. For the three types are *essentially different;* one is not merely a more perfect form of another. Yet the second type has all the perfection of the first, plus its own specific perfection. And the third has all the perfection of the second, plus its own specific perfection. These grades of life are called *vegetal* or *plant-life, sentient* or *animal-life,* and *rational* or *human life.* Life in living bodies is, therefore, at once of three *kinds* and of three *grades.* We assert the *essential* difference of the three grades of life in living bodies for the compelling reason that each superior grade of life has perfections or operations which are *essentially* beyond the reach of the lower grade or grades.

As we have said more than once, life in a living body is due to the presence of *a substantial principle of life* or a soul. The mass or material bulk of a body does not account for its life. The structure of a body as an organism does account for life-activity, but this very structure has to be built up according to a set plan before it is operative, and this building is due to an indwelling substantial principle which is not that thing which is built; even after building, the organic structure does not explain its permanence or its *actual* functioning, for in itself, it is only a structure *suited* for its functioning, and a substantial activating principle is still required to explain the fact that it does actually exercise vital operations. There must be, in a word, a *first* informing and substantial principle which makes the body *alive;* which determines the body as plant, animal, or man; which holds the body in its organic and functioning unity. This substantial principle we call *the soul.* Modern scientists do not like the word. They prefer *psyche,* or *entelechy,* or *bathmic energy,* or *vital direction,* or even *"the something over."* But philosophy cannot pause to quarrel about words. We call it *the soul,* and we say that it is the substantial principle of life which constitutes the organism and is substantially fused with the organism in the unity of a living body, and that it is the root of all operations of the living body, even those activities *which it uses as instruments* and which are in themselves mechanical or physico-chemical.

b) Vegetal Life

Vegetal life is the life of plants. For a plant is truly a *living* body. It is not only a body with physical, mechanical, and chemical activities; it has these, but they are under a precise direction and application which is the plant's, and not their own. A plant is a body that exists and lives by reason of its substantial form or vegetal soul.

A plant is alive, but it lacks any form of *knowing*. The fundamental form of knowing in bodies is that which is exercised by *a sense* or by *senses;* a living body with one or more senses is called *a sentient body* or is said to have *sentiency*. A plant is a body that is truly alive but lacks sentiency.

The vegetal operations (that is, *vital* operations) are three: *nutrition, growth,* and *vital generation* or *tendency to reproduce*. (*1*) *Nutrition:* Nutrition is the operation by which a living body feeds itself or nourishes itself. It does this by the marvellous power it has to take in alien substances and turn these into its own substance. Nutrition is a most complex process, involving a multitude of subsidiary operations; it is a mode of action essentially different from anything observable in non-living bodies. (*2*) *Growth:* A living body, by means of nutrition, tends to build itself up into a rounded and mature organism. This is accomplished by the wonderful multiplication of cells and the building of these cells into utterly diverse parts, all of which fit perfectly into a unified plan. (*3*) *Vital Generation:* A living body tends, by nutrition, to build itself into a mature being, and to be *fruitful* of other beings of the same essential type. Whether this tendency reaches its normal goal, whether it actually results in reproduction, is not here under discussion. The *fitness* of the living body to be a parent-body is the point we make, and towards this fitness a living body by its nature *strives* or *tends*.

These three vital operations are found in every living body. They are therefore found in plants. And since plants are the lowest in the scale of living things, these three vital operations are *all* the life functions possessed by plants.

Vital operations are produced by the respective *powers* or *faculties* of the soul or life-principle in a living body. For no created substance acts *immediately,* but through the mediation of *its powers to act.* These powers in a living body are, in themselves, qualities of the substance called the soul or life-principle. Hence, while we say truly that *the plant itself* exercises its vital operations, we speak more precisely when we say that the plant exercises these operations by means of the powers for such function which inhere in the plant-soul or principle of life. A plant, therefore, is a living body which normally possesses three vital powers or faculties, the nutritive power, the growing or augmentative power, and the generative or reproducing power.

The life-principle or soul in plants is called *a material principle.* Now, a thing is *material* for one of two reasons: either it is made of bodily matter, or it depends upon what is made of bodily matter. The plant-soul or life-principle is not *made* of matter. It cannot be severed from the plant and looked at separately. It is the substantial form of the plant, and a substantial form is simple and not made of parts. But the plant-soul *depends* for existence and function upon the organism (the arranged and articulated body) which it constitutes as an existing living body; which it builds up and activates. Without the organism, the functions of nutrition, growth, and vital generation cannot be exercised; and where the plant-soul can exist it can function. Therefore, without the organism the plant-soul cannot exist or function. It is, in consequence, called *a material life-principle,* not a spiritual life-principle as the human soul is.

The plant-soul is essentially simple, that is, not composed of parts. Hence, in itself, it is indivisible. Yet since the plant-organism is divisible, and since a suitable division of the plant-organism is ordinarily capable of retaining life as a new and separate plant, the life-principle of a plant is said to be *accidentally* divisible according to the divisibility of the plant-organism into such parts as will be able to retain and exercise plant-life. Thus the plant-soul is *actually one* but *potentially multiple.*

The plant-soul is generated as the plant itself is generated. It comes along, so to speak, as an essential constituent, determinant, or form. Similarly, the plant-soul perishes as the plant perishes. It is not a substance capable of independent existence, as a spirit is, but ceases to be with the cessation of the plant from being. This sort of *generation and corruption* is called *accidental.*

A plant-soul, accidentally generated, is said to be "educed from the potentiality of matter," and, accidentally corrupted, it is said to be "reduced to the potentiality of matter." In other words, the plant-soul is not created anew for each plant; nor is the plant-soul annihilated when the plant dies. It is drawn out of the capability of matter to be substantially constituted as a plant; it falls back into such unactualized capability when the plant dies.

c) Sentient Life

A *sentient* being is a living body which has all the perfections and operations of a plant and, in addition, has the essentially different and superior powers of *knowing* and of *acting on knowledge.* A sentient being is *an animal body.* We call a living animal body simply *an animal.* This philosophical use of *animal* differs from the scientific use. For we make no distinction of animals on the score of their structure; we do not distinguish philosophically among birds, insects, reptiles, and so on. All of these are *animals* as well as the larger beasts that are commonly called so in ordinary speech. Indeed, man himself is *an animal,* although he is also *more* than an animal, and is essentially other and greater than that which is animal merely. An animal is a living body with sentiency. From the amoeba to the elephant, this definition holds true.

A sentient body has powers of *knowing,* that is, of knowing in the lowest order of knowledge. A sentient body has *sentiency* or *powers of sense.* Sentiency is a knowing-power exercised through the body or part of the body. If a special part of the body serves for a special kind of knowing (as the eye, the ear, the nose) this part is called *a sensory* or *a sense-organ.*

A sentient body has not only the power of knowing by means of a sense or of senses; it has the power to act on knowledge. That is, it has the power to tend towards the attaining of what is sensed as desirable or good, and away from what is sensed as undesirable or bad. This power is called *appetition,* or *appetency,* or simply *appetite.* And, in most animals, this power of appetency is followed by *local movement.* Animals that can move from place to place have the power of *locomotion.*

Hence, the vital powers of an animal body are,—in addition to the nutritive power, the growing power, the reproductive power,—these three: the sensing-power, the appetizing-power, and, usually, the power of local movement. By these powers the animal exercises the vital operations of: *nutrition, growth, vital generation, sensation, appetition, locomotion.*

We defined a plant as a living body which lacks sentiency. We may define an animal as a living body with sentiency which lacks intellect or understanding. For no mere animal is intellectual, rational, or intelligent. We speak of "intelligent" animals in a metaphorical way; we mean that the animals are alert, that they use their marvellous sensing-powers in a striking way. But no animal that is not more than animal (as man is) has intelligence. We shall recognize the truth of this assertion when we come to study the intellect in man. Here it will suffice to notice these facts: that no activity of non-human animals is incapable of full explanation on the basis of sentiency alone; that any instance of real intelligence in animals is instantly regarded, even by lovers of animals, as an amusing thing, a joke; that if animals had intelligence they would have language, literature, and art; that if animals were intelligent they would *understand*, and grasp universal meanings and make definitions; that if animals were intelligent they would change and improve their mode of action, show signs of learning, and set up means of intellectual instruction.

The inner sense *of what is desirable,* whether to attain or to perform, is called *instinct*. It is this sense, more than any of the other senses, that manifests itself in the activities which lead the unthinking to speak of "intelligent animals." Now there are vast and essential differences between instinct and intelligence or intellect. Instinct is organic; it depends on a sensory or organ (which is a part of the brain); intellect is inorganic or spiritual. Instinctive knowledge is antecedent to experience; intellectual knowledge is acquired and presupposes experience. Instinct is fixed, not inventive; intellect is endlessly working out new things. Instinct is very limited; intellect is of seemingly boundless capacity. Instinct is changeless; intellect applies its knowledge in a multitude of ways.

The soul or life-principle of an animal is the animal's substantial form. That is, it is the substantial reality which joins with prime matter to constitute the animal as an existing body of the essential or specific kind that it is. It is a *material* principle, since it depends for existence and function upon the organism, the body, which it sets in being and activates. It is a principle "educed from the potentiality of matter" and is accidentally generated as the *animal entire* comes into being; it is "reduced to the potentiality of matter" when the animal is corrupted or dies, and thus it is accidentally corrupted.

Some animals have an organism that may be divided, and each part will endure as a complete organism. This is less common among animals than among plants, and in what we call *the higher animals* (those that appear to have all the senses with which man is equipped) this multiplication by partition or fission is not verified at all. For animals in the main are of much more complex and delicately balanced structure than plants are. The normal mode of reproduction among animals is by direct birth or by birth in egg-form which undergoes subsequent development until the full animal nature of the species is realized. Of the lower animals among which multiplication by fission or partition is a fact, the life-principle is, as in plants, *actually one but potentially multiple*. For a worm, for example, that may be divided carefully in such a way that each part will live as a complete worm, is, to begin with, one worm; its life is one life. Thus it is actually one, and its soul or life-principle is actually one. But, inasmuch as it can be divided into two worms, it is potentially multiple, and so is its life-principle.

The *senses* or *sentient knowing-powers* which may be found in animals are classified as *external* and *internal*. All animals have at least one exterior or external sense, and this is the sense generally called *touch*. This is the basic sense. It is indeed the bridge over which the sensing of all the other senses must pass. For a thing is not seen unless the eye come into *contact* or *touch* with its image; a thing is not smelled unless the air carry its minute particles and bring these into *contact* with the olfactory nerve; a thing is not heard unless sound-waves are carried to *touch upon* the auditory nerve. And since the interior or internal senses depend for their findings upon the preliminary activity of the exterior senses, it may truly be said that the sense of *touch* is basic to *all* sensing. A living body that gives no evidence of having the sense of touch (which may be loosely described as a sense of resistance, temperature, stimulus, irritation) is not an animal body, but a plant-body.

The higher animals, and man, have five exterior senses and four interior senses. The exterior senses are: *touch, taste, smell, hearing, sight*. (Under the head of *touch* we include the sense of resistance, the sense of temperature, the muscular sense, the sense of pleasure, the sense of pain.) The interior senses are: *sense-consciousness, imagination, sense-memory,* and *instinct*.

We shall speak of these in brief detail in our study of sentiency in man which we undertake in the next Article.

d) Species of Living Things

In a biological sense, a *species* is a class of living bodies, the members of which are similar in structure, and can breed indefinitely in their natural state. In the rather rare case of offspring from parent-animals of different species, we have a *hybrid*. The hybrid is usually sterile, but if it should have offspring, this will be an animal of the type of one of the parents of the hybrid. This fact is called *reversion to type*.

Minor groups of animals within the species are called *varieties*. When varieties are artificially cultivated, they are called *breeds* or *races*. The offspring of parent-animals of different breeds is called a *mongrel*. A mongrel often shows marked characteristics of one out of several ancestral breeds; this reversion is called *atavism*.

Different species which have some common characteristic make a *genus*. A genus grouped with other similar genera constitutes a *family*. Families of similar type make an *order*. Orders are grouped as *classes*. Classes are grouped into *phyla*. The *phylum* is the most general biological class of organisms, that is, of living bodies.

That there are different species of living things, and of animals, needs no proof. The question is not of the existence of species, but of the origin of species.

We have already noticed the fact of the origin of life. Life does not come from non-life. A living body is not the product of non-living bodies. Life in its first origin can have no explanation except in *creation;* life came by creation from the First Giver of Life, from God.

But did God endow the lower living things with powers to develop into higher types of things? Have the species of living things, and notably of animals, a common origin in one living body, or in one type of living body?

Of course, the Creator can make His world as He chooses. If He choose to have all plant and animal bodies develop from a single parent-body of a lower type than any existing plant or animal, who shall say that He may not do so? Yet He must, in that case, have equipped the original body with the powers to develop superior life-forms. For no living body has any tendency in the way of reproduction except *in its own kind*. Even for this, of course, the living body has to be equipped.

Geology seems to indicate that the forms of bodily life that appeared on our earth were increasingly more complex; that there was an ascending scale of development among living bodies. We leave man out of this account, for, as we have noticed, science simply does not know any ancestors of man. For the rest, we know the fact by supernatural revelation that man was the immediate handiwork of God. But even scientifically we may reach the same truth by showing that man's most notable and characteristic powers and activities are of a nature superior, —and *essentially* superior,—to *all* organic function, and hence cannot have their explanation in an animal development or evolution.

There are two theories about the origin of species. One maintains the *changelessness* of species, and declares that one species does not develop into another. Each species, while diversified by varieties, clings to its essential type and shows a fixed tendency to retain it always. No body, and hence no living body, has the suicidal tendency of destroying itself so that an essentially different (even if superior) body may exist in its place. The defenders of the changelessness of species say that the Creator made species as they are, either by a succession of creations at different times, or by a single creation of all species at once, although these species (like seeds all planted at the same time but destined to appear as plants at widely different seasons) have come into being at different stages of the earth's development.— The other theory about the origin of species is that of *transformed* or *derived* species; it declares that one species is derived or descended from other species. This theory is accurately called *transformism;* it is more generally, and less accurately known as *evolution.* Evolution is of three types: *monistic, Darwinian,* and *Christian. Monistic evolution* holds the theory that there is only one kind of substance, and that a material substance or bodiliness, which is diversified only by transient activity of a mechanical, physical, and chemical nature. We have already seen the self-contradictory character of monism in our study of The Cosmological Question. And we have noticed, in the present Chapter, the *essential* difference between living bodies and non-living bodies, as well as the fact, admitted by science, that life does not originate in non-life, and that living bodies come always from living bodies. The *monistic evolution,* which had its day of sweeping popularity in the 19 century under the influence of Ernst Haeckel, is now very generally abandoned as an explanation of the origin of life and of species. *Darwinian evolution* is the theory that species come from one or two types of organisms of the lowest order, and that this is effected by a constant tendency of living bodies *to acquire and transmit variations;* that there is *a struggle for existence* among living bodies in which *the fittest survive;* that existing species are survivors of the struggle by reason of their superior natures, and thus are here *by natural selection.* This theory accounts for *essential* differences in living bodies by assigning *accidental* differences (or variations) in their ancestors. Here we have not an adequate explanation. The effect is greater than the sum of all its causes. Darwinian evolution also conflicts with experience, for species are clearly and sharply differentiated, as the botanist and the biologist will maintain, and are not reaching out towards other species; indeed, they cling strongly to type. Hybridization is possible, and varieties can be produced, but there is effort needed to effect these results, and the phenomena of *reversion* and *atavism* are ever present. Darwinian evolution, in its pure form, has now very few defenders. It does not account scientifically for the origin of species. *Christian evolution* excludes man altogether (as reason demands) from any evolutionary process, but admits that lower forms of life than the human form have come into their present state by a process of evolutionary development. This type of evolution sets out these incontrovertible and scientific facts: (*1*) Matter is not self-existent, but comes from a Creator; (*2*) Matter is not the source of life; life comes from the Creator; (*3*) Living bodies develop into bodies of superior species by a power,—over and above the powers necessary for their proper existence and function,—specially conferred by the Creator. A Catholic may accept Christian evolution if he is satisfied with the evidence offered. But no type of evolution is scientifically established as a fact. Evolution is still *a hypothesis,* that is, a scientific guess. There is evidence that makes an evolutionary development of living bodies *appear likely;* there is no evidence that makes such a development a certainly known fact. It is to be noticed that any type of evolution demands a Creator who set the process in motion, a Conserver who sustains it, and a Concurrer who goes along with it to support its activity and achievements. No evolutionary theory can dispense with God.

Can a Christian hold the theory that man's *body* has an animal origin? That is, can it be held as a hypothesis,—since scientific knowledge on the point is out of question,—that the body of a single individual man was an animal body (ultimately formed from the slime of the earth) into which God breathed a human soul? For such a belief there is absolutely no evidence, yet the hypothesis *in itself* is not in open conflict with revelation.

Can a Christian hold the hypothesis that *a group of animals* were developed by an evolutionary process to such a stage as to render the inpouring of a human soul suitable, and that all or several of such animals were divinely made into men? No. Science as well as revelation informs us of *the solidarity of the human race,* that is, that man is the product of a single pair of first parents; revelation further informs us that the body of our first mother was taken from a purely human source,—the living body of the first man.

Summary of the Article

In this Article we have defined *life* both in basic fact (*in actu primo*) and in actual exercise (*in actu secundo*). We have described the manifestations of life *in living bodies.* We have seen that life in living bodies comes, in each case, from a substantial principle or source which is *the substantial form of the living body;* this substantial form is called *the life-principle* or *the soul* of the living body. We have discerned *an essential difference* between a living body and a lifeless body. We have learned that life in living bodies is of three essential *kinds,* and that these *kinds* are also essentially different *grades;* the three grades of life in living bodies are *vegetal life, sentient life,* and *rational or human life.* Of vegetal life, we have seen that it is characterized by three vital operations, *nutrition, growth,* and *vital generation.* Of sentient life, we have learned that it is essentially different from and essentially superior to vegetal life, and that it has all the operations of vegetal life plus its own proper operations of *sensation, appetition,* and, usually, *locomotion.* We have learned that the soul or life-principle in plants and in animals is *material,* inasmuch as it depends for existence and function upon the organism which it actuates; that it is generated and corrupted *accidentally,* inasmuch as it emerges and ceases to be with the organism as a whole; that it is educed from the potentiality of matter and reduced thereto as the animal or plant is generated or dies. We have discussed *the origin of species* and have mentioned various theories which seek to explain it.

Article 2. Life in Human Beings

a) Man's Soul; b) Man's Lower Faculties; c) Man's Higher Faculties.

a) Man's Soul

The substantial form of the human living body is called *the human soul.* As the substantial form of man, it is that substantial principle which makes a man *an existing being of the human species,* and it is the root-source in man *of all his vital activities.*

Now, man has the highest grade of life in living bodies. He has all the perfections and operations of plants and of non-human animals; he has the operations of nutrition, growth, vital generation, sensation, appetition, locomotion, and, in addition, he has his own proper or specific operations called *understanding* and *willing.* The activities or operations of understanding and willing are called *the operations of rational life.* And since *animal* means all that *plant* means plus the sentient powers and operations, so *man* means all that *animal* means plus the rational powers and operations. Man is therefore defined as *a rational animal.* As each of the three grades of life in living bodies is essentially different from, and essentially superior to the lower grade or grades, it is manifest that man, while possessing all the perfections and operations of plant and animal, is essentially different from these living bodies and essentially superior to them. He is *an essentially different kind of living body.*

While man has the perfections, powers, and operations of all three grades of life in living bodies, he is none the less *a single bodily being.* Each human being is one substance, not three. He has one substantial form, not three substantial forms. It is the one individual man who comes into existence by generation, who takes nourishment and grows, who feels and walks about, who thinks and makes free decisions. The human substance is a compound substance, as every bodily substance is, but it is a single substance, not a triple one. Man's one substantial form is *his one life-principle or soul.* This one soul is the root-source or principle in man of the *material* life of plant and animal which he possesses, and of the non-material or *spiritual* life which he manifests in his rational powers and operations. Since that which is superior can account for what is inferior, but not the other way about, we say that man's spiritual soul can account for even the material operations of man's life, but that a non-spiritual soul could not account for the spiritual operations of man. Hence we conclude that man's one soul is a spiritual soul. Of this we shall speak again in a moment.

The human soul is a substance; it is a simple or uncompounded substance; it is a spiritual substance; it is an immortal or deathless substance. We pause briefly upon each of these truths.

(*1*) The human soul is the substantial form of the human body. It is therefore a substantial thing, a substance. We shall presently see that it is a spiritual substance, and by that fact it is different from the other types of substantial form which actuate bodies whether living or lifeless; it is in itself *a complete substance.* It is not a complete *man,* that is, not a complete *human being;* it is only part of a human being. But it is a complete soul, capable of existence by itself without the body. For a complete substance is one that can exist and exercise its proper operations alone; an incomplete substance is one that requires another substance to be fused with it substantially so that it may exist and operate. That the human life-principle or soul is a substance, and not merely an accidental, is manifest, as we have said, from the fact that it is the substantial formal constituent of substantial man. Further, man's soul is the principle of man's vital powers, and these, in themselves, are accidentals, and must have,—as all accidentals in the order of nature must have,—a substantial actuality in which to inhere; *man's vital powers are rooted in a substantial principle,* that is, in *a substance,* which we call man's substantial form or *soul.*

(*2*) The human soul is a simple or uncomposed substance. It is not made of parts. Every substantial form is simple. For a body which exists as a definite kind of body by reason of its substantial form is one body. Even if the form be *potentially* multiple, it is never *actually* multiple. The life-principle of a plant, for example, is the substantial form of the plant; and each plant is a unified thing; it is one substance; it has one life. This life is manifested in root and stem and leaf and flower. But it is one life. You do not cut off *part of the life* when you pluck a flower or trim away a branch, though it may be that you produce, by partition, a completely new plant *with its own one life.* Thus every body that is truly one body, has truly one substantial form, and the substantial form *is itself without component parts,* even though the body has component parts. This fact is most obvious in living bodies. But what is true of the lower living bodies is *a fortiori* true of man who has all the perfections of all types of living bodies. For the rest, as we have seen, it is the one man who grows, who feels, who is moved by sentient appetite, who thinks, who wills. Man, who is a bodily being composed of bodily parts, is nevertheless *one* and *his life is one and indivisible.* In all his bodily parts man lives *a human life,* although he does not exercise all his human activities in each part. We declare, therefore, that the principle of man's life, his soul, is one and indivisible; that it has no parts of its own; that it is *simple.*

(*3*) Man's soul is a spiritual substance. Substances are of two possible kinds, *material* and *non-material or spiritual.* A material substance is either a substance composed of bodily matter, and hence made up of parts, or it is a substance which is itself simple but which depends for existence and activity upon what is bodily. We have seen that the soul of a plant and the soul of an animal are *material.* These souls are not made up of bodily matter; they are substantial forms, and hence simple; but they are dependent for their existence and their operations upon the organisms or living bodies which they actuate. Now, man's soul is neither made up of bodily matter or parts (as we have seen, since it is a substantial form), nor is it dependent upon the body for its own specific operations; hence, since it can operate without the organism, it can exist without the organism. How do we know that the soul of man can operate without the organism? Because it has operations, even while joined with the organism, which are essentially superior to any organic function and which are in themselves independent of bodily operation. Now, if the soul has operations which are essentially superior to, and independent of, bodily structure and function, then the soul itself is superior to and independent of bodily structure and function; it is then not dependent on matter; it is spiritual. For "operation follows on essence"; as a thing is, it acts; and if the soul is supra-organic in activity, it is supra-organic in essence; it is *itself* above the character of the body and is essentially independent of the body. Now, the soul has activities which are supra-organic. For the soul can (or, more properly, *man,* by reason of his soul, can) *think,* and *reflect,* and *decide.* The operations of understanding and of free-will are in no wise explicable in terms of the body, of the organism, or of the bodily powers of knowing and appetizing. There is an old and a true saying that "the senses are for individual perceptions, but the intellect is for universal grasps of reality." The eyes can take in an individual scene, or a series of such scenes; man, for instance, can see a tree, or a multitude of trees, or a succession of trees or of forests. But each visual perception is an individual thing. No number of such experiences amounts to the understanding of what *tree* means. Yet man has an understanding of what *tree* means; he can *define* tree, and the definition fits any and every tree that ever was, or is, or will be, or can be. No bodily knowing power (that is, no sentient faculty) can even begin to lay hold of an essence as the mind or intellect does. Even a little child of four or five knows what "a doll" or "a sled" means; the knowledge is not of this or these individual toys; it is knowledge of any and every possible doll, of any and every possible sled. In its own childish way, the infant has a grasp of *an essence,* of what would be expressed by *a definition* of doll or sled. Now, such a grasp of an essence is only possible to a supra-sensible power. For it is of the very nature of sense-knowledge that it lays hold of the knowable things according to their individual marks, limits, determinants. But the intellect pays no attention to such limiting things; it *prescinds* from them; it *abstracts* from them; it lays hold of an essence *in universal.* Thus in knowing what a doll is, a child does not need to know the size of some particular doll, or the color of its hair, or the material of which it is made, or any of the other *individuating marks* which make a doll this doll or that doll; the child knows what *doll-as-such* means, regardless of all individuating marks. It is manifest, we repeat, that no sentient power can thus grasp things in essence, in universal, by abstraction from individuating marks; on the contrary, it is by the individuating marks that a sentient power lays hold of any reality. Man has, therefore, a knowing-power which is superior to the bodily knowing-power called *sentiency.* In itself, the intellect is a power superior to and independent of sentiency, even though in this life the intellect has an extrinsic and accidental dependency on the senses. But if the intellect, which is the soul's knowing-power, is superior to and essentially independent of the bodily organs, the soul itself is superior to and independent of bodily limitations; for the function of the soul shows the essence of the soul; as a thing acts it is; what is superior to bodiliness in operation is superior to bodiliness in essence. The soul of man is, therefore, non-material; it is *spiritual.* Again, the soul can *reflect,* can turn the attention of the mind upon the mind; can think of itself thinking. No bodily power is capable of such an activity. The soul is, in consequence, superior to the body in its powers and operations; hence it is superior in its essence; it is not dependent in essence and operation on the body; it is not material; it is *spiritual.* Once again, man, by reason of the soul, can choose and decide, can exercise free-will. He can be swayed in his choice by the consideration of things beyond the reach of any bodily power, by thoughts of loyalty, of devotion, of friendship, of love; no sentient power has any means of grasping these things or of appetizing them. Therefore man has operations which are quite above the reach and character of bodiliness and sentiency. It follows that he has a principle of such operations which is itself beyond the character of the body, and is thus essentially independent of the body. In a word, it follows that man has a soul which is independent of matter, and is therefore *spiritual. The soul of man is a spiritual substance.*

(*4*) Man's soul is an immortal or deathless substance. Death is the separation of the substantial form of a living body and the material of which the body is made. It is a tearing apart of the life-principle (a substantial form) and the material substance which that life-principle in-formed and made a living body. In plants and animals death means the cessation from being of both organism and life-principle, for both are *material,* and they are mutually dependent for the constituting of the living body which now dies; and they are mutually dependent for their own existence on their union which is now dissolved. Thus plants and animals are *mortal,* or destructible by death, in their bodies and in their respective life-principles or souls. The soul of plant or animal has no activity independent of the body; hence it has no existence independent of the body; when the body-structure is no longer capable of supporting or subserving the functions of the life-principle in plant or animal, both the body and the life-principle cease to be the substantial things they were. With man the case is different. *Man* is mortal; *man* dies; *man* suffers the dissolution of his substantial constituting elements; but man's *soul* does not die. When a man dies, his soul endures in being. For his soul is a spirit, not a material thing; his soul is a complete substance as a soul, although it is not a complete human being. The human soul cannot conceivably cease to be except by *annihilation,* and we know from other sources that God does not annihilate. For the soul exists, it is independent of the body for its own existence and its proper functions of understanding and willing. And the soul is spiritual; it has no parts that can be thought of as severed or shattered so as to destroy it. *The human soul, being spiritual, is naturally immortal.* It is a deathless substance.

The human soul is spiritual, and therefore its only possible origin is in an absolute and entire production, that is, in *creation* by Almighty God. The human soul cannot be *generated* from the souls of parents, for the souls of parents are spiritual and have no parts to give off as seeds or germs of the soul of offspring. Each human soul is immediately created by Almighty God, and the moment of its creation is the moment of its substantial union with its body in the bosom of a human mother. The human soul does not pre-exist to the body. God by one and the same indivisible act creates each soul and unites it substantially with its body. The probable moment of the creation of the soul is the moment of conception.

The result of the union of soul and body is a human being, a human substance, a human *person.* For a person is a complete individual substance, constituted in its own specific nature, and belonging to the rational order. In other words, a person is a complete, individual, autonomous substance, endowed basically (or *in actu primo*) with understanding and free-will. Man is a complete individual substance; he is not a "soul in a body"; he is a single composed substance of body-and-soul-substantially-united. While the soul, once separated from the body by death, can and must continue to exist and to exercise its proper operations of understanding and willing; and while, even during bodily life, the soul is the root-principle of activities which are beyond the reach of bodily powers, it is none the less accurate to say that it is the *man,* the compound of body-and-soul, that is the author of all the operations called human. It is the *man* that understands and wills, just as it is the *man* that grows, senses, moves. A person rightly says, "*I* see, *I* feel, *I* walk, *I* thirst, *I* think, *I* choose"; he does not say that his body sees or that his eyes see, that his mind thinks, that his will chooses. For *actiones sunt suppositorum,* "activities are to be ascribed to the active substance as such, not to its parts or powers."

The substantial union of soul and body may be shown by a simple instance of their interaction. Suppose that a person of hearty appetite is about to begin upon a splendid dinner. A telegram is handed to him; he reads of the death of a near and dear relative. Immediately his appetite is gone. Now the appetite for food is manifestly of the body; it belongs, strictly speaking, to the vegetal order. But the understanding of marks on paper, that is, of the telegram, is an activity of the intellect, a soul-faculty. Yet the knowledge taken in by the intellect has an instant effect upon the appetizing activity of the body. Here the close interaction of body and soul indicates their substantial union; it is *the man* who has appetite; it is *the man* who reads and understands the calamitous news.

The spiritual soul is the one and only soul or life-principle in a man. It is *formally* spiritual and rational. But it is *virtually* vegetal and sentient. Just as a five-dollar gold-piece is formally gold, but it is virtually copper or nickel or silver (because it has the *virtue* or *power* or *force* or *meaning* of many coins of the inferior metals), so the human soul is *virtually* (or in effect or effectiveness) a vegetal soul and an animal or sentient soul, although in itself, as such, formally, it is a spiritual and rational soul.

Each human being has his own soul. It is the soul which *specifies* man, that is, makes him a being of this complete essence or species which we call the human species. But it is the material, the bodiliness which the soul in-forms and makes an existing human person, that is the principle of *individuation* in man. The soul makes a person an existing human being; but it is not the determinant of the figure, the sex, the nationality, and so on that mark the *individual* human being. In discussing The Ontological Question and The Cosmological Question we have learned that *the principle of specification is the substantial form,* and that *the principle of individuation is matter as marked by quantity.* How then is individuality preserved among separated souls, that is, among the souls that have left their bodies by death? St. Thomas holds that each soul is somehow extrinsically marked by *a real relation* to the body which it in-formed in earthly life, and thus each separated soul is equivalently "individuated" even in the absence of bodily matter.

The spiritual soul in a living man is in the entire body and in each part of the body. For the soul has no parts, it is not part here and part there; wherever it is it exists in its entirety. The soul does not exercise all the operations of which it is the principle in each part of the living body or organism. But it *exists,* and in entirety, in each living part. If a part of the living body is severed, the soul, the life-principle, is no longer in such a part. The soul cannot be mutilated as the body is mutilated; it cannot be cut down in size, for it has no size. Even a material soul or life-principle (like every substantial form) manifests this complete presence in the whole body which it in-forms. You may trim down a rose-bush to half its size, but the rose-bush is the same living substance after the trimming; its life is the same life; its life-principle has not been cut down.

b) Man's Lower Faculties

A *faculty* is a capacity or power for vital operation. We have already learned that man is in possession of all the faculties of living bodies. Man has nutrition, growth, and vital generation, like the plants. He has sensation, appetition, and locomotion, like the non-human animals. And he has understanding and will (at least *in actu primo*) like pure spirits. Because man has all these faculties, in addition to the bodily character of his being which he holds in common with non-living bodies, he has been called "a microcosm" or "a world in little."

Man's vegetal and sentient faculties are called his lower faculties. His understanding (that is, his mind, intellect, intelligence, reason) and his will are his higher faculties.

Faculties are powers or capacities, distinct from the substance which possesses and uses them, for the *immediate* exercise of vital operations.

Faculties are said to inhere in *a subject.* That which has faculties is the subject of these faculties. Man is, of course, the subject of all his faculties. But man is a composite being, and his faculties are to be more precisely assigned than they are in a general ascribing of them to man as a whole. Some of his faculties belong to *the living body,* some belong to *the soul.* In other words, some of man's faculties are *proper* to the composite of body-and-soul, while some are *proper* to the soul alone. We discern this fact even as we declare that man in his whole being **is** the possessor and user of faculties, and that man's soul (that is, his substantial form) is the root-principle of *all* his activities. The lower faculties have their *proper subject* in the composite of man's body-and-soul; the higher faculties have their *proper subject* in man's soul.

We need not pause upon man's vegetal faculties, for we have considered these in our study of vegetal life in general. It is manifest that man has the faculties of nutrition, growth, and generation. Man has, in a word, true plant-life.

(*1*) Man has also the sentient faculties, first of which is *sensation.* This word is used here in the meaning of "sensing-power" and "sensing-activity." In the common speech of every day, the word "sensation" suggests something startling or exciting; it has not that meaning in our present use of it. Here it means the *power* to know things by the use of special faculties called *senses,* and it is sometimes employed to indicate the *activity* of actually exercising this power.

Things *sensed* (or known by sensation) are said to be *perceived.* Each item sensed is *a percept,* and a man's sense-knowledge of anything is often a collection of percepts,—as, for example, his sense-knowledge of a rose may be a combination of percepts gathered by sight, smell, and touch.

Each sense, as we have seen in our discussion of The Critical Question, has its own *proper object.* The proper object of a sense is that which can be perceived by this sense alone. Objects that can be directly perceived by two or more senses are called *common objects.* Objects that are not directly sensed, but are known by experience to be associated with what is sensed, are called *accidental objects.* Thus, a man sees an apple; as *a colored object,* it is perceived by sight alone; as *a round object,* it can be known by sight and by touch; as *an object of sweet flavor* it can be known directly by the sense of taste alone, but the man who knows apples can *see* that it is a sweet apple, for he knows by experience that apples of that type are sweet; this "seeing" that the apple is sweet is *accidental* perception.

The system of bodily parts or organs by which man exercises sentiency is the cerebro-spinal system, which consists of the brain and the spinal cord, the cerebro-spinal nerves, and the external (or peripheral) sense-organs. The external senses (sight, hearing, taste, smell, touch) have their organs in the outer body, but their findings are conveyed to the brain by the nerves. The internal senses (sentient consciousness, imagination, sentient memory, and instinct) have their organs in the brain itself. External sensation is normally, and during man's waking hours, immediately recorded in imagination and consciousness. Imagination also retains and, under stimulus, evokes the recorded images of external sensations. Sentient memory has the single task of *recognizing* an evoked imagination-image as something experienced in the past. Instinct is an awareness of usefulness or harmfulness (of desirability or undesirability) in a sensed object.

(*2*) The second sentient operation is appetition or appetency. This operation is the tendency, the striving, towards what is sensed as desirable and away from what is sensed as undesirable or harmful. The tendency of any body (living or lifeless) to an activity is called *natural appetency;* such, for instance, is the tendency of a body to fall towards the center of the earth, or the tendency of a tree to grow to maturity and fruitfulness. The tendency *born of sense-knowledge* which inclines the sentient creature towards or away from an object, is called *sentient appetency.* We shall presently learn that the tendency *born of intellectual knowledge* of the desirability or undesirability of an object is called intellectual appetency or *the will.*

Since a sentient creature rather *undergoes* than elicits the tendency called appetition, the several classes of appetitive striving towards or away from an object are called *passions,* from the Latin *pati* "to undergo; to suffer." *Passion* in this present use means any manifestation of the sentient appetency. There are two main types of passions, called in an older day *the concupiscible passions* and *the irascible passions;* we may call these, respectively, "the appetites of simple tendency" and "the appetites of tendency in the face of some obstacle." The first class includes these appetites or passions: *love-hatred; desire-aversion; joy-sadness.* The second class comprises these passions: *hope-despair; courage-fear; anger.* The passions are all tendencies, positively or negatively, towards *good,* and they are all, in some sense, variants of *love.* The passions are good in themselves, although in fallen man they tend to be inordinate and thus productive of both physical and moral evil in a person who is not alert and decisive in holding them, at least in their effects, under the control of a well-disposed will.

(*3*) The sentient faculty of *locomotion* is the power of spontaneous movement from place to place. It is a power exercised in the light of sentient knowledge. Certain plants, like the tumbleweed, move about, but these have no faculty of locomotion, for their movements are not the result of knowledge. Locomotion is a faculty which, in many cases, makes possible the attaining of the object of appetition. Man's organ of locomotion (like that of all animals possessing this faculty) is the organism or living body, especially in its elements of muscles and the skeletal framework.

c) Man's Higher Faculties

Man's higher faculties are those that belong to the human spiritual soul as *their proper subject.* These faculties are two, *the intellect* and *the will.* The intellect is man's higher *cognitive* or *knowing* faculty. The will is man's higher *appetitive* faculty. And, since the will is "appetition born of intellectual knowledge," and since intellectual knowledge is frequently knowledge of possible action that is not necessitated, the will is *the faculty of free-choice.*

(*1*) The *intellect* is the knowing-power or faculty rooted in the spiritual soul. Man alone, of all bodily creatures, possesses *intellect.*

The intellect is a power for knowing things in an abstract and universal way. It is the power for knowing *essences.* Further, it is the power of *judging,* and the power of *thinking things out.* It is also the power of retaining or remembering *meanings* (that is, essences, judgments, conclusions, processes of thinking) ; the power of being understandingly aware (either instantly or by process of thought) of such meanings, and *of the human self;* the power of recognizing the agreement or disagreement of human conduct with the rule of what such conduct ought to be. In all its services, the intellect is a faculty or power for *essential knowing,* that is for the understanding grasp of *truth.* Truth is the *object* of the faculty of intellect. It seeks truth as the eye seeks light. It is a power connaturally formed to reach after truth and attain it and possess it. Its object is, therefore, the truth of thought (the truth *about* things, not the truth *of* things) ; in a word, its object is *logical truth.* The pupil will recall from our sketch of The Critical Question the various types of truth, and the definition of logical truth.

The name *intellect* is a general name for this spiritual knowing-faculty; so is the name *mind,* although many modern writers use the word *mind* to indicate any form of conscious life, even sentient life; we make *intellect* and *mind* synonymous. In its various services, the intellect is variously named: (*a*) Inasmuch as the intellect instantly recognizes truths that are self-evident, it is called *intelligence.* (*b*) Inasmuch as the intellect can think out, by connected steps, many truths that are not self-evident, it is called *reason.* (*c*) Inasmuch as the intellect is an understanding awareness of the *self* and of the mental and bodily activities, and of the world of things knowable, it is called *intellectual consciousness* (which is essentially different from *sentient consciousness,* an inner sense). (*d*) Inasmuch as the intellect (or more precisely *the intellect as reason*) thinks out the moral implications of a situation and judges on a point of duty, it is called *conscience*. (*e*) Inasmuch as the intellect retains its knowledge, it is called *intellectual memory*.

The intellect is not an *organic* faculty, that is, it is not exercised by the use of a special bodily sensory or organ. It is a supra-organic faculty, a *spiritual* faculty. It is not a spiritual substance, for in itself the intellect, like every faculty, is a quality of the substance it marks and serves. It is called *spiritual* because it is the faculty of the spiritual substance called the human soul. Since the intellect can exercise the activity of knowing in a manner wholly impossible to an organic faculty (for it can know in universal; it can grasp abstract essences; it can lay hold of things that are utterly beyond the power of senses to apprehend) we are forced to call it a supra-organic faculty. For *agere sequitur esse;* "function follows upon essence"; as a thing *is* it acts, and, conversely, as a thing *acts* it is. The intellect has supra-organic activities; therefore, necessarily, the intellect is itself supra-organic or spiritual. Hence a man does not think, reason, judge, with his *brain;* he does these things with the supra-organic faculty of mind or intellect, a soul-faculty. The brain is indeed the seat and center of *sensation* (that is, of sense-knowing). And *in this life of union of soul and body,* the soul-faculty of intellect cannot come *directly* at its object (the truth about things; the understood essences of things) but must find that object by working upon the findings of the senses. Hence, since we localize sensation essentially in the brain, we localize, by analogy, the activity of the intellect in the brain; but this is not a literally true localization, and, above all, it is not the attributing to the bodily member called the brain the spiritual operations of the intellect. There is, in other words, an *extrinsic dependence* of intellect on brain in this life; but it is distinctly not an intrinsic dependence. If the brain is diseased, a man's thinking usually goes wrong; the man is not sane; he cannot think and reason, judge and decide, as he could if his brain were healthy and normal. But this fact does not mean that the brain is the essential organ of thought, but only that it is extrinsically essential during man's earthly life.

The object of the intellect is truth. It is truth about things. And, since, in this life, there is an extrinsic dependence of the intellect upon the senses (especially as these have their findings focussed in the inner-senses of the brain) we say that the proper object of the intellect *in this life* is *the essences of material things,* the essences of things that can be sensed. The *adequate* object of the intellect is truth about all knowable reality.

The operations of the intellect are *apprehending, judging, reasoning.* Of these we have spoken in sufficient detail in our account of Aristotle's Logic in the First Part of this manual, and again in our study of The Logical Question and of The Critical Question in the Second Part. (*Cf. Part I, Chap. II, Art. 2, b; Part II, Chap. I, Art. 1, b; Part II, Chap. II, Art. 3, c.*)

The intellect, inasmuch as it actively abstracts essences, and so renders things understandable, or graspable in universal, is called *the agent intellect* or *intellectus agens.* The intellect inasmuch as it understandingly reacts to the impression of abstracted essences and expresses these within itself as ideas or concepts, is called the *intellectus possibilis* or *the actual understanding.*

The *idea* or the *concept* which is the first fruit of the intellect's first operation called *apprehending,* is drawn by the intellect from the findings of the senses as these are recorded in conscious imagination. Hence, the origin of ideas is to be found in *the abstractive power of the intellect working on the findings of the senses.* Ideas are not born in us, as *innatism* teaches. Ideas are not mere collections of sensations, as *sensism* teaches. Ideas are not revealed elements of knowledge handed down from generation to generation among men, as *traditionalism* teaches. Ideas are the legitimate fruitage of the abstractive activity of the intellect working upon the findings of the senses. And once possessed of ideas, the intellect is equipped for *judging* and *reasoning,* that is, for exercising all of its operations in its connatural drive or tendency to possess truth.

(2) The intellect is the knowing-power of the human soul. The *will* is the appetitive power or faculty of the human soul. It is the power of *intellectual appetition.* It is the faculty for going after, or away from, what the intellect presents as desirable (or *good*) or undesirable (or *bad*). Will therefore is rightly described by St. Thomas as *rational appetency.*

The will, like the intellect, is a supra-organic faculty. It is not intrinsically dependent upon any bodily member or organ, or upon the whole body itself. It is a spiritual faculty, for it is a faculty which inheres in the spiritual soul.

The will is a faculty *for appetizing understood good.* Thus, the object of the will is *good.* By the same token, it is a faculty for tending away from understood evil. *Good* is that which is appetizable, desirable. *Evil* is that which is unappetizable, undesirable, for it is a *negative* thing, and consists in *the absence of good.* Evil cannot be appetized for its own sake, but only under the aspect of good, that is, under the appearance of what is desirable.

We have noticed in an earlier stage of our study that "the intellect is capable of objective judgments which are morally indifferent." That is, the mind or intellect can let its light shine upon anything thinkable, and can discern in it elements of positive being which is always good, and elements of defect or absence of being which are bad. No matter what the mind lights upon may be seen in the aspect of what is factually there, or what fails to be there. The intellect can therefore judge as desirable what is truly not so, because it clothes, so to speak, the lack or absence of being with the appearance of being. And the intellect can judge as undesirable or evil what is actually good, because it can focus upon some point or detail of the good as deficient. Thus a murderer can envision the death of an enemy as good, as desirable, as *satisfying,* although it is really not so. Thus again, a lazy Christian can envision the Christian ideals as undesirable, unsatisfying, because his intellect can dwell upon the effort and delay exacted in their attainment. Hence, the intellect may set before the will (its appetency) an object which is *evil,* but only by clothing that object in the attractive features of *good,* that is, of what *satisfies.* This makes the choice of evil a possibility. For the will, be it repeated, cannot choose *evil as such,* but only when it appears *sub specie boni,* that is, only when it is masked as *good.*

It would appear then, at first sight, that *the intellect* (by its capacity for "objectively indifferent judgments") is the source of choice and the root of responsibility in man. But while the will always and inevitably follows upon *the ultimate practical judgment of the intellect,* it is nevertheless *the will* which allows the intellect to dwell upon an object and reach ultimate judgment on its desirability or undesirability, its good or evil. The intellect is like a spot-light which illumines an object, and may show up in that object points desirable and points unattractive, and may dwell on either, or may transfer, so to speak, the mask of desirability to what is unattractive in the object. The intellect is like such a spot-light. But the will is like the hand which controls the direction of the spotlight. To vary the illustration: A motorist driving his car at night, inevitably follows the headlights. But we do not say that the headlights choose the road for him. It is the motorist who chooses to turn the headlights on this road or that road. The intellect is like the headlights; the will is like the motorist. So, upon consideration, we discern the truth that though will follows intellect (as the motorist the headlights) it is the will that is the master-faculty in any deliberate choice of man. It is the will that is the root of responsible action.

The will is indeed influenced by the intellect, for a man cannot will what he does not in some measure know: *nil volitum quin praecognitum.* So we may say that the headlights of a car influence the motorist by suddenly revealing a fine stretch of smooth roadway leading off to left or right. Thus the intellect, acting in the manner of a final cause, attracts or invites the will. But the will influences and moves the intellect after the manner of an effecting cause, just as the motorist moves the headlights to illumine the "attractiveness" which comes of the fact that a rough road is the right road, and away from the suddenly revealed and illuminated attractiveness of the smooth side-road which will not carry him to his destination.

There was once much academic to-do about the ranking or the dignity of intellect over will or will over intellect. The question was about which faculty is *superior*. There are arguments for both sides. *To know,* regarded simply, is more perfect than *to tend;* under this consideration, intellect is superior to will. But to be *able to achieve* is better than to merely *know how* to achieve; and in view of this fact, will is superior to intellect. Yet when the struggle of life is done, the truly successful man who has attained his last end and has no longer to be concerned about choosing the way home, stands forever possessed of the Beatific Vision, which he beholds by *intellect* fortified by the light of glory. Thus, in the long run, intellect seems more noble than will. And still, even in beholding God, the *will* perfectly and endlessly cleaves to Him in loving joy.

The will is *free* by the freedom of *choice of means*. Man, made for happiness in the possession of Supreme Good, is not free to change that ultimate goal. Saint or sinner, a man goes after, inevitably, what he regards, rightly or perversely, as *ultimately fully satisfying*. Man is made for the City of Eternal Happiness (the City of God). And whether he goes north, south, east, west, he is striving towards that city. Even when his efforts are carrying him away from it, *it is that city which he is after*. So, even in the perverse (and not merely mistaken) conduct of the sinner there is manifest the tendency which man is not free to change or to reject,—the tendency towards what will completely and permanently *satisfy*. So the will is free *to choose means* to the ultimate end, and it may choose blindly, perversely, ruinously; but the will is not free to choose *the ultimate end itself;* towards that, all creation is inevitably set. If man does not choose the right means to the ultimate end, he will miss the ultimate end. The point we make is that it is the ultimate end *he is necessarily after,* whether he goes towards it or directly away from it. In the ultimate end, therefore, of human conduct, there is no choice, no freedom. Freedom is in *the choice of means* to the ultimate end.

The human will is truly free by this *freedom of choice,* or more accurately, by this *freedom of the choice of means.* Now since the Supreme Good is God, and since God is the fixed and necessary Goal of all creatures, there is no freedom in the quest of God. Saint and sinner, the devout man and the professed atheist, all alike are seeking God, although the sinner and the atheist are looking for Him where He cannot be found, and theirs will be the agony of endless defeat and pain. But it is God they are all after. This being fully understood, all responsible conduct (all *human acts,* as the ethician says), that is, every deliberate thought, word, deed, omission, effort, desire of man, is a matter of *means.* The human will is consequently *free in all its human acts.*

Man does not exercise freedom, and indeed he cannot exercise it, except in *deliberate* acts, that is, in acts of which he is fully aware, and over which he has control. That there are acts that man can know and over which he can exercise control is proved by daily experience. Many of our acts are more or less mechanical, even during our hours of full consciousness; perhaps most of our acts are of this type. But there is seldom a day when most of us have not some decision or other to make which calls upon some deliberation, some thought, before we "make up our minds." Often during life, at least, we have all had the experience of determining upon a course of action. *Before* we acted, we thought the matter over; perhaps we asked advice; perhaps we prayed for guidance. All the while we were clearly aware that the decision was "up to us," in our hands, so to speak, and dependent upon our own choice. Then, having decided, we took up the action in the full knowledge that it was our doing, and that we might act otherwise. Finally, *after* acting, we were satisfied or regretful, because we realized that the action was wholly of our choice. Thus, before, during, and after many of our will-choices, we have had the experience of a full conviction of our freedom in the matter. If this self-evident and universal human experience be deceiving, then what can we know for certain? And if we question all certitude, we are in the insanely impossible position of the skeptic.

The whole world recognizes human freedom of choice. It is factually recognized by the *determinists* who deny it in theory; by the *fatalists* who make our choice dependent upon some non-human thing like a star or a position of the planets at the time of our birth, or upon dreams, or upon a coincidence of numbers. Even the determinist and the fatalist recognize the need of the State, that is, of government and of laws. Now government and laws are controls suitable only to beings of free choice. We do not solemnly legislate for grass or for cows. We do not set up senates for stones, or build prisons for offending weeds. A human (that is, in this case, a civil) law is an admission that a man requires direction, that he might choose amiss without it, that he may choose amiss even with it, and therefore penalties are enacted. In every case, law is a recognition of the fact of human *choice,* that is of human free-will.

Indeed, every circumstance of life is an open profession of the inevitable doctrine of free-will. Even the determinists, seeking converts to their doctrine that free-will is a myth, are eager to offer argument, are anxious to have people *freely decide* to listen to these arguments. The advertising man in newspaper or on radio begs the housewife to exercise her free-choice, and to buy only the super-superlative brand of soap. The politician seeking votes is keenly aware that his constituency is free to vote for the other candidate. The sergeant drilling his awkward squad is more annoyed when they appear stubbornly perverse than when they appear naturally clumsy. The waitress handing a menu to a customer, awaits his free decision as he lets his eye wander through the columns of ostensible French. Freedom of the human will is a fact so obvious that not even the most determined determinist can evade it. One supposes that the determinist or the fatalist would not be serenely philosophic if a thief took all his property; he would have the law on the thief; he would recognize the fact that the thief is responsible, or, in other words, *free*.

Those who say that man's choice is only apparent, that what he thinks he chooses is merely the result of *chance,* are in conflict with experience and with reason. They stand condemned with the determinist on the score of experience. And they are in conflict with reason in assigning chance as a *cause*. For chance means what is unpredictable in an *effect*. Chance cannot be assigned as a cause. If the chance-theorists answer that they merely contend that all human choice is a chance effect, we inquire what is the cause of this effect? Is it some blind drive? Is it a star? Is it a constellation under which the human agent was born? All this throws us back to the position of the determinist which we have already discussed and disproved.

We conclude: The human will is endowed with true freedom of the choice of means to its ultimate end. The human will exercises its freedom of choice in every perfectly deliberate human act. The denial of human freedom of choice is a flat contradiction of reason, of all experience, of the exigencies of daily existence, and, if logically followed, it would turn the mind to the insanity of skepticism, and human society into a chaos of lawless disorder.

Summary of the Article

In this Article we have defined *man's soul* as the *spiritual substantial form of the living body*. We have seen that its *proper* faculties are those of *intellect* and *will*. We have noticed that man has three types of life,—*vegetal, sentient, rational,*—but we have learned that he can have but *one life-principle,* since he can have but *one substantial form,* and the life-principle or *soul* is this substantial form. We have seen that the human soul is *a complete substance,* although *not a complete human being*. We have learned that it is a substance that is *spiritual, simple, deathless* or *immortal*. We have learned that the substantial union of body and soul constitutes *a human person* who is the true author of his human acts. The one human soul is *formally spiritual and rational; virtually,* it is also *vegetal* and *sentient.* We have seen that the human spiritual soul exists in entirety *in the whole body,* and *in each living part of the body,* although it does not exercise all its operations in each part of the body. We have discussed the *faculties* of man, that is, his powers or capacities for vital operations. These we classed as *lower* and *higher,* calling *lower* those that are properly resident in the body-and-soul composite, and *higher* those that are properly resident in the soul alone. The lower faculties of man are those of *nutrition, growth, vital generation, sensation, sentient appetition, locomotion.* The higher faculties of man are his soul-faculties of *intellect* and *will.* We have seen that man's higher faculties are supra-organic; they are *spiritual faculties.* The object of the intellect is *truth;* the object of the will is *good.* We have seen that the will is the master-faculty during man's earthly life, even though it infallibly follows upon the ultimate practical judgment of the intellect. We have dwelt upon the great truth that *the will of man is free by a true freedom of the choice of means to man's ultimate end.*

CHAPTER VI

THE THEOLOGICAL QUESTION

The Theological Question is the question of the existence, nature, and operations of Almighty God. The department of philosophy which furnishes the answer to this question is called Natural Theology or *Theodicy.* The quest of philosophy for ultimate causes here discovers the First Efficient Cause and the Last Final Cause of all things. This study is a purely philosophical one, and draws no arguments from revelation; it is a truly metaphysical study, for it is a reasoned treatise on non-material real Being.

The Chapter is divided into the following Articles:

Article 1. The Existence of God

a) God; b) Demonstrability of God's Existence; c) Proofs of God's Existence.

a) God

The word *God* means, to the learned and the uncultured alike, a Being superior to this bodily world and all it contains; a Being that has produced the world, is in charge of it; a Being that is self-existent and self-explanatory; a Being that has no other superior to Itself, and is therefore Supreme. Rightly did St. Anselm say that "by the word *God* we mean the *greatest* Being that can be thought of." This is the meaning of the word *God,* even in the thoughts and speech of such persons as deny Him. For if a man says there is no God he confesses that he knows the meaning of the word *God* just as plainly as if he had said that there is a God. It would be impossible to have any discussion of this question of God's existence, nature, and activity, unless men were agreed upon the meaning of the terms of the discussion.

Our discussion centers upon the One Supreme Being. There are theories which appear to cloud this issue, but back of them all is this focal point: *unique Godhead, deity, divinity.* For our more ready understanding of all that is to follow, we list here the more notable theories on The Theological Question:

(*1*) *Theism* is a general theory of God; it is the doctrine that God exists.

(*2*) *Atheism* is a theory that there is no God.

(*3*) *Deism* is a belief in God, but not in His Providence or Government of the world.

(*4*) *Agnosticism* is the theory of God as the Great Unknowable.

(*5*) *Pantheism* in one way or another identifies God and creatures.

(*6*) *Monotheism* is the doctrine of one only God.

(*7*) *Polytheism* is the doctrine of a plurality of gods or world-rulers.

(*8*) *Ontologism* is the theory that the idea of God is the first idea acquired by man, and that this idea is necessary for the acquiring of any others.

(*9*) *Traditionalism* is the doctrine that the only certitude of God that man can attain comes to him, not by reasoning, but by receiving the human tradition which reports a primitive revelation made to our first parents.

(*10*) *Rationalism* is the theory that human reason can thoroughly investigate and understand all truth; that anything involving mystery is therefore fictional; that God, inasmuch as reason cannot fully comprehend Him, is to be denied or ignored.

b) DEMONSTRABILITY OF GOD'S EXISTENCE

A truth is *demonstrable* when it can be completely proved. A *strict* demonstration is *a reasoned proof,* as in the case of a theorem in geometry. A *less strict* demonstration is *an experimental proof,* as in the case of the laboratorian who shows by an experiment that water is H^2O.

A *strict* or *reasoned* or *philosophical* demonstration is either *a priori* or *a posteriori.* An *a priori* ("from beforehand"; "antecedent to experience") demonstration proceeds from the known nature and efficacy of a cause to the character of its effect. An *a posteriori* ("from afterwards"; "consequent on experience") demonstration proceeds from the fact and nature of an effect to the fact and nature of a cause adequate to account for the effect. If the argument is in this shape: "Here is a cause of a definite and known nature and efficacy; its effect will necessarily be so-and-so," it is an *a priori* argument. If the argument is in this shape: "Here is an effect of a definite and known nature; its cause must necessarily be of such-and-such nature and efficacy," it is an *a posteriori* argument.

A demonstration is *direct* or *indirect.* A *direct* demonstration shows that a thing is certain by setting forth its own causes or reasons (and *a cause* is anything that *produces or maintains; a reason* is anything that *explains*). An *indirect* demonstration shows that a thing is certain because *its denial* involves contradiction, or impossibility, or absurdity.

Can the existence of God be *demonstrated?* Can it be proved that there is one Supreme Being? There are persons who freely admit the existence of God, and who pay Him honor, worship Him, pray to Him, and yet who say that His existence is not a thing that can be *proved.*

If a thing cannot be proved, this fact is owing to one of two reasons: (*1*) the truth proposed is *self-evident,* and proof is neither needed nor possible; or (*2*) the truth is not subject to demonstration, and can be known only upon authority (of this type, for example, is all human historical truth). Now, neither of these reasons is here available.

Some, adducing the first reason, declare that God's existence is a self-evident truth which needs no demonstration and can have none. We answer that since God is the Necessary Being, it is true that the idea of the existence of God is a very part of the idea of God Himself; He is the Being that cannot be non-existent. The predicate "exists" belongs to the subject "God" just as necessarily as the predicate "round" belongs to the subject "circle." But, while we need no proof that a circle is round, but have this truth necessarily and self-evidently in our knowledge of what a circle is in itself, we do need proof of God's existence. For we have no such complete and adequate grasp of the idea *God* as we have of the idea *circle*. God is not a figure traced on a blackboard before our eyes. He is not manifest to the casual glance, like the rising sun. If we had minds capable of instantly taking in, with full clarity and distinctness, all the implications of the idea *God,* then the existence of God would be a self-evident truth to us. But, as a matter of fact, we have not such minds. We need *to reason out* the existence of God. And while no normal man can come to the full use of his mental powers without being aware, at least in a vague way, of the existence of a Supreme Being, this awareness is a *reasoned* awareness. We have here on earth no direct intuition, or immediate view, of God. Hence, although the truth of God's existence is *a self-evident truth in itself,* it is not *a self-evident truth to mankind.* Therefore, we can demonstrate or prove the existence of God.

Other objectors say that the truth of God's existence is not subject to demonstration. They maintain that we must stay within the realm of the laboratorian, in the world of "phenomenal things." Why, such persons would rule out of existence all pure mathematics. They would even cut the ground from their own position, for every laboratorian experiment rests ultimately upon reasoned truths or non-phenomenal assumptions. If we cannot trust human reason to work out a problem to its end, we cannot trust human reason to begin the problem.

We assert, therefore, that neither of the reasons which would render useless or impossible the demonstration of God's existence, has any force or value. We require a demonstration of the existence of God; such a demonstration can be had.

Our demonstration of God's existence is *direct, indirect, a posteriori.* It is *direct:* we assign reasons, and compelling reasons, which demand God's existence. It is *indirect:* we show the impossibility, the contradiction, the absurdity, the chaotic consequences, which come from the contradictory doctrine, that is, the doctrine that God does not exist. We cannot prove God's existence by an *a priori* demonstration, for, as we have seen, such a demonstration proceeds from cause to effect. Now, God is not an effect; God has no causes. He is *the First Cause Himself Uncaused.* Hence, our demonstration of God's existence must be *a posteriori.* (For St. Anselm's interesting argument *a priori,* —or, more accurately, *a simultaneo,*—see the First Part of this manual, *Chap. III, Art. 2, a*).

c) Proofs of God's Existence

We follow here the traditional proofs elaborated by St. Thomas Aquinas.

(*1*) *Proof from Motion.*—If there is motion in the world, there exists a mover, and, in last analysis, a First Mover which is itself not moved. Now, there is motion in the world. Therefore, there exists a mover, and, in last analysis, a First Mover which is itself not moved. This First Mover we call God. Therefore, God exists.

Motion is any *change.* There is change of substance, which is *corruption-generation;* there is change of quantity, which is *increase or diminishment;* there is change of quality, which is *alteration;* there is change of place, which is *local movement.* All these types of change are familiar to us in our daily experience. And each change is an example of *motion.*

The principle (that is the intellectual principle, the guiding truth) about motion is this: *Whatever moves is moved by something other than itself.* The word "moves" in this principle is to be understood as an intransitive verb. It is not difficult to see that this principle is absolutely justified. For what moves (the verb is intransitive) *receives* the motion, as the hand receives its motion from the man who writes or gesticulates. Anything *movable* is in a state of capacity or potentiality to receive motion. But to say that a thing moves itself is to say the thing gives motion to itself and receives motion from itself; it is to say that a thing is at once potential and actual; it is to say something as contradictory as that a man lifts himself by his boot-straps. Motion is not self-originating. Of course, there can be *a series* of movers. A man's fingers are moved, as he writes, by the muscles of hand and arm; these are moved into action by the motor nerves which center in the cerebro-spinal axis; these are set to motion or use by the man himself, and precisely by the man's will. But the will is a faculty used or set in motion by the soul. And the soul is set in motion when it is first created, and as it is preserved and concurred with by its Creator. Thus, we come back to a First Mover. A train of cars moving down the track is moved by the locomotive, although each car may be said to be moved by the one ahead of it which conveys the power or "pull" which moves it. The locomotive moves because its wheels move. The wheels move because the driving-rod moves them. The driving-rod is moved by the expansion of steam on the cylinder-head. The steam is moved to force and action by its compression in the cylinder. The compression of steam is owing to the action of fire on water. The action of fire, and the re-action of water, are due to their nature. Their nature is due to the Creator of nature, who moves them into existence equipped with certain powers, and who preserves them and concurs with them. Thus even the common spectacle of a moving train can carry the thinking mind straight to the First Mover, the self-existent, unmoved God. The First Mover cannot be moved, for it is *First*. It is purely actual (*Actus Purus*), "without change or shadow of alteration."

(*2*) *Proof from Co-ordinated Efficient Causes.*—If there exists an order of connected efficient causes, there is a First Cause which is itself not caused. Now, there exists all about us in this world an order of connected efficient causes. Therefore, there is a First Cause which is itself not caused. This First Cause we call God. Therefore, God exists.

An efficient or effecting cause is a cause which produces an effect by its own activity. There may be a series of such causes, each an effect of a prior cause. To illustrate: the sun causes sunburn; sunburn causes pain; pain causes irritability; irritability causes unpleasant social effects. Or again, the seed-wheat (together with subsidiary causes such as light, heat, moisture, and the chemicals of the earth) causes the crop; the crop is a cause of flour; flour is a cause of bread; bread is food which is a cause of energy in the man who eats it; energy is a cause of bodily action, and so on, almost endlessly. The world around us is a tissue of cause-and-effect. And each cause was an effect before it went to work as a cause of a further effect. But the chain of cause-and-effect cannot be infinite; no process unto infinity is possible in finite things. Hence, there is of necessity a First Cause. And since this Cause is *First* it is not an effect; it is not caused; for nothing can be prior to what is *first*. There is, therefore, a First Cause, Itself Uncaused. This we call God. Therefore, God exists.

(*3*) *Proof from the Contingency of Earthly Things.*—A thing is *contingent* (that is, dependent on its causes) when it has in itself no requirement, no demand, for existence. If a thing might conceivably *not be,* it is a contingent thing; it is marked by *contingency*. The opposite of contingency is *necessity*. A thing which *must exist,* and cannot conceivably be non-existent, is a necessary thing; it is marked by *necessity*. Now for our argument:

If contingent things exist, they demand as their ultimate explanation, a Being which is Necessary. Now, contingent things exist. Therefore, they demand as their ultimate explanation a Being which is Necessary. This Necessary Being we call God. Therefore, God exists.

It is manifest that contingency means *dependency in being.* Now, if a thing depends for its being on something else, what is the status of this something else? Is it also contingent? If so, what of the status of that further being on which it depends? Is this, too, contingent? But the chain of contingency cannot go on endlessly. If one link supports another, and is supported by another, this dependency is all upon some ultimate link which is supported *absolutely,* that is, by a power which, unsupported itself, supports the whole chain. Contingent being absolutely demands, as the "reason for its existence," *Being that is not contingent,* but necessary. Now, no sane man will question the contingency of things about us here on earth. Any one of the substances we look at,—our fellowmen, the grass and trees, the flying birds, the stones and streams,—might *not* have been. Indeed, there was a time when they *were not.* They *came* into being, and most of them will very quickly pass out of it, others more slowly. But, if these things were necessary and non-contingent, they would *have* to be; they would *have been* always; they could not perish or pass away. The world about us is a completely contingent thing. Thus, since contingency demands necessity as its explanation; since contingent things do not render an account of themselves but are accounted for only by the causes on which they depend; since, in a word, contingent things demand the existence of a Necessary Being, we assert the existence of such a Being. This Being is First; it is Ultimate. It has therefore no contingency on a *prior* thing. This Being, Non-contingent and Necessary, we call God. Therefore, God exists.

(4) *Proof from the Degrees of Perfection in Things.*—If there are, in things about us in this world, real degrees of greater

and lesser, then there must exist a Greatest. Now, there are, in things about us in this world, real degrees of greater and lesser. Therefore, there must exist a Greatest. This Greatest Being we call God. Therefore, God exists.

We speak here of *real* degrees of perfection in things, not of estimation or opinion in which this or that man holds things; we speak of the perfection of *things themselves.* Now, it is manifest that there are such real degrees in things. Consider man. He has all the perfection of being that belongs to a plant, and he has much more. He takes nourishment, grows, propagates, as a plant does. But man is moreover sentient and rational. Thus, man is *more perfect* than plant. And man is also more perfect than animal, for he adds in himself to all animal perfections, those of understanding and willing. The animal, in turn, is more perfect than the plant. For the rest, we are all aware that there are degrees of loyalty, of love, of friendship. We know that things are more or less noble, more or less good. Now, a thing is more perfect as it approaches to a greater *fulness of being.* This is the norm or rule and measure of perfection; in the application of this rule we discern the real grades or degrees of perfection in things. But that which *approaches* (more or less nearly, or more or less remotely) to the *fulness of perfection* or *the absolute plenitude of being,* must approach to *what is there.* Real grades or degrees of perfection would be illusory and meaningless unless they had reference to an Absolutely Perfect Reality actually existing. Now, this Absolutely Perfect Being we call God. Therefore God exists. Deny God, and you deny the essential superiority of mind over matter, of a man over the clod of earth he treads on, of Shakespeare over a stone by the roadside.

(5) *Proof from the Finality of Natural Things.*—Things are said to have *finality* when they are *made for a purpose,* when they are made for the attaining of an *end* or *finis* (hence the name *finality*). And things made for a purpose are *designed* or *planned* for the attaining of that purpose. This argument is, consequently,

often called the argument from *design.* Now, design is a plan; plan is a reasoned thing, it connotes *an intelligence.* Hence this argument points to the existence of Intelligence, and of First and Supreme Intelligence. The argument may be proposed as follows:

If the world, and things in the world, are manifestly designed for an end, then the world and things in the world have a designer, and ultimately a First Designer. Now, the world, and things in the world, are manifestly designed for an end. Therefore the world, and things in the world have a designer, and ultimately a First Designer. This Designer we call God. Therefore, God exists.

To discover design, we have but to look at any natural body. Living bodies particularly are such complex and balanced organisms that no sane mind could doubt their planning. If a building, or a timepiece, or any of the works of man's art and skill is unthinkable without a design, how much greater is the compelling reason which drives us to acknowledge design in things immeasurably above the capacity of man to envision or produce. That an eye is made for seeing, an ear for hearing, a heart for circulating and purifying the blood; that the seed is for the producing of a plant, that wings are for flying,—what mind could doubt the *purpose* of any of these things? Even lifeless things are manifestly designed. Can man who finds here on earth all that his nature requires,—food, air, water,—suppose that these things are not planned? Can he suppose that the rich deposits of oils, gases, metals, coal, which make the earth a profitable workshop for him, have all come about without any purpose or design? And if man shortsightedly complains that there are imperfections here on earth, we answer that there are indeed, and we know why. But the primal sin which hurt man and the earth, —yet rendered it the more suitable to exact man's labor, and to keep him reminded of the stern and pressing duty of attaining his eternal end, and to afford him means of necessary penance and discipline,—is not our present concern. The so-called imperfections of the earth are themselves proofs of perfection; unless a person knows *the standard* how shall he know what falls short of it? Unless he knows what the perfection of a reality is, how shall he know when it is imperfect? For the rest, any natural body is replete with such marvels of perfection, and exhibits such plan and purpose, that an honest mind cannot refuse the evidence. Such things as we call imperfections,—if they be imperfections at all,—are as nothing compared to the wondrous order, the complexity, the balance, the government to an end, that we observe all around us. And all this order, all this design, is multiplied for us by microscope and telescope. In small things and large, in the world as a whole and in its tiny part, we discern order, plan, purpose, design. Consider the full perfection of a design which operates without noise, without waste, without smoke and fuss, all of which are found in the operations by which man works out his artificial designs. There is no clamor of the mighty firmament as its countless solar systems and their parts move so surely in their proper orbits. There is no tapping of hammers, no hissing of steam, no sigh of expended effort, as the thick liquid within an egg-shell turns to the flesh and blood and bone and sinew of the fowl, and sets each delicate organ in its place. No one can honestly doubt or question design in the world. Now, if there is design there is certainly a designer, equipped with intelligence to plan and to execute. And if this designer were a creature, it would have a maker capable of producing the designer and all his powers. Ultimately we must come to a First Designer, in whom all the perfections and the plan and purpose of every creature must find its final explanation. This Designer must be self-existent, for He is *First*. We call this Designer God, the Supreme Intelligence. Therefore, God exists.

To these five traditional arguments we may add a few others:

(*6*) *Proof from Man's Desire of All Good.*—If man, by the irresistible drive of his nature, tends towards universal and boundless good, then such Good actually exists. Now, man, by the irresistible drive of his nature, tends towards universal and boundless good. Therefore, such Good actually exists. We call this Good by the name of *God*. Therefore, God exists.

Ethics and psychology tell us that man is made for the *summum bonum,* for boundless good. For in every deliberate thought, word, deed, of which man is the conscious master, he tends toward what pleases, towards what satisfies, towards what is desirable; in a word, he tends towards what is *good*. He may look for good in the wrong places, but it is good he is looking for. He may seek good in sin, in indulgence of self, even in cruelty or blasphemy; but it is *good* he is after. The will, author of man's deliberate acts, is a faculty which we define by its object, and we say that it is man's spiritual appetency, his power of going after good which is intellectually apprehended. The happiness of a man in his health, his home, his property; the misery of a man thwarted in his quest of what he desires; these things alike prove what man is *after*. He is after what will ultimately and completely *satisfy,* and this means that he is after *good*. For *the good* is defined as that which may be appetized, as that which can be striven for as a satisfaction. Now, man's nature which irresistibly impels him in the quest of good (however diversely different men may pursue the quest), is manifestly planned and designed for this quest. And our reason cannot accept the supposition that the planning was done to vex man and to see him involved in hopelessness, but assures us that the purpose for which man must strive is a purpose that can be achieved. Now only the Supreme and Boundless Good can satisfy man's natural tendency; man wants good; he wants all good; he wants it always. Only the Infinite Being can perfectly answer this connatural need and tendency of man. And reason, which sees that the satisfaction of man is objective and existing, acknowledges that this existing Goal is Infinite Good. But the First and Self-existent Being alone is infinite. Therefore man's nature points inevitably and infallibly to the existence of the First and Self-existent and Infinite Being. This Being is God. Therefore, God exists.

(7) *The Moral Proof.*—If man is aware that he is bound by a moral law to avoid evil and to do good, then a lawgiver exists, and ultimately a First Lawgiver. Now, man is aware that he is bound by a moral law to avoid evil and to do good. Therefore, a lawgiver exists, and ultimately a First Lawgiver. We call this Lawgiver by the name of *God*. Therefore, God exists.

When a human person ceases to be a baby, when he acquires some responsibility for his acts, he is aware of a requirement which reason itself manifests. He is aware that he is "to avoid evil and to do good." He may, in many things, ignore this law, but he cannot be ignorant of it. Every sane adult knows inevitably that there is such a thing as good, such a thing as evil, such a thing as duty. No talk of conventions, of "mores," of customs, will explain the manifest fact that *no* man can retain his sanity and honestly consider *all* things licit. One may call a certain thing evil, another may call it good, a third may call it indifferent. But the point we make is that all men know the meaning of these terms: *good, evil, indifferent*. Pride may make a stupid man believe that all things are lawful *to him;* but let another trespass on his rights, and see whether he have not fault to find and complaint to make as against *evil* done to him. The normal mind recognizes the *objective* character of moral good and evil. The normal mind acknowledges the truth that there is good, there is evil; that good is to be done and evil avoided. Well, all this means that there is a moral *law*. Now a law without a lawgiver is an effect without a cause. And an inescapable law, imposed on our very nature and made manifest by reason, is not the work of a lawgiver who has neither authority nor power. This is the work of a true lawgiver, one who actually can make his law known, and indicate enforcement. It is the work of a mind, of a will, that is, of a personality. There exists then a personal lawgiver for all men. But this must be, in last analysis, the First Lawgiver. This Lawgiver we call God. Therefore, God exists.

(8) *The Historical Proof.*—If all men of all times have reached the reasoned conclusion that God exists, then He must actually exist. Now, all men of all times have reached the reasoned conclusion that God exists. Therefore, He must actually exist.

When we say "all men of all times" we do not mean each and every individual; we mean men in general. Our assertion is that if belief in God, as a reasoned conclusion, has been a truly common and universal fact among men of all times, then God must exist. For the common consent of men on a matter of reasoned truth expresses the very voice of rational nature; and if this voice be false, we have no alternative but to lapse into the insane contradiction of skepticism. Men may be deceived about a fact of the material order which they judge too quickly upon appearances; so men have been wrong in judging that the earth is flat or that the sun moves across the sky each day. But when there is question of *reasoning* from certainly known data, this general error is not possible. Men may be wrong about the flatness of the earth, and about the movement about the sun; but they cannot be wrong in their conclusion that motion requires a mover or that a flat surface is mensurable by square measure. Now, the earth is a plain fact; its limitation and contingency are manifest; its order and design are undeniable. To argue from these facts to the adequate explanation of the facts is to follow a course of reasoning. In such reasoning the whole human race cannot be wrong. That all men have actually reasoned to the existence of God is plain from the fact that all men have had some idea of divinity as a power in control, a supra-mundane power. Even belief in false gods, or in many gods, is proof of the point. We do not assert that all men of all times have known the true God, or have known the true God truly. We do assert that all men of all times have had, as a reasoned conclusion, a conviction of divinity, of deity, of God. The voice of natural reason thus proclaims the existence of God, and this voice is not deceiving. Therefore, God exists.

(9) *Indirect Proof.*—A truth is proved indirectly when one shows that its denial leads to impossible consequences. Now, the denial of the truth of God's existence is *atheism.* Atheism leads to impossible consequences. Atheism therefore cannot be true. And if atheism cannot be true, theism must be true.

Atheism cannot be true because it cannot even be formulated as a positive doctrine. Man's mind cannot rest in sheer denial. The atheist never utterly denies God; he *replaces* God by something inferior, which he calls nature, or energy, or forces, or immanence, or even chance. Now, a doctrine which consists of sheer denial is not a doctrine at all, and, as we have seen, it cannot even be formulated as a doctrine. Hence, it is not true, for truth is expressible in a positive statement. The atheist cannot go on forever saying that God is not, and that the world, its contingency, its order, its design, and all the rest, are *not* to be explained by ultimate recourse to God. And the atheist, forgetting that he has nothing else to do but deny (for this is impossible), goes on to preach a positive doctrine which amounts to *theism.* For if "nature" explains things, then the atheist means by "nature" what we mean by "God," although he probably gives a narrow and imperfect character to "nature"—that is, he sets up inferior gods. But *some* gods he inevitably sets up.

Atheism is not true because it conflicts with reason. Reason rests upon a sure principle that "everything that exists has a sufficient reason for existing." There must be an explanation of the world, of bodies, of human life. And the minute a sufficient reason is assigned for any of these things, a god is set up. For the world of bodies does not explain itself; and if it did, the world itself would be a god. The idea of Godhead, of deity, is wholly inescapable.

Atheism is not true because it conflicts with man's best tendencies. It is in the right and reasonable recognition of his character as a *creature,* as one therefore bound to look with reverence and gratitude to a Creator, that man shows the best that is in him.

Atheism cannot be true, for it destroys all morality. If there is no God, then man is not answerable to any ultimate authority, and all he needs is craft to avoid being taken up by the police. Morality is then either a set of rules of etiquette, or a code of civil laws. And neither of these bodies of rules would have any true warrant for existing; they would both be imposed by tyranny. Now, any doctrine which cuts away the solid foundation of morality is a false doctrine, for it contradicts the requirements of man's life,—of his mind or reason, of his will, of his affections. Atheism therefore is a false doctrine.

Now, if atheism is false, then theism is true. God exists.

Summary of the Article

In this Article we have explained the meaning of the word *God* as fundamental to our discussion of God's existence. We have briefly defined various theories or doctrines that touch upon the existence of God or our knowledge of Him. We have shown that the truth of God's existence is capable of *demonstration* by true *a posteriori* proofs, both *direct and indirect.* We have seen that this truth requires demonstration, for while it is *a self-evident truth in itself,* it is not *a self-evident truth to mankind.* We have offered the five traditional proofs of the Scholastics, and have added several other proofs of lesser value. In conclusion, we must note that while we need these proofs for a philosophical study about God, we do not require them when we have the divine gift of Faith. Nor, having the Faith, do we coldly rationalize it by studying such proofs. But we have need of these proofs so that we may convince others, and lead them by the clear road of reason to the point where they may dispose themselves to accept the metaphysical certitude of divine Faith.

Article 2. The Nature of God

a) Essence and Nature; b) The Essence of God; c) The Attributes of God.

a) Essence and Nature

The *essence* of a thing is what constitutes it. The essence of a thing is what is expressed in a true definition of the thing.

A thing may be regarded in two ways: (*1*) as an *existible* reality, and (*2*) as an *understandable* reality. Hence, any reality may be *defined* in two ways; either according to its being as an existible thing, or according to its being as an understandable thing. Suppose we are to define *man.* As an existible thing man is a substantial compound of body-and-soul; as a thing that can exist among other things, man exists as body-and-soul. This is a definition of man, and it is called *a physical definition.* A definition *expresses an essence,* and the physical definition of man expresses the physical essence of man, that is, "body-and-soul-substantially-united." But suppose we define man as an *understandable* thing. We do not mean to define him according to the mere viewpoint of the mind; we mean to define him as a *reality.* But we mean to make our definition of *those points of reality* in man (not *physical parts* like body and soul) which render him intelligible. Now, how does an adequate mind or understanding lay hold of the *reality* called *man?* Well, first of all it knows man as some *thing.* Further, it knows man as a substantial thing, and as a complete substance; it knows man as *subsistent.* The mind knows man as *a subsistent thing.* But it knows him as distinct from such subsistent things as pure spirits; for it knows man as a *bodily*-subsistent-thing. And it knows man as other than mere bodies like sticks and stones; for it knows man as a *living*-bodily-subsistent-thing. And it knows man as something more than a living substance such as a tree; for it knows man as a *sentient*-living-bodily-subsistent-thing. And it knows man as something more than a sentient substance like a dog or cat; for it knows man as endowed with intellect and will, that is, it knows man as a *rational*-sentient-living-bodily-subsistent-thing. Notice that all the points the mind knows about man as understandable are *points of reality;* they are not points of the mind's view, they are points of fact in man himself; yet they are not physical parts. The six points of reality about man that make him intelligible or understandable are: thing, subsistent, bodily, living, sentient, rational. And you may take any one of these as predicate and say that man *is* such a thing: man *is* subsistent; man *is* alive; man *is* rational. Now the sum of all the points of reality which render a thing understandable constitutes *the metaphysical essence* of that thing. Thus the metaphysical essence of man is: "a reality or thing that is subsistent, bodily, living, sentient, and rational." Since the first five of these points of reality in man (that is, *thing, subsistent, bodily, living, sentient*) make the metaphysical essence of *animal,* we may merely add the word *rational* to *animal,* and we have, in shorter compass, the metaphysical essence of man. The metaphysical essence of man is expressed in the metaphysical definition of man: "Man is a rational animal."

The physical essence of man is his constitution as an existible thing; it is made up of man's fundamental and indispensable physical parts; it is constituted by man's body and soul.

The metaphysical essence of man is the sum of the points of reality about him that make him understandable; the sum of points of reality recognized by a mind that *knows* what man is; this metaphysical essence of man is constituted of animality and rationality.

Now, what we have said about the physical and metaphysical essence of man is true of the physical and metaphysical essence of *anything*. We have used *man* only as an illustration. In our present study we are to inquire into the physical essence and the metaphysical essence of God.

The *nature* of a thing is its essence regarded as the root or source of its operations. The nature of a thing is its *working essence*. Thus, while we say that the *essence* of a man is (physically considered) his body-and-soul, we say that the *nature* of man is his essence *as operative*. We say that it is *according to man's nature* that he thinks and wills; we say that it is *natural* to man to walk and to speak, and so on.

Now, the items of perfection that belong to a thing because it is of *such a nature,* are called *attributes* of the thing. It is essential (metaphysically) to man that he be *fundamentally equipped* for reasoning and willing; he has this fundamental equipment even as a baby when he is unable to use it; he has this equipment even if he be an imbecile that will never use it. But the actual ability to use this fundamental equipment belongs only to man when he is sufficiently matured, when he is conscious, when he is unprevented in its use. But granted that a man is fully constituted in being, that he is mature, awake, alert, unblocked in the exercise of his powers, it will follow of necessity *that he is able actually to reason and to use free-will.* This *actual* ability, we say, belongs to his *nature,* his operative essence; this ability follows upon that nature because it is such a nature. Therefore this actual ability is *proper* to man, it is to be *attributed* to man: actual reasoning and actual willing are *attributes* of man. An *attribute* is, therefore, the normal and necessary consequence of an essence fully constituted in its working capacity, that is, of an essence constituted as a nature. In brief, an attribute is a perfection that belongs by natural necessity to a nature.

We see, therefore, that an attribute (since it belongs to a nature because this *is* such a nature) is an index of the nature to which it belongs. If we know the attributes of a thing, we shall know by them the nature whence they flow, or to which they necessarily belong. Therefore, in our present study we shall investigate certain attributes of God, so that we may know *the nature of God.*

To sum up: Essence is that reality which constitutes a thing as *existible* (physical essence) or as *understandable* (metaphysical essence). Nature is essence considered as the source of operations. Attributes are perfections that belong by necessity to a fully constituted and unhampered nature.

b) The Essence of God

(*1*) *The Physical Essence of God.*—God is not a body; He is not made up of parts. God is not a creature; He is not limited or confined or in any way composed. Hence, the physical essence of God is a *unique* physical essence. We cannot illustrate it perfectly by showing what the physical essence of some creature is, and then drawing a comparison. But, since God is "constituted" (to use an imperfect word) in His being by *Himself,* and not as a sum of parts or of distinct elements or perfections, it may suffice to say that God's physical essence is his *infinite and indivisible being as pure spirit.* That is what God is as an existing thing: *a Spirit infinitely perfect.* More fully, God's physical essence is defined as *the one and only infinite and indivisible and all-perfect Spirit.*

Notice that we mention several *perfections* in setting forth this physical definition of God. We speak of the *oneness* or *unity* of God; of His *uniqueness* which we indicate by the word "only"; of His *simplicity* or *indivisibility,* for God has no parts; of His full *perfection;* of His *infinity;* of His *spirituality.* Now, it must be always understood that in God there is not only no distinction of parts (for He has no parts), but there is no real distinction of perfections; all that God *has* He *is.* We know supernaturally that in God there is one *real distinction;* it is the distinction of the Three Divine Persons. But aside from this (which philosophy has no right to investigate, since it is a truth known by revelation), there is no *real* distinction in God. God's unity, uniqueness, simplicity, full perfection, infinity, spirituality, are only *logically* distinct (that is, are only various aspects which our mind takes of one and the same actuality); they are not *really* distinct (that is, distinct as thing and thing). All these perfections are *in reality* one with God and one with one another; all are one in the Infinite Essence with which they are identified, and of which they are but various aspects taken by the finite mind.

(2) *The Metaphysical Essence of God.*—That is called the metaphysical essence of God which affords the mind its basic grasp of what *God* means. Theologians have ever differed in their opinion of what precisely is the point by which a creatural mind lays hold of God as understandable. Some have said that the fundamental notion or idea which the mind grasps in knowing God is His *radical infinity;* others have said that it is His *boundless knowing.* But others, with more show of reason, say that before we think of God as infinite or as all-knowing, we think of God as *there.* We think of Him as *existing.* And we think of Him as *existing of Himself,* or, in other words, we think of God as *Subsistent Being Itself.* In this we discern the metaphysical essence of God.

c) The Attributes of God

An *attribute,* as we have learned, is a perfection that belongs to a thing because the thing is *of such a nature.* It *belongs* to a nature. It *flows* from a nature fully and perfectly constituted and unprevented in function. To illustrate: as children we learned that the Church has certain *attributes.* One of these is infallibility. Now, consider what the Church is: an institution set up by Almighty God Himself when He walked the earth as man; an institution guaranteed by Almighty God for the teaching of truth and the leading of men to heaven. Such being the *nature* of the Church, *it necessarily follows* that the Church cannot teach error or lead men to hell. Therefore, infallibility necessarily *belongs* to the Church; it *flows* from the very nature of the Church. It is an *attribute* of the Church.

Now, there is an important observation to make here, or to repeat here, for we have made it before. Strictly speaking, God *has* no attributes. What we call His attributes are *Himself* regarded by our finite minds from different angles. God is simple, indivisible, not made of parts or elements. All that God *has,* God *is.* But we must use such terms as we can; we are finite and our language is not adequate for expressing infinity with full perfection. Therefore, as long as we know that what we call God's attributes are not things other than God which God merely possesses, we may use our inadequate terminology as the only available instrument for the expression of important truths.

We have already mentioned many attributes of God in our study of The Theological Question. We have spoken of God's oneness or unity, of His infinity, of His simplicity, of His uniqueness, of His supreme intelligence, of His supreme will, and of other divine perfections or attributes. Here we mention these again, together with some others. In studying the attributes of God, we are directly studying the nature of God.

(*1*) *Absolute Divine Attributes.*—"Absolute" means "freed from all *ifs, buts, hows, whys, conditions.*" The absolute attributes of God are those which belong to God as God, not to God as Creator, or Preserver, or Governor, but to God *simply.* Such are *infinity, immensity, immutability* or *changelessness, knowledge, wisdom.* Absolute divine attributes are either positive or negative. (*a*) *Positive* divine attributes express infinite perfection in God: *life, wisdom, understanding, will,* etc. (*b*) *Negative* divine attributes express absence of imperfection in God: *infinity* (which means that God is *not* limited); *indivisibility* (which means that God is *not* made up of parts); *immutability* (which means that God is *not* changeable), etc.

(*2*) *Relative Divine Attributes.*—"Relative" means having a relation to, a connection with, something else. Now, on the part of God, who is infinite and self-sufficing, *there are no real relations* whatever except the real relations of the Persons of the Trinity to one another. But creatures have essential relations with Almighty God, and these are *real.* God's relative attributes *bring creatures into relation with Him;* they do not bring God into any real relations with creatures. Relative attributes of God are, for example, His *power,* as creating, preserving, providing, governing the world and especially man; His *goodness* to His creatures; His *fidelity* to His saving word; His *truthfulness,* and so on.

In general, reason declares that since God is the fulness of all perfection in infinite degree; since He is Pure Actuality; since He is wholly Self-sufficing; since He is without the shadow of any imperfection (for *being* is perfection, and He is Infinite Subsistent Being Itself), He has as attributes *all pure perfections in a way far superior to that in which perfections are possessed or can be possessed by creatures.* The technical way of expressing this reasoned truth is this: *God has all pure perfections formally and eminently.* A pure or *unmixed* perfection is one that involves no imperfection, such as *life, knowledge.* A *mixed* perfection involves imperfection, such as *walking* or *reasoning.* For it is a perfection to be able to walk; but it is an indication of limitation (hence an imperfection) that a person must walk to reach another place and cannot be there instantly without walking. So it is a perfection to be able to reason out a truth; but it is an imperfection that one must think it out and cannot see it at once without mental labor. We say that mixed perfections are in God *virtually;* that is, the equivalent of all that is perfect about them belongs to God eminently. Thus, God who knows all things comprehensively (in such a way as to perfectly possess all possible knowledge about them) has no need of *reasoning,* that is, of studying things out; but He has all that such study or reasoning could possibly give; he has *all* knowledge; therefore we say that he has reasoning virtually or equivalently.

Now, the proof of all the perfections which can be listed as attributes of God rests upon the perfection of God in His metaphysical essence as Subsistent Being Itself. For such a Being is unconferred, unreceived, and hence not limited. Being that is received is received *in a measure.* Being unreceived must be unlimited, for only *a cause* can limit being as only a cause can confer it. So Being unreceived, unconferred, is being uncaused and unlimited. It is *Infinite Being*. Out of God's essence as Subsistent Being Itself appears the fundamental attribute of *infinity.* Upon infinity, as upon their proximate foundation (and their proof) rest the other divine attributes. Thus God is infinite or unlimited by time: He is eternal; He has the attribute of *eternity;* and this eternity is not limited or measured by days or hours or centuries; it has no *succession* (for this would involve limitation) : it is an everlasting *now,* without past or future. And God, as infinite, is unlimited by place; He is immense or immeasurable, not having *size,* which, however large, is a limitation. God thus has the attribute of *immensity,* of not being contained in limits of measurement or dimensions. And similarly God has the attribute, on this score, of *omnipresence* or *ubiquity;* God is everywhere, for *place* cannot shut Him out any more than it can enclose Him. And infinity involves *immutability* or *changelessness* in God, for any change means a loss and a gain, and a loss means a limit now, while a gain means a limit before the gain was made. Infinity in God means that he is not limited in *knowledge,* in *wisdom,* in *power,* in any perfection. Thus, infinity in God means simply that God is *all-perfect.* And since *personality* (that is substantial personality) is a high perfection, it must be in God in eminent degree. Human reason thus concludes inevitably that God is *a personal God,* not a "Cosmic Force" or an "Unconscious Absolute." Revelation informs us that God's personality is *threefold,* that God is Three Persons in One Undivided God. Reason cannot prove or disprove this truth directly. But reason cannot find conflict in it either. And reason can prove it indirectly; for if God exists (as reason proves) and if Christ is God (as history and reason demonstrate) then Christ's word is that of the Infallible God and is true. Now, Christ's own word, and the word of His Church which He has guaranteed, teaches the Trinity. Therefore, reason sees that this is a true word, and thus indirectly proves the existence of Three Persons in One

God. That God is *personal,* means in simple language, that God knows us, loves us, cares for us, provides for us, governs the world for our welfare.

Summary of the Article

In this Article we have learned the meaning of *essence, nature, attribute.* We have learned also what is meant by *the physical essence* and *the metaphysical essence* of a thing. We have discerned the physical essence of God in His infinite substantial spirituality. We have seen that His metaphysical essence consists in the fact that God is Subsistent Being Itself, Self-Existent Being. We have learned something of the *nature* of God by studying His essence and His attributes. We have carefully explained that an *attribute* in God is not merely a perfection possessed by God; it is God Himself in one aspect; it is God Himself seen from one angle by our finite minds. All God's attributes are one with His essence and one with each other in the Undivided Godhead. We have seen that God is a *personal* God.

Article 3. The Activity of God

a) Operations of God; b) Immanent Divine Operations; c) Transient Divine Operations.

a) Operations of God

By an *operation* we mean an activity performed; we mean the product of a power for acting or doing. Now, infinite power is an attribute of God. But, as we have learned, this attribute is not something that God *has;* it is something that God *is.* God *is* Infinite Power. In creatures, an operation is the product of a power which is not the active or operating creature itself, but something distinct from the creature which the creature *possesses.* A creature cannot act or operate *immediately;* it must act or operate through the *medium* or by the *means* of a power to act; it operates *mediately*. But with God this is not so. Hence, when we speak of the operations of God, or of the divine operations, we speak of God Himself exercising Godhead.

An operation is either *immanent* or *transient*. An immanent or "indwelling" operation stays in its main effect within the being which operates; we call this being *the agent,* from the Latin *agens* "the actor, the doer, the performer, the accomplisher." A transient operation (from the Latin *transiens* "going across") goes across, so to speak, from the agent and finds its main effect in something outside the agent. The operation or activity of *growing* is an immanent operation in a child. The tearing of a garment by growing is a transient activity or operation of the growing child. The operation of thinking is immanent; the operation of bat against ball is transient.

Now, since God is the author of all positive being or perfection, there is nothing outside God for Him to work upon except such things as His power has placed there, and which His power keeps in existence. And so there is no positive being, no actual creature, which is utterly independent of God, and which exists as a wholly alien thing for Him to exercise transient operations or activities upon. Besides, a transient activity always involves (in creatures, where transient activity in its perfection is possible, and where *alone* it is possible) a kind of "kick-back," an effect on the agent itself. If the bat hits the ball, the bat itself receives an impact; the bat itself is affected. But this connatural property of transient activity or operation is not found in God's operations. And thus we perceive that the phrase *transient operation* or *transient activity* is not strictly and literally predicable of any of God's operations. But we use such language as we possess; it is imperfect language, but it is the best we have. And so we *call* by the name of *transient divine activity* the operations of God which affect creatures.

The immanent operations of God are those that are "indwelling" in God, and indeed are *identified* with the very essence of God in His Undivided Infinite Self-Subsistent Being.

b) Immanent Divine Operations

The immanent operations of God (apart from the eternal generation of the Son by the Father, and the eternal procession of the Holy Ghost from the Father and the Son—operations which philosophy is not competent to discuss) are the operations of God as *Intellect* and of God as *Will.*

(*1*) *God as Intellect* is God the Omniscient, God the All-knowing. Since God is infinite, there is no limitation to God's knowledge; *it exhausts the knowability of everything.* It is truly *comprehensive* knowledge which takes in not only what things *are* or *have been* or *will be* or *can be,* but all that, under other and non-existing circumstances, they *could* be. God's knowledge is knowledge of all things in all their actual and possible relations. This must be so, as reason sees, otherwise God's knowledge would be limited; and God (who *is* His knowledge) is infinite. God's knowledge is not the product of *learning.* It is not conserved in *memory* or anticipated in *expectation.* For God has no past and no future; He knows all knowables (in all actual and possible relations) *now,* in an eternal *now;* for God's knowledge is His eternal *Self.* God's knowledge does not operate to the prejudice of his free creatures, men and angels. For God's knowledge regarded as the *operation* of knowing, is immanent. It is *the will* of God that provides and governs and gives free creatures every possible help to their happiness. The fact that God knows whether I shall be saved or damned does not save me or damn me. We do wrong to speculate on this point, for our speculation always imposes on God our own limitations; we always speak or think of God *looking forward to our final state as to a future event.* And this view of the matter is calamitously false. Such a mistaken imposing of limitation on God results also in the silly cry, "If God *knew* [past tense] that I shall be lost [future tense] why did [past tense] He create me?" But God has no past and no future, and such a cry is a hopelessly falsified expression of a state of affairs. I had better say: "I am part of a magnificent and eternal plan. How I fit into it is my own doing, for I am made in God's image and my best gift is my freedom. But whether I fit into the plan to my own happiness or my own misery, I do not spoil the plan. God's work is perfect in any case; it gives Him external, formal, and objective glory, no matter whether I proclaim His goodness in heaven or His justice in hell. God's work does not fail, nor can I make it fail. I can make *my own* work fail, but I had better not do so. Meanwhile, I must not idly and impiously inquire why God made His glorious creation of which I am a part, and utter silly cries of objection that the whole thing should have been omitted because *I* was going to ruin my own happiness by my own free choice. God's knowledge of my success or failure in my own work does not compel or necessitate me. I am free. Besides, let me soberly consider this: God knows whether I am going (future tense, *for me,* not for God) to heaven or to hell. But *I* do not know. What I *do* know, and it is sufficient, is that I can go to heaven if I choose to do so and if I express my choice by living rightly according to God's will."

God's knowledge (which is God as Intellect) embraces all things perfectly. God knows Himself, which is only saying that He *is* Himself. God knows all creatures in Himself. We human beings *learn,* we *come* to know; we apprehend what things are *in themselves* after the things are there. But God knows all knowables *eternally*. In our language, God knows things perfectly *before* they are there. If He did not know them, they could not be planned and created and put there. Their *very possibility* rests upon God's knowledge. Thus God knows all things *in Himself,* not *in themselves,* as we know things. We know things by taking in their mental image or species, as it is called. But God Himself is the adequate *species* of all existible creatures. No image or species is impressed on God, or expressed in God, for such impression and expression is necessarily limited, and God's knowledge is His Infinite Essence and *unlimited.* But we say, technically (if inaccurately), that in God are the "archetypes,"

—that is, the first molds, the primal designs,—of all things knowable and creatable. Sometimes we call these "archetypal ideas" or "archetypal images" or "archetypal species." The primary object of God's knowledge is Himself; the secondary object of God's knowledge is all knowable creatures, and these He knows eternally in Himself.

Philosophers (and theologians) make a distinction (not real, but logical with a basis in reality) in the knowledge of God, and speak of God's *Simple Understanding* and God's *Vision.* By the Knowledge of Simple Understanding, God knows all things *possible.* By the Knowledge of Vision, God has *present* knowledge of all things *actual,* whether, in our view, these are past, present, or to come. Some learned men make a further distinction and say that there is a type of knowledge which lies midway between these two types; they call it *Scientia Media* or Middle Knowledge, and they assign to this type of divine knowledge the things, not merely and sheerly possible, and not truly actual, but *such things as a creature would certainly do if certain circumstances and conditions were verified, but which are not, in fact, going to be verified.* Thus God knows perfectly what I would do if I went out into the street tomorrow and found a thousand-dollar bill. But, as a fact, I am not going to find any such bill. *What I would do* is not sheerly possible, but something that *would be actual* if conditions were met (and they are not going to be met); nor is it *truly actual* but only what *would be actual* in the unrealized circumstances. Such a thing is *knowable,* and God knows it. But in the human scheme of distinguishing God's knowledge into a sort of set of two compartments (Simple Understanding or Simple Intelligence and Vision) such a thing does not seem to fit; we make a third compartment called *Scientia Media* for this thing to fit into. Now, these things that are not going to happen, but *would certainly happen,* if conditions (which are not going to be realized) were in fact realized, are called *futuribilia.* So we may sum up this matter and say that philosophers and theologians distinguish in God (*a*) *Knowledge of*

Simple Understanding or *Knowledge of Simple Intelligence,* by which God knows all things *possible;* (*b*) *Knowledge of Vision,* by which God knows all things *actual;* and (*c*) some philosophers add what others call unnecessary, the third distinction called *Scientia Media* or *Middle Knowledge,* by which God knows *futuribilia.*

(*2*) *God as Will* is God the Almighty; it is God as Infinite Love. For love is the proper act of will. God loves Himself infinitely, which is only saying that God *is* Himself. We must not impose upon God our creatural thoughts or expressions, and think of self-love in God as we think of it in creatures. For will is a thing which a free creature *has,* not what he *is*. Besides, "self-love" in a creature is really not love of self; it is "selfishness" and does *harm* to the creature afflicted by it; true love of self would not do *harm* but *good* to the self. So we must be on our guard, lest mistaken human expressions should make us attribute something unworthy to God. In God love of Self is the highest perfection; it is Infinite Godhead. And God loves all creatures, for they are the product of His will, that is, of His Almighty Love. The primary object of God's will is Himself; the secondary object of God's will is creatures. Creatures are the object of God's will or love in proportion to their actuality or perfection or being. Hence, men and angels, the most perfect of creatures, are peculiarly the object of God's will or love.

Philosophers and theologians distinguish in God an *antecedent* and a *consequent* will. God's will is called *antecedent* when it wills simply; it is called *consequent* when it wills in view of special conditions and circumstances, especially those that come from the free-will of a creature. Thus, *antecedently* God wills all men to be saved. But men are free, and can abuse their freedom, and so can be lost. *Consequently* upon their choice, God wills their punishment if they choose to be lost.

God wills or loves all things. But *evil* is not *a thing. Thing* or *being* means actuality, and actuality means *perfection.* Evil is *the absence* of perfection. Thus God does not will evil. But *physical* evils (like hunger, sickness, hardships, a bad climate, etc.) may be really *good* inasmuch as they help a man to virtue, such as patience, penance, hope of eternal life, striving towards heaven. Inasmuch as these are *good,* God is said to will physical evils *accidentally* and not *per se* or in themselves. Thus a loving father whose son has been extravagant may profitably allow the young man to suffer inconvenience and threat of arrest, or even arrest itself, as a lesson that will be of inestimable profit to him in time to come. The father does not will the suffering of the son *in itself* or *per se;* he wills it *accidentally* or *per accidens* inasmuch as it comes along with the good he wishes his son to take from a tight situation. Or, to use another analogy, a man who must undergo a painful, dangerous, and expensive operation if he is to recover health, wills the pain, the danger, the expense (all types of deprivation, absence, evil) *accidentally* and not *in themselves;* for he wills his recovery of health, and these things "go along." So we say, God does not will physical evils *per se,* but only *per accidens* inasmuch as they are the means to good for His children. But God does not will *moral evil* or *sin* either *per se* or *per accidens,* for sin is a contradiction of God and God does not will (that is God *is* not) a contradiction in Himself. Sin is man's own doing; it is an abuse of free-will; and, like all evils, moral evil or sin is not a *thing,* but the absence of a thing; it is the absence (that is, the failure) of agreement between man's conduct and the rule of what it ought to be. Sin is a failure *to measure up.* It is a defection from the true moral rule, which is God as Infinite Understanding and Will.

c) Transient Divine Operations

As we have warned the reader above, there are no *literal* or *strictly-so-called* transient operations of God. But we *call* transient the divine operations which reach out, so to speak, to God's creatures.

(*1*) *The first of these operations is creation.* There is, as we have seen in the first Article of this Chapter, no ultimate explanation of the world of creatures except *an absolute beginning,* an *emerging out of nothing* under the power and activity of the First Cause. Creation is therefore a fact. And, as we have also seen, only truly infinite power (which is God) can account for such an emergence. For creation is *the producing of a thing in its entirety out of nothing.* Creation is an operation so proper to Infinite Power that a creature cannot serve even as an instrumental cause. For an instrumental cause is a cause employed upon something which is *there* to work upon; and in the case of *creating* there is *nothing* to work upon.

(2) *The second of the divine transient operations is conservation* or preservation of creatures. For not only does a creature fail to explain its *coming* into existence, it fails to account for its *continuing* in existence. Contingent things (and all creatures are contingent) depend utterly upon causes to *produce* them and to *maintain* them. Hence, in last analysis, the creating power (without which the world is wholly impossible) must be extended to be also *the preserving or conserving* power. Now, preserving a thing may be *direct* or *indirect.* A man who catches a delicate vase as it is about to fall, *directly* preserves it. If he then locks it up in a case where nothing can come near to break it, he *indirectly* preserves it, and he may go off about his business and forget the vase entirely; still he is indirectly preserving it by the fact that through his activity it is now locked up and safe. Now, God must preserve creatures *directly.* For creatures are wholly contingent, and unable to preserve themselves for an instant unless they are actually and actively held out of nothingness. They cannot be locked in a forgotten case, for God would also actively hold the case in existence. Thus conservation is a divine activity that is continuous. It is called "a continuous creation," and the phrase is justified. For the same divine power that is required to bring creatures to existence is required to keep them in existence. If God were to refuse conservation, this would be *annihilation of creatures.* Speaking absolutely, God *could* annihilate; but when we consider that God is not only

creating and conserving Power, but is also Infinite Wisdom, Infinite Mercy, and Infinite Goodness, we say that He *cannot* annihilate, for this would conflict with His perfections. The technical way of putting all this is: God, by His absolute power, can annihilate; by His ordinated power (that is, power as seen in line with the other divine perfections) He cannot annihilate.

(*3*) *The third of the divine transient operations is concurrence* by which God supports creatures in their activity. By *conservation* God supports creatures in *being;* by *concurrence* He supports creatures in *doing.* When we read in Scripture that man "cannot so much as say the Lord Jesus but by the Holy Ghost" we find the fact of necessary divine concurrence neatly expressed; man (or any creature) can do *nothing* except by the concurrence of God. But what about sinning? Remember that the actual physical activity that may be connected with a sin (such as the bodily exertions of the murderer) are *in themselves* good; a murderer might use the same muscles, the same movements, in saving a life that he uses in destroying a life. The bodily actions of the sinner are *in themselves* good. It is their direction and their result as determined by free-will that is bad. It is the free-will that *fails* to bring them into line with God and so make them *morally,* as well as *physically,* good. But what of the free-will action itself? This is sinful inasmuch as it *fails,* is *defective,* is an *absence* of agreement with the moral law. For, as we have seen elsewhere, *evil,* whether physical or moral, is not a thing but the absence of a thing. A thing, a positive being, as such, is *good.* So God does not concur with sinful activity as *sinful,* for this phase of the activity, being negative and defective, is not positive being or activity. But God does necessarily concur with physical activity, even in a sinner, and He *permits* the abuse and defection whereby the sinner *fails* to make his act a good act. God is *in no sense* the author of sin; man is responsible for sin by defection, by failure, by absence of the work and effort needed to bring his activity into line with moral goodness. Sin requires, in itself, no *effecting* cause, but a *defecting* cause; not a cause that produces being, but a cause that fails to produce being as it should. Hence, God, the sole *Primary* Effecting Cause of all being and all real activity, is not the cause of sin; this, as we say, is a *defecting* cause; it is the *failing* will of man.—We distinguish types of divine concurrence. (*a*) *Mediate* concurrence is that by which God supports in creatures their *power* to act. (*b*) *Physical* concurrence is that by which God supports *the actual exercise* of such power. (*c*) *Moral* concurrence is that by which God draws or invites free creatures to good action. (*d*) *Previous* concurrence is the divine support or influence on the agent *before* the operation and in view of it. (*e*) *Simultaneous* concurrence is the divine support in the doing or operating of the creature at the actual instant that such operating takes place. (*f*) *Efficacious* concurrence is that which infallibly takes effect. (*g*) *Indifferent* concurrence has its effect dependently upon the co-operation of the creatural cause (or *secondary* cause). (*h*) *General* or *Indeterminate* concurrence is not directed to a definite effect. (*i*) *Special* or *Determinate* concurrence is directed to one determinate effect. (*j*) *Intrinsic* concurrence is intertwined in the very essence of the operation of the creatural cause. (*k*) *Extrinsic* concurrence is, so to speak, an outer influence.— Now, *how does God concur with man's free acts?* Some say that God's concurrence with man's free acts is immediate, moral, indifferent, simultaneous, and extrinsic. (Such is the theory of Molina, famous Jesuit theologian and philosopher of the 16 century.) Others maintain that God's concurrence with man's free acts is physical, previous, immediate, special, intrinsic, and also simultaneous. (Such is the theory of "Physical Pre-motion.") We cannot pause here upon a point of controversy. Suffice it to say that, whichever theory best expresses the fact of God's concurrence with man's free will, *God so concurs with the human free-will as, on the one hand, to retain in Himself the creating power necessary for the first origin of all activity, and, on the other hand, to keep man's deliberate activity truly free.* There is mystery here, of course; but the facts remain: God alone is necessary and primary Cause; man is actually free in all his deliberate moral conduct.

(4) *The fourth of the divine transient operations is the governing of the world.* God is Infinite Wisdom. He has made the world, therefore, for a most wise purpose. Hence He has a most wise *plan* for the working of the world to its end. This plan of God we call *divine Providence.* The working out of the plan is *divine Government.* Providence and Government extend to everything and every activity in the world, not only in a general way, but in every particular and detail. God supports and moves all creatures according to their nature (that is, *their working essence* which He has made), and where man's *free* nature brings in, by its *failure,* the evil of sin, even here God's Providence and Government so shape things, by eternal plan, as to bring good out of evil, as, for example, the great good (the sanctity) of the martyrs is drawn out of the crime of those who put them to death. Mystery is here too, but reason sees that Providence and Government must be factual, and experience of honest minds testifies to the actual working out of Providence in the Government of creatures. In many matters we are in the dark about just *how* such and such a thing fits in with God's Providence and Government; we are like the puzzled child undergoing a painful operation at the hands of his surgeon-father; the child cannot see *how* his own father can hurt him so. Yet the hurt means life to the child. We have compelling evidence each hour of God's provident love for us. We must sanely trust Him, and not imprudently seek to know all the workings of His loving Providence. Reason and experience, as well as faith, testify that indeed God "moves from end to end mightily and disposes all things sweetly."

Summary of the Article

In this Article we have learned what is meant by *a divine operation.* We have listed the divine operations as *immanent* and *transient,* making careful explanation that the term *transient* is not used literally in this instance. We have studied the divine immanent operations of God's Intellect and God's Will. We have seen that the divine knowledge does not destroy human freedom. We have discussed the object of God's knowledge, and have distinguished God's *knowledge of simple intelligence,* God's *knowledge of vision,* and the disputed type of divine knowledge called *scienta media.* We have seen the essential love of the acts of the divine Will, and have shown that these do not make God the author or approver of moral evil, and that God wills physical evil only accidentally or *per accidens.* We have seen that God is the necessary *Creator, Conserver, Concurrer, and Governor* in the relations creatures bear to Him; in these offices we discerned God's transient operations or activities. In point of divine concurrence, we have briefly discussed the Molinist Theory and the Premotionist Theory on the mode or manner of divine concurrence. We have noticed that God's providence and governance extend to all creatures in general and in special down to the last and least, and that this divine activity is neither destructive of human freedom nor in conflict with the fact that man, by failing his true nature, can sin.

CHAPTER VII

THE ETHICAL QUESTION

The Ethical Question is the question of the morality of free and responsible human conduct. It is the question of *right,* of *wrong,* and of *duty,* in man's conscious and deliberate activity. The department of philosophy which answers this question is called *Moral Philosophy* or *Ethics.* This science grows out of the rest of philosophy. For when we have a philosophical grasp of the existence of God, of man's dependence on God, of the possibility of achieving certitude and of right formulas for reasoning out truth, of the inadequacy of self or this world to fulfill man's nature; then we are necessarily aware of the need of the true programme for right human living. Thus, out of the Theological Question, the Psychological Question, the Critical Question, the Logical Question, and the Cosmological Question, we find emerging the Ethical Question. We turn our special attention to this question in the present Chapter.

The Chapter is divided into two Articles:

Article 1. General Ethics

Article 2. Individual and Social Ethics

Article 1. General Ethics

a) Human Acts; b) Ends of Human Acts; c) Norms of Human Acts; d) Morality of Human Acts; e) Properties and Consequences of Human Acts.

a) Human Acts

The term *human act* has a fixed technical meaning. It means an act (thought, word, deed, desire, omission) performed by a human being when he is responsible; when he knows what he is doing and wills to do it. An act is *perfectly* human when it is done with full knowledge and full consent of the will, and with full and unhampered freedom of choice. If the act is hampered in any way, it is *less perfectly* human; if it is done without knowledge or consent it is not a human act at all. An act done by a human being but *without* knowledge and consent is called an *act of a person* but not a *human act.* In the terminology of Scholastic philosophy, a human act is *actus humanus;* an act of a person is *actus hominis.*

The essential elements of a human act are three: *knowledge, freedom, actual choice.* (*1*) *Knowledge:* A person is not responsible for an act done in ignorance, unless the ignorance is the person's own fault, and is therefore willed (*vincible ignorance*), in which case he has *knowledge that he is in ignorance* and ought to dispel it. Thus, in one way or another, *knowledge* is necessary for responsible human activity. (*2*) *Freedom:* A person is not responsible for an act over which he has no control, unless he deliberately surrenders such control by running into conditions and circumstances which rob him of liberty. Thus, in one way or another, *freedom* is necessary for every human act. (*3*) *Actual choice* or *voluntariness:* A person is not responsible for an act which he does not *will,* unless he wills to give up his self-control (as a man does, for instance, in allowing himself to be hypnotized, or by deliberately becoming intoxicated). Thus, in one way or another, *voluntariness* or actual choice enters into every human act.

Now, a human act is a *willed* act. It proceeds from the will, following the knowledge and judgment of the mind or intellect. Since what refers to the free-will is usually described as *moral,* a human act is a *moral* act. Since the will is free, a human act is a *free* act.

A human act comes from the will directly or indirectly. When the act itself is the choice of the will, it comes directly from the will and is said to be willed *in se* or *in itself.* When the act comes indirectly from the will, inasmuch as the will chooses rather what causes or occasions the act than the act itself, it is said to be willed *in its cause* or *in causa*. Thus a man who wills to become intoxicated, wills it directly or *in se;* a man who does not wish to become intoxicated, but who seeks entertainment where, as experience tells him, he is almost sure to become intoxicated, wills the intoxication indirectly or *in causa*. This distinction of *direct and indirect willing* (or *direct and indirect voluntariness*) raises a notable issue, and we have here two of the most important principles (that is, fundamental guiding truths) in all ethics. These are:

(*1*) *The Principle of Indirect Voluntariness: A person is responsible for the evil effect of a cause directly willed when three conditions are met, viz.,* (*a*) *when he can readily forsee the evil effect, at least in a general way;* (*b*) *when he is free to refrain from doing what causes the evil effect; and* (*c*) *when he is bound to refrain from doing what causes the evil effect.*

But is the agent (that is, the doer of an act) not *always* bound to avoid what causes an evil effect? Is not the fact that the effect is evil a sufficient reason for rendering the act which leads to it unlawful? Not always, for sometimes the act has two effects, one good and one evil. In this case, the following principle applies.

(*2*) *The Principle of Twofold Effect: A person may lawfully perform an act which has two effects, one good and one evil, when the following conditions are met, viz.,* (*a*) *when the act which has two effects is not in itself an evil act;* (*b*) *when the evil effect does not come before the good effect so as to be a means to it;* (*c*) *when there exists a reason, proportionately weighty, which calls for the good effect;* (*d*) *when the agent* (*that is, the doer or performer of the act*) *intends the good effect exclusively, and merely permits the evil effect as a regrettable side-issue.*

Sound human reason vindicates the value and trustworthiness of these two leading ethical principles. The basic law of morals, —called *the natural law,*—is summed up in this plain mandate of reason: *We must do good; we must avoid evil.* And, developing the second point,—that is, the avoidance of evil,—we have this basic rational principle: *We must never do what is evil, even though good may be looked for and intended as a result of it.*

Human acts are modified, that is, affected, and made less perfectly human, by anything that hampers or hinders any of the three essentials of human action: knowledge, freedom, voluntariness. Chief of the modifiers of human acts are these:

(*1*) *Ignorance.* Ignorance that may be overcome by due diligence is called *vincible ignorance* or *culpable ignorance;* ignorance that cannot be expelled by due diligence is called *invincible ignorance* or *inculpable ignorance.* The reasoned ethical principle on this point is: *Invincible ignorance destroys voluntariness and relieves the agent of responsibility; vincible ignorance lessens but does not remove voluntariness and responsibility.*

(*2*) *Concupiscence.* By *concupiscence* we mean any of the human impulses or tendencies technically called *the passions.* These are: love, hatred, grief, desire, aversion, hope, despair, courage, fear, anger. When concupiscence sweeps upon a person without his intending it, it is called *antecedent concupiscence;* when a person wills it (as in the case of a man who nurses his injuries, or stirs himself to revenge, or who allows a suddenly envisioned obscene image to remain in his mind or before his eyes) it is called *consequent concupiscence.* The ethical principle here is: *Antecedent concupiscence lessens voluntariness and responsibility but does not take them away; consequent concupiscence does not lessen voluntariness and responsibility.* Of all the types of concupiscence which influence human acts, *fear* has a peculiar significance, and we have a special reasoned principle for it: *An act done from a motive of fear is simply voluntary; the agent is responsible for it, even though he would not do it were he not under the sway of fear.* Of course, if the fear is so great that it renders the agent insane at the moment of his act, he is incapable of a human act and is not responsible. Civil law and ecclesiastical law make provisions for the nullifying of *contracts* made under the stress of fear (that is, of *threat,* or *duress*), for the common good requires that people be protected from the malice of unscrupulous persons who would not hesitate to enforce harmful bargains by fearsome means.

(3) *Violence. Coaction* or *violence* is external force applied by a free cause (that is, by human beings) to compel a person to do something contrary to his will. The ethical principle with respect to violence is: *An act owing to violence to which due resistance is made, is not voluntary, and the agent is not responsible for it.*

(4) *Habit.* Habit is a readiness, born of repeated acts, for doing a certain thing. The ethical principle is: *Habit does not take away voluntariness; acts done from habit are voluntary, at least in cause, as long as the habit is permitted to continue.*

b) Ends of Human Acts

An *end* is a purpose or goal. It is *that for which* an act is performed. It is *the final cause* of an act.

An end intended for itself is an *ultimate* end; an end intended as a measure or means of gaining a further end is an *intermediate* end. The first end (in order of attainment) is *proximate;* other ends are *remote.* An ultimate end is ultimate in a certain series of ends, or it is the crowning end of all human activity. The ultimate end of a series is called *relatively ultimate;* the crowning end of all human activity is called *absolutely ultimate.*

A young man entering medical school has, as proximate and intermediate ends, the passing of his exams, and the advance from the first to the second class; more remote ends are the exams and classes further on; the ultimate end of the whole series of his studies and efforts is the status of a physician. But this end is relatively ultimate, not absolutely so. Why does he wish to be a physician? Perhaps to do good and to have an honorable means of livelihood. But why does he want this? For a full life, a rounded satisfaction in his earthly existence? But why does he want these things? Inevitably, in view of a still further end. For *all* human ends are directed, in last analysis, to an all-sufficing *absolutely ultimate* end. This is the *completely satisfying* end or good; it is the Supreme and Infinite Good; it is the *Summum Bonum;* it is God.

An end as a thing desired or intended is called *objective*. The satisfaction looked for in the attainment and possession of the objective end, is the *subjective* end.

Man, in every human act, strives for the possession of good (for *end* and *good* are synonymous), and for infinite good or God. This is *the absolutely ultimate objective end* of all human activity. And man strives for the infinite good as that which will boundlessly *satisfy;* he looks for *complete beatitude* or *complete happiness* in the attainment and possession of God. This is *the absolutely ultimate subjective end* of all human activity.

Saint and sinner alike are striving towards God. The Saint is striving in the right direction, and the sinner in the wrong direction. But it is the one Goal they are after, that is, the full, everlasting, satisfaction of all desire. The good man in his good human acts and the evil man in his evil human acts are like two men digging for diamonds; the one digs in a diamond mine, the other perversely digs in a filthy heap of rubbish; the one works where diamonds are to be found, the other's work is hopeless of success. *But it is to find diamonds that both are working.*

Man necessarily (and not freely) intends or wills the supreme and absolute end of all human acts. Man freely (and not necessarily) chooses *the means* (that is, intermediate ends) by which he expects, wisely or perversely, to attain that end.

c) Norms of Human Acts

A *norm* is a rule; it is the measure of a thing. The norm of human acts is the rule which *shows whether* they measure up to what they should be, and *indicates the duty* of bringing them up to full standard of what they ought to be. The norms of human acts are *law* and *conscience*. More precisely, the one norm of human acts is *law applied by conscience.*

(*1*) *Law* is an ordinance of reason promulgated for the common good by one who has charge of society.

Fundamentally, law is an ordinance of Infinite Reason for all mankind and for every creature. In this sense, law means *the Eternal Law* which is God's plan and providence for the universe. Inasmuch as this law is knowable by a normal mind which reasons to it from the facts of experience, the Eternal Law is called *the natural law.* For when a person ceases to be a baby and becomes responsible, this is owing to the fact that he recognizes the following truth: "There is such a thing as *good;* there is such a thing as *evil;* I have a *duty* to avoid evil and to do good." A child of ten that knew no distinction between lies and truth, theft and honesty, obedience and disobedience, would rightly be classed as an imbecile. Indeed, we say that a person "comes to the use of reason" when he begins to have a practical grasp of three things: *good, evil, duty.* In other words, reason makes evident the basic prescriptions of *the natural law.*

The natural law is general. But man needs, in addition to general prescriptions for conduct, special determinations of the law. The Ten Commandments are special determinations of the natural law. So are the enactments of State and Church in civil and ecclesiastical laws.

Law is for the common good. Special regulations for individuals or groups are called *precepts.* A precept is like a law inasmuch as it is a regulation or an ordering unto good. A precept is unlike a law inasmuch as it is rather for private than for common good. In *human* laws and precepts, a further distinction is made. A law is territorial; it binds in a certain place and not in other places; a precept is personal, and it binds the person subject to it wherever he may be. Again, a law endures even though the actual persons who formulated and promulgated it are dead and gone; a precept ends with the death (or removal from office) of the preceptor. Divine laws, like the Ten Commandments, are both laws and precepts. They are for all mankind, the world over, at all times, and they are also for the individual and private good of men.

True law is a liberating force, not an enslaving one. A true law may be compared to a true map. The map does not enslave the traveller, but enables him to make his journey without hindrance or mishap. The man who says he will not be enslaved by maps, is a prey to ignorance, and is thus truly enslaved; the man who uses the map is liberated from the enslavement of ignorance and is freed to make the journey. For liberty does not include in its essence *the ability to do wrong.* This ability is a sad condition of earthly human existence; it is not a part of liberty itself. God can do no wrong, yet God is infinitely free. The souls in heaven can no longer sin, and yet they have not lost freedom, but have used freedom and brought it to its crowning perfection. Man's freedom is *freedom of the choice of means* to his ultimate end; when the end is attained, means are no longer needed, and the freedom which won to success is forever crowned in full perfection.

Law that is set down in recorded enactments is called *positive* law. The moral law as knowable to sound human reason (that is, the Eternal Law as so knowable) is called, as we have seen, *the natural law.* A law is called *moral* if it binds under guilt, that is, under sin. It is called *penal* if it binds under penalty (such as a fine). It is called *mixed* if it binds under both guilt and penalty. It is a debated question among ethicians whether there can be a law that is entirely and exclusively penal.

All true laws have *sanctions,* that is, inducements (of reward or punishment prescribed) sufficient to make those bound by them obedient to their prescriptions. Human positive law usually has the sanction of penalty, not of special reward. The sanctions of the Eternal Law are heaven and hell.

In individual human acts, law is applied by conscience.

(2) *Conscience* is the practical judgment of human reason upon an act as *good,* and hence permissible or obligatory, or as *evil,* and hence to be avoided.

Conscience is the reasoned judgment of the mind. It is no instinct, no sentiment, no prejudice born of custom or what moderns call *mores;* it is no "still small voice"; it is no "little spark of celestial fire." It is the pronouncement of reason, the reason with which we work out a problem in mathematics,—only, to be called *conscience* it must be the working out of a judgment or pronouncement in the domain of morals, of duty.

When the judgment of conscience squares with facts, conscience is called *correct* or *true.* When the conscience-judgment is out of line with facts, conscience is called *false.* When the conscience-judgment is wholly assured and unhesitant, conscience is called *certain.* When the conscience judgment is hesitant, and amounts to no more than opinion, conscience is called *doubtful.*

Doubt is *speculative* when it is a lack of certainty about *what is true;* it is *practical* when it is a lack of certainty about *what is to be done.* A doubt is *positive* when the mind hesitates between two opposites because there seems good reason for each; it is *negative* when the mind hesitates because there seems no good reason on either side. A most important reasoned principle is the following: *It is never lawful to act while in a state of positive practical doubt.* The doubt must be dispelled and replaced by at least moral certitude.

To dispel positive practical doubt, a person must use *the direct method* of study, inquiry, finding all the facts. If this method prove unsuccessful, or if it cannot be applied, then *the indirect method* (called *the appeal to the reflex principle*) must be employed. This means that the person in doubt *about the licitness or illicitness of an act* can make sure that he is not bound by applying the reflex principle: *A law that is of doubtful application cannot beget a certain obligation.* In this case, certitude is attained, not of the case itself, but of the person's freedom from obligation; thus, it is an *indirect* certitude.

Out of the use of the reflex principle just mentioned, emerges the theory called *Probabilism*. It amounts to this: If there exists a solidly probable opinion against the applicability of a law in a given case, that law is of *doubtful* applicability. In other words, it is a doubtful law. But a doubtful law cannot beget a certain obligation. Therefore, if there exists a solidly probable opinion against the applicability of a law in a given case, there is no obligation.

The moral system of Probabilism is of value only when there is question of the lawfulness or unlawfulness of an act; it has no place when the question is one of the validity or invalidity of contract or Sacrament. Further, the phrase "a solidly probable opinion" does not mean a strong inclination or liking on the part of the agent; it means a *reasoned* opinion, especially such as is defended by men of known learning and prudence.

Probabilism, or the application of the reflex principle, *a doubtful law does not bind,* cannot be employed except in the failure or the inapplicability of the direct method of solving a doubt. Nor can it be used when there is question of a clear and definite end to be achieved. Thus a man who is looking for the true Church cannot give up the search for any such reason as this: "I've inquired into this religion and that; I am unable to determine which is the true one. I am therefore in doubt about my duty of joining a church. I rely on the reflex principle, and consider myself as free to join any church I please, or perhaps no church at all." In this case there is a definite end to be achieved, that is, the finding of truth, the salvation of a soul. No probability will serve to absolve from duty here, or to lighten it or lessen it. But, indeed, in such a case direct means are *always* available for the finding of truth with certitude; they are *never* exhausted and found absolutely and permanently fruitless.

d) Morality of Human Acts

Morality is the relation of human acts to the norm or rule of what they ought to be. As we have seen, the norm of human acts is law applied by conscience. And the basic law is the Eternal Law, especially as this is knowable by sound human reason (it is then called *the natural law*). The squaring up of free and responsible human conduct with *law* as applied by *conscience* is the *morality* of human acts; the lack of such agreement of human acts with their norm is *immorality*. But, as we have indicated, *morality* is generally used to signify the *relation* (whether of agreement or disagreement) of human acts to their norm or rule. Thus we speak of morally good acts and of morally bad acts.

A human act considered *as such,* as an act, as a deed performed, stands in agreement or out of agreement with the norm of what it ought to be. Thus it has *objective* morality. Many mistaken people of our day, especially those of university training, are fond of talking as though a human act took all its morality from the intention of the agent, or from his viewpoint. They are full of expressions such as, "As I see it . . . ," "To my mind . . . ," "I don't look at it in that way . . . ," "It's all in the point of view . . ." etc. Now, there is an immense field for human *opinion.* Where certitude cannot be had, opinion is the best man can achieve. But in matters of essential morals, certitude can be had (as we have seen, by direct method, or, *this failing,* by the reflex method). Hence the lawfulness or unlawfulness of an act,—its morality, in short,—is never a matter of opinion, viewpoint, prejudice, or preference. It is a matter of fact. It is an *objective* thing. Human acts have *objective morality.*

A person blamelessly mistaken about the objective morality of an act is exempt (by reason of invincible ignorance) from responsibility for such act. Thus, a person who is invincibly ignorant of the fact that a lie is *always* unlawful, and who is convinced with full certitude that in certain circumstances a lie is permissible, is not guilty of formal falsehood for telling such a lie. But this does not mean that the objective morality of a lie is a fiction or an illusion; it does not mean that the morality of an act depends on the agent's convictions. The lie is objectively evil and remains so. Only, in the case mentioned, invincible ignorance excuses the agent from responsibility for it. And so much the worse for the agent, for ignorance is always a blight and a burden.

Some acts have their objective morality in themselves by reason of their nature. Murder, lying, calumny, impurity, injustice, are examples of acts *intrinsically evil.* Respect for life, truthfulness, charity, purity, justice, are examples of acts *intrinsically good.* Other human acts have their objective morality by reason of positive law, which is an extrinsic determinant. Thus, hunting out of season, violating the speed laws, neglecting to pay definite assessed taxes, are acts objectively but *extrinsically* evil. Obeying civil ordinances, performing the duty of true citizens as expressed by law, are, in the main, acts objectively but *extrinsically* good. The basic virtue of being a good citizen, however, is intrinsically good.

In the concrete, as a deed done, *every* human act has true objective morality. But when a human act is considered in the abstract, in general, and not as a concrete deed performed, it is sometimes found to be *indifferent,* and neither good nor bad. In other words, some human acts are not *intrinsically* good or *intrinsically* evil in themselves as abstractly considered. But *in their actual performing,* they take on morality (and truly objective morality) from the circumstances.

For the *determinants* of morality are *the act performed* and *the circumstances of the act performed.*

(*1*) *The act performed* is technically known as *the object.* Human acts that have intrinsic morality are good or evil by reason of the object, that is the act itself. Such acts, if evil, are never permissible. If good, and if circumstances do not vitiate them, they are lawful. Some of them are not capable of being vitiated by circumstances, and these are always lawful, and also of obligation. Such, for example, is the duty of honoring God, of professing the truth, of working justice to all men.

(*2*) *The circumstances of an act performed* determine its morality when the object does not do so. Circumstances are various, but the most important are those of person, of the intensity of the act, of place, of time, of helping influences in the act, of manner, and of intention. The last named (that is *intention* of the agent or doer) is the most notable circumstance.

(*a*) Of circumstances in general, the ethical principles are these: An indifferent act is made good or evil by circumstances; a good act may be made evil by circumstances but an evil act cannot be made good by circumstances; an act is made better or worse by circumstances; a circumstance gravely evil ruins the morality of the whole act and makes it evil; a circumstance slightly evil, which is not the entire motive of a good act, does not utterly destroy its goodness.

(*b*) Of intention in special, the ethical principles are these: A good act done for a good intention has an added goodness from the intention, and a bad act for a bad intention has an added evil from the intention; a good act for a bad intention is wholly evil if the intention is gravely evil or if it is the whole motive of the act; a good intention cannot make a bad act good, but a bad intention vitiates a good act; an indifferent act may be made good or evil by its intention.

For an act to be lawful, that is, *morally right and good,* it must square with *all* the requirements of object, circumstances, intention. For an act to be evil, it must fail to square with any *one* of the rquirements. The axiom is: *An act to be good must be entirely good; it is vitiated* (*wholly or partially*) *by any defect.*

e) Properties and Consequences of Human Acts

A *property* of an act is anything that belongs by natural necessity to the act. Now, a human act is a free and deliberate act of a responsible being who is its author. It follows, that such an act is *imputable* to its author, to his credit or discredit, that is, as a *merit or a demerit.* Thus, properties of human acts are *imputability, merit, demerit.*

A human act once performed sets a precedent for the agent. It marks a path which he has traversed. It cuts a groove, so to speak, for his action. And therefore he tends to act in the same way again. In a word, human acts tend to follow patterns called *habits*. By *habit* in the present instance we mean *an operative habit,* a habit of acting. Such a habit is *an inclination, born of frequently repeated action, for acting in a certain way.*

An operative habit that is morally good is called *a virtue*. An operative habit that is morally bad is called *a vice.* Virtues and vices are the consequences of human acts.

The chief virtues are prudence, justice, fortitude, and temperance. These are called *the cardinal virtues* (from the Latin *cardo,*—stem *cardin-,* "a hinge") because all other virtues depend on them as a door depends on its hinges.

Vice, or habit of evil doing, is a habitual defect, a habitual failure to measure up to the norm of right conduct and of the virtues. A single bad act is a *sin,* but not a vice. Vice is the habit of sin. It stands opposed to virtue either by defect or by excess, but in either case it is a habitual failure (a negative thing) to measure up to the standard of what a human act ought to be.

Summary of the Article

In this Article we have defined *human act,* and have determined its essential elements as *knowledge, freedom, voluntariness.* We have learned that other names for the human act are *free* act, *moral* act, *willed* act. We have discussed voluntariness *in se* and *in causa,* and have learned two outstandingly important principles, viz., *the principle of indirect voluntariness* and *the principle of twofold effect.* We have considered the modifiers of human acts: *ignorance, concupiscence, violence, habit.* We have seen that a human act is necessarily directed to an *end,* and, in last analysis, to *the absolutely ultimate end* or Supreme Good which is God. We have noticed that man's freedom is *freedom of choice of means* to the ultimate end, not freedom to set up a new ultimate end. We have learned the norm of human acts as *law applied by conscience.* We have defined *law,* and have studied several classifications of it, and have contrasted it with *precept.* We have seen that conscience is *the judgment of practical reason* in matters of right and wrong, and not some mysterious inner voice like Kant's Categorical Imperative. We have noticed the necessity of man's acting with a *certain* conscience, and we have studied the *direct* and the *indirect* method of banishing doubt and achieving certitude. We have spoken of *Probabilism.* We have defined the *morality* of human acts, and have investigated its *determinants.* We have indicated the properties of human acts as *imputability, merit,* and *demerit;* and we have seen that human acts tend to consequences called *virtues* and *vices.*

Article 2. Individual and Social Ethics

a) Terms; b) The Individual's Rights and Duties; c) Social Rights and Duties.

a) Terms

The term *Individual Ethics* means the philosophical science of morality as it affects human persons individually. *Social Ethics* is the philosophical science of morality as it affects groups of human beings: the family, the State, the Church, the whole race.

Ethics as here applied in the domains of the individual and of society speaks ever of rights and duties. A *right* is a moral power residing in a person, or in unified groups of persons, of doing, possessing, or exacting something. A *duty* is the correlative of right; it is the moral obligation of doing or avoiding something. Rights and duties are of different classifications. A right or duty is *natural* or *positive* according to its basis in the natural law or in positive law. For every right and duty rests ultimately on law, which is the norm of all human activity. A man's right to life, and his right to freedom from enslavement, are *natural* rights. A man's duty to keep the speed laws is a *positive* duty; his duty to respect the life and property of others is a *natural* duty.—A right is either a right *of property* or a right *of jurisdiction.* A right of property is a right of disposing of possessions at will. A right of jurisdiction is a right of rule. My right to my books and clothing is a *property* right. The right of the parent to be obeyed, of the judge to have his rulings enforced, of the teacher to be respected and attended, are *jurisdictional* rights.—A right is *alienable* when it may be surrendered in any circumstances; it is *inalienable* when it may not be surrendered except in extraordinary circumstances. The right to property is alienable, for property may be sold or given away. The right of parents to care for their children is inalienable. Inalienable right is also strict duty.—A right is juridical or *perfect* when it is strictly enjoined or supported by law and strict justice. A right is moral or *imperfect* (and constitutes *a claim*) when it is founded on some other virtue than justice, usually on charity.—A duty is *affirmative* when it *exacts* the doing of something; it is *negative* when it *forbids* the doing of something.

Rights have certain characteristics or properties. A right is *enforceable,* but good order requires that *personal violence* be employed only as a last resort. A right is *limited* by the rights of others. When rights *collide,* that right prevails which is the more important or rests on the stronger title. Duties, too, have characteristics, chief of which is that certain duties admit *exemption,* of which we may state the principle as follows: *No necessity exempts from a negative natural duty; extreme or grave necessity exempts from an affirmative duty, provided there is no involved violation of negative natural duty. Common or ordinary necessity never exempts from duty.*

Rights and duties belong to *persons.* In this world, human beings alone are persons. Animals have neither rights nor duties. But this does not mean that we may treat animals cruelly or fawn upon them in an inordinate way. For *we* have rights and duties towards animals, or rather towards the owner of all animals who is God, and who has given them to us for our benefit.

By cruelty to animals a man violates a negative natural duty to God, a duty which requires his abstaining from inordinate and inhuman conduct; and for such cruelty a man could even miss his eternal happiness and suffer eternal damnation. Where animals are not helpful but hurtful or bothersome (as flies and mosquitoes) they may be killed without the least blame. And where their death is for our use (as in supplying food or clothing) there is nothing inordinate in killing them. But wanton destruction, or mere meanness to animals is a violation of the fundamental duty of men to their Creator and Preserver. So too is a fondness for animals that makes them more important than human children.

b) THE INDIVIDUAL'S RIGHTS AND DUTIES

Each man stands in essential *relations* to God and to fellowmen. And each man has the fundamental duty of living his own life rightly. Therefore, the rights and duties of the individual are those of each man towards his own life, towards God, towards neighbor. The question is rather of duties than of rights, but we recall that a right in one person is a duty in all others, for others must respect rights. And so we shall talk of duties (with involved rights) of individual man to God, to self, to neighbor.

(*1*) *A Man's Duties to God.*—Man has a strict duty to face truth, for he has been furnished a mind to know truth; he has a strict duty to honor what his mind shows to be excellent, to love what he knows to be worthy, to be thankful for what he knows is a benefit, to be obedient to what he knows is just rule. Reason indicates the fact and the strictness of these duties. Now, God is Truth; God is all-excellent; God is all-lovable; God is the bestower of every good gift; God is the supreme ruler. Therefore, man must know God, he must honor God, he must love God, he must be grateful to God, he must obey God. In other words, each individual man must have *the virtue of religion.*

Further, each man must find and embrace the objective religion established by God as the one means for eternal salvation.

The duty of *religion,*—which sums up man's duties to God, directly considered (although all duty rests ultimately on the Eternal Law, or God),—is here shown to be a *natural* duty. Reason makes it clear. And the converse of the duty "have the virtue of religion" is the negative natural duty (from which there is *never* an exemption) "do not be without religion." The man who professes and practices no religion is in offense of the negative prescriptions of the natural law; he is guilty of evil, and vainly does he protest that he "does no harm" by his failure to live religiously. He does harm; harm to himself; harm by example to his neighbor; harm or insult to God.

Besides, since man, as reason shows, has the duty of living a life in conformity with the law of morals, the natural law, he must have religion. For without religion there is no solid morality. Without God, all-excellent, all-ruling, the prescriptions of law and even the Ten Commandments are but codes of etiquette. But to regard such basic morality as mere etiquette would turn the world into chaos. Hence, God must be recognized. And due recognition of God means religion, and,—so far as possible to the individual,—the objectively true religion. Every man has the strict duty of knowing the true religion and embracing it and living up to it.

Religious indifferentism is therefore intolerable and immoral. Indifferentism is of two types, the one being an indifference to *religion* or *no religion,* the other being an indifference to *this religion* or *that religion* objectively considered. The man who says that it makes no difference whether a person practises religion or not is an indifferentist; so is the man who says all religions are equally good, all different paths to the same heaven. Both types of indifferentism are against the prescriptions of the natural law. Both types fail to face truth, to seek and know God, to honor and obey God, to love and thank God as *He* would be loved and thanked. Indifferentism of either type is the outgrowth of human laziness and absorption in worldly and selfish interests, even when these low motives are masked as *tolerance*. For we are not to *tolerate* our fellowmen and their practices; we are to *love* our fellowmen, and to do our best prudently and reasonably to bring them to true practice. This is the prescription of reason, of the natural law.

Religion as a virtue is *subjective,* it resides in a man as its *subject*. It is defined as the virtue which inclines a man to render constantly to God the honor and the homage that is due to Him. —Religion considered as an *object* is the system of truths, laws, and practices, which regulate a man's worship of God. To have the true objective religion is a duty.

The exercise of religion is essentially *divine worship*. The chief acts of divine worship are devotion, prayer, adoration, sacrifice. The first two of these acts are fundamentally *internal,* the other two naturally express worship in an *external* way. Man has an internal and an external life. Both are from God. Both must recognize God. Hence, man is bound to exhibit to God both internal and external divine worship.

(2) *A Man's Duties to Himself.*—The duties of a man in respect to himself are duties of *soul* and of *body*. Duties of soul are those of the mind or intellect, and those of the will, for intellect and will are the faculties or operating-powers of the soul. In point of intellect, man has the duty of knowing what is necessary for the attainment of his purpose in existing. Thus, man has the duty of knowing God, of knowing what makes acts morally good, of knowing how to keep his own acts morally good. For the rest, man does well to acquire such free (or non-necessary) knowledge as will enable him to live becomingly on earth and to support his dependents. This secondary duty is strict in some (as in those who have dependents) and less strict in others, and non-existent in an exceptional few. In point of the will, man must steadily choose what is morally right and good. Hence, he must love and serve God.

Duties of a man towards his body and its life, as well as towards certain other things connected more or less directly with life, are both positive and negative. Thus, a man must conserve life and bodily integrity (this is an inalienable right and a duty, and only exceptional circumstances which offer place for *heroism* constitute an exemption or rather a higher interpretation of this duty). A man does not own his body. He cannot take his life, he cannot mutilate his body, he cannot unreasonably suffer its enslavement by his own will, he cannot sell it or its irreplaceable members. Here we see the negative side of the duty of a man towards his body and its life.

In addition to the goods of body and soul which man must preserve and not wantonly destroy, there are other goods which man has *ordinarily* the duty to procure and maintain. Such are his good name, his honorable status in life, sufficiency of means for decent support of self and dependents. If no injury to others is involved, a man may *heroically* sacrifice some or all of these goods for a higher motive and for his higher perfection.

(3) *A Man's Duties to His Neighbor.*—Man has the duty in *justice* of rendering to everyone what is due to him. With regard to a neighbor's body and its life, man has the strict duty of respecting life, liberty, integrity of body. Man has also the negative natural duty (in *justice*) of avoiding injury to the neighbor on any of these scores except in the case of *blameless self-defense* against unjust attack. With regard to the soul of a neighbor, a man owes (in *justice*) truth to the neighbor's mind, and good (especially good example) to the neighbor's will. Negatively, a man must abstain from all that would injure a neighbor in these matters. He must not deceive his neighbor, he must not lead him astray.

An important duty is that of telling truth and avoiding lies. A lie is a serious statement contrary to the knowledge (or the honest conviction) of the speaker. A lie is never lawful. There are no white lies, no innocent lies. Certain fictions, like that of Santa Claus, are not lies. They are not serious; they are jocose; and it is surprising how quickly the very young child enters into the spirit of the joke; a pleasant, jolly pretense. But *a lie* cannot be justified.

Concealment of truth from those who have no right to it, is another thing. A man who lies is like a man who offers counterfeit money for goods received; a man who legitimately conceals truth is like a man who keeps his money in his pocket and declines to buy. Concealment is unjust when the inquirer has a right to know the truth. Otherwise it is not unjust. Concealment is effected by silence, by diversion of the subject of conversation, by evasion. Concealment is necessary and a duty in case of *secrets*. But the so-called *mental reservation* is usually only a tricky lie, and is forbidden. Certain well-known formulas of speech (such as "I'm delighted to meet you"; "Mr. Smith is not in"; "I'm anxious about your sick brother") are everywhere recognized as *formulas of politeness,* and are not accepted as strict statements, necessarily true. To say that a man is not in when he is in is not true; but it is a universal human practice of dismissing a caller without offense, and it is not a lie. If the caller is deceived, this is not the fault of the speaker who uses a phrase which people everywhere perfectly understand in its real meaning.

With regard to a neighbor's *good name* and *honor,* a man has a strict negative natural duty founded on justice; he must not injure a neighbor in these matters. Every man has a right to his good name until he loses it publicly. To tell truths to the hurt of a neighbor is the evil and sin of *detraction;* to tell harmful lies is the evil and sin of *slander* or *calumny*. Both evils call for such restitution as is possible by the person guilty of them.

With regard to a neighbor's property, man has the negative natural duty of respecting it, and not causing injury by theft or action that would render it of less value. Stolen goods must be restored in themselves, their kind, or their equivalent, according to the measure of the thief's ability. Right to the private ownership of property, especially of the land, is a necessary right for man's well-being. Theories such as Socialism and Communism are inept, unjust, and full of threat to peace and even to decent morals.—A person acquires just title to property by first occupation of what belongs to nobody; by finding, when the true owner is not discovered by the exercise of due effort; by accession or natural increase; by prescription; and by contract of promise or sale. *Prescription* is a process of transferring ownership; the property of one may become the property of another who has possessed it for many years (the number set by civil law) in the full belief that it is his own, and who has some show of title for that mistaken belief. A *contract* is a method of transferring property; it is an agreement of transfer, and it begets an obligation in one or both of the parties agreeing. For a contract to be just and valid, it must be upon a matter properly subject to such transfer (one could not contract lawfully to deliver stolen goods for a price); the parties must be capable, not minors or others naturally or civilly incapacitated for making contracts; there must be full and free consent of the parties; there must be some formal sign of the consent, such as a signed document, or a public declaration before witnesses.

c) Social Rights and Duties

A *society* is a stable moral union of two or more persons established for the purpose of achieving a common end by the use of common means.

The whole human race is a society, and a natural society. All men are united in point of their common rational nature, the common ultimate end for which they were created, and the common means,—intellect and will,—with which they are furnished to attain that end. Often when people speak of "society" they mean the human race.

Within the human race there are many societies, some *natural,* some *conventional* or arbitrary (depending on the choice of men who set them up), and one *supernatural,* namely, the true Church. Among natural societies the first and by far the most important is *conjugal society,* that is, the society of husband and wife, which normally turns soon into *the family* or *the domestic society.* Upon the family, as upon no other institution, rests the fabric of civilization and decent living on earth. Another important natural society is *civil society* or *the State. The family, the State, and the Church* are the outstanding societies. Among free or conventional societies, vocational groups and workmen's unions are important societies.

(*1*) *The Family.*—The family has its first origin in conjugal society which is effected by marriage. No solid family can exist which is not founded upon a true, indissoluble marriage of one husband and one wife. Conjugal society is founded for the purpose of begetting and rearing children and for the mutual support and helpfulness of the spouses. It is not founded for romance alone, or for feelings, or for compatibility, or for a career. It is founded for the welfare of children and the peaceful happiness of the married couple. Here are its *ends* in their order of importance. Anything that conflicts with these ends conflicts with the very nature of marriage and of conjugal society, which is a *natural* institution, not to be tampered with by human enactments in the name (falsely assumed) of *laws. Divorce* is impossible, no matter what the law-courts say. The only divorce is effected by the death of one of the spouses; the other is then free to set up a new conjugal society. The marks of true marriage, the foundation of the family, are: *unity,* that is one husband and one wife during the time both live, and *indissolubility* or perpetuity without possibility of being dissolved or divorced. Reason manifests the necessity of these marks. For marriage is for the *welfare* of children (for their begetting and proper rearing), and without a true home which only monogamous marriage can secure, the welfare of children is not served. Also against the welfare of children is the horrible practice of birth control by artificial or unnatural means. The sole means of "controlling births" lies in the free abstinence of the spouses.

Since the welfare of children is the first end or purpose of marriage and the family, it is manifest that the right and duty of *educating* children belongs to parents. The State is to furnish opportunity for the schooling of children, and it may compel delinquent parents to see that their children are given a minimum school training. Beyond this the State cannot lawfully go. For the State exists for families, not families for the State. The State cannot, without injustice, assume *the control* of education.

(2) *The State* is civil society. It is a perfect natural union of families established for their common good under a definite government and in a definite territory.

The State is a *natural* society, for it answers a natural need of men when many individuals and families are to live as neighbors and to work harmoniously together. The old theory of Rousseau, Hobbes, and others, that the State is an artificial institution set up by some *social contract,* is now defended nowhere. The State is called a *perfect* society because it has within itself all means of carrying out its purposes, and has no essential dependency on any *similar* natural society for its functions. Of course, the State depends on the family, for families constitute it; but it has no dependency on other States, but is complete in its own sphere among similar States. The form of government in a State is a matter of the choice of the people governed, at least in its origins. No form of government can be declared *absolutely the best.* Only a government *relatively the best* can be hoped for; that is, a government which is best *in relation* to the needs, temperament, geographical situation, and physical conditions, of a given people at a given time.

The State has authority, for no society can exist without authority. Since the State is a natural, and therefore a necessary, institution, its authority is fundamentally from the Author of

Nature, from God. The *limits* of State authority are determined by its nature and purpose. The State has no right to interfere with the rights of individuals and of families in matters personal and private. It has no right to control the education of children, nor to herd families into homes of its choosing, nor to legislate in matters of religion or conscience. When families or citizens unlawfully extend their own rights, even when they try to justify such extension by the cry of "personal liberty" or "religious liberty," it is sometimes lawful, sometimes imperative for the common good, that the State intervene; for such people are "making liberty a cloak for malice." But when personal activities have not a bearing upon the common civic well-being, the State has no right to take command.

The State has the positive duty of protecting citizens and families and helping them in the exercise of their normal rights. It must remove obstacles to personal liberty, it must repress violations of the rights of its people, it must seek to keep off all that is harmful to itself and its family-members,—such things as wars, oppressive taxation, political trickery which is cancerous in its effect upon the body politic. It should help families and individuals in matters where these cannot help themselves; thus it should open and improve ports, rivers, canals, and national highways; it should conduct public works, especially when private enterprise fails to provide employment to many; it should maintain necessary offices and institutions, such as armed forces in adequate number, postal systems, customs offices; it should establish and carefully regulate to the best interests of all a system of monetary exchange. The State requires, for the task of maintaining all its useful institutions, the support of the citizens through *equable taxation.*

The State must be watchful to prevent ill and to foster good among its citizens. Because human nature is a fallen nature, abuse is ever tending to appear. The State has a connatural tendency towards absorbing too much power and taking over the rights of citizens in either a harsh or a tenderly paternal fashion.

Against this, both families and officers of State should be constantly on guard. Citizens should be loyal to their State, and alert to prevent its rule from turning into paternalism or into tyranny.

When a State is tyrannous beyond ordinary endurance, it is the right of the citizens to resist its evil activities, and, in last resort, to revolt and set up a new State. Of course, citizens must make many sacrifices and endure much, for the State is perfect only in a technical sense, and not in the full range of its effects upon the families and individuals that compose it. Only when conditions become intolerable is *revolution* lawful, and then only when no other means of remedying evils exists or is available.

(*3*) *The Church,* that is, the one true Church,—is a perfect society, supernatural in character, set up on earth by God, for the teaching of eternal, necessary truth, and for the governing unto salvation of all mankind through human instruments consecrated to their task and divinely guided and protected.

Without offense, it may be plainly stated that only a Catholic has any true conception of "the Church," and only a Catholic uses that term with any definite meaning. For others it is a blanket-term, a term which signifies not one society, but a multitude of societies largely in disagreement. None the less, the Church as we have defined it is here in the world; it is God's own institution for the eternal welfare of man. It is manifestly every man's strictest duty to find, to recognize, to enter, to live up to, the one true objective religion in the one true Church.

In the foggy modern conception of "the Church" is the source of the many resentments and the many erroneous opinions about the relations of "Church and State." No one is in doubt about the State; every citizen is aware of it, and of its purpose, and of what its character ought to be. It is small wonder that people so clear in one conception and so muddled in the other should tend to stress the claims and the importance of what they know and to minimize the place and function of what they foggily accept as a kind of necessary nuisance.

There is no true clash of interest or operation between Church and State. Each is a perfect society in its own sphere. But when the State, which is a human society, extends its authority unduly, as it often does, at the expense of the Church, which is superior, then the State is wrong and tyrannous. The State cannot set up its own Church, as has been done in England; for the true Church is not a human, but a divine institution. The State must not interfere with the Church in matters of spiritual import. Nor must the Church interfere with the State in what is purely temporal. The State must not ignore the Church, but must support its efforts and protect it. The Church must not ignore the State, but must teach obedience to just civil authority as a matter of moral duty, and must foster sane *patriotism,* which is not high feeling but "a well-ordered love of country."

It is the business of the State in its relations with other States to promote peace which, as St. Augustine says, is "the tranquillity of order." War, or armed and active conflict between or among States, is sometimes a regrettable last resort for the establishing of justice. Therefore, there can be a just war. The conditions necessary for a just war are these: (*a*) that it be declared by competent authority for a just cause and that it be undertaken for an honest purpose; (*b*) that it be engaged in only when the most important issues are at stake and no other means exists to serve them; (*c*) that it be essentially a defensive activity and not an offensive one (though this does not involve a prohibition of *offensive tactics* during the actual prosecution of the war); (*d*) that there be a reasonable prospect of success in the war, else it is wrong to subject peoples to all the horror and misery of such a conflict (this does not make unlawful *the heroic stand of a whole people* willing to perish rather than endure great injustice; it merely forbids those in power from inflicting an unwelcome war when success is known to be impossible); (*e*) that the war be conducted in a manner approved by civilized peoples.

(4) *Associations of Laboring Men* are important free or conventional societies. Man has a strict right, in the virtue of justice, *to join with his fellowmen* for the better attainment of worthy purposes which separated individuals could not otherwise well attain. Hence labor organizations are lawful, and any State would be tyrannous which sought to prevent or destroy them.

Labor organizations must constantly seek to have justice done to both members and employers. They must work for the payment of a just wage, they must also strive for the rendering of honest work. These organizations must therefore refrain from exorbitant demands, nor must they bring unnecessary hardships on people by going to extreme measures to obtain assent to trifling demands.

The *just wage* to which a laboring man is entitled should be such a return for honest labor as will enable a man to live decently and frugally in the circumstances of his times, to set up a family and take care of it, and to lay by something for a time of exceptional hardship (sickness, operations, deaths, births, unemployment, etc.). Therefore, a just wage is *a living wage, a marrying wage,* and *a family wage.* Employers who cannot pay such a wage have no right to be employers. Some closely cooperative method of owning and operating factories and other institutions of modern industry is doubtless the best method of insuring justice for employer and laborer alike.

To enforce justice, organizations of laboring men sometimes resort to *strikes* and *boycotts.* A strike is a cessation of labor by agreement of the workmen for the purpose of exacting just conditions for labor or just returns for labor. A boycott is a refusal to have business dealings with a certain institution, to compel its owners or operators to meet the demands of just dealing. The conditions for *just* strikes and boycotts may be summarily set forth as follows: (*a*) these extreme measures must not be undertaken except as a last reluctant resort when no other means of securing justice is available; (*b*) they must promise some success, else it is wrong to inflict on men and their families the terrible hardships that often accompany such measures; (*c*) they must be undertaken only for the most important reasons, not for the enforcement of slight or trifling demands; (*d*) the prosecution of these measures must be kept free from acts of injustice, such as violence, destruction of property, etc.

Summary of the Article

In this Article we have defined the terms used in discussing individual and social ethics; we have seen the meaning of *right, duty, property, jurisdiction.* We have noted that rights and duties belong to *persons* alone. In special, we have considered the rights and duties of man, the individual, towards God, towards himself, and towards his neighbor. And we have considered social rights and duties of man in the family, the State, the Church, and in associations such as organizations of laboring men.

INDEX

Numbers refer to pages

Anita McKeon